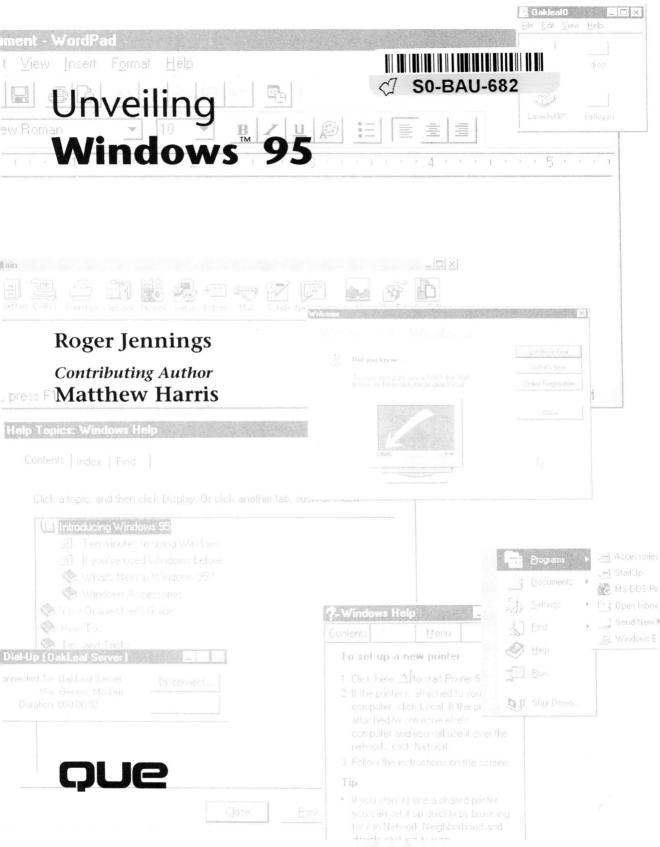

Unveiling
Windows™ 95

Roger Jennings

Contributing Author
Matthew Harris

que

Unveiling Windows 95

Copyright© 1995 by Que® Corporation

Library of Congress Catalog No.: 94-68825

ISBN: 0-7897-0061-1

98 97 96 95   4 3 2 1

Interpretation of the printing code: the rightmost double-digit number is the year of the book's printing; the rightmost single-digit number, the number of the book's printing. For example, a printing code of 95-1 shows that the first printing of the book occurred in 1995.

Publisher: David P. Ewing

Associate Publisher: Joseph B. Wikert

Associate Publisher-Operations: Corinne Walls

Managing Editor: Kelli Widdifield

Dedication

This book is dedicated to my wife, Alexandra Tillman-Jennings.

Credits

Publishing Manager
Steven M. Schafer

Acquisitions Editor
Fred Slone

Acquisitions Coordinators
Patricia J. Brooks
Angela C. Kozlowski

Product Director
C. Kazim Haidri

Production Editor
Mike La Bonne

Technical Editors
Donald W. Doherty
Scott Mauvais

Book Designer
Sandra Stevenson

Indexer
Michael Hughes

Graphic Image Specialists
Becky Beheler
Brad Dixon
Jason Hand
Denny Hager
Clint Lahnen
Cheri Laughner
Michael Reynolds
Laura Robbins
Dennis Sheehan
Craig Small
Jeff Yesh

Production Team
Claudia Bell
Stephen Carlin
Mike Dietsch
Chad Dressler
Lorell Fleming
Karen L. Gregor
John Hulse
Deb Kincaid
Bob LaRoche
Elizabeth Lewis
Erika Millen
Steph Mineart
Vic Peterson
Kris Simmons
Scott Tullis

Composed in *Stone Serif* and *MCPdigital* by Que Corporation

About the Authors

Roger Jennings is a principal of OakLeaf Systems, a Northern California consulting firm specializing in Windows database and multimedia applications. He's had more than 25 years of computer-related experience, and is an amateur musician, arranger, and composer. Roger is the author of Que's *Using Access 2 for Windows*, Special Edition; *Access Hot Tips*; and *Discover Windows 3.1 Multimedia*. He was a contributing author to Que's *Killer Windows Utilities*; *Using Windows 3.11*, Special Edition; and *Excel Professional Techniques*. Roger is a contributing editor for Fawcette Technical Publication, Inc.'s *Visual Basic Programmer's Journal*. Roger's CompuServe address is 70233,2161, and you can reach him via the Internet at rogerj@mcp.com or as Roger_Jennings on The Microsoft Network.

Contributing author **Matthew Harris** has been involved with the microcomputer industry since 1980 and began programming applications for IBM PCs and compatibles in 1983. He has provided programming, technical support, training, and consulting services to the 6th International Conference on AIDS, the University of California at San Francisco, and many private firms. Matthew is the author of Que's *The Disk Compression Book*, coauthor of *Using FileMaker Pro 2.0 for Windows*, and was a contributing author to Que's *Using Word for Windows 6*, Special Edition; *Using Excel 5*, Special Edition; *Excel Professional Techniques*; *Using Paradox 4.5 for DOS*; *Using Paradox for Windows 5.0*; and *Using MS-DOS 6*. You can reach Matthew via CompuServe 74017,766 or over the Internet at 74017.766@compuserve.com.

Acknowledgments

Microsoft's **Frank Wong** graciously provided much of the detailed information about Windows 95's new Audio Compression Manager and Wave Mapper that appears in Chapter 9, "Playing and Recording Hi-Fi Sound and Music." **Jeff Stone** of Microsoft Online Services provided valuable insights for Chapter 13, "Joining The Microsoft Network." **Pam Hazelrigg**, who is unquestionably the most active MSN beta tester, made the General Chat sessions a fun place for all participants. **Sandy Garrett's** advice on The Microsoft Network and in the CompuServe Windows 95 beta forum is much appreciated. Special thanks also go to **Michael Paoli** for his expert assistance in making the Internet connections and using the FTP (file transfer protocol), as described in Chapter 14, "Hooking Up to the Internet."

Donald Doherty and **Scott Mauvais** were the technical editors for *Unveiling Windows 95;* their sharp eyes for technical slipups and their suggestions for improvement contributed greatly to the accuracy of this book. Any errors or omissions, however, rest squarely on the shoulders of the authors.

Thanks to associate publisher **Joe Wikert** for editorial guidance, to product development director **Chris Haidri** for development assistance, and to senior editor **Mike La Bonne** for production editing this book.

Trademarks

This book is based on information on Windows 95 made public by Microsoft as of 10-28-94. Because this information was made public before the release of the product, we encourage you to visit your local bookstore at that time for updated books on Windows 95.

If you have a modem or access to the Internet, you can always get up-to-the-minute information on Windows 95 direct from Microsoft on WinNews:

On CompuServe:	GO WINNEWS
On the Internet:	ftp://ftp.microsoft.com/PerOpSys/Win_News/Chicago
	http://www.microsoft.com
On AOL:	keyword WINNEWS
On Prodigy:	jumpword WINNEWS
On Genie:	WINNEWS file area on Windows RTC

You can also subscribe to Microsoft's WinNews electronic newsletter by sending Internet e-mail to enews@microsoft.nwnet.com and putting the words SUBSCRIBE WINNEWS in the text of the e-mail.

We'd Like to Hear from You!

As part of our continuing effort to produce books of the highest possible quality, Que would like to hear your comments. To stay competitive, we really want you, as a computer book reader and user, to let us know what you like or dislike most about this book or other Que products.

You can mail comments, ideas, or suggestions for improving future editions to the address below, or send us a fax at (317) 581-4663. For the on-line inclined, Macmillan Computer Publishing now has a forum on CompuServe (type **GO QUEBOOKS** at any prompt) through which our staff and authors are available for questions and comments. In addition to exploring our forum, please feel free to contact me personally on CompuServe at 74143,1574 to discuss your opinions of this book.

Thanks in advance—your comments will help us to continue publishing the best books available on computer topics in today's market.

Chris Haidri
Product Development Specialist
Que Corporation
201 W. 103rd Street
Indianapolis, Indiana 46290
USA

Contents at a Glance

Contents

Introduction

Microsoft Corporation's extravaganza celebrating the retail release of Windows 95 is likely to result in Bill Gates & Company displacing Ringling Bros. and Barnum & Bailey as the proprietor of the "Greatest Show on Earth." Windows 95, originally code-named Chicago, was in its second formal beta testing stage, called Beta 2 or M7, when this book was written, so it wouldn't surprise anyone if Microsoft rented the entire city of Chicago some time in the first half of 1995 for an 8-hour (or longer) soirée. After all, Microsoft has invested hundreds—perhaps thousands—of programmer-years in the development of Windows 95 and the 32-bit Windows NT operating system, much of which has been absorbed into Windows 95. When you consider that a programmer-year probably costs Microsoft more than $100,000 (including administrative and program management overhead), the numbers add up to tens or hundreds of millions of dollars. What's a few million to rent a namesake city?

Even in the beta stage, Windows 95 promises to be a sure-fire winner; Windows 95's an operating system with something for everyone. Computer neophytes will find that the apparent demise of DOS makes getting started with the PC vastly easier than with Windows 3.1+. Windows 95's spiffed-up user interface helps users navigate the operating system and adds a Start button at the bottom of the display. (Windows 95 even displays an animated `Click Here to Begin` message to make sure that Windows *naifs* don't suffer from rodentoclickaphobia—fear of clicking the mouse.) The accessory applets (small applications included with Windows 95) offer the functionality you expect from full-fledged applications. As an example, WordPad, which replaces Windows 3.1+'s Write and Notepad applications, can read and save files in Microsoft Word 6.0, rich-text, Windows 3.1 Write, and ASCII text formats. Not coincidentally, WordPad is a mini-Word 6.0, complete with a toolbar and a ruler.

> **Note**
>
> The term *Windows 95* refers to the retail version of Microsoft Windows 95, which Microsoft states will be released in the "first half of 1995," unless otherwise noted in the text. The Beta 2 version of Windows 95, build 224, which was released to about 30,000 beta testers in early November 1994, is called M7 (for Milestone 7) in this book. (Microsoft assigns sequential build numbers to versions of Windows 95 released for internal and external testing.) In this book, *Windows 3.1+* includes Windows 3.1 and 3.11, plus Windows for Workgroups 3.1 and 3.11. The term *Windows NT* includes both Windows NT 3.5 Workstation and Windows NT 3.5 Server, unless explicit reference is made to the Workstation or Server version.

An old Chinese curse says: "May you lead an *interesting* life." Adapting to Windows 95's new desktop-style user interface will be an *interesting* experience for long-time Windows 3.1+ users, and may cause temporary culture shock. Windows power users, however, get a full 32-bit, multithreaded, multitasking operating system. But power users are likely to be forced to wait from six to nine months for upgrades to Windows 3.1 applications that fully support multithreaded operation. In the meantime, 32-bit OLE 2.01 and ODBC 2.0 provide adequate compensation for the lack of threads in the first 32-bit versions of major productivity applications. (See Chapter 6, "Upgrading to 32-Bit Productivity Applications," for translations of OLE, ODBC, and other Windows 95 acronyms.)

Many Windows developers and power users who initially choose to use Windows NT 3.5 may be drawn into the Windows 95 fold, after they overcome resistance to using terms such as *My Computer* and *Network Neighborhood*, and the apparent lack of Windows 3.1's familiar Program Manager and File Manager applets. However, according to the "Windows NT Gets Face-Lift" story in the December 26, 1994 issue of *Information Week*, Windows NT 3.5 users will have the option of grafting the Windows 95 user interface onto Windows NT "within 90 days of Windows 95's release." Dhiren Fonseca, the Microsoft Windows 95 product manager quoted in the story said, "The Interface won't be part of an NT upgrade. Rather, it will be part of the normal NT service packs we send out to users." If Windows 3.1+ and upgraded Windows NT 3.5 *aficionados* don't want to use Explorer instead of File Manager, Microsoft has thoughtfully provided Windows 95 versions of both ProgMan and FileMan for the unconverted.

The magazine publishing industry has reaped a Windows 95 bonanza; articles about Windows 95, Microsoft, and/or Bill Gates fill tens of thousands of column inches in publications ranging from *ComputerWorld* to *Business Week*, and even the *New York Times* carries the occasional Windows 95 story. You'll also see many snippets in this book that quote late-1994 issues of *Information Week*, *PC Week*, and *Datamation*. But book publishers, including Que Corporation, haven't been so lucky. Microsoft's repeated postponement of the retail release date for Windows 95 causes publication schedules for updates to best-selling, step-by-step guides to Windows, such as Ron Person's *Special Edition Using Windows 95* (by Que Corporation), to slip in unison. Slipping publication schedules drive book publishers nuts.

On the other hand, Windows 95 is the foundation of the *convergence* (discussed in Chapter 1) of low-cost PC hardware, easy-to-use software, pre-installed CD-ROM drives, and simple access to the *infobahn* that will drive the burgeoning home computer market in the second half of the 1990s. According to Andy Grove, president of Intel Corp., the late 1990s will see worldwide PC sales of 100 million or more units per year. Book publishers, hardware manufacturers, and software suppliers alike will reap the late harvest sown by Windows 95.

Microsoft's contribution to convergence, The Microsoft Network (MSN), has stirred a maelstrom of controversy since MSN's official announcement at the November 1994 COMDEX computer show in Las Vegas. MSN, described in Chapter 13, "Joining The Microsoft Network," represents Microsoft's entry into the world of commercial online information services. Some commercial online services consider including the client software for MSN with Windows 95 and integrating the MSN client within the Windows 95 operating system to be "unfair competition." Microsoft contends that MSN will increase the size of the online information services market, benefiting all of the participants. Regardless of who's right on the "fairness" issue, MSN is likely to become the leading online service, according to the December 1994 issue of the *Windows Watcher* newsletter. As noted in Chapter 13, many industry pundits believe that MSN will have a greater effect on the PC industry than Windows 95 itself.

Aiming at a Moving Target

When this book was written, Windows 95 was still a moving target. Writing a guide to a product whose user interface and feature set are in a perpetual state of flux is a chancy proposition. An article titled, "Windows 95 Slims Down: Features Sacrificed to Meet Deadlines," in the Aug. 15, 1994, issue of *Information Week* quoted Brad Chase, general manager of Microsoft's personal systems group, referring to the Beta 1 (M6) version: "If Capone isn't ready when Windows 95 is rock solid, we'll probably release the operating system without the universal inbox features." *Capone* is an upgrade to Windows 95's Exchange electronic mail (e-mail) application, called *Info Center* in Beta 1, that collects a user's mail from everywhere, ultimately including voice mail, in a single spot. Microsoft Exchange looks good in M7 and Exchange is required to send and receive MSN e-mail, thus there's little likelihood that Capone will miss the final cut. (You'll have to wait a bit longer for voice mail features to be implemented by a new Microsoft application code-named "Tazz," according to the "Microsoft Answers the Call" story by Mary Hayes in the Dec. 19, 1994 issue of *Information Week*.) The August *Information Week* article disclosed that the planned Internet interface will be missing from Windows 95, and it isn't in M7. Thus, an Internet interface isn't likely to appear in the retail version, but MSN promises to provide access to Internet e-mail and Usenet "news groups." (Don't worry, though; Windows 95 *will* support TCP/IP and direct dialup to an Internet host via PPP, the UNIX Point-to-Point Protocol, and SLIP, the Serial Line Interface Protocol, through commercial providers of Internet access. Both PPP and SLIP work in Beta 2, as demonstrated in Chapter 14, "Hooking Up to the Internet."

Cutting back features, if necessary, is a better strategy than adding further delays to Windows 95's release, according to most Windows 95 writers. Not just book publishers, but computer suppliers, hardware manufacturers, and software publishers have invested hundreds of millions of dollars getting ready for Windows 95, which originally was scheduled to ship in early- to mid-1994. Making Windows 95 compatible with the 60 or 70 million PCs running DOS and Windows 3.1+ now appears to be Microsoft's biggest hurdle. In the fall of 1994, Microsoft promised Windows 95 would be available "in the first half of 1995." Brad Silverberg, senior vice-president of Microsoft's Personal Systems Division announced on December 19, 1994 that the retail release date for Windows 95 "might" be pushed back to August 1995. According to Silverman, the further delay is due to "installation, compatibility and configuration" problems with Windows 95.

Who Should Read This Book

As you've probably gathered from the tone of this introduction, *Unveiling Windows 95* isn't a step-by-step guide to Windows 95. Instead, this book describes the nuts and bolts of the Windows 95 operating system and Microsoft's design philosophy for the product. The goal of *Unveiling Windows 95* is to paint the picture of Windows 95 so you can determine whether it's as great an operating system as it's cracked up to be, and Microsoft says it is. (Remember that it was P.T. Barnum who said, "There's a sucker born every minute.") Thus, there's a substantial amount of editorial content, opinion, and an occasional touch of sarcasm in this book.

Unveiling Windows 95 also contains its share of guesswork and rumors about the final feature set of Windows 95. Material of this ilk doesn't belong in a how-to-use-it, step-by-step tutorial. The authors of this book have collectively written several tutorial books for Windows database applications, programming, and multimedia, and have contributed many chapters to other Windows guides. It's an engaging experience to abandon the "Choose Open from the File menu to display the *whatever* dialog" style in favor of a narrative that instead describes the significance of a new product and its features.

This book is intended for an eclectic audience, encompassing the following *personae*:

- People and families making the decision to purchase a home computer, the "information appliance" of the late 1990s

- Current users of Windows 3.1+ considering migrating to Windows 95 in either a business or home environment

- Windows 3.1+ power users needing esoteric information on features such as multitasking, multithreading, OLE 2.01 compound documents, and OLE Automation

- Information systems (IS) managers planning to evaluate Windows 95 for use throughout the enterprise

- Network administrators and PC support people who must live with the decisions made by their IS managers

- Software publishers and hardware manufacturers wanting an independent analysis of the pros and cons of Windows 95 and the size of the market for their Windows 95-oriented products

Including first-time computer users in the audience for this book requires incorporation of introductory material, such as the descriptions of commonly used PC bus structures that appear in Chapter 2, "Making Hardware Plug and Play." Computer specifications include a variety of exotic terms and acronyms that prospective computer users must understand to make an informed purchasing decision; experienced PC users can skip these sections.

An Important *Caveat*

This book was written using the Beta 2 version of Windows 95, also known as M7. The user interface (UI) of Windows 95 wasn't "frozen" in Beta 2; some elements of the feature set of Beta 2 were incomplete, help files were few and far between, and documentation for the operating system and accessory applications was scant, to be generous. The Microsoft Network was in its early beta-testing stage. Microsoft scheduled the third beta version of Windows 95, tentatively labeled the "Preview Edition" (M8), for release to about 400,000 beta sites in early 1995, after this book was sent to the printer. (Most users of M8 must purchase the beta release for about $30.) If Windows 95 follows a pattern established by previous Microsoft Windows beta testing programs, there may be more than one Preview Edition or release candidate. Thus, you can expect conflicts between some of the figures in this book and the corresponding display of the final retail version of Windows 95. Such discrepancies, however, are likely to be minor and should not detract from the usefulness and your enjoyment of this book.

As noted in the earlier section "Aiming at a Moving Target," Microsoft announced in early August 1994 that some uncompleted features that might delay the release of Windows 95 beyond the revised target date of "early 1995" would be dropped. Thus, you may find accessory applets and other features described in this book to be missing from Windows 95. If this is the case, it's very likely Microsoft will offer you later in 1995 the opportunity to buy the missing elements as add-on applets (for a nominal charge).

How This Book Is Organized

Unveiling Windows 95 is organized into five parts that address the major new feature sets of Windows 95. The chapter-by-chapter content of each section is described under the headings that follow.

Part I, "Introducing Windows 95"

Part I provides an overview of Windows 95, the new Windows 95 User Interface (UI), and running Windows applications under the Windows 95 operating system. A description of Windows 95's Plug and Play features and a guide to the PC hardware you need to run Windows 95 precede the sections describing the UI, because you might not even see Windows 95's UI if you don't have a sufficiently capable PC.

■ Chapter 1, "Building the 'Information Appliance' of the 1990s," describes how the convergence of the Windows 95 operating system, low-cost Intel-compatible PC hardware, and instant access via modem to worldwide information sources will bring about a 100 million PC per year market by the late 1990s.

■ Chapter 2, "Making Hardware Plug and Play," describes the single most important feature of Windows 95 for new computer users and those who plan to upgrade their PCs—automated Plug and Play installation of adapter cards in desktop PCs and of PCMCIA devices used with laptops. Chapter 2 also includes descriptions of today's most popular PC bus structures, plus a recommended specification for buying a Windows 95-compatible PC.

■ Chapter 3, "Exploring the Windows 95 Interface," explains the new desktop-oriented Windows 95 user interface, file and document management with Windows 95, the upgraded Control Panel, and how Windows 95's UI relates to Windows 3.1+ and the Apple Macintosh operating system.

■ Chapter 4, "Using the Built-In Accessory Applets," gives you a quick tour of each productivity application built into Windows 95, such as WordPad and WinPad, that appear in the Accessories folder. Descriptions of the multimedia applets, CD Player, Media Player, and Sound Recorder, appear in Part II.

■ Chapter 5, "Running Your Current Applications under Windows 95," describes how existing Windows productivity applications take on the Windows 95 look and feel and how your favorite Windows 3.1+ applications take advantage of new Windows 95 features.

■ Chapter 6, "Upgrading to 32-Bit Productivity Applications," examines how Windows 95's 32-bit preemptive multitasking and multithreading will enhance performance of future Win32 (Windows 32-bit) productivity applications, such as word processing and spreadsheet programs.

Part II, "Exploring Windows 95's Multimedia Features"

Multimedia is where the action is in the home PC market, and the business world is finally beginning to adopt multimedia in earnest. Windows 95's 32-bit multimedia feature set, including the new 32-bit CD-ROM file system (CDFS), brings needed ease of use and performance improvements to Windows multimedia entertainment and educational products. The following chapters of Part II summarize what you can expect from Windows 95 in the multimedia scene, and which accessory devices take best advantage of Windows 95's new multimedia features.

■ Chapter 7, "Interacting with Windows 95 Multimedia," is an overview of the multimedia market of 1995 and beyond, version 2 of the

Multimedia PC standard, and how Windows 95 fits into the multimedia scene, including the ephemeral *Information Superhighway*.

■ Chapter 8, "Using CD-ROM Drives with Windows 95," examines the new triple-speed and quad-speed CD-ROM drives, explains the differences between new and existing CD-ROM drive interface standards, and describes Windows 95's new integrated CD-ROM device drivers plus the 32-bit CDFS.

■ Chapter 9, "Playing and Recording Hi-Fi Sound and Music," explains how Windows 95's new voice and music compression algorithms based on ADPCM (Adaptive Differential Pulse Code Modulation) let you store more sound files on your fixed disk. Windows 95's new Audio Compression Manager and Wave Mapper also are covered.

■ Chapter 10, "Watching *Real* Digital Video," shows you the most important advancement in Windows 95 multimedia: 32-bit Video for Windows. Together with MPEG (Motion Picture Experts Group) compression, which requires an MPEG adapter card for decompression, Windows 95's 32-bit operating system finally makes full-screen, full-motion digital video a reality.

■ Chapter 11, "Taking Advantage of Windows 95's Game Features," looks at how enterprising computer game publishers are taking advantage of Windows 95's new WinG (high-performance Windows Game) graphics, digital joystick support, and other Windows 95 multimedia features to create a new generation of challenging, high-performance PC games.

Part III, "Telecomputing with Windows 95"

The Internet has been 1994's hottest computer topic, and virtually every computer now has a modem installed. Windows 95's built-in modem support and new HyperTerminal applet simplify the process of connecting your computer to the outside world. The built-in client for The Microsoft Network makes joining MSN an almost-automatic process. Windows 95's built-in ISDN (Integrated Signaling Digital Network, a high-speed telecommunication protocol) support makes telecommuting to the office and teleconferencing practical. The chapters of Part III discuss Windows 95's handling of modem-based communication in detail.

■ Chapter 12, "Connecting to the Outside World," leads you through Windows 95's telecommunication features, including automatic modem detection and support, using the HyperTerminal applet, and how to install an ISDN connection.

- Chapter 13, "Joining The Microsoft Network," gives you a preview of Microsoft's new online information service, which is likely to be your primary source of technical support for Windows 95.

- Chapter 14, "Hooking Up to the Internet," explains the UNIX TCP/IP (Transport Control Protocol/Internet Protocol) used by the Internet, connecting to the Internet with PPP (Point-to-Point Protocol) and SLIP (Serial Line Interface Protocol), and how to use the TELNET terminal applet included with Windows 95.

- Chapter 15, "Faxing with Microsoft At Work Fax," describes Windows 95's built-in fax reception and transmission capabilities, and provides an introduction to Microsoft's TAPI (Telephony Application Programming Interface).

Part IV, "Networking Windows 95"

By the end of 1995, experts estimate that more than 60 percent of all PCs will be connected by networks classified as local area networks (LAN) and wide area networks (WAN). Like Windows for Workgroups 3.11, Windows 95 includes its own 32-bit peer-to-peer networking system based on the NetBEUI (Network BIOS Extended User Interface) protocol, but Windows 95 also adds built-in support for Novell IPX/SPX and TCP/IP protocols. You can even create your own simple WAN using the remote access services (RAS) provided by Windows 95 and low-cost ISDN lines. The chapters in Part IV describe the gamut of the networking features offered by Windows 95.

- Chapter 16, "Using Windows 95 Clients with Existing Networks," describes Windows 95's 32-bit networking features, how to install the necessary protocols to connect to existing Novell, LAN Manager, LAN Server, TCP/IP, and Windows for Workgroup networks, and explains how Windows 95's Network Neighborhood and Printers windows provide quick access to network resources.

- Chapter 17, "Creating Workgroups with Windows 95's Peer-to-Peer Networking," shows you how to quickly set up a simple Windows 95 file and printer sharing network at a cost of less than $150 per PC.

- Chapter 18, "Messaging with Windows 95's Exchange Client," describes Microsoft Exchange, a "universal inbox" that gathers e-mail from network mailboxes, the Internet, CompuServe, AT&T Mail, MCI Mail, and other e-mail service providers. You also get a brief tour of 32-bit Extended MAPI (Messaging API 1.0), which serves as the foundation for Microsoft Mail 4.0 and Microsoft Exchange Server.

■ Chapter 19, "Synchronizing Your Notebook Computer with Briefcases," describes how Windows 95 briefcases overcome the single biggest problem of mobile computing, keeping the files on your desktop PC and your laptop PC in synch.

■ Chapter 20, "Using Windows 95's Deal-Up Networking," shows road warriors how to use Windows 95 RAS with desktop and laptop PCs to connect to their own office PC or to a network that provides dialup access.

■ Chapter 21, "Managing Networked PCs with Windows 95," gives IS managers and PC support people a guide to Windows 95's remote configuration and management features for networked PCs running Windows 95.

Part V, "Digging into the Windows 95 Operating System"

Part V gets into the technicalities of the Windows 95 operating system, with emphasis on operating system design, setting up and running Windows 95 in a multiple operating system environment, the intricacies of Windows 95's new Registry database, Windows 95's implementation of 32-bit OLE 2.01 within the operating system, and how DOS applications run under Windows 95.

■ Chapter 22, "Understanding Windows 95's Operating System Architecture," expands Chapter 6's description of multitasking and multithreading to provide a complete overview of the design of Windows 95.

■ Chapter 23, "Setting Up and Managing Windows 95," explains the significance of your choice(s) when you install Windows 95: Overlaying your present Windows 3.1+ installation or starting with a clean slate in a new directory. Setting up dual-boot and triple-boot operation with Windows 95, Windows 3+, and Windows NT also is covered.

■ Chapter 24, "Replacing WIN.INI, SYSTEM.INI, and REG.DAT with Registry," presents Windows 95's Registry, the new registration database that includes entries that hold information on every facet of your computer and the applications you install under Windows 95.

■ Chapter 25, "Running DOS Applications under Windows 95," describes Microsoft's implementation of MS-DOS as a subset of the Windows 95 operating system and the influence of this new architecture on how existing DOS applications run under Windows 95.

Part I

Introducing Windows 95

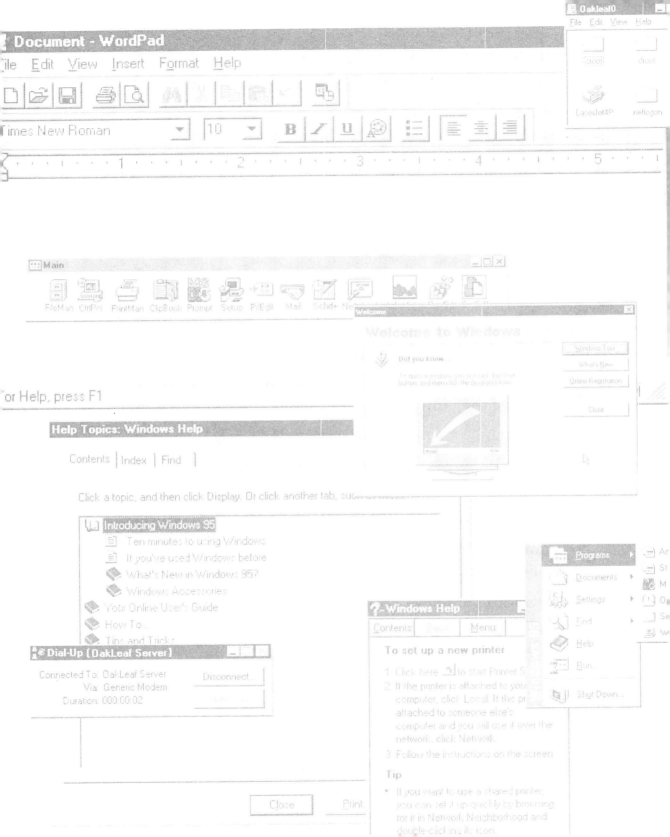

Chapter 1

Building the "Information Appliance" of the 1990s

The advent of Windows 95 will introduce yet another new device to millions of American homes: *information appliance*. The information appliance is a modem-equipped personal computer, plus a CD-ROM drive, sound card, and laser printer. In 1995 and beyond, the information appliance will take its place next to other home electronic essentials, such as videocassette recorders and microwave ovens, achieving "must have" status. Mass production and chain-store distribution bring economies of scale and inevitably lower prices. Andy Grove, president and chief executive officer of Intel Corporation, stated in his June 1994 keynote speech at PC Expo: "By the late 1990s, we expect 100 million PC units to ship worldwide each year—more than cars and TVs." Businesses will buy a substantial percentage of these PCs, but the majority will end up in homes. According to an article by Steven H. Wildstrom in the Aug. 1, 1994, issue of *Business Week* magazine, "70% or so of American homes [today] remain computerless."

PC makers have made several attempts to create a truly "personal" PC for the home market. The most notable failure was IBM's early PC Junior, with its "Chiclet" keyboard. Other firms that focused on the home computer market, such as Commodore, also have fallen by the wayside. Apple Computer, on the other hand, which emphasized the home PC market with its Apple II and Macintosh product lines, has managed to gain a domestic foothold by reducing the price of the Mac. The question arises: Why will PCs successfully penetrate the home market barriers in the last half of the 1990s, in the light of previous failures? The answer is *convergence*. This chapter discusses convergence as it applies to both the home and business elements of the new PC market of 1995 and beyond, with emphasis on Windows 95's role in achieving the necessary critical mass.

Convergence in the PC Market

Convergence is a term associated with the merging of high-speed telecommunication and digital entertainment on the information superhighway. The *infobahn*, as the highway's commonly called, someday will deliver interactive, on-demand video entertainment and educational features by phone lines, cable, and satellite to a variety of display devices, ranging from PCs to wireless personal digital assistants (PDAs). Microsoft cofounder and chief executive officer Bill Gates discussed convergence in his keynote address, "Information at Your Fingertips—2005," at the November 1994 COMDEX computer exposition:

> "Of course, at the center of this will be the idea of digital convergence. That is, taking all the information—books, catalogs, shopping approaches, professional advice, art, movies, and taking those things in their digital form, ones and zeroes, and being able to provide them on demand on a device looking like a TV, a small device you carry around, or what the PC will evolve into. All of these form factors will count. But we'll need to have a common architecture so we can take all the authoring, the work done to prepare this media, and make it easily available to people using these different devices. So this is what we're reading about all the time, with all the different stories. The communications companies have to think about this because it is their future. Media companies, from TV to cable, to Hollywood studios, need to get involved because it is their future. The consumer electronics industry is coming into this and will need to be one of the ones building these devices. Certainly, for the PC industry, this is what it's all about. Lots of advances, lots of things that we can draw on to have growth in years ahead. So even at 40 million [PC] units a year we still have lots of frontiers to conquer and lots of impact."

Today, the high-speed infobahn is a technological vision that's likely to remain only a vision, until at least the late 1990s. On the other hand, the following set of conditions are resulting in personal computing convergence *now*:

▶ See Chapter 3, "Exploring the Windows 95 Interface"

■ *The promise of a new operating system, Windows 95, that makes PCs less intimidating to new users.* Although Windows 3.x greatly expanded the business market and opened the home market for Intel-based PCs, Microsoft designed Windows 95's graphical user interface (GUI) specifically for new computer users. (Present users of Windows 3.x may find adapting to Windows 95 a bit unsettling at first.)

■ *Access to a broad range of entertainment and educational material in PC-compatible formats.* Affordable CD-ROM drives, a wide variety of CD-ROM titles (including the new CD-Video discs), low-cost sound cards, and easy access to The Microsoft Network and the Internet make the interactive PC an attractive alternative to passive watching of commercial and educational TV programs. Windows 95's built-in dial-up networking features ease direct access to the Internet. The Microsoft Network promises to deliver Internet e-mail and Usenet "newsgroups."

■ *Rapidly decreasing cost of PCs and peripherals.* Andy Grove's rule of thumb is that PC power doubles about every 18 months at constant or lower cost. Intensive competition has drastically lowered the cost of computers using Intel 80486 chips and similar devices from other semiconductor manufacturers. Figure 1.1, a slide presented by Bill Gates at Microsoft's Professional Developer's conference in late 1993, shows the PC's price-performance trend from early 1990 to mid-1994.

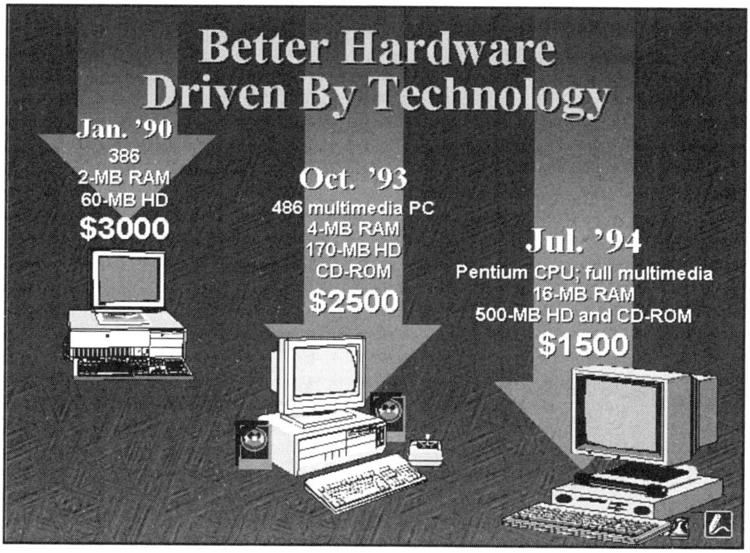

▶ See Chapter 8, "Using CD-ROM Drives with Windows 95," Chapter 9, "Playing and Recording Hi-Fi Sound and Music," Chapter 10, "Watching *Real* Digital Video," and Chapter 14, "Hooking Up to the Internet"

Introducing Windows 95

Fig. 1.1
Price-performance trends in the PC industry, 1990 to 1994 (courtesy of Microsoft Corporation).

■ *Widespread distribution of home PCs in specialty and discount stores, which offer extended credit terms on purchases of this magnitude ("No down payment, 24 months to pay, and make your first payment after 90 days!").* Although chains such as Costco-Price Club, Circuit City, and the Good Guys have carried PCs for several years, mid-1994 saw a dramatic increase in the amount of display area devoted to PCs and peripherals. Figure 1.2 is a slide from Andy Grove's PC Expo presentation that shows the growth of shipments of PCs using the Intel 80x86 architecture. Much of the projected increase for 1994 shipments can be attributed to the home PC market.

> **Note**
>
> Bill Gates's 1994 projection that an Intel Pentium PC with CD-ROM drive, sound card, 16M of RAM, and a 300M fixed disk drive would sell for $1,500 in July 1994 appears to have been a bit optimistic. This price-performance target, however, likely will be met by the time Windows 95 reaches the retail market.

Fig. 1.2
Shipments of PCs using Intel 80x86 architecture, 1989 to 1994 (courtesy of Intel Corporation).

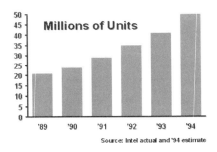

▶ See Chapter 12, "Connecting to the Outside World"

■ *Availability of middle-band telecommunication capability at low cost.* High-speed Integrated Signaling Digital Network (ISDN) telephone lines are available today in most metropolitan areas. ISDN provides almost a tenfold increase in data transmission rate, compared with today's standard 14,400 bps (bits per second, 1,440 characters per second) modems. ISDN reduces the time required to transmit a 1.44M (1.44 million characters, bytes not bits) file from about 20 minutes to about 2 minutes at 128,000 bps. ISDN likely will be the link that brings low-cost teleconferencing to businesses and even homes. By 1996 or 1997, ISDN lines should be widely available, even in rural locations.

▶ See Chapter 13, "Joining The Microsoft Network"

■ *Wide-band transmission of digital data via satellite to small satellite antennas (called* dishes) *you can mount just about anywhere that has an unobstructed view of the southern sky.* Hughes Network Systems, a unit of GM Hughes Electronics, expects to introduce its DirecPC service in spring 1995. DirecPC provides 12-Mbps (about 1.2 megabytes/seconds) PC connectivity to the Internet and delivers a variety of multimedia content from a Hughes Galaxy satellite through a PC adapter card. Microsoft is reported to be considering using Hughes' DirecTV high-power direct broadcast satellite, DBS-3 (to be launched in mid-1995), to downlink information from The Microsoft Network to your PC.

It's the convergence of PC and telecommunication technology that's creating the demand not only for home PCs, but also for the myriad notebook and subnotebook PCs available today. Higher-performance computers bring the need for higher-speed telecommunications, and vice versa. "The bigger the communications pipeline," says Andy Grove, "the more powerful the computer needs to be to handle the data flowing through the pipeline. And the more powerful the processor, the bigger the pipe required to transmit data to it. The computing/communications spiral is the determining force for both industries in the 1990s."

What's Wrong with Yesterday's PCs and Operating Systems?

A computer, whether a PC or a mainframe, is totally lifeless without an operating system to perform basic functions such as accepting keystrokes, painting the display, and reading data from and writing data to disk drives. According to the article, "Next Stop, Chicago," in the Aug. 1, 1994, issue of *Business Week*, there were then about 120 million users of Microsoft's MS-DOS operating system worldwide, including 55 million Windows 3.x users. MS-DOS is designed solely for use with Intel 80x86 architecture, so at least 120 million IBM-compatible PCs likely were in existence as of mid-1994. Based on Intel's estimate of sales of 50 million 80x86 PCs in 1994 and wide-scale retail availability of Windows 95 in the third quarter of 1995, the number of DOS users will have grown over this six-month period to more than 150 million, of which some 70 million or more also will have Windows 3.1+ or Windows 95 installed. Microsoft and Intel are likely to report record earnings for 1994. According to *Forbes* magazine, quoted in the August 1994 issue of Jesse Berst's *Windows Watcher* newsletter, Microsoft's Bill Gates this year replaced Warren Buffet as the richest person in the U.S. and the sixth richest person in the world, excluding monarchs and dictators. If the DOS and Windows PC business is so good, why make waves with Windows 95?

The fact is that PC technology is running full steam ahead, but DOS and Windows 3.1+ quickly are running out of steam. Similarly, yesterday's conventional bus structure, called the ISA (Industry Standard Architecture) bus, is the bottleneck to painting Windows' display and accessing data on fixed disk drives. Following is a list of problems that plague most of the 150 million PCs in use today:

▶ See Chapter 22, "Understanding Windows 95's Operating System Architecture"

- *A cumbersome 16-bit DOS operating system, a legacy from the original 16-bit Intel 8080 microprocessor.* Present versions of DOS ignore the capability of 80386 and higher microprocessors to run in 32-bit *protected mode*, a far more efficient method of using memory than DOS's 16-bit *real mode*. Windows 3.1 runs under DOS, so Windows and its applications suffer the real-mode-out-of-memory blues. Many Windows users are blissfully unaware of DOS's cryptic command-line prompt until Windows suddenly won't load automatically. Apple Computer's System 7.x and IBM's OS/2 are 32-bit operating systems. Microsoft's Windows 95 and Windows NT 3.5 both are 32-bit operating systems, although Windows 95 retains some 16-bit operations to minimize its memory requirements and provide compatibility with existing 16-bit DOS and Windows applications.

- *High hardware acquisition cost for most alternative operating systems.* Windows NT 3.5 provides a fully 32-bit operating system, but requires 12M to 16M of RAM (random access or chip memory) to run effectively. The average PC in use today probably has about 2M of RAM, with 4M now the standard for most prepackaged home PCs. Windows 95 and IBM OS/2 *can* run in 4M. (Larger Windows applications require at least 8M to attain reasonable performance.) At about $50 per megabyte, adding enough RAM to just run Windows NT 3.5 costs at least $400. It's likely that 8M of RAM will become the prepackaged-PC standard for 1995 and beyond.

- *Rapid hardware obsolescence.* Just two to three years ago, the "standard" PC used an 80386 microprocessor on an ISA bus and ran at 25 to 33 MHz. Now the standard is an 80486DX2 (clock-doubled) processor running at 66 MHz, with the Video Electronics Standards Association's (VESA) video local bus (VLB) or Intel's Peripheral Control Interface (PCI) bus. Either a VLB- or PCI-equipped computer is now standard with a Windows accelerator card for users who enjoy full-color graphics. 100-MHz clock-tripled chips are becoming common. Intel's Pentium processor promises to speed operations by another 50 to 100 percent. Many buyers are just making the last payment on what they now find to be their obsolete home PC. Windows 95 runs comfortably on an 80486 computer of any speed with 8M of RAM. It remains to be seen how well Windows 95 runs your favorite applications in 4M.

■ *Difficult hardware upgrade procedures.* Adding a sound card, a CD-ROM drive, or even a modem to yesterday's PC can be a nightmarish process, even for PC gurus and technicians. Manuals discuss jumper settings, IRQs, and DMA and device addresses as though these were household terms. To make things worse, you must install driver software, often for DOS and Windows. Windows 95's new Plug and Play feature lets the software automatically configure the hardware when you install (or remove) an adapter card in your desktop or notebook PC. Unfortunately, you're likely to need a new Plug and Play-compatible PC motherboard (or at least a new BIOS chip) and a new set of Plug and Play adapter cards to take full advantage of automatic self-configuration.

▶ See Chapter 2, "Making Hardware Plug and Play"

Note

By early 1995, most new motherboards will be Plug and Play compatible, but whether a full slate of Plug and Play adapter cards will be ready for the release of Windows 95 still is an open question.

■ *Growth pains in Windows 3.x and its applications.* Microsoft introduced Windows 3.0 on May 22, 1990. Windows 3.0 set the standard for the graphical user interface with its Program Manager and File Manager applications. Subsequent upgrades, such as Windows and Windows for Workgroups 3.10 and 3.11, built on the Windows 3.0 foundation, adding object linking and embedding (OLE) 1.0, electronic mail, and network file-sharing features. New Microsoft applications tack OLE 2.01 onto a straining Windows, often with unforeseen effects. Windows 95, on the other hand, is a unified operating system that encompasses OLE 2.0, Microsoft Mail and other messaging systems, and networking clients within the operating system itself, not as afterthoughts. Program Manager and File Manager now are combined into a single, integrated entity called My Computer that uses the folder metaphor for subdirectories, combined with icons for programs and documents (much like the Apple Macintosh's desktop), as figure 1.3 shows.

▶ See Chapter 16, "Using Windows 95 Clients with Existing Networks," and Chapter 18, "Messaging with Windows 95's Exchange Client"

Fig. 1.3
Windows 95's
hierarchy of
windows that
use folders to
represent sub-
directories and
icons for programs
and documents.

▶ See Chapter 6,
"Upgrading
to 32-Bit
Productivity
Applications"

It's possible to ruminate for an entire day or two over the shortcomings of
yesterday's PCs and MS-DOS, such as file names limited to 8 characters plus a
3-letter extension. Windows 95 lets you give files names up to 255 characters
long. Windows 3.1+'s out-of-memory messages are especially frustrating
when you just upgraded to 16M, thinking you'd never see that infamous
message again. Windows 95 solves most, but not quite all, of the system resource memory limitations of Windows 3.1; you must upgrade to Windows
NT and/or obtain 32-bit versions of your Windows applications to fully es-
cape the system resource barrier.

Turning the PC into an Information Appliance

The original IBM PC, like most of the microcomputers that preceded it, was
designed for computer aficionados. Only a nerd could truly appreciate and be
willing to learn all the ins and outs of MS-DOS, decipher its interrupts and
idiosyncrasies, and confidently type command-line instructions at DOS's
cryptic C:\> prompt. This techie orientation meant that the average PC user
was provided with a simple menu from which she or he could choose which
program to run; if the program wasn't on the menu or something went
wrong, you were simply out of luck. In many respects, using MS-DOS required the same degree of perspicacity, skill, and luck as programming an

early VCR to record your favorite soaps. A computer that relies on DOS won't likely become a universal home appliance. The following three sections describe what's required for PCs to achieve the same status as the ubiquitous VCR.

Emulating the Macintosh with an OS/2 Flavor

The first and foremost requirement is to eliminate "new-user trauma." The Apple Macintosh established the standard for ease of use against which all other computer operating systems are compared. The Macintosh graphic user interface was designed from the ground up, with a bit of help from former members of Xerox Corp.'s Palo Alto Research Center (PARC), with the novice computer user in mind. Thus, it isn't surprising to find many Mac-like features incorporated in Windows 95. If you're a seasoned Mac user, you'll likely find yourself more immediately at home with Windows 95 than many Windows 3.1+ gurus. The behavior of Windows 95's menus, for instance, is similar to (but not exactly the same as) those of the Mac. Figure 1.4 shows the four-level Technicolor cascade of Windows 95's hierarchical menus that emerge when you take Microsoft's advice on launching Windows 95 and Click Here (the Start button of the task bar) to Begin, then, holding the left mouse button down, successively position the mouse pointer on the Programs, Accessories, and Games choices.

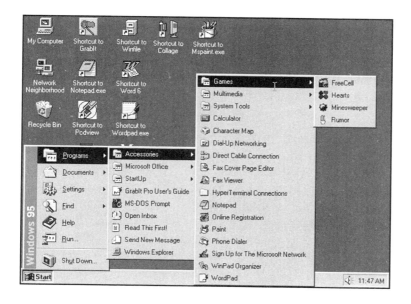

Fig. 1.4
The hierarchy of Windows 95's application launching menus displayed from the taskbar's Start button.

Microsoft and IBM collaborated for many years on the development of OS/2, until Microsoft abandoned OS/2 in favor of Windows NT in 1993. Thus, Windows 95's operating system also retains a bit of an OS/2 heritage, such as the desktop that underlies figures 1.3 and 1.4. Just because Apple's System 7.x for the Macintosh and IBM's OS/2 are losers in the PC numbers game doesn't mean that these operating systems don't have a good feature set—they do. Both operating systems simply were steamrolled by the overwhelming success of Microsoft's Windows 3.x.

> **Note**
>
> Did you notice in figure 1.4 that accelerator key combinations (Alt+*key*) were missing from the Start button's cascading menus at the Program level and lower? You still can run Windows 95 from the keyboard with the cursor and Enter keys if you're a die-hard typist, but a mouse is truly a necessity if you want to use Windows 95 effectively.

A Not-So-Sad Farewell to DOS

The second necessity is to get rid of DOS, or at least make DOS invisible. One of the primary objectives of Microsoft Windows was to hide Microsoft's greatest all-time cash cow, MS-DOS, from the average computer user. If your objective is to hide DOS from users, why not eliminate DOS altogether? That strategy won't fly because many prospective users of Windows 95 are habituated to the DOS prompt and wouldn't even *think* about converting to an operating system that can't or won't display c:\>. There are many PC games that run only under DOS, and you need DOS device drivers for some sound cards and other peripheral hardware until the manufacturers supply 32-bit Windows 95 virtual device drivers (VxDs) for their products.

▶ See Chapter 25, "Running DOS Applications under Windows 95"

OK, so what's the answer? Make Windows the operating system and emulate DOS. Sure enough, if you click Start, then mouse to Programs, a DOS window appears when you click the MS-DOS Prompt choice. Type **dir /p** at the command line and press Enter. All your favorite DOS applications appear in the form of EXE files in the \WIN95\COMMAND directory, some of which are listed in figure 1.5. Although Microsoft has mentioned a product called MS-DOS 7.0, you'll probably have to buy Windows 95 to use it, because future versions of DOS undoubtedly will be a subset of the new Windows operating system.

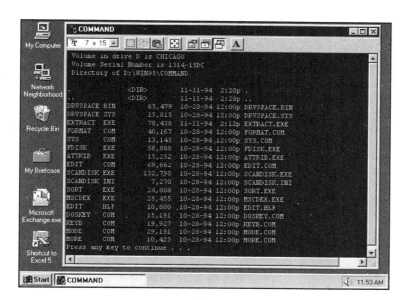

Fig. 1.5
Windows 95's
MS-DOS window
displaying a few of
the DOS execut-
able files in the
\WIN95\COMMAND
directory.

Introducing Windows 95

I

Here's some good news for new users and PC administrators. Computers that support Plug and Play and equipped with Plug and Play adapter cards don't need CONFIG.SYS and AUTOEXEC.BAT files. Each time you start Windows 95, the operating system checks to see what adapter cards and what peripheral equipment, such as printers and video display units, are installed in your PC. It next assigns each card its own parameters: interrupts (IRQ), direct memory address (DMA) channel, and port address. Finally, the startup (boot) process loads only the driver software needed to support the installed hardware. If you have a notebook computer with one or more PCMCIA slots, Plug and Play provides a process called *hot swapping*. When you exchange a PCMCIA network card for a PCMCIA modem, the Plug and Play portion of the operating system detects the card swap, unloads the network driver, and installs the modem driver.

Of course, Windows 95 supports adapter cards and other legacy devices that don't implement Plug and Play. If these devices, such as sound cards with attached CD-ROM drives, require DOS drivers and DOS terminate-and-stay-resident (TSR) applications (MSCDEX.EXE, as an example, for CD-ROM drives), you need entries in CONFIG.W40 and AUTOEXEC.W40, Windows 95's substitutes for CONFIG.SYS and AUTOEXEC.BAT. When you install Windows 95, the Setup application automatically creates these entries for you. If you use fixed disk data-compression utilities, such as Stacker 3.x, Windows 95 adds the necessary entries to CONFIG.W40 and appears to have no problems handling compressed disk volumes.

▶ See Chapter 8, "Using CD-ROM Drives with Windows 95," and Chapter 9, "Playing and Recording Hi-Fi Sound and Music"

Paving the On-Ramp to the Information Superhighway

▶ See Chapter 12, "Connecting to the Outside World," Chapter 14, "Hooking Up to the Internet," and Chapter 18, "Messaging with Windows 95's Exchange Client"

Finally, you need to make it easy to merge onto today's information super-highway, the Internet. A substantial percentage of home PC purchases are the result of the Internet craze that became epidemic in 1994. Literally millions of new users have joined the Internet in 1994, and many more will make the Internet connection in 1995. Books about joining the Internet are best-sellers for every publisher and bookstore chain. Internet service providers, who supply you a dial-up connection to the Internet for a monthly or per-hour fee, are popping up like mushrooms after a spring rain, each trying to get a piece of the Internet action. Every commercial online information service, including CompuServe, America Online, Prodigy, and Delphi, either delivers Internet connectivity to your PC today or promises to do so in the near future.

Windows 95 provides the basic components you need, such as dial-up TCP/IP (the protocol used by the Internet) services with PPP (UNIX's Point-to-Point Protocol) or SLIP (Serial Line Interface Protocol), to connect to the Internet, and simple TELNET terminal and FTP file-transfer applications. What's more important, however, is that Windows 95 includes full support for public domain and shareware WinSock (Windows sockets, version 1.1) applications for navigating the Internet, such as Mosaic, WinWAIS, and WinGopher. If you have an Internet host on your company's network, the Microsoft Exchange client, Windows 95's universal e-mail inbox, integrates Internet e-mail with other networked e-mail systems.

▶ See Chapter 13, "Joining The Microsoft Network"

The magnitude of Internet content, however, is likely to intimidate most PC neophytes. The Microsoft Network (MSN), announced at the November 1994 COMDEX exposition in Las Vegas, is Microsoft's entry into the online information services fray. If Windows 95's Setup program detects a modem in your PC, you'll be invited to sign up for MSN, which is considerably easier to navigate than the Internet. Windows 95 includes the MSN client application, which is fully integrated with Windows 95's Explorer and its Exchange client. Figure 1.6 shows the first beta version (M7) of MSN's opening window, which Microsoft calls both the *front page* and *home base*. The home base provides access to MSN's basic services: e-mail, bulletin boards (BBSs, the equivalent of CompuServe's forums), online chat sessions, and technical support for Microsoft products (including Windows 95).

Fig. 1.6
The opening
window (front
page or home
base) of The
Microsoft Network
that appears when
you connect to
MSN.

When this book was written, MSN was in its first beta-testing stage. Microsoft
had not announced the monthly and hourly charges for a subscription to
MSN, nor had Microsoft disclosed what you can expect from MSN's third-
party content providers. Microsoft Online Services (MOS) representatives say
that cost of membership in MSN will be "competitive or better," when compared with competing online information services. Press releases accompanying the announcement of MSN at COMDEX promise news, sports, and
financial information, plus "rich multimedia content." These extended services, which may carry surcharges levied by their providers, aren't likely to be
in place and fully operational until Windows 95 reaches the retail shelves.

Leveraging the Information Appliance into a Business Tool

So far, this chapter has dealt primarily with Windows as a domestic information appliance, because home computers are likely to represent the largest
initial market for Windows 95. Microsoft is expected to release an OEM (original equipment manufacturer) version of Windows 95 to computer makers
before releasing it for retail shelves. From that time forward, all Intel-
architecture PCs destined for retail distribution will leave the factory with
Windows 95 installed, possibly with a choice of dual-booting Windows for

Workgroups 3.11. (The dual-boot option is likely to appeal to purchasers of new computers to run existing Windows 3.1+ business applications.) According to an article by Lisa DiCarlo in the July 25, 1994, issue of *PC Week* magazine, Microsoft will discontinue retail distribution of Windows 3.11 and Windows for Workgroups 3.11 after Windows 95 ships. If you want to buy either product, however, you'll likely be able to order copies directly from Microsoft.

PCs used for business applications now constitute the majority of the installed base and represent the largest potential market for Windows 95. Companies that depend heavily on PCs to conduct everyday operations, however, are very reluctant to change their operating environment. This is especially true for an as-yet-unproved product that replaces both the operating system and the graphical operating environment. The cost of installing Windows 95, retraining employees to use it, and lost productivity during the Windows 95 learning curve easily can exceed $1,000 per PC. If a firm has 10,000 PCs (which many do), the cost of the upgrading process might reach $10 million.

Note

Studies show that about 80 percent of the long-term costs of business PC ownership arise from installing, configuring, and managing the PC, and training PC users; the remaining 20 percent is for hardware. The Gartner Group, a prominent market research firm, reported in its *PC Research Note: Personal Computing Costs, A Chicago Model* on Aug. 15, 1994, that the cost of supporting Windows 95 will be $1,180 less per user per year than supporting Windows 3.1+.

On the other hand, businesses will benefit from the advent of Windows 95. Here are a few of these benefits:

▶ See Chapter 16, "Using Windows 95 Clients with Existing Networks"

■ The improved networking features of Windows 95—especially Novell (IPX) and UNIX (TCP/IP) networks—and ease of navigating the network with Windows 95's Network Neighborhood window will greatly reduce installation, training, and support costs. By the end of 1994, it's probable that 60 percent or more of all PCs in the business environment will be connected to a network. Simple peer-to-peer networking capability is built into Windows 95, so even the smallest businesses can interconnect their PCs at very low cost. The primary source of today's Windows networking problems are the DOS network client programs for Novell and UNIX networks loaded by CONFIG.SYS and AUTOEXEC.BAT files. Windows 95 eliminates the need for these DOS programs by supplying its own set of 32-bit network drivers.

■ Remote access by field agents and telecommuters to the office network is simplified by Windows 95's built-in dial-up networking features and ease of modem installation. (The M7 beta version of Windows 95 uses the term *dial-up networking* to replace M6's *remote access services* or *RAS* terminology.) Windows 95 dial-up networking provides support for NetBEUI (the protocol used by Microsoft NT and LAN Manager networks, as well as IBM's LAN Server), Novell's IPX, and UNIX's TCP/IP. Even if you don't have a network, you can connect your home computer to your office computer if both have Windows 95 and a modem installed. Where ISDN is available, telecommuters can gain a 10-times performance boost at nominal cost. Figure 1.7 shows a typical dial-up networking connection in process. (The telephone number and codes used to make the connection have been disguised in figure 1.7.) After you're logged on to the remote network, the directories to which you have access appear in the Network Neighborhood window.

▶ See Chapter 20, "Using Windows 95's Dial-Up Networking"

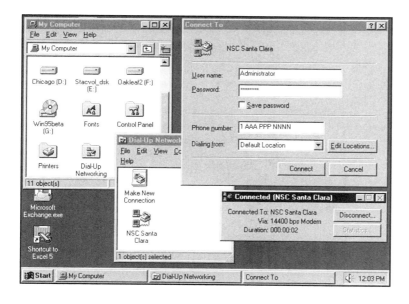

Fig. 1.7
Connecting to a remote network with Windows 95's Dial-Up Networking.

■ Windows 95 includes a set of administrative tools that allows network managers to remotely control the configuration data of networked PCs. The network manager creates "policies" for users and groups of users using the Policy Editor application (see fig. 1.8). These policies, stored in the POLICIES.DAT section of the Registry, override the settings established by the user. The network manager also can remotely read from and write to each user's Registry file.

▶ See Chapter 21, "Managing Networked PCs with Windows 95"

Introducing Windows 95

Fig. 1.8
Connecting to a
remote network
with Windows
95's Dial-Up
Networking.

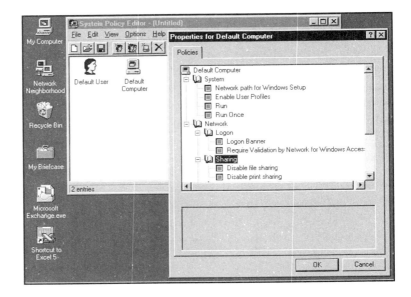

- Windows 95's new user interface will greatly reduce training time and
  cost for neophyte computer users. Unfortunately, this cost saving initially will be overshadowed by the cost of training current users of
  Windows 3.1+.

- Widespread installation of home information appliances will provide
  the business community with new recruits who are computer literate.
  If Windows 95 is as successful as expected by most industry observers,
  these new recruits already will be self-trained to use Windows 95. The
  proliferation of home computers also will provide a larger pool of potential telecommuters.

- The economies of production scale brought about by the increasing
  numbers of PCs entering the retail market will reduce substantially the
  purchase cost of business PCs of similar configuration. The trend toward more powerful home computers with larger fixed disk drives
  makes it possible to standardize on a single PC model, which businesses
  also can offer to employees at a volume discount.

It remains to be seen whether the larger members of the business community
will be "early adopters" of Windows 95. In all probability, committees will
take the safe route: "Let's wait for Windows 95.1. Remember that Windows 3
wasn't really stable until Windows 3.1 appeared." Power users undoubtedly
will use Windows 95 or Windows NT 3.5 to gain the benefits of 32-bit

operation, whether or not these products are blessed by the Information Systems department. For sales of Windows 95 to soar, mass migration to Windows 95 by large corporate Windows users is necessary. Large firms spend long periods evaluating new operating systems before adopting them. Only time will tell whether firms with tens of thousands of PCs will buy into Windows 95 on a company-wide basis or will wait for "Windows 96."

Chapter 2

Making Hardware Plug and Play

If you've added a sound card to your PC, there's a very good chance that the card—and possibly your PC—didn't work the first time you tested the installation. So you pulled out the card, changed some miniature jumpers on the sound card or one of the other adapter cards in your PC, and then tested the card again. (This assumes that you didn't lose the jumper under your desk.) The most common refrain during this process is, "Let's see, what IRQ and DMA and device addresses did I try last time?"

Plug and Play abolishes jumpers and software configuration programs; plug in a Plug and Play adapter card, and your Plug and Play-compatible computer makes it play the first time around. Figure 2.1 shows the first window of the New Device Installation Wizard that appears when you double-click the New Device icon in Control Panel. To install a Plug and Play device, you're told to shut down your computer and install the hardware. When you restart your computer, if Windows 95 can't use one of its built-in software drivers for the card, it asks you to insert the manufacturer's floppy disk in drive A. You don't even have to read the manual. (Sound card documentation often appears to be written in Pidgin.) This chapter tries to explain how Plug and Play's magic works.

Fig. 2.1

The first window
of the New Device
Installation
Wizard.

Plug and Play is a computer-industry standard to automate the process of adding new capabilities to your PC or changing PCMCIA adapters in your notebook PC. (PCMCIA stands for the Personal Computer Memory Card Interface Association.) The Plug and Play standard is a joint development of Intel Corporation and Microsoft Corporation. Other industry leaders, such as Phoenix Technologies Limited, Compaq Computer Corporation, NEC Technologies, Inc., and Toshiba Computer Systems Division, contributed their expertise to the development of the set of eight specifications that make up the Plug and Play standard.

Windows 95 is the first operating system to support the Plug and Play standard fully, but you also can gain the advantage of a limited set of Plug and Play features under MS-DOS 5+, Windows 3.1+, and Windows NT 3.5.

You might wonder why a chapter devoted to hardware precedes the chapters that describe the wonders of Windows 95's new graphical user interface and the many new features incorporated within Microsoft's new operating system. The reason is simple: it's likely that many prospective buyers of Windows 95 and 32-bit Windows applications don't have computer hardware that will run Windows 95, let alone run it with acceptable performance. This is especially true of those who now run character-based applications under DOS quite successfully but want to upgrade to Windows 95. When this book was written, Microsoft assured users that Windows 95 will run Windows applications at the same speed or faster than Windows 3.1+ in the same amount of memory (with a minimum of 4M). Only the final, retail release of Windows 95 can verify that Microsoft's assurance remains valid. Speed comparisons between an early beta version of one operating system and a finely honed released version of another operating system is invalid; beta software is seldom optimized for speed until the last stages of its development.

Many readers of this book may not be familiar with microprocessor and PC architecture, so this chapter begins with an explanation of common PC architectural terminology. If you're a prospective home computer user, you should understand at least the principal PC buzzwords so you can make an informed decision when buying your Windows 95-based information appliance. Buying a new Windows 95-capable PC involves an expenditure of at least $1,000 and more likely $1,500 to $2,000; most people or families consider such an expenditure to warrant serious study of alternatives. Experienced PC users with 80486 or faster computers, however, may want to skip the next few sections and continue with the detailed description of the Plug and Play specification that follows.

A Quick Ride on the Computer Bus

This book is devoted to PCs that use microprocessors using Intel 80x86 architecture. These microprocessors often are referred to as CISC (complex instruction set computing) devices, in contrast to the newer RISC (reduced instruction set computing) chips, typified by IBM/Apple PowerPC and Digital Equipment Corporation's Alpha processors. Windows NT was designed as a multiplatform, scalable operating system; it can run on both CISC and RISC computers, and you can improve Windows NT's performance by adding more processors if your computer has a motherboard that supports multiprocessing and has empty sockets to hold the chips. Windows 95, like its Windows 3+ predecessors, is a single-platform, single-processor operating system that runs only on computers that use the Intel architecture.

The motherboard, also the systemboard, is the main printed circuit board that usually holds the processor, memory chips, and connectors for adapter cards. Figure 2.2 shows the Properties for System sheet that appears when you double-click the System icon in Control Panel. Double-clicking the System icon in Control Panel lists the devices on the motherboard that Windows 95 recognizes. Figure 2.3 shows the Resources page that appears when you select a device and then click the Properties button.

Fig. 2.2
The Properties for
System sheet that
displays devices
Windows 95
recognizes.

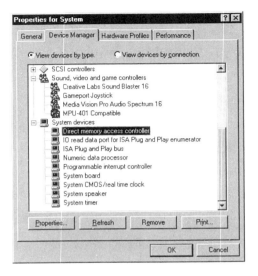

Fig. 2.3
The Resources
page for the
DMA channels
of your
computer.

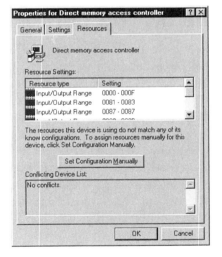

There are, however, significant differences in the architecture of the computers that use Intel 80x86 and compatible processors. The differences relate primarily to the structure of the bus that interconnects the adapter cards that connect to the video display unit, fixed disk drive, printer, and other external (peripheral) devices. Some desktop PC manufacturers integrate on the motherboard many functions that otherwise require an adapter card. Laptop PCs don't use conventional PC adapter cards; instead, most laptops provide one or two slots that accept small PCMCIA adapter cards. At first, PCMCIA cards were intended only to expand the random-access memory (RAM) of laptop computers; now you can buy fax modems, network interface cards, and even fixed disk drives in the PCMCIA format. The new PCMCIA cards support Plug and Play at the hardware level.

The sections that follow describe the most common bus structures found in today's PCs, in the approximate order of their sales in 1994, starting with the most popular bus.

The Industry Standard Architecture (ISA) Extended ISA (EISA) Buses

The original IBM PC used the Intel 8080 microprocessor, an 8-bit device, and offered a floppy-disk drive as an option. (An audio tape-cassette drive was the standard method of storing programs and data in those bygone days.) Subsequently, IBM introduced the PC-AT, which used an 80286 processor, had a 16-bit bus, could hold two floppy disk drives, and included a fixed disk drive. (The first of the PC-ATs offered a choice between a 5M and a 10M drive.) IBM's competitors rapidly adopted the PC-AT's 16-bit bus, which is now called the Industry Standard Architecture (ISA) bus. The largest percentage, by far, of the installed base of PCs and about 90 percent of all adapter cards use the ISA bus design and come in 8-bit and 16-bit versions. The problem with the ISA bus is that it runs at a fixed, 8M per second speed, no matter how fast a processor is installed on the computer motherboard. Thus, the ISA card creates a data bottleneck between the device on one end of the adapter card and the processor connected to the other end.

To overcome the speed limitations and take advantage of the 32-bit data path of the Intel 80386 and higher processors—as well as to compete with IBM's Micro Channel Architecture bus (MCA, described in a later section)—an industry association of PC manufacturers (excluding IBM) got together and designed an extended version of the ISA bus, called EISA. Motherboards that used these buses and adapter cards for the EISA and MCA buses were more expensive than the ISA variety, so neither of these architectures enjoyed great popularity. Today, computers using the EISA bus are employed primarily as central file and application servers for networked PCs, but the ISA bus remains the most popular—at least, as of late 1994.

The Video Electronic Standards Video Local Bus (VLB)

The Video Electronic Standards Association (VESA) is an industry consortium that creates the specifications for video display units (VDUs, or monitors) and VDU adapter cards. The introduction of Windows 3.0, with its heavy-duty graphics requirements, demonstrated that the ISA bus bottleneck slowed the capability of computers to redraw Windows displays, especially with VGA (Video Graphics Array) displays and adapter cards that could render 256 or more colors. Thus, VESA came up with a design that added a second bus, called a video local bus (VLB), to the original ISA bus. The VLB bus is, in effect, connected directly to the processor, eliminating the 8M per second speed limit of the ISA bus. The VLB bus rapidly gained acceptance among computer manufacturers, and most 80486 desktop and laptop PCs today offer VLB as a standard feature. VLB also supports other high-speed adapter cards; VLB disk drive adapter cards can greatly improve the performance of today's fast fixed disk drives at relatively little additional cost, compared with a combination ISA floppy-disk/fixed-disk controller card.

> **Note**
>
> If you decide on a desktop PC that incorporates VLB, make sure that both the video display adapter and the fixed disk adapter card are connected to the VLB. A few unscrupulous computer assemblers have been reported to provide a VLB motherboard, but with very-low-cost video and fixed-disk adapter cards installed on the ISA bus.

Most ISA-bus desktop PCs have eight adapter-card connectors (called slots) of which one is 8-bit and seven are 16-bit. Usually, three of the 16-bit slots have added VLB connectors. Figure 2.4 is a diagram of a typical VLB motherboard. In a standard ISA-bus PC, three of these slots are occupied by the video, combination fixed disk/floppy disk, and serial-parallel input/output (I/O) card. You connect the mouse and printer to the I/O card. An internal modem occupies another slot. Thus, you have four slots remaining for other, special-purpose adapter cards, such as an audio-adapter (sound) card. Open slots are exceedingly valuable, especially if you plan to take full advantage of Windows 95's digital and analog multimedia features, either immediately or in the future.

> **Note**
>
> Some "small-footprint" desktop PCs, which minimize desktop real-estate consumption, have as few as two expansion slots. Before you commit to buying a desktop PC, determine the number of free expansion slots after the basic video, disk, I/O, and modem functions are implemented, either by adapter cards or by the motherboard. If the number is less than three, you're likely to find yourself running out of expansion slots in six months or less.

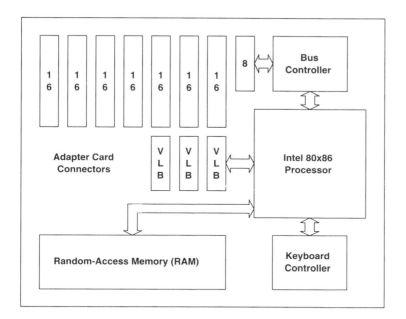

Fig. 2.4
A diagram of a typical motherboard with three VLB connectors.

The Peripheral Control Interface (PCI) Bus

The Peripheral Control Interface (PCI) bus was designed by Intel Corporation in conjunction with the development of the Pentium processor. (At one time, the Pentium was referred to as the 80586.) The PCI bus, which abandons the original ISA bus connector entirely, incorporates some of the basic Plug and Play requirements. Most motherboards that implement the PCI bus have seven active slots: four slots are 16-bit ISA, two slots are 32-bit PCI, and one slot has a shared set of ISA/PCI connectors into one of which you can plug either type of adapter card. Figure 2.5 is a diagram of a typical PCI motherboard, based on the Gateway 2000 P4D series. These motherboards compensate for the one-slot differential between ISA and PCI by integrating the functions of the floppy-disk drive and I/O adapter card on the mother-board. Some, including the Gateway P4D boards, also provide an integrated IDE connector for fixed disk drives. (IDE is explained later in the section "The Integrated Device Electronics (IDE) Interface.") You'll need a mouse with an IBM PS/2 round (DIN) connector or a PS/2 mouse adapter for most PCI motherboards, because mouse support also is provided by the system. If you choose to use a standard serial mouse, you lose one of the two serial (COM) ports.

Fig. 2.5
A diagram of a typical PCI/ISA motherboard.

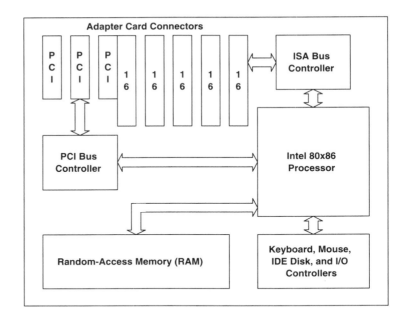

Although the PCI bus got off to a slow start, the fact that the PCI bus was designed by Intel carries a great deal of weight in the PC industry. Most Pentium-based computers use the PCI bus, and the PCI bus is Plug and Play-ready. When this book was written, the PCI bus was catching up with the VLB bus in popularity; sales of PCI motherboards will likely surpass those of VLB motherboards in 1995. Several manufacturers offered non-Plug and Play PCI video accelerator cards, and Plug and Play SCSI-2 adapter cards for the PCI bus were being field tested in the fall of 1994. The SCSI bus is the subject of a section that follows shortly.

IBM's Micro Channel Architecture (MCA) Bus

IBM introduced its Micro Channel Architecture (MCA) bus in conjunction with its PS/2 computer product line. Unlike the IBM PC and PC-AT buses, IBM considered the MCA bus to be a proprietary design. To build a PS/2 clone or MCA bus adapter cards, manufacturers had to sign a license agreement with IBM and pay a royalty on each unit sold. This change in IBM's strategy, combined with comparatively high prices for PS/2-series computers, provided a market for MCA adapter cards with only a fraction of the volume of the ISA card sales. Low production volume costs forced manufacturers to charge a substantial premium for MCA adapter cards. Even IBM abandoned the MCA bus for its competitively priced PC product lines.

The MCA bus is no longer a PC architecture of significance to most PC users but, like the PCI bus, it has the advantage of hardware compliance with Plug and Play. Windows 95 includes Plug and Play support for MCA adapter cards. PS/2 and IBM laptop PC users may be able to obtain an upgrade SurePath Gator 1.2 Plug and Play BIOS from IBM.

The Small Computer Systems Interface (SCSI-2)

The Small Computer Systems Interface (SCSI, pronounced scuzzy) bus isn't a PC architecture—it's a means of multiple peripheral devices, such as fixed disk drives, CD-ROM drives, tape backup drives, and graphic scanners, to the PC. You can connect up to seven internal or external SCSI devices to a single SCSI adapter card. Figure 2.6 is a diagram of a typical SCSI setup, with an internal SCSI fixed disk drive, external CD-ROM and tape backup drives, plus a page scanner.

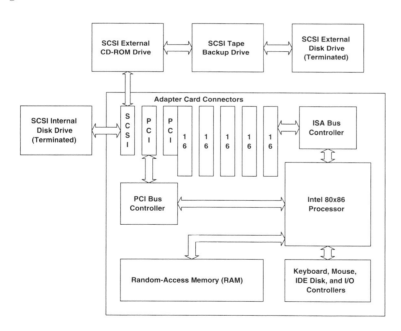

Fig. 2.6
A typical SCSI installation using a PCI host adapter.

Apple Computer was the first manufacturer to support the SCSI bus; SCSI was the only means of attaching most external devices to the Macintosh. Most CD-ROM drives use the SCSI bus, and many sound cards include a simple SCSI adapter to connect CD-ROM drives. The advantage of the SCSI bus is that the devices connected to the bus have built-in "intelligence"—circuitry that takes some of the processing load off the PC. SCSI devices can "talk" to each other, as well as to the PC. The extra circuitry for this intelligence causes SCSI devices, such as disk and CD-ROM drives, to carry prices somewhat higher than devices with IDE or proprietary interfaces. (The IDE interface is the subject of the next section.)

The original SCSI specification was a rather loosely worded document, and the SCSI devices sold by one manufacturer often wouldn't work with another manufacturer's products. The second specification, SCSI-2, tightened up the spec and provided a substantial increase in bus operating speed. Today, all SCSI-2 devices are fully compatible with one another. SCSI-2 has become the standard architecture for the high-capacity disk drives used in network file servers and client-server computing. Windows NT 3.5, for example, is designed specifically for SCSI devices; you need a SCSI drive to install Windows NT 3.5 from the distribution CD-ROM. (Windows NT 3.5 also is available for installation from floppy disks.)

Note

The SCSI-2 connector is much smaller than the SCSI-1 connector. Most SCSI-2 adapter cards have a 50-pin internal SCSI connector that connects to SCSI devices, such as fixed disk and CD-ROM drives, mounted in your PC's housing. You'll need a special SCSI-2 to SCSI-1 cable to connect between the external connector the new SCSI-2 adapter cards to conventional 50-pin "Micro Blue Ribbon" connectors used by most of today's external SCSI devices, such as scanners.

A recent improvement to the SCSI-2 bus, called Fast-SCSI, increases bus speed from about 5M per second to 10M per second. Wide-SCSI uses a 16-bit or 32-bit bus structure to provide a theoretical 40M per second data rate. The performance of the basic SCSI-2 bus is adequate for all but the most demanding network file server and client-server duties.

The Integrated Device Electronics (IDE) Interface

Fixed disk drives in early IBM PC-ATs and clones required an adapter card that held most of the electronics required for the drive to communicate with the ISA bus. Subsequently, PC and fixed disk drive manufacturers determined that there were technical and economic advantages to moving the circuitry from the adapter card to the drive itself. The result was the Integrated Device Electronics (IDE) interface standard for fixed disk drives. Today, most drives of less than 500M use IDE. Standard IDE adapter cards connect two floppy disk drives and two fixed disk drives, and most now include the functions of the I/O card, providing two serial ports and one or two parallel ports. Many PC manufacturers now incorporate the IDE interface on the motherboard.

In mid-1994, the IDE specification was upgraded to provide a higher data rate (11M per second), accommodate up to four fixed disk drives, support larger disk drives, and provide for Plug and Play support. The Gateway 2000 P5D motherboards use the enhanced IDE interface. Most manufacturers of CD-ROM drives now offer IDE versions; by the time Microsoft releases Windows 95, it's likely that IDE, rather than SCSI, CD-ROM drives that support Plug and Play will be the standard for moderately priced, multimedia-ready PCs. This means that audio adapter card manufacturers can eliminate the CD-ROM drive interface, so the cost of sound cards will decline further.

What Makes a Windows 95-Ready PC

At this point, you may have more than you ever wanted to know about PC architecture. Not only is familiarity with acronyms such as PCI, VLB, and SCSI necessary to distinguish between offerings of suppliers who sell PCs carrying the "Designed for Microsoft Windows 95" logo, but also to understand the Plug and Play specification described in the rest of this chapter. If you're planning to buy a new PC or upgrade your present PC for Windows 95, follow these guidelines to assure a Windows 95-ready PC:

- The 80486DX2/66 will be 1995's "standard" processor for running Windows 95. Clock-tripled, 100 MHz 80486DX4s and Pentiums provide significantly improved performance, but Windows 95 runs like a champ on the "standard" processor. High volume and intense competition in the 80486 market will give clock-doubled 80486DX2 computers the price-performance edge. One of the differences between 80486DX2-based computers will be the size of the high-speed cache memory offered. A 128K cache is adequate; it's difficult to discern the performance improvement offered by a 256K cache.

- Don't even *think* about buying a PC that doesn't have a VLB or PCI bus. Plain-vanilla ISA PCs are obsolete. Even if you don't plan to experiment with digital video or playing and recording hi-fi sound today, it's likely you'll be tempted to upgrade when you discover the new 32-bit multimedia features of Windows 95.

- Buy as much RAM as you can afford. Like money, you never can have too much RAM (or fixed disk space). 8M is the practical minimum for running today's Windows 3.1+ applications, and Windows 95 will very unlikely require significantly less RAM than Windows 3.1+. The good news is that Windows 95 makes much better use of added RAM than Windows 3.1+; 12M will be optimum for most users, but 16M gives a noticeable performance boost to 32-bit Excel 5.0 and Word 6.0.

■ If you're interested in graphics and/or multimedia, make sure that you include a VLB or PCI video accelerator card in your purchase specification. If you're seriously interested in digital video, consider buying a video accelerator card with hardware MPEG decompression on board. Video accelerator cards with on-board MPEG decompression will be readily available by early 1995 but will cost more than a conventional accelerator card. A Plug and Play-compatible VLB or PCI SCSI-2 adapter, such as NCR Microelectronics' NCR8100S PCI to SCSI host adapter, is the better choice for a multimedia setup because SCSI-2 fixed disk drives offer better performance than the current crop of IDE drives. You also have a wider choice of CD-ROM drives, and most scanners attach to the SCSI bus.

▶ See Chapter 8, "Using CD-ROM Drives with Windows 95," and Chapter 9, "Playing and Recording Hi-Fi Sound and Music"

■ Make sure that you buy a fixed-disk drive with a 300M or larger capacity. Windows 95 with all its options occupies only about 15M, but you should reserve 20M to 30M for Windows 95's swap file, which automatically expands and contracts as space is needed. (You don't need a permanent swap file to achieve top performance with Windows 95.) Remember that full installations of productivity applications, such as Microsoft Excel 5.0 and Word 6.0, each occupy about the same amount of disk space as Windows 95 itself. Multimedia eats disk space big time. Quantum Corporation's new 300M and 500M SCSI-2 Lightning-series drives are Plug and Play-compliant and are priced competitively with IDE drives of similar capacity. You'll find Windows 95's new 32-bit disk and file access speeds up loading and running large applications and provides much better performance when playing or recording digital audio and video.

■ Verify that the adapter cards or the equivalent circuitry on the motherboard is Plug and Play-compliant and that the fixed disk and CD-ROM drives support Plug and Play. This is especially important for SCSI-2 controllers, as you'll see in the section devoted to the Plug and Play-SCSI specification. You'll also want to make sure that the internal modem and sound card, if included, also support Plug and Play.

■ If you're buying a laptop computer, make sure that the PCMCIA cards and the docking station you buy are Plug and Play-compliant. Otherwise, you won't gain the advantages of "hot swapping" and "hot docking."

The Plug and Play Standard

Microsoft defines a Plug and Play computer system, qualifying for the "Designed for Microsoft Windows 95" logo, as having the following three components:

■ *Plug and Play BIOS version 1.0a.* Plug and Play BIOS (basic input-output system) provides the basic instructions to identify the devices necessary to boot the computer during the POST (Power-On Self-Test) process. The standard minimum set of devices is a display, keyboard, and a disk drive to load (bootstrap) the operating system—in this case, a fixed disk drive to load Windows 95.

■ *Plug and Play operating system.* Windows 95 is the first Plug and Play operating system, but limited support for Plug and Play can be obtained with MS-DOS 5+ and Windows 3.1+. Hopefully, Microsoft will add Plug and Play to a future version of Windows NT.

■ *Plug and Play hardware.* Plug and Play hardware is a set of PC devices that are autoconfigurable by the Plug and Play operating system. Plug and Play hardware primarily consists of adapter cards or their equivalent circuitry on the PC's motherboard; however, printers, external modems, and other devices connected to the PC's COM (serial) and LPT (parallel) ports also may support Plug and Play. PCI and MCA adapters qualify as Plug and Play hardware. ISA and EISA adapter cards require modification for Plug and Play autoconfiguration. When this book was written, it wasn't clear whether all adapter cards included in a computer bearing the "Designed for Microsoft Windows 95" logo were required to support Plug and Play installation.

By early 1995, virtually every PC manufacturer and assembler will be offering products claiming Plug and Play compliance and displaying the "Designed for Microsoft Windows 95" logo. Simply replacing the motherboard's BIOS chip with one that meets the Plug and Play BIOS Specification 1.0a, described in the following section, doesn't make an assembled computer Plug and Play-compliant. The adapter cards, fixed disk and CD-ROM drives, and other components of the system also must comply with the appropriate Plug and Play specification. Following are the eight specifications that comprised the Plug and Play standard when this book was written:

■ Plug and Play BIOS Specification 1.0a, developed by Compaq, Phoenix Technologies, and Intel. This is the basic document that defines how Plug and Play works. The Plug and Play BIOS specification is described in additional detail in the next section.

■ Plug and Play ISA Specification 1.0a, developed by Microsoft and Intel. The purpose of the Plug and Play ISA specification is to define how non-Plug and Play and Plug and Play-compliant cards can co-exist on the ISA bus without getting in each other's way.

■ Plug and Play SCSI specification 1.0, developed by Adaptec, AT&T Global Information Solutions, Digital Equipment Corporation, Future Domain, Maxtor, and Microsoft. The SCSI 1.0 spec defines the SCSI host adapter card. Additional specification, SCAM (SCSI Configured AutoMagically), defines the means by which individual SCSI devices, such as fixed disk drives, support autoconfiguration features similar to Plug and Play. The SCSI standard is maintained by committee X3T9.2 of the American National Standards Institute (ANSI).

■ Plug and Play IDE Specification. The IDE specification wasn't available for public review when this book was written.

■ Plug and Play LPT Specification 1.0, developed by Microsoft, defines the method by which devices connected to the parallel port identify themselves to the Plug and Play BIOS. Printers, modems, network adapters, and parallel port SCSI adapters are among the devices defined by the Plug and Play LPT specification. If you plug a Hewlett-Packard LaserJet 4M into your computer's parallel port, Windows 95 finds the driver for the printer and automatically loads the driver.

■ Plug and Play COM Specification 0.94, developed by Microsoft and Hayes Microcomputer Products, defines how serial devices such as mice, modems, printers, and uninterruptible power supplies identify themselves. Windows 95 usually is quite capable of identifying the type of mouse and modem installed, even without Plug and Play identification. The Plug and Play COM spec was a draft version when this book was written.

■ Plug and Play APM specification 1.1, developed by Microsoft and Intel, handles advanced power management for laptop and energy-efficient desktop PCs.

■ Plug and Play Device Driver Interface Specification for Microsoft Windows and MS-DOS 1.0c, developed by Microsoft, provides limited support for Plug and Play assignment of I/O, IRQs, DMA, and memory ranges under DOS and Windows 3.1+.

> **Note**
>
> In addition to the specifications of the preceding list, the ATAPI specification defines the identification process for Plug and Play-compatible CD-ROM drives that attach to the enhanced Plug and Play-compliant IDE interface. The Extended System Configuration Data (ESCD 1.0) specification is designed to provide additional information about ISA and EISA adapter cards to the Plug and Play BIOS.

The primary reason for boring you with the preceding list of specifications is this: you may need to ask whether a computer, motherboard, or device you are planning to buy is truly Plug and Play-compatible. The ability to name the applicable specification precisely is more likely to elicit a forthright response than "Is whatever Plug and Play?" A second reason for the list is that you can download current copies of each of the preceding specifications (except the IDE spec) from the libraries of the Plug and Play forum (GO PLUGPLAY) on CompuServe. Copies of these specifications aren't readily available elsewhere. A white paper, Microsoft Windows and the Plug and Play Framework Architecture, WINPNP.ZIP, containing WINPNP.DOC, is available from Library 1 of the PLUGPLAY forum and as PNP.ZIP from the WINNEWS forum. (PNP.ZIP includes Word 6.0, ASCII text, and PostScript versions of the backgrounder.)

The Plug and Play BIOS Specification 1.0a

Clearly, the most important element of a Plug and Play computer system is the Plug and Play System BIOS. Plug and Play BIOS Specification 1.0a adds the following three major new components to the conventional PC's system BIOS:

▶ See Chapter 6, "Upgrading to 32-Bit Productivity Applications," and Chapter 22, "Understanding Windows 95's Operating System Architecture"

- Resource management handles the basic system resources: direct memory access (DMA), interrupt requests (IRQs), input/output (I/O), and memory addresses. These system resources are shared by various devices, which often leads to the conflicts discussed at the beginning of this chapter. The Plug and Play BIOS resource manager is responsible for configuring boot devices on the motherboard, plus any Plug and Play devices.

- Runtime management of configuration is new to PCs. Plug and Play BIOS includes the capability to reconfigure devices after the operating system loads. This feature is particularly important for notebook PCs with PCMCIA devices that you can change at will. Previously, the operating system considered all devices detected by the BIOS to be static; this required that you restart the notebook after swapping a PCMCIA device.

■ Event management detects when devices have been removed or added to the system while the computer is running. Plug and Play BIOS 1.0a provides event management only for notebooks' PCMCIA devices because hot-swapping of adapter devices of desktop PCs isn't a safe practice. Event management relies on run-time management to reconfigure the system.

Phoenix Technologies, one of the coauthors of the Plug and Play BIOS Specification 1.0a, is the leading independent supplier of PC system software, BIOS ROMs (read-only memory chips), and BIOS utilities. According to Albert Sarie, Phoenix Technologies' senior marketing manager for advanced technology, Phoenix has 65 percent of the non-captive market for these PC system products. (Compaq and IBM developed their own BIOS.) Sarie says that all Phoenix Technologies customers are designing Plug and Play BIOS into their PC product lines. The only PCs that ultimately might not implement Plug and Play are high-powered systems used as network file and application servers.

If your PC doesn't have a BIOS ROM chip that meets the requirements of Plug and Play BIOS Specification 1.0a, you're likely to be out of luck in the Plug and Play department. The only exceptions are if:

■ Your computer has flash BIOS that you can upgrade with a floppy disk from the computer or motherboard supplier. Flash BIOS is a non-volatile memory chip (NVRAM) that retains the BIOS instructions when the power is turned off.

■ The supplier of your computer or motherboard offers a Plug and Play BIOS 1.0a upgrade kit. In this case, you simply remove the existing BIOS chip(s) and plug in the replacement(s).

If the manufacturer or assembler of your computer doesn't offer one of the two preceding options, you'll need to replace the motherboard to gain the benefits of Plug and Play.

Note

Some brands of computers whose motherboards were produced in 1994 display messages during the boot process indicating that the motherboard supports Plug and Play. Many of these motherboards have early versions of the Plug and Play BIOS that don't conform to the 1.0a specification. If your computer displays a message containing Plug and Play, you can determine whether the BIOS is current with two DOS test utilities, PNPINF.ZIP (Intel, rev. 1.21) and BIOTST.ZIP (Microsoft, rev. 1.0), that you can download from Library 6, BIOS, of the PLUGPLAY forum on CompuServe. You receive a Plug and Play BIOS not found message if your BIOS doesn't conform to the 1.0a specification.

How the Windows 95 Operating System Orchestrates Plug and Play

When you start a Plug and Play computer, the following five steps occur:

1. The system BIOS identifies the devices on the motherboard (including the type of bus), plus external devices such as disk drives, keyboard, video display, and other adapter cards.

2. The system BIOS determines the resource (IRQ, DMA, I/O, and memory address) requirements of each device. Some devices don't require all four of these resources. At this step, the system BIOS determines which devices are legacy devices that have fixed resource requirements and which are Plug and Play devices whose resource requirements can be reconfigured.

3. The operating system (Windows 95) allocates the resources remaining after allowing for legacy resource assignments to each Plug and Play device. If many legacy and Plug and Play devices are in use, it may require many iterations of the allocation process to eliminate all resource conflicts by changing the resource assignments of the Plug and Play devices.

4. Windows 95 creates a final system configuration and stores the resource allocation data for this configuration in the registration database (Registry).

5. Windows 95 searches the \WIN95\SYSTEM directory to find the required driver for the device. If the device driver is missing, a dialog appears to request that you insert the manufacturer's floppy disk with the driver software in drive A. Windows 95 loads the driver in memory and then completes its startup operations.

Figure 2.7 shows the preceding steps in the form of a simple flow diagram. Although the process appears simple on the surface, there's a substantial amount of low-level BIOS and high-level programming code required to implement the Plug and Play feature set. Compaq, Intel, Microsoft, and Phoenix Technologies deserve congratulations for making the magic work.

Fig. 2.7
A simplified diagram of the Plug and Play system configuration process.

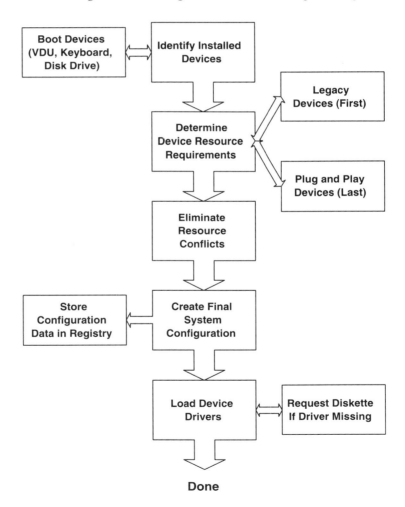

Chapter 3

Exploring the Windows 95 Interface

The Windows 95 user interface (UI) provides a wealth of features and functionality and, surprisingly, keeps the complex feature array relatively simple to use. Although it may seem odd, the most confused new Windows 95 users will most likely be experienced Windows 3.1+ and DOS users—the new desktop model and document-oriented and object-oriented features of the Windows 95 UI require a slightly different mind-set to operate than most of the software to which Windows 3.1+ and DOS power users are accustomed.

The first few sections of this chapter discuss some of the transition issues for Windows 3.1+ users and the basic components of the Windows 95 UI. Other sections explain the desktop-oriented Windows 95 UI model, and then describe the central program and task-management features of Windows 95—the command centers for activities in Windows 95. Windows 95's file-management system also is discussed, giving an overview of long file names and file searches. The last two sections in this chapter describe various power-user features incorporated in the Windows 95 UI, and the different ways that Windows 95 provides built-in help and coaching for experienced and novice users. A few comparisons between Windows 95's environment and the Macintosh operating system are made throughout this chapter.

Moving to Windows 95: New Views for Windows Users

The transition from Windows 3.1+ to Windows 95 will pose some minor difficulties for experienced Windows users, mostly in areas relating to the way Windows 95 structures its working environment and handles file and task management.

The Windows 95 desktop model (explained more fully in a later section) is sufficiently different from the Windows 3.1+ operating environment that you may find yourself momentarily confused in the new landscape. In Windows 3.1+, nothing really happens on the desktop—the Windows 3.1+ desktop is used only to display the icons of running, minimized applications, and to display pretty wallpaper. In Windows 3.1+, the real action is divided between the Program Manager and the File Manager. Windows 95 uses neither; instead, all the equivalent functionality is built directly into the desktop itself.

If you are a Windows 3.1+ user who has some Macintosh experience, you may comprehend the Windows 95 desktop model more readily than users with only Windows and DOS experience. Indeed—assuming that it's possible to pry Macintosh users away from their beloved machines to even look at Windows 95—they will find that many ways of getting work done in Windows 95 are implemented in a fashion similar to that of the Macintosh.

This isn't to say that Windows 95 copies the Macintosh operating system in any particular way. Windows 95, like the Macintosh operating system, was designed from the ground up with the primary goal of making a computer that novices can easily use (a feature that's generally accepted as the primary basis of the Macintosh's appeal). As you might expect, similar approaches are used to meet the ease-of-use goals in both systems, resulting in similar features in both systems. Indeed, the authors of this book think that many new Windows 95 users will be first-time computer buyers looking for a home or hobby computer that's as easy to use as the Macintosh they remember from school or a store display, but is more easily affordable. (Although Macintosh prices have declined steadily over the past couple of years, equivalent Intel-based hardware is still substantially less expensive.)

Although Windows 3.1+ users can expect to find many differences in Windows 95, they don't need to worry that they'll have to completely relearn a new operating system. Windows 95's basic operations are very similar to operations in Windows 3.1+, and many differences are only cosmetic.

The greatest hurdle that experienced Windows 3.1+ users will encounter is making the adjustment to the Windows 95 desktop model and its inherent differences in file and program management. Beyond that, operations in Windows 95 are almost identical to operations in Windows 3.1+.

The main differences Windows 3.1+ users may notice stem from Windows 95's primary design goal, which was ease-of-use for novices; compatibility for Windows 3.1+ was a secondary goal. Don't let this last statement make you sweat, however, if you're a Windows 3.1+ user. Although Windows 3.1+ compatibility may have been a secondary goal in the Windows 95 design, it hasn't been neglected. Making the transition from Windows 3.1+ to Windows 95 should be relatively painless—both environments have many similarities.

Note

Microsoft says that Windows 3.1+ compatibility areas are the most likely to change between the current Windows 95 beta version and the final release—with more Windows 3.1+ compatibility to be added.

Windows 95's interface is full of symbols and controls that Windows 3.1+ users will immediately recognize. For example, Windows 95's drop-down menus still use a right-facing triangle (▶) after a menu choice to indicate that it opens a submenu, and an ellipsis (...) still indicates that a menu choice will open a dialog box. Windows 3.1+ users will easily recognize the check boxes, radio buttons, and command buttons of Windows 95's dialog boxes. Also, Windows 3.1+ power users will find that most or all of their familiar keyboard commands—such as Ctrl+Esc and Alt+Tab to switch applications, or Alt+F4 and Ctrl+F4 to close screen windows—produce the same results within Windows 95's context that they do in Windows 3.1+.

Other similarities between Windows 95 and Windows 3.1+ include the presence of a Startup folder, which fulfills the same purpose of the Windows 3.1+ Startup program group. For Windows 3.1+ users who feel helpless without the familiar Program Manager and File Manager, Windows 95 includes its own versions of Program Manager and File Manager as an alternative to performing program and file management directly in the Windows 95 desktop.

> **Note**
>
> Some Windows 3.1+ users may find an immediate mystery in the Windows 95 interface—how do you exit from Windows 95 so you can turn off the computer? Because Windows 95 is the operating system, you don't exit from Windows 95 like you have to exit from Windows 3.1+; instead, you execute a specific shut-down command (a feature familiar to Macintosh users) that causes Windows 95 to clear all its internal buffers and disk caches, save the desktop, and perform other housekeeping tasks so you can turn off the computer without any data loss. (The later section "Windows 95's Command Centers: Task Bar, Explorer, and Control Panel" describes how to find the Shut Down command.)

The next section describes the Windows 95 Welcome dialog box and its Tour and What's New features. Following sections describe the basic Windows 95 UI components and the basic skills that Windows 95 users must have. Differences between operating DOS programs in Windows 3.1+ and Windows 95 are the topic of Chapter 25, "Running DOS Applications under Windows 95."

The Welcome Dialog Box: Windows 95 Introduces Itself

The first thing you'll see after installing Windows 95 is the Welcome dialog box shown in figure 3.1. The Welcome dialog box is Windows 95's way of introducing itself to you. *Welcome* always displays a helpful hint for using Windows 95, and provides an up-front opportunity to see an explanation of Windows 95's new features, or to take a guided tour of Windows' features.

Fig. 3.1
Windows 95 displays the Welcome dialog box, which shows you helpful hints for using Windows, allows you to take a quick Windows tour, or just see what's new in Windows 95.

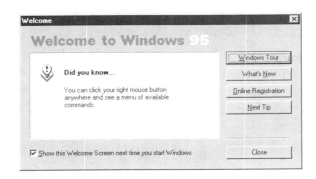

> **Tip**
>
> If you get tired of the Welcome dialog box, you can tell Windows 95 to stop displaying it by clearing the Show the Welcome Screen next time you start Windows checkbox at the bottom of the dialog box.

The Windows Tour, What's New, Next Tip, and Close command buttons always appear in the Welcome dialog box. The Online Registration command button appears only if you have a modem and have installed The Microsoft Network software either during Setup or by using the Add/Remove Applications icon in the Control Panel. (The Microsoft Network is a new online information service, which competes with CompuServe, America Online, and Prodigy. The Microsoft Network software allows you to connect to this service to register Windows 95; subscribing to The Microsoft Network is optional.)

► See Chapter 13, "Joining The Microsoft Network"

Clicking the Next Tip button displays additional hints about how to use Windows 95. The effects of clicking the Windows Tour and What's New buttons are described next.

> **Note**
>
> The Welcome dialog box is actually displayed by a special Welcome applet stored in the same folder in which you installed Windows 95 (usually named Windows). If Windows 95 doesn't display the Welcome dialog box after starting your computer, you can manually run the Welcome applet by double-clicking its icon in any folder window, or by using the Run command on the Start menu.

Windows Tour

Clicking the Windows Tour button in the Welcome dialog box starts the Windows Tour—a special feature in the Windows online Help system. The Windows Tour is a short tutorial for using Windows 95 that covers all of the essential skills you need to get started using Windows 95.

> **Tip**
>
> You can also start the Windows Tour directly from the Windows online Help system, described at the end of this chapter.

Windows Tour contains the following tutorial lessons:

- *Starting a Program.* This lesson teaches you how to use the Start button and its menu to run programs, and how to use the Close button on a window's title bar to close the window.

- *Exploring Your Disk.* This tutorial shows you how to use windows to find disk drives, files, folders, and programs on your computer.

- *Finding a File.* This lesson—important to both novice and experienced computer users—teaches you the rudiments of using the Find command on the Start menu. The Find command is an indispensable tool for quickly locating just about any folder, document, or application stored on your computer.

- *Switching Windows.* This tutorial shows you how to use the Task Bar to switch among open windows and programs, and how to use the Minimize button in the window's title bar.

- *Using Help.* This final lesson shows you how to use the Help system's index to find specific topics; it also shows you some special features of the Help system: shortcut action buttons and the What's This button (these last two features are described in more detail at the end of this chapter).

> **Note**
>
> Although Windows Tour teaches you all the essential skills to get started in Windows 95, it is really only a simulation. Consequently, you'll find a couple of minor discrepancies between what you see in Windows Tour and what really happens when you use Windows 95. First, Windows Tour uses a simulated desktop and My Computer window, so your actual desktop and My Computer will probably be different. Second, the simulated submenus in Windows Tour require a separate mouse click for each submenu choice; the real submenus in Windows 95 pop up automatically, as described in a following section.

> **Tip**
>
> If you're using the Windows Tour, and you're not sure where a control such as the Close or Minimize button is, click the Show Me button to display a large arrow indicating the desired command button or other screen object.

What's New

Like the Windows Tour, clicking the What's New button in the Welcome dialog box starts the Windows 95 online Help system, and displays the special topic covering new features in Windows 95. (As you might expect, you can also display the What's New help topic directly from the online Help system.)

The What's New help topic provides text information that answers the following questions:

- How do I start programs?

- What happened to my program groups?

- What happened to File Manager?

- What happened to Control Panel?

- Where did the MS-DOS prompt go?

- What happened to the Run command?

- How do I copy files?

- How do I switch between tasks?

As you can see, these topics cover all of the basic tasks you'll need to perform in Windows 95—they also address the most obvious differences between Windows 95 and previous versions of Windows. The information in What's New is geared more toward experienced Windows 3.1+ users than toward first-time Windows users. Only experienced Windows 3.1+ users will actually know enough to wonder what happened to File Manager, program groups, the Run command, and so on. With the exception of the information on copying files, What's New contains little information for novices that isn't covered in the Windows Tour.

Now that you've seen how Windows 95 introduces itself, read the next few sections for a more formal introduction to Windows 95.

Basic Components of the Windows 95 User Interface

No matter how "intuitive" an operating system is, every user must have a basic vocabulary and set of skills before being able to use that operating system. You can't use a real-world object without knowing a little bit about it.

To use a telephone, for example, you need to know that you must lift the receiver from the hook, and then press buttons (or twirl the rotary dial) on the telephone to call someone.

In Windows 95 (as in Windows 3.1+, the Macintosh, and most other graphical user interfaces), one way of meeting the ease-of-use goals is to keep the required starting skill set as small as possible. To get started using Windows 95, you really need to know only the following minimal information:

- The different parts of a screen window

- How to select items in lists or make choices in menus and dialog boxes by clicking with the left mouse button

- How to initiate actions by clicking or double-clicking an icon or button with the left mouse button

- How to move or resize objects seen on-screen by dragging with the mouse

Users with previous experience in any graphical user interface (GUI) will have no problem working in Windows 95; the sculpted look of Windows 95's GUI makes buttons and menu choices easily identifiable to novice users. Further, this basic skill set is increasingly becoming a part of our culture—even some TV commercials for cars and soft drinks use animations of computer screens showing a mouse pointer making command button and menu choices.

The Parts of a Windows 95 Window

Figure 3.2 shows a typical Windows 95 window and identifies its essential components. The icon at the top left corner of each window changes, depending on what's now displayed in the window: if the window is a folder, the icon is an open file folder; if the window is for a specific application, the application icon appears. In figure 3.2, the window displays the contents of My Computer (explained later), and shows the My Computer icon.

Although their appearance is different, the purpose and function of the window parts and controls shown in figure 3.2 will be familiar to users of Windows 3.1+, Macintosh, and OS/2. Every window has a menu bar, title bar, and several sizing controls. To reposition a window on-screen, drag its title bar to the new location; to resize a window, drag the window frame's sides or corners.

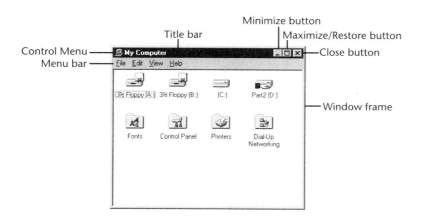

Fig. 3.2
Basic parts of a
Windows 95
window: new
look, same
functionality.

A new window control for Windows 3.1+ users is the Close button at the
extreme right of the window's title bar. Clicking this button closes the window. This one button may be one of the most annoying changes to which
experienced Windows 3.1+ users may have to adjust. Because the control
button at the extreme right side of the title bar in a Windows 3.1+ window is
the maximize/restore button, many Windows 3.1+ users will find themselves
inadvertently closing windows that they really intended to maximize. (You
can still close a window in Windows 95 by double-clicking the icon at the
extreme left of the title bar.)

The menu bar in a Windows 95 screen window functions exactly the same as
the menu bar in a Windows 3.1+ window—clicking a word in the menu bar
opens a drop-down menu from which you make additional choices. Every
window has the File, Edit, View, and Help choices; other choices depend on
the specific window or application that's open.

Windows 95's windows have many different viewing options. Figure 3.3, for
example, shows the same window from figure 3.2, but with the window's
toolbar turned on. The toolbar's buttons provide shortcuts to several frequently used commands. The Explorer drop-down list box—a miniature version of the Explorer described later in this chapter—allows you to select the
information displayed by the window from a tree diagram of folders on the
computer. The Parent Folder button displays the folder that contains the
current folder, while the Map Drive and Disconnect Drive buttons provide a
quick way to connect or disconnect network disk drives. The remaining four
buttons select the format of the window's displayed contents: large icons,
small icons, a list with file names and icons only, or a list with full details

about a file's size, type, and date/time last modified. Viewing options such as the window toolbar are designed to make things easier for experienced computer users.

Fig. 3.3
One of Windows 95's many different viewing options for its windows.

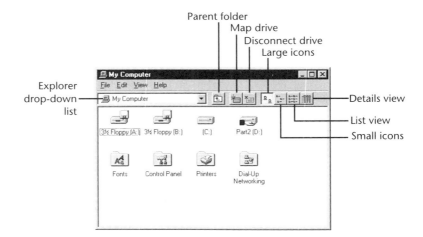

As in Windows 3.1+, each window "remembers" its size, position on-screen, and current viewing option settings, so the next time you open the window, it appears and behaves exactly the same as it did the last time you had the window open.

How Windows 95's Menus Work

Although Windows 95's menus work essentially the same as drop-down menus in any application or operating system, they incorporate some interesting and useful new functionality. In general, Microsoft has designed Windows 95 to minimize the number of mouse clicks necessary to accomplish various tasks. This design goal is apparently intended not only to speed up a user's work, but also to reduce the possibility of acquiring carpal tunnel syndrome or repetitive stress injuries while using Windows 95. Whether altruism or product liability lawsuits are the source of this goal is irrelevant: many users will welcome this change in the UI.

As in Windows 3.1+, you open the top-level menu by clicking once on the menu name in a window's title bar; Windows 95 displays the drop-down menu. Unlike Windows 3.1+, Windows 95 tracks the position of the mouse cursor and moves the highlight bar in the drop-down menu to correspond to the mouse pointer's position. If the highlight rests over a menu choice that leads to a submenu, Windows 95 automatically displays the submenu.

Figure 3.4 shows four different menus opened with a single mouse click. A single click on the Start button (at the bottom left of the screen) displayed the first menu at the left. Moving the mouse pointer over the Programs option caused Windows 95 to automatically display the next submenu to the right. Each additional submenu was displayed simply by holding the mouse pointer over the menu choice. (The Start button is described later in this chapter, along with the Task Bar.)

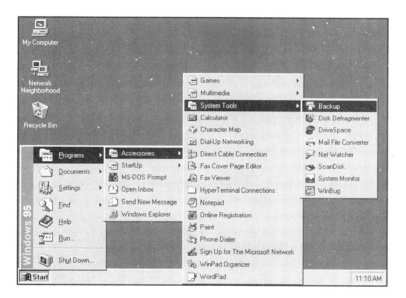

Fig. 3.4
Windows 95 automatically opens submenus for you, reducing the total number of mouse clicks you must make to activate a particular command or action.

To actually select a command, only one additional mouse click is required. If the user made a selection from the fourth submenu (the one at the extreme right of figure 3.4), only two mouse clicks are required, instead of the five mouse clicks that would be required in Windows 3.1+. Incidentally, this system is even easier to use than the menu system in the Macintosh—in the Macintosh, users must hold the mouse button down to display cascading menus.

Understanding Windows 95's Desktop Model and Document Orientation

Windows 95 is an object-oriented operating system, which means that Windows 95 tries to create a work environment for your computer that models an actual physical working environment—your desk. In the same way that your real desk is a piece of furniture on which you place various objects (such as paper, telephone, calculator, pencil, notebook, and report) the Windows 95 desktop is a piece of "furniture" on which you place the computer equivalents of the documents and tools you might find on your real-world desk. Just as your real desk provides a place to store and keep handy the things you work with, so does Windows 95's desktop.

Novice computer users may actually adapt to the Windows 95 desktop faster than experienced Windows 3.1+ users habituated to the Program Manager and File Manager. The Windows 95 desktop incorporates the functionality of Program Manager and File Manager invisibly into the desktop. When you move a real object on your desk, you don't usually use a special tool—you just pick the thing up and move it to its new location. Similarly, on the Windows 95 desktop, you don't need a special tool (File Manager) to move or copy an object—you just move the object to its new location by dragging it there with the mouse.

Novice users, with no preconceptions, are more likely to try moving things around on the Windows 95 desktop as they would on a real desktop—which is the purpose behind the Windows 95 desktop design. The Windows 95 desktop provides many different ways to accomplish the same task or get at the same features. This variety allows Windows 95's desktop to behave more like your real desktop, where you have few restrictions regarding how you work—the only restrictions are imposed by you.

Windows 95's Common Desktop Elements

Figure 3.5 shows a Windows 95 desktop as it appears immediately after installing Windows 95 (the desktop wallpaper has been set to "none" for clarity). The solid bar with the Start button at the bottom of the screen is Windows 95's Task Bar, described later in this chapter.

Fig. 3.5
Windows 95's
initial desktop
display.

Every Windows 95 desktop contains the first three icons at the top left area of figure 3.5: My Computer, Network Neighborhood, and Recycle Bin. The fourth and fifth icons, My Briefcase and Microsoft Exchange, are optional Windows 95 components you can install when you set up Windows 95, or by using the Add/Remove Programs applet in the Control Panel. Microsoft Exchange is for users of Microsoft Mail, while My Briefcase is a file-synchronization tool for use with notebook, laptop, or other portable computers.

▶ See Chapter 18, "Messaging with Windows 95's Exchange Client," and Chapter 19, "Synchronizing Your Notebook Computer with Briefcases"

Icons on Windows 95's desktop fulfill many different purposes. An icon on the desktop can represent a single object, such as an application (just like the application icons in Windows 3.1+) or a document. Icons on Windows 95's desktop can also represent some kind of container, such as a folder or a disk drive. Folders, like real file folders on a real desk, are containers for other objects. A folder may contain documents, application programs, or other folders.

Note

Folders are really the same as the subdirectories that DOS and Windows 3.1+ users are familiar with; *document* is now the generic term for any data file stored on your disk drive. Windows 95's file system is discussed more fully later in this chapter.

All Windows 95 icons—whether on the desktop or contained in a folder—are opened or activated by double-clicking. If the icon represents an application program, Windows 95 starts the program when its icon is double-clicked. If the icon represents a folder, disk drive, or other container, Windows 95 opens a window on the desktop that displays the container's contents: applications, documents, or other folders.

Each icon (My Computer, Network Neighborhood, Recycle Bin, My Briefcase, and Microsoft Exchange) shown in figure 3.5 represents a container; these are special folders on the desktop, with special purposes:

- *My Computer* contains icons representing all the objects that belong to the computer you're using. When you open the My Computer folder, you see icons for all the disk drives installed in your computer or connected through a network, along with the Control Panel, Fonts, and Printers folders. (The Control Panel folder provides access to Windows 95 configuration utility applets; the Printers Folder contains the tools to configure and control your printers while the Fonts folder lets you manage your installed fonts.) If you've installed Windows 95's software for connecting to remote networks via modem, the Dial-up Network folder also appears in My Computer. Control Panel, Fonts, Printers, and the Dial-up Network folders are discussed more fully later in this chapter.

- *Network Neighborhood* contains icons representing the computers connected to yours on the network, and a folder containing Windows 95's remote access tools. Consolidating access to network computers in the Network Neighborhood—and access to the local computer's resources in My Computer—helps avoid confusion for new and experienced users about how to get access to a particular resource.

- *Recycle Bin* is part of a deletion-protection system that allows you to retrieve documents or folders that you might have deleted from the disk drive accidentally. The Recycle Bin is described in more detail later in this chapter.

- *My Briefcase* is an optional component for Windows 95 that helps automate the synchronization of copies of the same documents between your office and home computer, or between your office and notebook computer.

- *Microsoft Exchange* is another optional component that contains management tools for using Microsoft mail and other telephony activities such as faxing.

▶ See Chapter 19, "Synchronizing Your Notebook Computer with Briefcases," Chapter 16, "Using Windows 95 Clients with Existing Networks," Chapter 18, "Messaging with Windows 95's Exchange Client" and Chapter 15, "Faxing with Microsoft At Work Fax"

Introducing Windows 95

> **Note**
>
> When you work with windows on the Windows 95 desktop, keep in mind that you use a window on-screen to view an object. You can use a single window to view different objects at different times, you can use many different windows to view several different objects at the same time, or you can use many different windows to view the same object.

It won't occur to a novice computer user to even wonder, but if you're a DOS and Windows 3.1+ expert, you may end up asking yourself, "If an object is on the desktop, where is it really stored in the file system?" Windows 95 maintains a hidden folder (subdirectory) in its installed directory named DESK-TOP. (If you installed Windows 95 in a directory named WINDOWS, then the DOS path for the desktop is \WINDOWS\DESKTOP.) All the items that Windows 95 displays on the desktop are stored in this subdirectory. If you create a new folder and place it directly on the desktop, for example, Windows 95 creates a new subdirectory inside the DESKTOP subdirectory. As another example, if you drag a document onto the desktop, Windows 95 moves or copies the file into the hidden DESKTOP subdirectory.

Windows 95 is aware of where you drag disk drive icons, however, and prevents you from doing things such as trying to copy the entire contents of a hard disk into the desktop. Instead, Windows 95 will ask you if you want to create a shortcut for the disk drive. (Shortcuts are described later in this chapter.)

Object Properties

As already mentioned, Windows 95's desktop uses an object-oriented model to emulate the way you work with real objects on a real desk. In the real world, a given object has specific properties: weight, size, shape, and color, to name only a few. To implement its model of a desktop, Windows 95 treats all objects—windows, icons, applications, disk drives, documents, folders, modems, printers, and so on—as self-contained objects. Each object keeps track of its own properties. Typical object properties include things such as the object's name, size, position on-screen, and color, among others.

> **Tip**
>
> You can inspect an object's properties by viewing its property sheet. Access an object's property sheet by right-clicking on the object, or by using the File menu's Properties command in a folder window.

In general, this object-oriented model really does deliver the promised ease-of-use. Rather than use a tool such as Windows' File Manager or the DOS RENAME command to rename a folder or document, you work directly with the document or folder. For example, to rename a document or folder in Windows 95, use the File menu's Properties command to change the object's name property, or just click the text label displayed under the document's or folder's icon and type the new name.

Some aspects of working with Windows 95's object properties can be a little confusing, however. You may forget (or just not know) that things such as a document's name are properties of the document, and may waste time looking for a command or utility that isn't present because it isn't needed. Unless you run the Windows 3.1+ File Manager substitute supplied with Windows 95, you'll never find a command to rename a document file—because you do so by altering the document's name property.

At times, it may not be obvious that some piece of information you want to get is one of an object's properties, or that you are inspecting the correct object's properties. For example, free space on a disk drive is a property of that drive. To find out how much free space is left on a disk drive, you must inspect the drive's properties.

Because you can't move a disk drive out of the My Computer folder, Windows 95 allows you to create a Shortcut icon that you can place on the desktop or in any folder to provide more convenient access to a disk drive. (Shortcuts are described in more detail later in this chapter.) If you inspect the properties of a disk drive Shortcut, you are inspecting the Shortcut properties, not the actual drive's properties—as a result, you can't find out how much free space is left on the drive. Instead, you have to inspect the properties of the original disk drive icon in the My Computer folder to find out its free space.

> **Tip**
>
> If you can't figure out how to change the configuration of some item in Windows 95, try looking at the object's property sheet.

The Desktop's Document-Oriented Features

Another important aspect of Windows 95's desktop model is that the Windows 95 operating system is more document-oriented than Windows 3.1+. Working in DOS or Windows 3.1+ tends to be application-oriented. To create a letter, spreadsheet, database, or other "document," you start an application, create or open the document, and then work with it.

Windows 95's operating system allows you to create and work with documents without explicitly opening an application first. The idea behind this document orientation is to provide a more natural way for people to work. If you want to, say, balance your checkbook, most people don't start out by setting up a calculator first—instead, they grab their check register and statement, and use a calculator or other tools as necessary.

Object linking and embedding (OLE) in Windows 3.1+ was the beginning of a document-oriented structure in Windows. OLE 2.0 provides in-place editing. When you edit an OLE object in a document, the document you see on-screen doesn't change; instead, the window around the document changes, providing access to the application tools needed to edit or create that portion of your document.

Windows 95 extends the in-place editing concept to the entire operating system. The File menu in Windows 95's folder windows includes a New command, which (as you might expect) allows a user to create a new folder inside the current folder, or to create a new Shortcut (described later in this chapter). As you can see in figure 3.6, the New command also allows you to instantly create a document for any application that's properly entered in Windows 95's Registry, without starting that application first—possibly without even knowing which specific application owns the document. Once you create the document, you double-click it to begin editing—all without ever explicitly starting a particular application program.

▶ See Chapter 24, "Replacing WIN.INI, SYSTEM.INI, and REG.DAT with Registry"

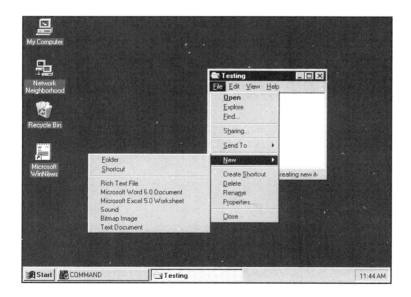

Fig. 3.6
Create new documents with the File menu's New command without first starting a specific application.

I

Introducing Windows 95

Windows 95 reinforces its document orientation in subtle ways. In Windows 3.1+, every application window has a title bar that displays the name of the application, and usually also displays the name of the currently active document. In Windows 95 applications, every application window has a title bar that displays the name of the document first, and then displays the name of the application you're using to edit that document. This reinforces the idea that it's the document that's important, not the tools that you use to manipulate the document. (Although existing Windows 3.1+ applications will still display the application name first, all Windows 95 applets and applications that carry the "Designed for Microsoft Windows 95" logo will display the document name first, and then the application name.)

Another way Windows 95 reinforces its document-oriented approach is to include built-in file viewers, so it's possible to view (but not edit) the contents of a document without actually opening (or even owning) the application that created it. File viewers are described in the section "Browsing Files with File Viewers" later in this chapter.

Windows 95's document orientation may seem like a trivial feature in the operating system, but it's an important concept in the desktop model and in meeting ease-of-use goals for novices. Most novice computer users tend to want to manipulate an object directly, as they would with real physical objects. Only those of you who are used to procedural systems such as DOS and Windows 3.1+ tend to think of tasks in terms of applications working on files. Chicago's document-oriented features make it easier to emulate the free-form work approaches possible with real objects on your real desk.

Windows 95's Command Centers: Task Bar, Explorer, and Control Panel

Windows 95 consolidates the control of running applications, system resources, and system configuration into three main areas: the Task Bar, the Explorer, and the Control Panel.

Windows 95's Task Bar

The Task Bar is the tool you use to start an application or to switch back and forth between running applications. The Task Bar combines all the functionality found in the Windows 3.1+ Program Manager and Task Manager for starting a program or switching to it while it's already running.

The Task Bar makes Windows multitasking capabilities more obvious and more accessible. (Based on the author's own experience, and according to user surveys conducted by Microsoft, Windows 3.1+ multitasking features tend to be underused by many.) By default, the Task Bar is always visible at the bottom of the screen (refer to figs. 3.5 and 3.6). The Task Bar uses a combination of push buttons and pop-up menus to provide easy access to all your programs, file-searching capabilities, system configuration tools, and on-line help topics.

Figure 3.7 shows the Task Bar after clicking the Start button and moving the mouse pointer over the Programs choice. You can start any program installed on the computer (and properly registered) from the Programs menu. No more hunting through Program Manager's program groups to find the application you want—just look for it in the Task Bar's menus.

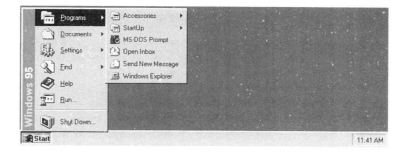

Fig. 3.7
The Windows 95 Task Bar's Start menu and Programs menu. The specific contents of the Programs menu varies from computer to computer, depending on what applications are installed.

Each choice on the Programs menu with a folder icon to its left and a right-facing triangle (▶) on the right, leads to a submenu of other programs; these are analogous to the Windows 3.1+ program groups. In fact, if you upgrade from Windows 3.1+ to Windows 95, the Windows 95 Setup program creates a choice on the Programs menu corresponding to each program group that was in Program Manager at the time you upgraded. In figure 3.7, the Accessories and Startup choices on the Programs menu each lead to a submenu of other programs and group folders.

Note

Notice the Startup choice on the Programs menu in figure 3.7. This folder fulfills the same purpose as the Startup program group in Windows 3.1+. Any programs or Shortcuts in this folder are started each time Windows 95 boots.

Like the desktop, Windows 95 keeps track of what items should appear on the Start menu by creating a Start Menu subdirectory (or folder) in the installed directory. If you installed Windows 95 in a subdirectory named Windows, all the items that appear on the Start menu are stored in a subdirectory whose complete DOS path is \Windows\Start Menu. (Yes, the Start Menu subdirectory name really has a space in it—it's one of the new Windows 95 long file names described in a following section.) Any applications, folders, or shortcuts in the Start Menu folder will appear on the Start Menu on the Task Bar.

Similarly, Windows 95 keeps track of what items should appear on the Programs menu by creating a Programs subdirectory in the installed directory. You can also start programs by displaying a window to view the contents of the Programs folder, and double-clicking the application icon.

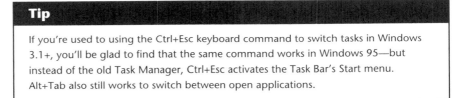

Tip

If you're used to using the Ctrl+Esc keyboard command to switch tasks in Windows 3.1+, you'll be glad to find that the same command works in Windows 95—but instead of the old Task Manager, Ctrl+Esc activates the Task Bar's Start menu. Alt+Tab also still works to switch between open applications.

Each time you start a new application or open a new window, Windows 95 adds a command button for application or window to the Task Bar, as shown in figure 3.8. This command button remains on the Task Bar as long as that application or window is open. To switch to an open window or application, click the corresponding button on the Task Bar, and Windows 95 switches to the selected window. This feature eliminates any need to search the desktop for minimized window icons—any user can immediately see which windows and applications are open by looking at the Task Bar.

Fig. 3.8
Each open application or window gets its own button on the Task Bar.

Having a command button for an open window or application appear on the Task Bar is useful apart from providing a means of switching among windows or applications. Windows 95 doesn't display an icon for minimized windows or applications (to avoid confusion with other items already on the desktop), so the only way to find an open, minimized window is to look for its command button on the Task Bar.

> **Note**
>
> If you now use Microsoft Office, you may notice that the Windows 95 Task Bar works much the same way the Microsoft Office toolbar works—it's always on-screen and provides quick access to a variety of programs. The Task Bar, however, is more flexible and dynamic than the Microsoft Office toolbar.

The one drawback to the command buttons on the Task Bar is that the Task Bar may become crowded. As each new command button is added to the Task Bar, the existing buttons keep getting smaller and smaller so that their legends are less readable. Figure 3.8 shows a moderately crowded Task Bar. Already you can see that the name of the window or application on each command button is truncated, and (although the icon on the button helps) it's difficult to tell exactly to which application a button refers.

Fortunately, when you hold the mouse pointer over a command button on the Task Bar, Windows 95 displays ToolTip (that is, a text label attached to the mouse pointer like the ToolTips in Excel 5 and Word 6) that displays the name of the window or application. Also, you can enlarge the Task Bar so that it holds two rows of buttons, instead of just one.

In general, you can customize the Task Bar to fit your particular work habits. If you like, you can drag the Task Bar to the top of the screen or to a vertical position at the left or right edge of the screen. If you don't want to see the Task Bar all the time, you can change its properties so that it remains hidden unless you press Ctrl+Esc or move the mouse pointer to touch the edge of the screen where the Task Bar is located.

You can add items such as documents, folders, or applications to the Programs menu by placing them in the Programs folder, or by changing the Task Bar's properties. If there are programs that you use frequently, you can add them directly to the Task Bar's Start menu by changing the Task Bar's properties or by dragging and dropping a Shortcut icon onto the Task Bar's Start button. Windows 95 stores any Shortcuts or folders you add to the Start menu in a directory named Start Menu in the Windows 95 installed directory.

The preceding paragraphs explain the Task Bar's purpose and the general functions of the Task Bar and the Programs menu. The Start menu of the Task Bar provides access to several other Windows 95 operating system features (refer to fig. 3.7):

- The Documents menu choice displays a menu of the last 15 documents you had open, regardless of the application with which you opened them. This feature provides a quick way to recall the last documents on which you worked. (Remember, a document is any file; the Documents menu displays word processor, spreadsheet, or recently edited files of any type.)

- The Settings menu provides rapid access to all the tools to alter Windows 95's hardware and software configuration or settings. The Settings menu provides a quick jump into the Control Panel, Start Menu, or Printers folders, as well as access to the Task Bar's own properties. (The Control Panel and Printers folders are described later in this chapter.)

- The Find menu allows users to search local and network disk drives for a particular file or folder, or to search over the network for a particular computer. This feature is similar to the File menu's Search command in the Windows 3.1+ File Manager, but is much more flexible and powerful. For one thing, you don't have to use DOS wild-card characters to search for partial file names. You can also use a file's extension, time and date last modified, or size as part of the search criteria. You can even base a search for a document on text in the document—Windows 95 will read each document to see whether it contains a particular word, phrase, or expression. The text-in-file search criteria can be highly useful—you may have forgotten what name you gave to the document containing your quarterly sales report, but you'll probably be able to remember a particular heading or title in the report that Windows 95 can find. (UNIX and DOS utility users will recognize this search capability as a GREP type search through the contents of files.)

- The Help Topics choice leads to the top level of Windows 95's on-line help system, described later in this chapter.

- The Run menu choice is essentially the same as the Run command on the Windows 3.1+ Program Manager's File menu, allowing you to execute programs (usually installation programs for new software) directly, without an installed icon.

- The last choice on the Start menu, Shut Down, is at least as important as the Programs menu. Because Windows 95 is the entire operating system, not just an addition to an operating system, it has no Exit from Windows command anywhere. Exiting from Windows 95 is the same as turning off your computer. Because Windows 95 maintains an internal disk cache, and because Windows 95 must be able to save or update the desktop, turning off your computer while Windows 95 is running will almost inevitably lead to some type of data loss. The Shut Down command on the Task Bar's Start menu lets you safely shut off your computer. When you choose Shut Down, Windows 95 clears all its internal caches and disk buffers, preserves the desktop, and lets you know when it's safe to turn the computer off. The Shut Down command also lets you restart the computer, or log off the network without restarting Windows 95.

The Explorer

Although the Windows 95 desktop puts few restrictions on how you work, and the Windows 95 UI may seem somewhat chaotic to experienced DOS and Windows 3.1+ users, Windows 95 actually organizes its components in a strict hierarchy. (It's the great number of possible lateral moves in the hierarchy that allows the sort of free-form work approach supported by the Windows 95 desktop.) The Explorer is the tool that reveals Windows 95's hierarchical structure, while also providing a means to access all of your system's available local and network resources.

Figure 3.9 shows a maximized Explorer window, with a view of the hierarchy corresponding to the desktop shown in figure 3.5. Many Windows 3.1+ users will find similarities between the Explorer and the old File Manager. The left pane of the window displays a tree diagram of your system's resources, while the right pane displays the contents of the item selected in the left pane. Explorer provides many more capabilities than the File Manager does, however. Through the Explorer you view not merely the file system but all available resources, including attached peripheral devices.

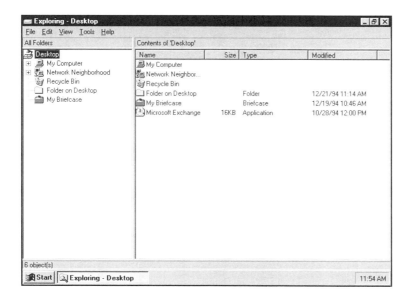

Fig. 3.9
Windows 95's Explorer lets you access documents, folders, and programs through a tree diagram of your computer's resources, as well as illustrate Windows 95's organizational hierarchy.

The Explorer works much the same way the Windows 3.1+ File Manager does. You can view the contents of various folders by expanding and collapsing branches of the tree diagram in the left pane of the Explorer window. You can open documents, open folders, or start applications by double-clicking on the icons in the right pane of the Explorer. Figure 3.10 shows the same Explorer window from figure 3.9, except with the branch of the tree diagram for the My Computer folder expanded. (The Desktop folder in the left pane of the window is still selected, so the right pane of the Explorer window hasn't changed.)

Fig. 3.10
The Explorer uses expanding and collapsing branches in its tree diagram, much like the Windows 3.1+ File Manager.

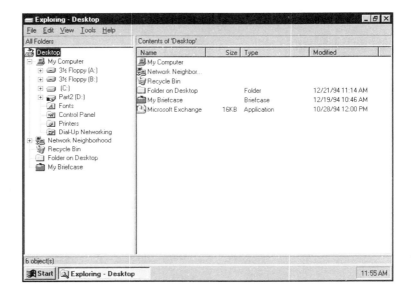

Windows 3.1+ users who find that the Windows 95 desktop gets cluttered too quickly with open windows, or who prefer the less open-ended management style of File Manager, may prefer to operate almost exclusively in the Explorer.

The Explorer offers many of the same viewing and toolbar options as other Windows 95 windows, allowing a variety of sorting and display methods.

Every Windows 95 folder window can display a sort of mini-Explorer. As described earlier, one of the viewing options for a folder window displays a toolbar for the window (refer to fig. 3.3). Figure 3.11 shows a folder window (in this case, for the Desktop folder) with the Explorer drop-down list displayed. This list contains a tree diagram like the one that appears in the left pane of the Explorer's window, with all branches of the tree expanded.

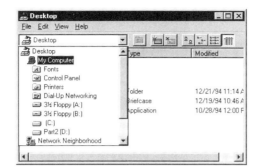

Fig. 3.11
Every folder window in Windows 95 contains its own mini-Explorer on its toolbar.

I

Introducing Windows 95

Control Panel

If you're a Windows 3.1+ user, many items in the Windows 95 Control Panel will look familiar (see fig. 3.12). Windows 95's Control Panel fulfills the same purpose as the Windows 3.1+ Control Panel—to provide a centralized location for all the utilities needed to set up or configure your computer system's software and hardware.

Fig. 3.12
The Windows 95 Control Panel, like the Windows 3.1+ Control Panel, consolidates the utilities for configuring your computer's hardware and software configuration.

The Date/Time, Keyboard, Mouse, Multimedia, and other icons in the Control Panel look the same as those in the Windows 3.1+ Control Panel and carry out essentially the same functions. Some of the Control Panel applets have been added to or enhanced. The Date/Time applet for setting the system's date and time, for example, now includes a time zone map of the world, used to set the time zone for your location.

Like almost everything else in Windows 95, the Control Panel is really just a folder in Windows 95's installed folder. Also like everything else in Windows 95, you can access the Control Panel in several different ways: use the Settings choice from the Start menu on the Task Bar, open the Control Panel folder directly from its icon in the My Computer folder, or go through the Explorer.

▶ See Part II, "Exploring Windows 95's Multimedia Features"

Windows 95's Control Panel does have several differences from Windows 3.1+, however. For example, system sounds, Sound Mapper, MIDI Mapper, and other audio/visual device driver controls are now consolidated in the Control Panel's Multimedia applet.

Other Control Panel differences include the Display, Network, Microsoft Exchange Profiles, Modems, Security, System, Add New Hardware, Printers, Add/Remove Programs, Microsoft Mail Postoffice, and Accessibility Options applets.

▶ See Chapter 12, "Connecting to the Outside World," and Chapter 18, "Messaging with Windows 95's Exchange Client"

The Network applet provides control of all your computer's network configuration options. (Network administration is carried out in the Policy Manager—see Chapter 21, "Managing Networked PCs with Windows 95.") The Microsoft Exchange Profiles, Modems, and Microsoft Mail Postoffice applets all relate to configuring your modem hardware and to configuring Windows 95's built-in Mail capabilities.

The Security applet allows you to set or change security passwords for network access to your computer, enable remote network administration, or permit different users to have different profiles. A profile is the information about your desktop settings—wallpaper, pattern, open windows, and so on. If more than one person uses the computer, you can let each user have her/his own profile.

Control Panel's System allows you to review all the physical hardware devices present in your computer and, where possible, change their configuration. The System applet even lets you view hardware items such as your CPU, RAM, and hard disk controllers. The Add New Hardware applet helps you install and configure new hardware devices in your computer, such as CD-ROM drives, sound cards, hard disks, scanners, and so on.

The Accessibility Options applet lets you set up special options for disabled computer users. The Accessibility Options are described in more detail in the section "Life with Windows 95: Making It Easier" at the end of this chapter.

The Display applet in Control Panel consolidates all the controls that affect your computer's screen display. The Display applet lets you change or preview desktop patterns, wallpaper, and screen savers. Display also lets you customize the colors used to display active and inactive windows, and to choose the typeface, font size, and color used to display text in windows—similar to the Windows 3.1+ Colors applet.

◀ See Chapter 2, "Making Hardware Plug and Play"

Perhaps most importantly, the Display applet in Control Panel allows you to configure your display type—you can choose the number of colors (16, 256, etc.) and the screen resolution (640x480, 800x600, etc.). Making these settings in the Control Panel makes much more sense—and is much more convenient—than having to run the Windows Setup program as you do in Windows 3.1+. Even more convenient, Windows 95 uses hot-switching of video modes—meaning that, if you have the right kind of hardware, Windows 95 can change video modes without having to be restarted.

The Add/Remove Programs applet is another sensible addition to the Control Panel. The Add/Remove Programs applet allows you to install and uninstall Windows 95 programs, and to add or remove optional Windows 95 components (such as the backup utility, Microsoft Exchange, Briefcases, Dial-Up Networking, desktop wallpaper, and so on) at any time. Like changing the display mode, it makes sense to be able to configure Windows 95's optional software components from the same place you control all of its other features—the Control Panel.

The Printers Folder
Although a Printers icon does appear in Control Panel, the Print Manager doesn't exist in Windows 95. Instead, all printer setup and control is consolidated in the Printers folder in My Computer. Clicking the Printers icon in Control Panel merely activates a shortcut to the Printers folder in My Computer. You can also open the Printers folder from the My Computer window.

The Printers folder looks much like any other Windows 95 folder window. It contains the Add Printer applet to help you install a new printer, and icons that provide access to a particular printer's configuration.

The Fonts Folder
Like the printers, font management is now in My Computer, and isn't directly part of Control Panel, although an icon for the Fonts folder does appear in the Control Panel window. Like the Printers folder, clicking the Fonts icon in Control Panel activates a shortcut to the Fonts folder in My Computer.

Font management is much simpler than in Windows 3.1+. Figure 3.13 shows the open Fonts folder. Use the Install New Font command on the Fonts window's File menu to install a new font. To delete a font, just use the Delete command on the Fonts window's File command. The Fonts window allows you to view fonts depending on how similar they are to each other, if you wish. Figure 3.13 has this viewing option turned on.

Fig. 3.13
Use the Fonts folder to view a list of your installed fonts, and to add or delete fonts.

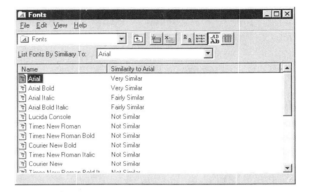

You can also see or print a sample of what your installed fonts look like by selecting a font and then opening it with either the File Open command or by double-clicking. Figure 3.14 shows a Font Sample window for the Arial font.

Fig. 3.14
You can open font files in order to see or print samples of your available fonts.

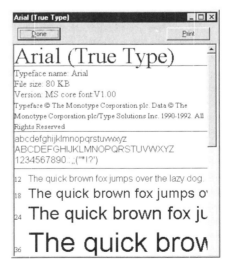

Managing Files in Windows 95

The file system is the core of the operating system. Windows 95's designers believe, on the basis of user surveys and testing with novice users, that exposed file hierarchies (like you see in the Windows 3.1+ File Manager and the Windows 95 Explorer) are intimidating to new users. (This belief may be a little surprising to those of you who remember when all work was performed at the DOS command line, and were grateful for File Manager's graphical representation of directory trees and the ability to view more than one disk directory at a time.)

As a result, Windows 95's file system, although arranged in a strict hierarchy just like the DOS directories and subdirectories that Windows 3.1+ users are familiar with, actually goes to some lengths to make sure that the file system appears more or less "flat." Only in the Explorer does the hierarchical structure underlying Windows 95's file system become visible.

In Windows 95, you are expected to locate specific documents by opening a series of windows. If you're a novice user, you'll likely know that a particular document is stored on your own computer, so you'll open the My Computer folder, and then open a window for the disk drive on which you stored the document. Next, you'll open additional folder windows until you reach the desired document. Figure 3.15 shows a Windows 95 desktop after performing such a search for a particular document.

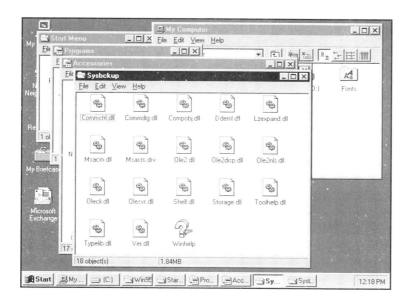

Fig. 3.15
Novice users will locate files by opening a series of folder windows on the desktop. Experienced users may find this proliferation of open windows annoying or confusing.

If you think about the way you work with physical papers and file folders on your real desk, this system doesn't seem quite so strange—most people end up with a variety of papers and notes scattered all over their desks, with some papers covering other papers, and so on. Remember, the Windows 95 desktop is an emulation of a physical desk.

Microsoft claims that the ability to find what you look for, and feel comfortable while doing it, is more important than efficiency or speed in the method you use to find what you're looking for. Whether or not you agree, this principle is obviously carried out in Windows 95. Probably, only those of you who are used to the tree-based browsing methods of the Windows 3.1+ File Manager will object to this system of browsing documents. If you prefer a tree-structured method of browsing files, you can use Explorer or the Windows 95-compatible version of File Manager. (Incidentally, the merits of the Windows 95 approach to file browsing for novice users are evidenced by the success of the Macintosh operating system—Mac users have been using a similar system for years and apparently regard it with great affection; Mac users typically sneer at the tree-based file browsing methods used in Windows 3.1+.)

> **Note**
>
> One drawback of using the Windows 95-compatible version of File Manager is that it doesn't support long file names (described in the next section of this chapter), and may hamper your adaptation to Windows 95's way of doing things, which means you may miss out on some of Windows 95's better features. If you really prefer a tree-based diagram of your file system, use the Windows 95 Explorer to browse files, or use the mini-Explorer drop-down list on a folder window's toolbar (described earlier).
>
> Windows 95 installs its version of the File Manager in both dual-boot and upgrade installations (see Chapter 23, "Setting Up and Managing Windows 95").

If you prefer to view documents and folders through a window rather than in the Explorer, you can reduce the amount of clutter on-screen (refer to fig. 3.13) by changing the viewing options of the window you use to browse files. By default, Windows 95 opens a new window for every folder that you open. You can change a window's viewing options, however, so that the window "follows" the view—each time you open a new folder, the current window displays the contents of the newly opened folder, rather than opening another window.

The Windows 95 file system includes many "intuitive" enhancements incorporated directly into the desktop. Some of these operations are already familiar to Windows 3.1+ users, such as moving a document to a new location by dragging it there (Ctrl+drag to copy files also works in Windows 95). Windows 95, however, lets you cut, copy, and paste entire documents and folders from one window to another, or onto the desktop—just as you would with individual text or graphics items within an application (you use the Edit menu in a folder window on the desktop). One way to copy a document from one folder to another, for example, is to select the document you want to copy, choose the Edit Copy command, and then use the Edit Paste command to copy the document into another folder.

Windows 95 avoids explicitly exposing the file hierarchy even in the new standard File Save As and Open File dialog boxes. Figure 3.16 shows a File Save As dialog box from the WordPad applet supplied with Windows 95. This dialog box is only slightly similar to the File Save As dialog boxes found in Windows 3.1+ applications, and actually has more in common with Windows 95's desktop folder windows.

Fig. 3.16
Windows 95's standard File Save As dialog boxes contain some of the same controls found in other folder windows, and also help conceal the file system's hierarchy.

Except for the File name text box and the Save as Type drop-down list (both are located at the bottom of the dialog box in figure 3.16), the Save File As dialog's controls are mostly borrowed from the Windows 95 folder windows. The large window in the dialog box shows all of the folders and documents contained in the current folder; the name of the current folder is shown in the Save in drop-down list at the top left of the dialog box. The Save in drop-down list contains the same mini-explorer tree diagram as the toolbar for the desktop folder windows described earlier, and works the same way.

Three of the four buttons to the right of the Save in drop-down list in the File Save As dialog box (see fig. 3.16) are the same as those on any Windows 95 folder window's toolbar. The two buttons at the right control the list view of folders and documents in the large window of the dialog box; you may choose either a small icon list (as shown in the figure), or a list showing the details of each item's size, type, and date/time last changed. The button next to the Save in drop-down list is the Parent folder button, which moves one level higher in the file system. The only button that does not also appear in a folder window's toolbar is the New Folder button, which allows you to create a new folder—a real convenience for most users.

The Windows 95 standard Open File dialog box contains the same controls as the File Save As dialog box in figure 3.16, and works essentially the same—except to open files instead of saving them.

> **Note**
>
> Windows 3.1+ applications running under Windows 95 do *not* use the Windows 95 File Save As and Open File standard dialog boxes. Instead, they continue to use the same tree diagram and list box with which Windows 3.1+ users are already familiar.

Built-In Deletion Protection: The Recycling Bin

Almost all computer users with more than a few hours of experience have accidentally erased a disk file. The proliferation of deletion-protection utilities for DOS, and the eventual inclusion of an UNDELETE utility as part of MS-DOS itself, attests to the frequency and seriousness of this type of human error. Windows 95's Recycle Bin will help you save yourself from such accidents.

Figure 3.17 shows the Recycle Bin desktop icon. When the Recycle Bin is empty, it looks like the icon on the left; when the Recycle Bin contains deleted disk objects, it looks like the icon on the right.

Fig. 3.17
The Recycle Bin icon, shown here both empty and full, is your key to retrieving accidentally deleted folders and documents.

Whenever you delete a document, folder, application, or any other item stored on one of your hard disks, Windows 95 puts it in the Recycle Bin instead of completely erasing the item from your disk drive. If you later decide that you deleted an item in error, you can get it back by retrieving it from the Recycle Bin—sort of like rooting around in the wastebasket under your desk for a memo you threw away, but much cleaner.

You retrieve items from the Recycle Bin by double-clicking on the Recycle Bin's icon to open a folder window that displays the Recycle Bin's contents, and then moving or copying the item from the Recycle Bin to some other folder on your computer. The Recycle Bin's folder window is essentially the same as the folder windows described at the beginning of this chapter.

Although the Recycle Bin is similar to the famous Macintosh trash can, Windows 95 does not automatically empty the Recycle Bin when you shut down your computer. The Recycle Bin stores deleted items indefinitely, with only one limitation (explained next). This indefinite retention of deleted disk files is an important feature, because it may be hours, days, or even weeks before you realize that you really do need a particular document that you deleted previously.

By default, the contents of the Recycle Bin can occupy up to 10 percent of the total space on your hard disk. (You can change the amount of space that the Recycle Bin is allowed to use by altering the Recycle Bin's properties.) The only time that Windows 95 automatically removes items from the Recycle Bin is when the Bin's disk space limit is reached. Each time you delete a disk file, Windows 95 moves it to the Recycle Bin. When the total combined size of the items in the Recycle Bin exceeds the percentage of disk space allotted to it, then Windows 95 permanently discards only the oldest items from the Recycle Bin, and only enough items to make room for the newly deleted item. You can also manually discard one, some, or all of the items in the Recycle Bin.

Windows 95 implements the Recycle Bin by creating a hidden folder named RECYCLED in the root directory of each of your hard disks. Whenever you delete a disk file, Windows 95 moves the deleted file into the RECYCLED folder, keeping track of the total space taken up by files in the RECYCLED folder and only permanently deleting one or more of the oldest deleted files whenever the space limits for the Recycle Bin are exceeded.

Caution

Once you "empty"—that is, delete—an object from the Recycle Bin, it is truly gone, and can no longer be recovered.

Using Quick View to Inspect File Contents

If you're like most computer users, you'll eventually find a file that you just can't remember what you put in it. More often, you may be looking for a particular bit of information and just can't remember which one of several different files in which you put it. In Windows 3.1+, you have to start the application that created a particular file (or one that can read that file's format) to look inside that file. Taking a quick peek at a file's contents without spending the time to load a complete application just wasn't possible.

In Windows 95, however, you can examine the contents of files on your disk without first starting an application. Windows 95 has, built into the desktop, the capability to view many different types of files directly, without starting an application. Windows 95 includes a variety of file viewers. To view the contents of a disk file, select the file in a folder window, and use the Quick View command from the folder window's File menu. Figure 3.18 shows the WinNews text file (part of the documentation provided with Windows 95) in a Quick View window.

Fig. 3.18
Use Quick View to quickly check the contents of various text, spreadsheet, or graphics files.

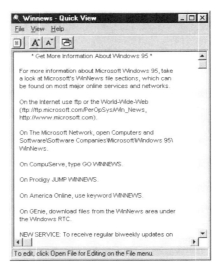

You can use the Quick View command to view text, word processor, worksheet, and graphics files in a variety of different formats. If you decide you do want to edit the document you're looking at in Quick View, the Quick View window provides menu and toolbar commands that start the appropriate program for the document you've selected.

Understanding and Using Long File Names

One of the greatest conveniences for novice and experienced DOS and Windows 3.1+ users is the advent of long file names in Windows 95. Most DOS or Windows 3.1+ users have had the experience of exhausting their imagination trying to think of a meaningful eight-character name for a particular document (the three-character extension often can't be used as part of the file name, since the extension is usually used to indicate the type of the file).

Eight-character file names caused Macintosh users to scorn and pity DOS and Windows 3.1+ users—even UNIX users have been astonished at the eight-character file name limit. Those days are gone: Windows 95 permits file names up to 255 characters long, which may include space characters or other punctuation. You can now give files expressive names, such as Second Quarter Sales Report, instead of code names such as 2QSLSRPT.

The fact that Windows 95's file system retains compatibility with the file system in earlier versions of MS-DOS leads to some interesting complications with long file names. First, until everyone has applications written expressly for Windows 95, most application software won't be able to use long file names. For these applications, Windows 95 will translate a long file name to an eight-character equivalent so you can open the file, but you won't be able to create new files with long names from within the application. (If the application is properly registered in Windows 95, you could create a document for that application with a long file name directly from a folder window with the File menu's New command, however.)

Caution

Although the FAT (file allocation table) structure of Windows 95's file system is compatible with earlier DOS versions, don't use defragmenting utilities from earlier versions of DOS on your Windows 95 hard disk—this is especially important if you have made a dual-boot installation of Windows 95. Defragmenting your disk will result in a loss of all long file names, leaving only the DOS file names. Windows 95 has its own defragmenting utility, which is compatible with long file names. Use the Windows 95 utility only.

The way Windows 95 handles long file name translation to maintain compatibility with earlier DOS versions is to make a distinction between a file's long name and its so-called DOS name. Windows 95 maintains a FAT compatible with earlier DOS FAT structures, and keeps long file information in a virtual FAT (VFAT). Windows 95 enters an eight-character (plus three-character extension) file name in the DOS FAT, and enters the long file name in the VFAT.

▶ See Chapter 25, "Running DOS Applications under Windows 95"

Windows 95 typically uses the first eight letters of a long file name to create the DOS name. For example, a document with the Windows 95 long name *Letter to Dave* has its name entered in the DOS FAT as LETTERTO. Windows 95 handles conflicts between DOS names by adding tilde characters (~) and numbers to the DOS name. For example, if you have two documents in the same folder—one named *Letter to Dave* and the other named *Letter to John*—Windows 95 uses LETTERTO as the DOS name for the first document, and LETTER~1 for the second document. If you add a document named *Letter to Susan* to the same folder, its DOS name will be LETTER~2.

Applications that don't support Windows 95's long file names—such as Windows 3.1+ or DOS programs running under Windows 95—will display and use the DOS name for a file. As you can see from the example in the preceding paragraph, it may be possible for your DOS file names to become even more confusing and cryptic when translated from Windows 95 long file names. As a result, most users will probably migrate very slowly to long file names.

Another consequence of Windows 95's file system compatibility with previous versions of DOS is that Windows 95 still uses the three-character file extension to determine a file's type—that is, to determine whether a file is an application program, a font, a document belonging to a registered application, or some other type of file.

Although a file extension to indicate a file's type may seem incompatible with the concept of long file names, Windows 95 works it out reasonably well. Windows 95 considers any characters that appear after the last period (.) in a file's name to be the file's extension. In the file name Test.executable.txt, for example, Windows 95 considers *txt* to be the file's extension, indicating that this is a text document. If more than three characters follow the last period in the file name, Windows 95 uses the first three letters to determine the file extension. As far as Windows 95's file type determination goes, the two documents *File.exe* and *File.executable* both have the *exe* extension, and Windows 95 expects them to contain executable program code. (In fact, the DOS name for both *File.exe* and *File.executable* is FILE.EXE.)

If you are an experienced DOS and Windows 3.1+ user, you'll quickly notice that most file name extensions don't appear in any folder window, no matter what viewing options you use (large or small icon, list, or details). This is because Windows 95, by default, hides the extension for any file type that's properly registered in Windows 95's Registry. (You can change this by setting a folder window's viewing options, if you want to see file extensions.) Rather than show the file extension, Windows 95 displays an icon for the file that corresponds to its type, as determined by the Registry. This relieves novice users from ever having to be aware of a file's extension or type—Windows 95 handles that part of the file system's machinery behind the scenes. Windows 95 displays a file's extension only if the extension isn't in the Registry.

If a file's extension appears in the Registry, you can't change the extension (and hence, the file's type) when you rename or copy the file. Because Windows 95 maintains the file's extension as hidden information, the extension isn't accessible for alteration unless you've changed the viewing options for the window to show all file extensions, even those that appear in the Registry. Notice that you can't possibly rename a file such as *Test.executable* to *Test.exe* because Windows 95 complains that the file already exists—the complaint is based on the DOS names for the file.

Taking Shortcuts through Windows 95

Even novice computer users will probably quickly tire of the tediousness of opening several different windows to view specific documents or folders. More advanced users will also want ways to accelerate their work, particularly when making various menu selections to change an object's properties. Windows 95 provides various different techniques to speed up work for power users and novices alike.

Shortcut Icons: The Quick Way to Programs and Folders

Even the newest of computer users will eventually protest the need to open the My Computer folder on the desktop every time they want to browse through files on their hard disks. More advanced users will start out decrying what seems to be the hard way to get to a particular folder or document— opening a variety of windows on the desktop.

Windows 95 provides a special link to jump quickly to a particular application, folder, or document: the Shortcut. A Shortcut, similar to a program item in Windows 3.1+, displays an icon representing the item to which it refers, and has a related disk file that contains information that Windows 95 needs to locate the referenced item. (Shortcuts are created by using the Create Shortcut command on the File menu in a folder window, or by right-dragging an application to a new location.)

Shortcuts on the desktop provide a quick way to get at particular programs, folders, or documents. As mentioned earlier, you don't have to start an application first to open or edit a document; instead, you can double-click any document's icon to open that document directly. Because of this feature, you can speed up your work by doing things such as putting a Shortcut that points to a particular document on your desktop. You can then open that document with one double-click, rather than having to first locate and start an application and then loading the desired document into the application. For example, you might have a calendar program file that you use frequently for scheduling meetings and appointments. You might create a Shortcut for the calendar document on your desktop. You could then open and edit your appointments in the calendar document without first starting your calendar program.

You can have as many Shortcuts as you want, and you can place Shortcuts anywhere on the desktop or in any folder—you can even put Shortcuts in other documents. As many Shortcuts as you want can all point to the same folder, program, or other item.

Shortcuts are distinguished from other icons on the desktop and in folders by the "jump" arrow that appears on the Shortcut icon. Figure 3.19 shows a folder window containing several Shortcut icons. (When you create a Shortcut, Windows 95 adds the phrase *Shortcut to* the name of the item you made the Shortcut for—you can change this name, if you want.)

Fig. 3.19
Shortcuts can be anywhere on the desktop or in any folder for rapid access to documents, folders, and programs.

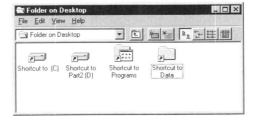

A Shortcut contains all the information necessary to open whatever folder, device, or application it points to—just double-click the Shortcut. You can have as many Shortcuts as you want scattered throughout your system, all of which refer to the same item. Deleting a Shortcut doesn't delete the item to which the Shortcut refers, just the Shortcut itself—again, much like the program items to which Windows 3.1+ users are accustomed.

Note

Pay attention to Windows 95's deletion confirmation messages, especially when deleting Shortcuts—if you accidentally delete the original item, then the file, folder, or application is gone. Shortcuts always have an extension of LNK, so you can tell whether you're deleting a Shortcut or the actual file to which a Shortcut refers.

Windows 95 keeps all your Shortcuts synchronized with the source items to which they refer. If you delete a file or folder, Windows 95 deletes all the Shortcuts that refer to the deleted item. If you rename an item that has Shortcuts pointing to it, Windows 95 doesn't rename the Shortcuts, but does ensure that the Shortcuts still point to the renamed item.

Clicking the Right Way: Using the Other Mouse Button

For years now, Microsoft and compatible mice have had at least two (and sometimes three) buttons. Only recently have any software engineers found a consistently useful application for the right mouse button, however. If you've used some of Microsoft's more recent applications for Windows 3.1+ (Excel 5, Word 6, and others), you may be familiar with the concept of right-clicking— that is, clicking with the right mouse button—to bring up various shortcut menus.

Windows 95 also makes use of the right mouse button in a similar fashion. Right-clicking on any object on the desktop or in a folder window displays a shortcut menu of actions or options applicable to that object. You can even produce shortcut menus for blank areas of the desktop or a folder window. For example, to change the properties of the desktop (wallpaper, pattern, screen resolution, etc.), you can right-click on any blank area of the desktop, and then choose Properties from the pop-up menu that appears.

Right-clicking is a fast way to access frequently needed commands and options, such as setting an object's properties or creating a new folder, Shortcut, or document. Actions you can perform by right-clicking all have corresponding choices that you can access through the window menus—right-clicking is a non-intuitive shortcut method, intended mostly for the convenience of advanced users.

Dragging objects by using the right mouse button also has special effects in Windows 95. For example, if you right-drag an item from a window onto the desktop, Windows 95 displays a shortcut menu when you release the mouse button that gives you the opportunity to specify whether or not you want to move or copy the object to the new location, or whether you want to create a shortcut icon for the dragged object.

Life with Windows 95: Making It Easier

Windows 95 provides a large number of features intended to smooth operations for novice users. One of the greatest hurdles for novice users is getting over the "What-do-I-do-now?" question that arises the first time they sit down at a computer. Windows 95 provides continuous hints and pointers for getting started.

Hints and ToolTips

The most obvious of the operating hints that Windows 95 provides are those in the Welcome dialog box that Windows 95 displays whenever it starts up. (The Welcome dialog box was discussed at the beginning of this chapter.) Unfortunately, few of these hints actually say what might happen—you really do have to perform the experiment yourself to discover the outcome of the suggested action.

Windows 95 also displays ToolTips for most command buttons in folder windows and for all buttons on the Task Bar. (A *ToolTip* is text added to the mouse pointer that labels the control the mouse pointer is now over.) For example, a ToolTip appears when you move the mouse pointer over an application button on the Task Bar—the text label contains the name of the running application corresponding to that button on the Task Bar. As another example, ToolTips appear for all the buttons on a folder window's toolbar.

Windows 95 Wizards

Windows 95 contains a variety of Wizards to help you perform various tasks—usually installing or configuring a new hardware or software device. A Wizard is really a special applet that guides you step-by-step through a particular process, rather than make you deal with a raw, fill-in-the-blanks dialog box. Windows 95's Wizards include the Add Printer Wizard (started by double-clicking the Add Printer icon in the Printers Folder) to help you install new printers, and the Add New Hardware Wizard (started by double-clicking its icon in the Control Panel) to help you install new hardware devices and their software drivers. Typically, you'll need to use the Add New Hardware Wizard to install any hardware devices that aren't Plug and Play.

Windows 95's Help System

Windows 95's help system is similar to the on-line help system with which Windows 3.1+ users are familiar, but has a simplified interface, and keeps individual help topics shorter so that you aren't overwhelmed by too much information at one time.

Apparently, many novice users were confused by the differences between using the Windows 3.1+ help system's Search and Index features, so Windows 95's on-line help system combines the old Search and Index into a single new Index—which still allows you to search for items as you do by using the old Search dialog box. Figure 3.20 shows the new Windows 95 help Index. You can either scroll through the alphabetic indexing listing in the lower part of the window, or type a specific topic to search for in the text box at the top of the dialog box.

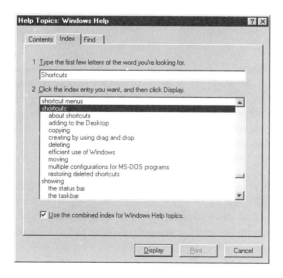

Fig. 3.20
Windows 95's on-line help system combines the index list and topic searching into a single dialog.

Windows 95's on-line help system uses a much-improved table of contents. This table of contents uses expanding and collapsing branches to display or hide subheadings. Figure 3.21 shows the expanded branch of topics for the

Introducing Windows 95

Introducing Windows 95 table of contents entry. Notice the open book icon to the left of the Introducing Windows legend in the figure. The open book icon indicates an expanded branch of the table of contents, while a closed book indicates that there are hidden topics. The page icon indicates a help topic that you can display.

Fig. 3.21
The table of contents for Windows 95's on-line help system.

Note

Because all Windows 3.1+ applications use the same help engine (supplied by Windows itself) to display help topics, the help displays in your existing Windows 3.1+ applications will take on the look and feel of Windows 95's new help system.

Although the old Search feature in the online Help system has been merged with the new Index, Windows 95 adds a powerful Find feature to its help system. Figure 3.22 shows the Find sheet of the Windows 95 Help system. The Help Find sheet has three parts: a text box at the top where you enter the topics or subjects you want to find help for, a list from which you can select matching words to help describe what you want to find, and (at the bottom) a list of found help topics.

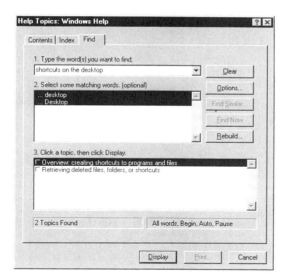

Fig. 3.22
The Help system's Find feature helps you find help topics matching simple descriptions you type in, or by searching for particular keywords.

The Find feature has several options regarding how it uses the text you enter. You can look for topics that contain one or more keywords that you enter, or you can look for topics that contain particular phrases. In essence, the Find dialog lets you type in a simple English phrase describing what you want to find help for—like "shortcuts on the desktop" in figure 3.22. (Actually, Find searched for topics containing both the keywords "shortcuts" and "desktop," but the results are the same.)

> **Note**
>
> The first time you use the Find feature, you must let the Help system build a special database of the words in your Help files. You can include all of the installed Help files, or limit the index to only Help files you select. Find can only search for topics in the Help files included in its database. If you don't seem to turn anything up with Find, you may need to rebuild Find's word database to include additional Help files. You can rebuild the Find database anytime by using the Rebuild command button in the Find dialog box.

Many topics in Windows 95's Help system not only contain hypertext links to additional topics and word definitions, but also contain "jump" buttons that take you directly into the activity that you're reading about. If you want to find out how to install a new printer, for example, you might look up the topic in the online Help system. Figure 3.23 shows the Help topic for installing a new printer. Notice the command button in the text of the Help topic (it's in step 1 of the instructions). Clicking this button actually starts up Windows 95's Add Printer Wizard.

Fig. 3.23
Windows 95's Help system includes "jump" buttons that actually start the application or utility under discussion. The button in step 1 of this Help topic starts the Add Printer Wizard.

The What's This? Button

As a final bit of extra help, many Windows 95 dialog boxes include a What's This? Help button. Figure 3.24 shows the Date & Time dialog box from the Date/Time applet in Control Panel (these dialog boxes are referred to as property sheets). Notice the button with a question mark on it at the top right corner of the dialog box, next to the Close button.

Fig. 3.24
The Date & Time properties sheet in the Date/Time Control Panel applet, showing the What's This? button and the pop-up Help window it produces.

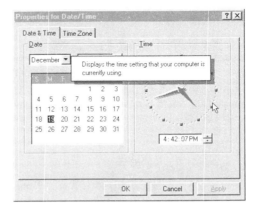

When you click this button, Windows 95 puts a question mark icon next to the mouse pointer. Move the mouse pointer over any control or area of the dialog box that you are having trouble with, and click it. Windows 95 will display a pop-up window containing an explanation of that item, if there's one available. In figure 3.24, the What's This? button was clicked, and then the mouse was clicked over the clock face, resulting in the pop-up help window shown in the figure.

Accessibility Features

Windows 95 provides extra help for some users in one final area—the Accessibility features, which are configured through the Accessibility Options applet in the Control Panel. For some time now, MS-DOS has contained various accessibility tools to make using a computer easier for persons with disabilities. Up to now, these tools have consisted of a suite of special device drivers and TSR programs whose installation and use required more than a little skill and knowledge.

In Windows 95, however, the Accessibility tools are integrated directly into the operating system and are easily activated and configured through the Windows 95 Control Panel. The Accessibility Options applet in Control Panel allows you to configure all of the accessibility options quickly and easily, including serial-key devices. Using the Accessibility Options applet, you can activate or configure the following special features:

- *Sticky Keys*, which makes it possible to enter key combinations such as Ctrl+Esc by pressing the Ctrl and Esc keys one after the other, instead of both at the same time.

- *Filter Keys*, which causes Windows 95 to ignore brief or quickly repeated keystrokes.

- *Toggle Keys*, which tells Windows 95 to sound a tone whenever the Caps Lock, Num Lock, or Scroll Lock keys are pressed.

- *Sound Sentry* makes Windows 95 flash part or all of the screen whenever Windows or an application generates sound through the PC speaker or multimedia sound card.

- *Show Sounds* causes Windows 95 to tell running applications to display a caption for any speech or sound they make. To the author's knowledge, there are currently no applications that can receive this message, but perhaps close-captioned multimedia is in our future?

■ *High Contrast* display mode, which causes Windows 95 to use a high-contrast color scheme for its windows, command buttons, menus, and so on, is specially designed to increase the readability of the screen.

■ *Mouse Keys* allows you to move the mouse cursor by using the arrow keys on the keyboard.

Chapter 4

Using the Built-In Accessory Applets

Like Windows 3.1+, Windows 95 includes a variety of applets intended to assist your personal productivity, whether at home or in the office. (An *applet*, by the way, is a general term for any small-scale application.) Windows 95's applets don't necessarily have all the features that you'd find in a full-blown application program, but they do provide you with some handy, basic tools with which to get started—and you can't beat their cost (free with Windows 95).

This chapter gives you a quick tour through the productivity applets installed in Windows 95's Accessories folder. Because several of the Accessories applets are similar to those provided with Windows 3.1+, this chapter pays most attention to the newest additions to the Windows applet family: WinPad, WordPad, and Windows 95's system maintenance applets.

Note

This chapter doesn't cover the Control Panel or multimedia (Media Player and Sound Recorder) applets. For information on Control Panel's functions, refer to Chapter 3, "Exploring the Windows 95 Interface." The chapters in Part II, "Exploring Windows 95's Multimedia Features," cover the various multimedia applets.

The Usual Assortment

To fill the Accessories folder, Microsoft rounded up many of the "usual suspects" with which Windows 3.1+ users are already familiar. Although these applets now have the basic look and feel of any other Windows 95 application, they haven't changed substantially from previous versions of Windows.

Accessory applets that will be familiar to Windows 3.1+ users include:

- *Calculator.* The Calculator applet works much like any pocket or desktop calculator—use it to add, subtract, multiply, and divide. Scientific mode allows you to perform computations in different number bases: hexadecimal, decimal, octal, and binary, as well as standard trigonometric functions (see fig. 4.1).

Fig. 4.1
The familiar
Calculator applet.

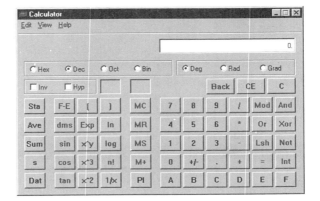

- *Character Map.* The Character Map allows you to select special symbols from any fonts you have installed on your computer and copy those characters to the Windows Clipboard for insertion into other documents (see fig. 4.2).

Fig. 4.2
The Character
Map applet is
another feature
familiar to
Windows 3.1+
users.

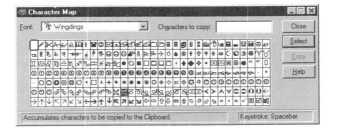

- *NotePad.* The NotePad applet allows you to edit plain, text-only files, such as DOS batch files or a Windows program's INI file. A text-only file contains just the text of a document, without any special formatting information to specify fonts, paragraph formatting, and so on. Figure 4.3 shows NotePad being used to view a text file. Many people use NotePad to compose electronic mail messages while offline, as well as to create or edit DOS batch files. The NotePad can edit text files up to about 64K bytes long; if you try to open a text-only document that is too large for NotePad, then NotePad will offer to start the WordPad applet for you. (WordPad is described at the end of this chapter.)

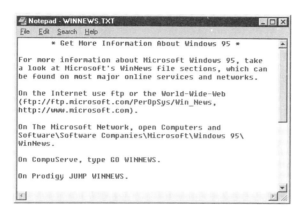

Fig. 4.3
The NotePad applet has many uses.

■ *Paint*. The Paint applet is essentially the same as the Paintbrush applet provided with Windows 3.1+ (see fig. 4.4). The Paint applet allows you to create or edit graphics in Windows Bitmap (BMP) file formats, only. Paint supports monochrome, 16-color, 256-color, and 24-bit color BMP formats. The toolbars and color palettes have changed slightly, but all the features found in the old Paintbrush program still exist in Paint.

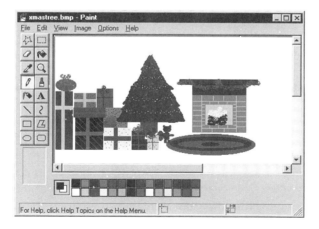

Fig. 4.4
The Paint applet also has many uses.

As you can see from the preceding descriptions and their accompanying figures, many productivity applets provided with Windows 95 have not changed much from previous versions of Windows. You may notice, however, the absence of the Calendar, and Cardfile applets that were included with Windows 3.1+. These last few applets have been replaced with new applet utilities specifically designed for Windows 95. (Microsoft has stated that it may include some of the old Accessory applets in the Windows 95 release for users of previous Windows versions.)

The new WordPad applet greatly expands the features formerly found in the Windows Write program. WordPad is discussed in a separate section later in this chapter. Like Write, the Calendar and Cardfile applets from Windows 3.1+ have been replaced by a single new applet, WinPad. WinPad also is discussed in a separate section later in this chapter.

Tools for Your Computer System

Windows 95 provides several different tools to help you get greater use from your computer, to keep the vital data on your computer safe, and to facilitate your transition into Windows 95. The Accessories folder contains the System Tools folder, which contains the following system maintenance tools:

> **Note**
>
> Many of the applets in the System Tools folder continue Microsoft's practice of providing disk diagnostic and maintenance tools (begun with DOS 5), and disk compression software (begun with DOS 6). Windows 95 *is* the next version of MS-DOS, and contains most of the disk utilities that users have come to expect from MS-DOS.

■ *Backup.* This applet is similar to the MSBACKUP (for DOS) and MWBACKUP (for Windows) utilities provided with DOS 6. Backup allows you to back up files to floppy disks or tape. As with most backup utility programs, you have a variety of choices about how you back up or restore files. Backup options include making complete or incremental backups, or backing up selected files only. Restore options include choosing whether to overwrite existing files, and whether to restore files to the same directory they were backed up from. Figure 4.5 shows a backup being prepared with the Backup applet.

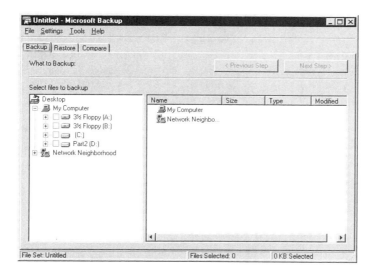

Fig. 4.5
Use the Windows
95 Backup utility
to backup files to
floppy disk or to a
tape drive.

■ *Disk Defragmenter*. Use this applet to defragment your disk drive to speed up your computer system's disk performance. Data is stored on your disk in chunks called *clusters*. A single file stored on disk may be composed of many different clusters. As the data stored on your disk drive changes, both your data files and the free space on your disk become increasingly *fragmented* as their disk clusters become scattered around the surface of the disk. Defragmenting your disk drive makes all of the file clusters contiguous, and leaves all of the free clusters in one contiguous block. Having all the used and free disk clusters contiguous speeds up your computer system because it takes less time to find all of the clusters that make up a file, or to find a free cluster to write new data on your disk. Figure 4.6 shows the dialog box that the Disk Defragmenter displays while defragmenting a drive.

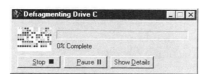

Fig. 4.6
The Disk
Defragmenter
applet displays a
dialog box as it
defragments your
hard disk. Clicking
the Show Details
button displays a
more detailed
progress chart.

■ *DriveSpace*. Use the DriveSpace applet to compress disk drives under Windows 95, and to configure or maintain existing DoubleSpace and DriveSpace compressed drives. DriveSpace is the Windows 95 version of the disk compression utility provided with DOS version 6.22, which superseded the DoubleSpace disk compression provided with DOS 6. Compressing a disk drive causes all of the data stored on the disk, now and in the future, to be stored in a special compressed format. Using disk compression, you can theoretically store twice as much information in a given amount of disk space. Figure 4.7 shows DriveSpace getting ready to compress a disk in drive A.

Fig. 4.7
Use DriveSpace to compress both hard and floppy disk drives. Creating compressed disk drives increases the amount of data you can store on the disk.

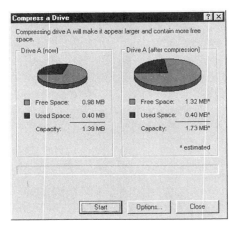

> **Note**
>
> To use a DoubleSpace or DriveSpace compressed disk, you must have the Windows 95 DriveSpace device driver installed. If you already had a DoubleSpace or DriveSpace compressed drive at the time you installed Windows 95, then the Windows Setup program installed the DriveSpace device driver. Otherwise, the DriveSpace applet will install the DriveSpace device driver when you compress your first disk drive.

- *Mail File Converter*. This optional applet converts Microsoft Mail documents into a format that Microsoft Exchange can read. Microsoft Exchange is discussed in Chapter 18 "Messaging with Windows 95's Exchange Client."

- *Net Watcher*. This applet lets you monitor information about things such as shared printers and disk drives on your own computer or on other computers in the network. This network administration tool is discussed in Chapter 21, "Managing Networked PCs with Windows 95."

- *ScanDisk*. Use the ScanDisk applet to check the integrity of, and to repair, the file system on your disk drives; you can also use ScanDisk to check for physical defects in the surface of your disk drives. Like the CHKDSK program from early versions of MS-DOS (and the SCANDISK program provided in DOS 6) the Windows 95 ScanDisk applet tests for, and optionally repairs, lost file clusters and cross-linked files. The Windows 95 ScanDisk applet, however, can also check your drive for file or folder names that contain invalid characters in their names, or have invalid date/time stamps. Figure 4.8 shows the opening dialog of the ScanDisk applet, preparing for a standard test of drive C. ScanDisk's Advanced options allow you to control which method ScanDisk uses to repair or reclaim cross-linked files (make copies of the cross-linked files, delete them, or ignore them), and to recover lost file clusters (convert them to files, or simply make them available as free space).

Fig. 4.8
Use ScanDisk to find and repair lost disk clusters, cross-linked files, and files or folders that have invalid names.

- *System Monitor*. This option allows you to monitor the number of bytes per second read from or written to your disk drives, the amount of free or allocated memory in your computer, the amount of memory used by Windows 95's disk caches and swap file, the percentage of time that the CPU is actually in use, and many other bits of information relating to your computer's performance. System Monitor is primarily a network administration tool. In addition to displaying information about your own computer, System Monitor also allows you to gather information about system usage on other computers, and to monitor the number of bytes per second transferred through various network connections, how much memory is in use by various parts of the network software, and so on. System Monitor is only installed on your computer if you install the optional network administration features.

> **Tip**
>
> You can use the Add/Remove Programs applet in the Control Panel to install optional Windows 95 features at any time. Chapter 3, "Exploring the Windows 95 Interface," discusses the Control Panel and the Add/Remove Programs applet.

Reaching Out with the Phone Dialer

Because Windows 95 has many built-in telephony capabilities, including a phone dialer makes sense—if nothing else, to demonstrate Windows 95's inherent capability to use the telephone.

To use the Phone Dialer, you must have a modem installed in your computer and (obviously) a telephone handset attached to the same line as the modem. The Phone Dialer is for establishing voice connections to other users, not for data calls. You use the Phone Dialer to dial the number, and then pick up the handset to speak to the person you've called.

Figure 4.9 shows the Phone Dialer ready to dial a number. You can use the Phone Dialer's numeric pad to dial a phone number or use the speed-dial buttons to dial numbers you've entered previously (the Phone Dialer's speed-dial buttons are all blank until you enter numbers). You can also type the number to dial directly into the Number to Dial text box. When you use the numeric pad to dial, each number you select is entered into the Number to Dial text box. You must click the Dial button to actually dial the number. When you use the speed-dial buttons, the number associated with the speed-dial button gets entered in the Number to Dial text box, and the Phone Dialer dials the number immediately.

Figure 4.9 also illustrates an interesting capability of the Phone Dialer. In the figure, the Correct Time speed-dial button was selected just before the screen was captured for this figure. In California, the mnemonic word for the phone company's time announcement service is "popcorn" (767-2676). The user who made this speed-dial entry typed the mnemonic word instead of the actual number. The Phone Dialer interprets the characters in the Number to Dial text box and correctly dials the digit corresponding to each character.

Fig. 4.9
The Phone Dialer
showing its speed-
dialing capability.

Another interesting feature of the Phone Dialer deserves mention. As the Phone Dialer dials each number, it maintains a log of each call. If the call is put through successfully—that is, a person, voice mail, or an answering machine picks up the line—the Phone Dialer enters the number, date, and time of the call into the log. You can then view the log, and print or save it as a text file. Of course, you'll also be able to copy entries from the log by using the Clipboard. This feature is very handy for users with home offices, who need to record individual business calls from their home telephones for tax purposes.

Managing Personal Information in Windows 95 WinPad

The potential capability for a computer to help with personal information management—appointment schedules, milestones in long-term projects, records of personal and business contacts, and so on—is one of the areas that frequently attracts new buyers into the PC marketplace. Every magazine is full of advertisements for one type of PIM (Personal Information Manager) or another.

The new WinPad accessory supplied with Windows 95 won't put any PIM publishers out of business, but it certainly provides the two essential features of any PIM: an appointment calendar and an address book. WinPad also contains several other useful features; each major WinPad feature is described in the following sections.

Calendar

Figure 4.10 shows the WinPad calendar open in a weekly view. WinPad's calendar allows you to view your schedule in a daily, weekly, or monthly format. You also can view a yearly calendar whenever you need to take a look into the future. (Select the view by clicking one of the tabs visible at the right edge of the Calendar page shown in figure 4.10.)

Fig. 4.10
WinPad's calendar allows you to enter and view your appointments or other scheduled events.

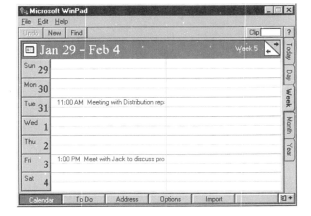

As you might expect, clicking the New button allows you to enter a new appointment or schedule an event, and the Find button lets you search for a particular event. Figure 4.11 shows a new appointment being entered into WinPad's calendar.

Fig. 4.11
When you enter a new appointment, you can set the time, specify the duration of the event, and set alarms to alert you of an upcoming appointment.

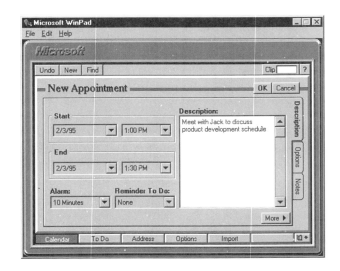

Address Book

WinPad also includes a rather comprehensive address book. Figure 4.12 shows an address book page. The tabs along the top edge of the address book let you choose the alphabetic listing you're looking at. The window at the right of the page shows a list, alphabetized by last name, of people you've entered in the address book (figure 4.12 has only one entry in the list). The file card window at the left of the address book shows the details of the entry selected in the upper window.

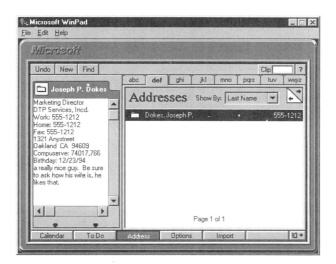

Fig. 4.12
The WinPad address book lets you enter information about your personal or business contacts.

Figure 4.13 shows a new address book entry being created. Notice the row of tabs along the top edge of the address book page. Clicking one of these tabs displays a different part of the address book's data-entry system. The address book not only allows you to record a person's name, address, and phone numbers, but also allows you to enter e-mail addresses and keep notes about that person.

To Do List

Most PIM programs include a to-do list that is linked to the appointments and events schedules. WinPad is no slacker in this respect. Figure 4.14 shows a page in WinPad's To Do list. Each entry in the To Do list is linked to a particular date. (The To Do list always shows a blank space at the end of the list for new entries.) Notice the tabs along the top edge of the To Do list. You can add or view items on the To Do list for today, this week, or an entire month. WinPad also allows you to enter To Do activities for your spare time, as shown in the figure.

Fig. 4.13
WinPad's Address book lets you record a person's name, phone numbers, e-mail addresses, and notes about the person.

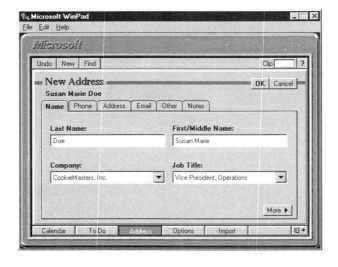

Fig. 4.14
WinPad's To Do list helps you organize daily, weekly, and monthly goals or objectives.

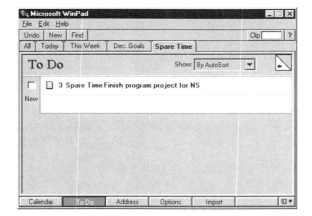

WinPad Options

WinPad's Options screen lets you select among WinPad's various configuration options. Figure 4.15 shows the WinPad Options page. (Figure 4.15 looks different from earlier figures of WinPad because it uses the screen orientation option described in the following options.) The following list summarizes each option setting:

- *Personal.* This option lets you enter your own name into WinPad or use WinPad as a "guest." This feature is primarily related to WinPad's capability to be shared over a network, so that several people can use the same calendar. For example, you might allow another user to review your appointment calendar to see what times you have available to schedule a meeting.

■ *Screen.* This option lets you determine whether you view the WinPad pages in a vertical format (as shown in fig. 4.15) or in a horizontal format (as shown in the previous WinPad figures).

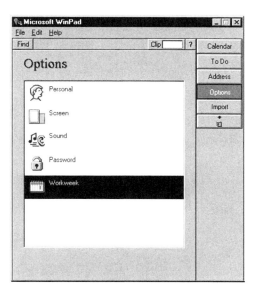

Fig. 4.15
Viewing the WinPad pages in a vertical format.

■ *Sound.* This set of options allows you to select what events you want WinPad to sound an alarm for. You can tell WinPad to sound an alarm for appointments or a clock alarm. You can also select whether WinPad makes a keyboard-click sound from the PC speaker as you type.

■ *Password.* This option lets you set passwords in WinPad. When you set passwords, you can hide various items in the appointment book, address book, notes, to-do lists and other areas of WinPad. Because you can share WinPad over the network for scheduling within your entire workgroup, users can set their own name and password. The password options also let you select whether the password should be entered on a daily or weekly basis.

■ *WorkWeek.* This interesting option isn't found in many calendar or appointment book programs. Use the WorkWeek option to tell WinPad what your work week is: when your work day starts and ends and which days of the week are business days for you. WinPad uses the information about your work week to distinguish between activities scheduled for working hours and activities scheduled for your spare time.

Getting a Leg Up

If you previously used the Cardfile or Calendar applets in Windows 3.1+, you may be admiring WinPad's more comprehensive features but dreading having to transcribe your entire address book and calendar information. No fear; WinPad includes an import feature specifically for bringing existing Cardfile and Calendar files into WinPad. Figure 4.16 shows WinPad's Import page. To import a file, simply indicate the file format by choosing Cardfile or Calendar in the System drop-down list, enter the name of the specific file you want to import in the File Name text box, and then click the Import button. WinPad handles the rest of the work for you.

Fig. 4.16

WinPad lets you import your existing Cardfile and Calendar data.

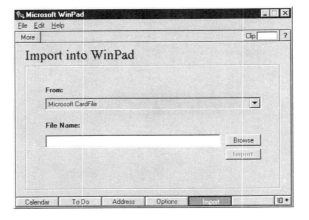

Note

WinPad can *only* import Cardfile or Calendar data files.

Son of Windows Write: Windows WordPad

As mentioned earlier in this chapter, the old Windows 3.1+ Write applet has been replaced by a new applet, named WordPad. By default, whenever you open WordPad, it assumes you want to create a formatted document, and displays a window like the one shown in figure 4.17.

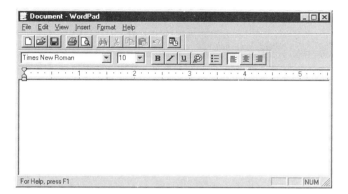

Fig. 4.17
WordPad displays
this window for
formatted
documents.

In figure 4.17, notice the two toolbars at the top of the window; if you've
used MS Word 6 for Windows, these toolbars will be somewhat familiar. The
first toolbar contains (in order from left to right) buttons to create a new
document, open an existing document, save, print, zoom, find, cut, copy,
paste, and undo; the final button inserts a time and date stamp into the
document. The second toolbar contains formatting controls: font, font size,
font style (bold, italic, underline), font color, bulleted lists, and paragraph
justification (left, centered, right).

WordPad can read formatted document files in Word for Windows 6,
RTF (Microsoft Rich Text Format), and Windows Write formats. However,
WordPad can save formatted document files only in Word for Windows 6 or
RTF. Whether you are editing a Word 6 or RTF document, WordPad displays
both of the toolbars shown in figure 4.17.

WordPad's capability to read and save RTF documents may be particularly
useful if you exchange documents between different operating systems and
different word processors. RTF-formatted documents are essentially plain text
files that contain special character sequences that tell the word processor how
the text in the document should be presented on-screen or when printed
(bold, centered, justified, font style and size, and so on). As a result, you often
can exchange RTF files between different operating systems or different word
processors more easily than a document in another format. Provided the
other system can also read and save RTF documents, there's no need to
convert the document from one format to another.

You can also use WordPad to create or edit a text-only file. (Text-only documents don't include any paragraph or font formatting information in the file; they contain only plain ASCII text. If you open a document file in a format that WordPad does not recognize, WordPad opens that file as a text-only file. Figure 4.18 shows a document opened as a text file.

Notice that only the toolbar for file (open, save, print), clipboard (cut, copy, paste) and the find and time stamp commands appear at the top of the WordPad window. Because text formatting is not permitted in a text-only document, WordPad does not display the text formatting toolbar. The toolbar shown in figure 4.18, however, is always visible, no matter what type of document you're editing.

Fig. 4.18
You can use WinPad as a text editor, similar to NotePad. WinPad, however, can edit text files much larger than is possible with NotePad.

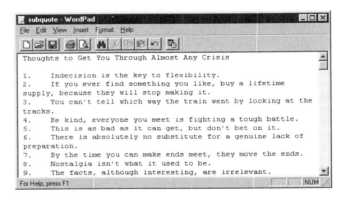

Chapter 5

Running Your Current Applications under Windows 95

According to figures published by Microsoft, Windows 3.1+ software now exceeds sales of software for any other operating environment in all categories (except games). The existing user base for Windows 3.1+ applications is, therefore, quite large. Microsoft can't expect to sell many copies of a new operating system if that operating system won't completely support existing applications.

Few users will upgrade to Windows 95 if they can't use their existing software packages. Even if the operating system upgrade is inexpensive (the anticipated upgrade price for Windows 95 is under $50, and under $100 for first-time buyers), no one will use Windows 95 if they also have to spend hundreds or thousands of dollars upgrading their productivity or recreational software. Windows 95's designers and marketers are well aware of this fact, so Windows 95 incorporates a high degree of compatibility for Windows 3.1+ applications, while improving their performance and overall reliability in several ways.

This chapter describes how Windows 95's architecture and features affect your existing Windows 3.1+ applications, starting with a description of how your existing applications will look and perform under Windows 95. This chapter then describes features of Windows 95's internal architecture that maintain compatibility with Windows 3.1+ applications. Next, you'll hear how Windows 95's system-wide features enhance various aspects of existing

Windows 3.1+ applications' performance. This chapter concludes with a description of Windows 95's mechanisms and features that improve the overall reliability of your system while running your existing Windows 3.1+ programs.

Using Windows 3.1+ Applications under Windows 95

In general, you'll install and use Windows 3.1+ applications in Windows 95 the same way you now install and use them in Windows 3.1+. The most obvious differences you'll notice when running your existing 16-bit Windows 3.1+ programs under Windows 95 are changes in your program's on-screen appearance. Otherwise, you'll use these applications exactly as you do under Windows 3.1+.

> **Note**
>
> You can expect any of your company's custom Windows software written by in-house programmers or programming consultants to run successfully under Windows 95—if that software runs successfully under Windows 3.1+. Applications written in Visual Basic or Visual Basic for Applications for use in Windows 3.1+ will run successfully under Windows 95. Any applications written for Windows 3.1+ in languages such as C, C++, Pascal, Assembler, Smalltalk/V, or others will also run under Windows 95—again, if they run successfully under Windows 3.1+ in the first place.

Inheriting the Windows 95 Look and Feel

Figure 5.1 shows a document being edited in Microsoft Word for Windows 6 running under Windows 3.1+. Compare this screen to figure 5.2, which shows the same view of the same document, this time being edited in Word for Windows 6 running under Windows 95. Notice the differences in Word's title and menu bars, and how the Word 6 maximized window has made itself smaller, leaving room for the Windows 95 Task Bar at the bottom of the screen.

The document's appearance is the same in both figures, as is the appearance of Word's toolbars, status bar, and scroll bars. What's different are Word's title bar and menu bars. Notice the different presentation of the application and document name in the title bar of figure 5.2 and the corresponding differences in the Close, Minimize, and Maximize/Restore buttons. Notice also the differences in the document Close button (at the left of the menu bar), and the document Minimize/Maximize button (at the right of the menu bar). If you look closely, you also notice some slight differences in the drop-down lists on the toolbars in each figure.

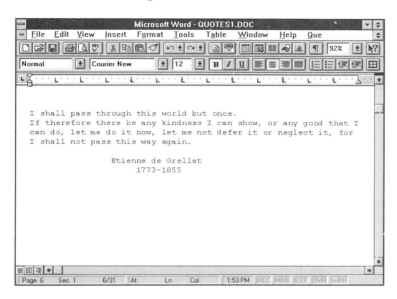

Fig. 5.1
Editing a document in Word for Windows 6 under Windows 3.1+.

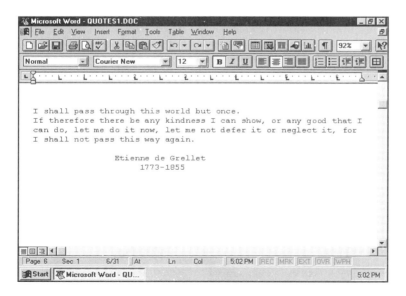

Fig. 5.2
Editing the same document from figure 5.1 in Word for Windows 6 under Windows 95.

Windows applications—assuming they're programmed correctly for Windows—use routines provided by the operating environment (whether Windows 3.1+ or Windows 95) to display title bars, menu bars, and various dialog controls such as check boxes, option buttons, drop-down lists, and so on. A Windows application displays standard program elements (such as a menu bar) by requesting the operating environment to display the element. The Windows application merely gives a description of the element—such as a list of the choices that should appear on a menu—to the operating environment and then lets the operating environment handle the work and housekeeping involved in displaying the requested element. As a result, program elements that you see on-screen when running your Windows 3.1+ applications under Windows 95 will have the look of the Windows 95 operating system.

◀ See Chapter 3, "Exploring the Windows 95 Interface"

Program elements such as menu bars, title bars, and dialog controls not only end up with the Windows 95 look but also end up with the Windows 95 feel. Drop-down and pop-up menus in Windows 3.1+ applications running under Windows 95 all operate the same as any other Windows 95-style menu.

Figure 5.3 shows an opened menu and submenu in the Micrografx Picture Publisher program. These menus—generated by Windows 95 at the request of the Picture Publisher program—work the same way as any menus generated by Windows 95. A single mouse click on the Window menu name opens the first drop-down menu. The Arrange submenu in the figure is displayed by simply holding the mouse pointer over that choice—Windows 95 automatically displays the submenu. Like other Windows 95 menus, the final action selection is made with one additional mouse click.

Fig. 5.3
Menus in Windows 3.1+ applications also end up with the look and feel of Windows 95's menus.

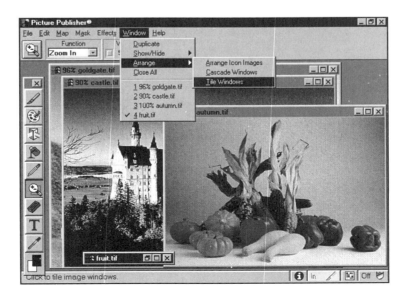

As you can see from these figures, all Windows 3.1+ applications "inherit" certain user interface features from Windows 95. Essentially, any Windows 3.1+ program element produced by using the common dialogs library or other built-in resources from the operating system end up with the distinct Windows 95 feel, as well as the Windows 95 look.

Because Windows 3.1+ applications inherit the look and feel of Windows 95's control elements, you'll probably be able to use many of your existing Windows 3.1+ applications a bit more efficiently—the drop-down menus shown in figure 5.3 illustrate this. In Windows 3.1+, a total of three mouse clicks are needed to select the Tile Windows command (refer to fig. 5.3): two mouse clicks to open the menus and a third click to make the actual command selection. If the exact same program is running under Windows 95, only two mouse clicks are required to select the Tile Windows command: one click to open the Window menu and one click to select the actual command.

Although this example represents a very small time savings (by one click), deeper menu layers still require only two mouse clicks under Windows 95—one to open the first menu level and one to select the actual command (Windows 95 automatically opens all intermediate submenus as the mouse pointer passes over the choices leading to them). The cumulative time savings over several hours of work may be fairly substantial—not to mention the reduced wear and tear on your hands and your mouse. Double-clicking is a fairly stressful activity for your hands (in relation to a possible risk of repetitive stress injuries or carpal tunnel syndrome). Much less importantly, double-clicking probably accelerates wear and tear on your mouse—one of this book's authors (we're not saying who) typically wears out four or five mice a year.

Other On-Screen Differences

Figure 5.4 shows an operating session using CompuServe's WinCIM program running under Windows 95. As you would expect from the preceding discussion, a Windows 3.1+ application's child windows (such as the Services window in figure 5.4) display the Windows 95-style title bar with Windows 95's Minimize, Maximize, and Close buttons—just like the parent window.

In Windows 3.1+, when you minimize a child window, the child window displays as an icon inside the application's main window. In Windows 3.1+, minimized child window icons look much like program icons in the Windows Program Manager. Windows 95, however, uses a different way to display minimized child windows. (Windows 95 never displays minimized program or window icons on the desktop—they always appear on Windows 95's Task Bar.)

Fig. 5.4

Child windows in Windows 3.1+ applications running under Windows 95 also use the Windows 95-style title bar. Also, minimized child windows don't appear as icons anymore; instead, they appear as shortened title bars with no windows.

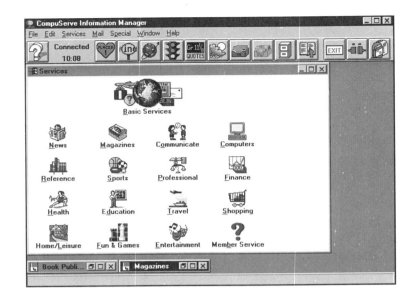

Notice the minimized child windows in figure 5.4 below the Services window—each minimized child window looks like a truncated title bar (without an accompanying window) but with slightly different control buttons. The action of each control button is summarized in order from right to left:

- Like every Windows 95 title bar, the control button on the extreme right of the title bar is the Close button; clicking this button closes the minimized child window.

- The button to the left of the Close button is Windows 95's usual Maximize button; clicking this button maximizes the child window.

- The third button in the three-button cluster is the Restore button; clicking this button restores the child window to whatever size it had before you minimized it.

- Finally, clicking the icon at the left edge of the minimized child windows' title bar displays the standard menu for any minimized child window; this menu displays the usual window control choices to Restore, Move, Size, Minimize, Maximize, and Close the window.

The difference in the way Windows 95 displays minimized child windows may, like reducing the number of mouse clicks necessary to make a menu selection, slightly increase the efficiency of your work. In Windows 3.1+, you can double-click a minimized child window's icon to restore the window to whatever size it was before you minimized it. If you want to close or maximize the minimized child window, you must either click the minimized child window's icon once to display the control menu for the child window, or restore the window and then use one of the control buttons on the window's title bar. In Windows 95, the most commonly used controls (restore, maximize, and close) are available as buttons on the minimized window's title bar. This situation also reduces the number of mouse clicks or other commands you need to issue, with consequent benefits.

Installing Windows 3.1+ Applications in Windows 95

Because there probably will be some lag time between the final release of Windows 95 and the common availability of truly logo-compliant Windows 95 applications, many early upgraders to Windows 95 will probably find that some or all of the new software titles they buy are actually written for Windows 3.1+. As a result, Windows 95 users will probably find themselves installing Windows 3.1+ applications. You may also end up installing Windows 3.1+ applications in Windows 95 if you installed Windows 95 as a dual-boot system. When you install Windows 95 in a dual-boot configuration, you must reinstall all your Windows 3.1+ applications.

▶ See Chapter 23, "Setting Up and Managing Windows 95"

> ### Tip
>
> Logo-compliant means that an application meets the strict requirements that Microsoft has set for new Windows 95 applications; only logo-compliant applications may bear the "Designed for Windows 95" logo licensed from Microsoft. Logo-compliant applications for Windows 95 must be fully 32-bit.

Whether you need to install Windows 3.1+ applications in Windows 95 because you installed Windows 95 in a dual-boot configuration or find it necessary to buy a Windows 3.1+ application because you can't wait for the logo-compliant Windows 95 version to arrive, you'll find that process for installing Windows 3.1+ applications is essentially the same in Windows 95.

▶ See Chapter 6 "Upgrading to 32-Bit Productivity Applications"

In Windows 3.1+, you typically use the File menu's Run command in Program Manager to install programs by executing a special setup or install program for the application you want to install. The process is essentially the same in Windows 95, except that you use the Run command from the Task Bar's Start menu. (Alternatively, you can use the Add/Remove Programs applet in the Control Panel; this applet will execute the Windows 3.1+ application's setup program as well.)

Because the setup or install programs for Windows 3.1+ applications are usually also Windows 3.1+ applications, the setup program's dialogs and title bars display the same differences in Windows 95 as those just described for other Windows 3.1+ applications running under Windows 95. Figure 5.5 shows the Microsoft Office Setup program in action.

Fig. 5.5
Windows 95 runs the Setup or Install programs for your Windows 3.1+ programs with the same differences apparent in any Windows 3.1+ program running under Windows 95. Notice the Windows 95-style title bars and check boxes.

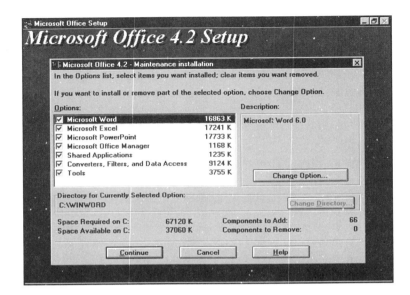

One difference between Windows 95 and Windows 3.1+ may cause some confusion when you install or maintain your Windows 3.1+ programs in Windows 95. Many of the Windows 3.1+ installation programs—particularly the installation programs for Microsoft Office, Microsoft Word for Windows, and Microsoft Excel—install components that may be shared by several applications (such as spelling dictionaries, graphing tools, and so on). Any setup or install program that installs or updates shared components must be the only application running on your system. This is because the setup program can't update any shared program component while it's being used by an application that's running concurrently with the setup program. Setup and install programs that do update shared program components typically check the operating environment to find out whether other processes are active and asks you to shut them down if they are.

So far, this process of switching to and exiting concurrently running applications poses no problems in Windows 3.1+ or Windows 95. A point of confusion arises when the Windows 3.1+ setup or install program displays its warning message asking you to terminate any other running processes. Many

Windows 3.1+ setup and install programs ask you to use the Task Manager to switch to and then exit the other running programs. The Task Manager doesn't exist in Windows 95. Instead, you must use the Windows 95 Task Bar to switch to any other programs that might be running. This issue doesn't represent any change or loss of functionality; it just means that you need to use slightly different tools and terminology to get some Windows 3.1+ applications installed.

Windows 95's Compatibility with Windows 3.1+ Applications

Windows 95 is designed to provide compatibility with Windows 3.1+ programs. In fact (as described in the next section of this chapter), Windows 95 includes a complete subsystem specifically designed to run Windows 3.1+ programs.

> **Note**
>
> Compatibility for executing Windows 3.1+ programs isn't necessarily the same as compatible interface operation. Refer to Chapter 3, "Exploring the Windows 95 Interface," for information on how Windows 95's interface provides Windows 3.1+ user controls.

Windows 95 does display a high degree of compatibility with existing Windows 3.1+ programs. In general, you can expect to run or install any of your commercial Windows 3.1+ applications successfully under Windows 95. Even fairly esoteric products, such as Smalltalk/V for Windows, will run successfully under Windows 95. Figure 5.6 shows a graphics and animation demonstration from Smalltalk/V running on the Windows 95 desktop.

Windows 3.1+ shareware and Windows 3.0 programs may pose some problems, however. Although most shareware and vertical market applications are written by skilled, professional programmers, many are also written by persons whose primary profession is something other than software design and programming. Shareware and public domain applications are frequently written by individuals whose primary occupation relates to the specialty niche for which the software is intended and to whom programming and software design is a secondary profession.

Fig. 5.6.
Window 95's
compatibility for
Windows 3.1+
application
includes even
complex and
demanding
programming
environments
such as Small-
talk/V.

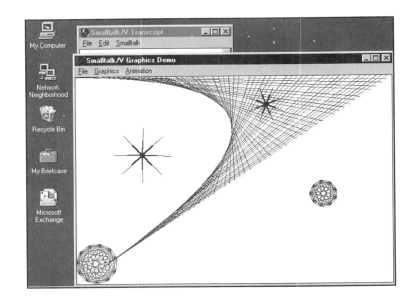

Note

Some Windows programs—especially programs such as disk optimizing or repair utilities—make very specific version checks before they execute, and may refuse to run under Windows 95. These programs don't refuse to run because they are incompatible with Windows 95, but because they have been specifically designed, for safety, to refuse to run under any version of Windows other than the one for which they were specifically designed. In such cases, you'll usually see an error message stating that you should upgrade your program. As an example, Norton Utilities 8 is programmed to run *only* under Windows 3.1, and will refuse to run under any other version—the error message is generated by Norton Utilities, not Windows 95.

Such programs may not always follow the best programming and design principles for Windows applications; the programmers may inadvertently include code that's overly specific to Windows 3.1+ or accidentally create programs that aren't good Windows citizens—that is, programs that monopolize memory or hardware resources or interfere with Windows 3.1+'s message queue operations.

> **Note**
>
> A few of the Windows 3.1+ shareware programs tested in Windows 95 by the au-
> thors either crashed outright, or Windows 95 simply refused to run them—in the
> latter case, Windows 95 displayed a message stating that the program was prepared
> for an earlier version of Windows and suggesting that the user obtain an updated
> version of the program.

▶ See Chapter 12,
"Connecting to
the Outside
World"

Apart from minor difficulties with shareware applications, some programs
written for Windows 3.0 may not run successfully in Windows 95. For example, communications applications written for Windows 3.0 won't execute
in Windows 95. When you try to start one of these applications, Windows 95
displays an error dialog complaining that the application you're trying to run
was written for an earlier version of Windows and that you should obtain an
upgrade.

This behavior isn't too surprising when you think about it. Communications
programs by their nature must access one or more of your computer's COM
ports (used for serial communications devices, such as modems). Windows
95's internal methods for handling COM ports (and other input/output devices) have changed substantially since Windows 3.0—and Windows 3.1+, for
that matter. As a result, there's a high probability that a Windows 3.0 communications program may try to use a COM port in a way that isn't compatible with Windows 95. Windows 95's refusal to run Windows 3.0 applications
that have a high probability of causing problems isn't only to be expected,
it's highly appropriate.

▶ See Chapter 22
"Understanding
Windows 95's
Operating
System
Architecture"

For the same reasons, Windows 95 may also refuse to run other Windows 3.0
applications that use network ports, printer ports, COM ports, or similar system resources.

Windows 95's Accommodations for Windows 3.1+ Applications

Windows 95's internal architecture includes an entire 16-bit subsystem devoted exclusively to running Windows 3.1+ applications. Figure 5.7 shows a
block diagram illustrating the relationship of the 16-bit subsystem to the
overall Windows 95 internal environment.

Essentially, the 16-bit subsystem runs within Windows 95 as though it were
another 32-bit application, allocating its own memory and receiving messages from the system's main message queue. All your Windows 3.1+ applications run as a separate thread within the 16-bit subsystem.

Fig. 5.7
Windows 95 provides a complete 16-bit subsystem for running Windows 3.1+ 16-bit applications.

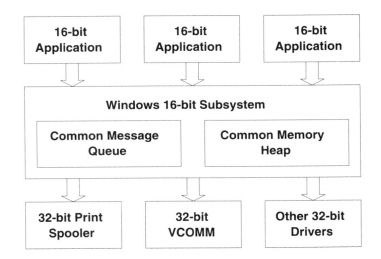

The 16-bit subsystem is preemptively multitasked with any 32-bit applications that are running. When an event message (such as a mouse click or characters you type at the keyboard) occurs, it goes into the 32-bit message queue. If the recipient of the event message is a 16-bit Windows 3.1+ application, Windows 95 transfers the message to a separate message queue in the 16-bit subsystem. The 16-bit subsystem's message queue is then cooperatively multitasked within the 16-bit subsystem, just like the message queue in Windows 3.1+. (Chapter 22, "Understanding Windows 95's Operating System Architecture," explains the difference between preemptive and cooperative multitasking.)

Because 32-bit applications use your computer's memory differently than Windows 3.1+ 16-bit applications, the 16-bit subsystem allocates and manages a shared memory heap for all the 16-bit Windows 3.1+ applications that are running—again, just like the shared memory heap used in Windows 3.1+.

> **Note**
>
> Windows 95 keeps track of each application that's now running, along with information that lets Windows 95 determine whether the application is a Windows 3.1+ program or a 32-bit Windows 95 program. Windows 95 obtains this information from the application's program files at the time Windows 95 loads the application. This technique is referred to as thread tracking.

Although this arrangement makes it possible for Windows 95 to run your Windows 3.1+ applications, it doesn't mean that your Windows 3.1+ applications can take advantage of Windows 95's multithread and preemptive multitasking architecture. Windows 3.1+ applications simply don't contain the code necessary to use threads and preemptive multitasking— multithreaded programs must be written from the ground up to use Windows 95's multithread features.

Windows 95's Improvements for Windows 3.1+ Applications

In addition to the special 16-bit subsystem for running Windows 3.1+ applications, Windows 95 has new memory management features to explicitly improve the robustness of Windows 3.1+ applications. (A program that doesn't crash, even when various user or system errors occur, is said to be a robust program.) Windows 95 also has several inherent features that tend to enhance the performance of your Windows 3.1+ applications.

Improved Memory Management

In Windows 3.1+, each application program must free up any memory resources that it reserved whenever that application exits. Windows 3.1+ itself won't free up memory allocated by an application. This simple fact is the source of the notorious Windows 3.1+ "memory leaks" that plague many Windows users. (This "memory leak" problem manifests itself when a user receives out-of-memory error messages at times when plenty of memory should be available—like when running a single program on a machine with 16M of RAM.)

Unlike Windows 3.1+, Windows 95 does free up any memory allocated by an application whenever that application exits. If an application's programmer forgot to free up all the memory his or her program reserves, Windows 95 forces that memory to become available again. Unfortunately, this doesn't work with Windows 3.1+ programs.

Because programmers know that Windows 3.1+ doesn't force reserved memory to be freed up, some programmers exploit this fact to reserve memory blocks in Windows 3.1+ for later use by shared applications or for more or less continual use by DLL routines. Although this isn't necessarily the best programming practice, it does happen.

If Windows 95 forced the memory reserved by a Windows 3.1+ application to be freed up when the application exits, Windows 95 would "break" the few Windows 3.1+ applications that exploit Windows 3.1+'s failure to force reserved memory to be freed up. Rather than force individual Windows 3.1+ memory allocations to be freed up, Windows 95 waits until no Windows 3.1+ applications are running. As soon as the last Windows 3.1+ application exits,

Windows 95 forces all memory allocated by the 16-bit Windows 3.1+ subsystem to be freed. In this way, Windows 95 minimizes or eliminates possible memory leak problems, without risking interference with any Windows 3.1+ applications.

32-Bit API Effects on Windows 3.1+ Applications

Essentially, any time a Windows 3.1+ application uses an API call, it receives the benefits of a 32-bit operating system. (API stands for application program interface, the name given to the group of common routines built into Windows that allow applications to display menus, windows, and dialog controls or to read or write information to the disk.)

Because the bulk of Windows 95's operating system uses 32-bit technology, any Windows 3.1+ program receives the benefit of Windows 95's 32-bit operating system every time that application uses the common menu, dialog, disk, or other of Windows 95's built-in routines—with one exception. Most of the routines in the GDI (graphics device interface, the subgroup of API functions related to drawing windows on-screen) are actually 16-bit routines rather than 32-bit routines. This was done specifically to maintain compatibility between Windows 95 and Windows 3.1+ applications and helps ensure that your Windows 3.1+ applications run successfully.

In particular, you may notice a significant improvement in your Windows 3.1+ application's printing performance. You'll probably notice a faster return to your application when printing. Not only does the entire printing system use a 32-bit technology, but the print spooler has been redesigned to improve the speed at which printer data is spooled onto the disk.

Tip

The deferred printing feature included to support laptop computers is also useful on your desktop computer. Use deferred printing if you lose your connection to the network printer or if your local printer is disabled for repair. When you use deferred printing, Windows 95 sends the printer spool file to disk and then prints it whenever the printer next becomes available.

Chapter 6

Upgrading to 32-Bit Productivity Applications

If you use Windows 3.1+, you or your employer (or both) are likely to have a substantial investment in 16-bit Windows productivity applications. If you're new to Windows, you'll probably end up investing several hundred dollars or more in shrink-wrapped software for Windows 95. Productivity applications are the mainstream software products: word processors, spreadsheet programs, database management systems, presentation graphics, and project management software. These five software categories, the first four of which now are bundled in "software suites," probably provide most of the operating income of two of the three major players in the Windows software business: Micro-soft, Lotus, and the Novell/WordPerfect conglomerate. (Novell derives most of its income from network operating systems.) "Suite wars" and "competitive upgrade" battles between these software behemoths have reduced the effective street price of suite member applications to about $125 each. This price is a far cry from the $250 average just a couple of years ago.

When this book was written, only a few 32-bit Windows productivity applications had reached retailers' shelves. One of the principal reasons for the failure of Windows NT 3.1 to live up to Microsoft's original sales projections was the lack of popular 32-bit productivity applications, such as Microsoft Word and Excel or Lotus Ami Pro and 1-2-3 for Windows NT 3.1. Why would the average user buy Windows NT 3.1 and upgrade to 16M of RAM just to run existing Windows 3.1 apps with a 10 percent speed penalty? Windows NT looks and feels much like Windows for Workgroups 3.11. IBM's OS/2, originally a joint IBM-Microsoft product, faces the same Catch-22 situation, because there are few 32-bit productivity applications designed for OS/2.

Like Windows NT, most users of OS/2 predominately run 16-bit Windows 3.1+ applications. So far IBM's OS/2 has outsold Windows NT by a substantial margin, but Windows NT 3.5 was coming on strong in corporate PC networks in early 1995.

> **Note**
>
> Windows NT 3.5 overcomes the performance problems of 16-bit Windows applications running under Windows NT 3.1, with about a 50 percent speed improvement. Each 16-bit Windows application runs in its own address space, making Windows 3.5 a much more robust operating system. The second release of Windows NT adds many new features, including full support TCP/IP networking and PPP (UNIX's Point-to-Point dialup protocol most commonly used for Internet access; SLIP, the Serial Line Interface Protocol, also is included). Windows NT 3.5, which is available both in workstation and server versions, is now truly a "world-class" operating system for both applications and networking. Memory requirements for the workstation version have been reduced to 12M, and the server version brings a major performance boost to Microsoft SQL Server for Windows NT 4.21a. (SQL Server for Windows NT is Microsoft's candidate for ultimate dominance of the enterprise-wide client-server computing environment of the late 1990s.)

Microsoft seldom repeats a marketing faux pas; Microsoft is very adept at learning from past embarrassment. In late 1995, Microsoft released 32-bit versions of Excel 5.0 and Word 6.0. (You can upgrade your 16-bit versions of Excel 5.0 and Word 6.0 to the 32-bit version at a very nominal cost; Microsoft calls this process a *sidegrade*.) Both of these 32-bit applications support long file names and run in their own protected address spaces, but neither is multi-threaded. According to rumors in the trade press, it's likely that Microsoft will introduce Excel 95 and Word 95, with enhanced performance and Window 95 compatibility, when Windows 95 is released, or shortly thereafter. It's questionable, however, whether Lotus and Novell/Word-Perfect's mainstream productivity applications will make Windows 95's 32-bit starting gate.

> **Note**
>
> If you're a heavy-duty user of 16-bit Excel 5.0 and Word 6.0, you've probably received the dreaded Out of memory message at some critical juncture in your work. Windows 95 reduces the chances of your getting this message with 16-bit applications, because it uses shared memory more efficiently, but 32-bit software virtually guarantees the demise of this very frustrating message.

Waking Up to a 32-Bit Upgrade World

Columnists writing for the computer publications lament that the major software publishers have abandoned potential new users of their products in favor of selling product upgrades to existing users. Microsoft has such a large share of the software suite market—70 or 80 percent by some estimates—that the firm's marketers are unlikely to significantly increase Microsoft's market share no matter how hard they sell. One of the major costs of publishing software is the cost of technical support; employees can't spend much time helping a person use a product that has a gross margin of $50 or less. Selling upgrades to experienced users minimizes the cost of product support and maximizes the bottom line. On the average, Microsoft issues a major upgrade of its mainstream applications and programming languages about every 18 months.

If you're a registered user of any Microsoft product, your mail box will be flooded with "special value" 32-bit upgrade offers when Microsoft releases Windows 95. You can bet that the package which holds your Windows 95 disks or CD-ROM will be stuffed with coupons offering 32-bit Word 6.0 and Excel 5.0 versions at a bargain price "for Windows 95 users only." Whether you take the bait then or not, you ultimately will be hooked. Microsoft has stated publicly that there will be no further major upgrades to the 16-bit versions of its productivity apps. If you're looking forward to improvements in Microsoft Word, Excel, and probably Access and Project too, plan on emigrating to 32-bitland. If you're considering taking up C++ programming, bear in mind that Microsoft Visual C++ 2.0 is a 32-bit product that runs only under Windows NT or Windows 95.

What 32-Bitness Brings to the Table

The first wave of 32-bit upgrades will bring billions of dollars to Microsoft's coffers, but what will it do for you? The following sections describe the benefits of fully 32-bit Windows (Win32) applications. It's likely that there will be some 16-bit code hanging around in the first set of every publisher's productivity application upgrades, just as Windows 95 includes some 16-bit code in the operating system. In time, however, all 16-bit Windows applications will migrate to the full Win32 standard.

Improved

It remains to be seen how the performance of the final Win32 versions of Excel 5.0 and Word 6.0 compares with their 16-bit (Win16) predecessors. Windows 95's 32-bit disk and file operations make all applications launch faster, as well as speed the opening and saving of files. Windows for Workgroups 3.11 offers 32-bit disk and file access (except for SCSI drives), so this isn't a big plus for the 32-bitters. Apparent improvement performance due to 32-bit disk and file operations ranges from about 10 percent to more than 200 percent, depending on a variety of circumstances. Win16 and Win32 apps share equal improvement here.

Improvements in performance depend on how you use the Win32 applications. You'll see no startling benefit to simple operations on small documents, such as a one-page Excel spreadsheet or a Word 6.0 letter. The following list describes the uses of Win32 productivity applications that show the greatest improvement in performance:

- Integrated applications that use object linking and embedding (OLE) 2+ to create compound documents benefit from Windows 95's 32-bit implementation of the OLE 2+ dynamic libraries (DLLs). Figure 6.1 shows a Word 6.0 compound document with an embedded Excel 5.0 chart. OLE 2.01, the current version when this book was written, was designed from the beginning as a 32-bit application. Starting with a 32-bit design, even if you have to implement the design initially in a 16-bit version, usually results in significantly better performance than the retrograde approach. All the applications that participate in creating the compound document must be 32-bit to take full advantage of 32-bit OLE 2+. 32-bit OLE 2+ clients that use Visual Basic for Applications to manipulate 32-bit OLE 2+ server objects benefit from the speed increase, too.

Fig. 6.1

A Microsoft Word 6.0 compound document containing an embedded Excel 5.0 chart.

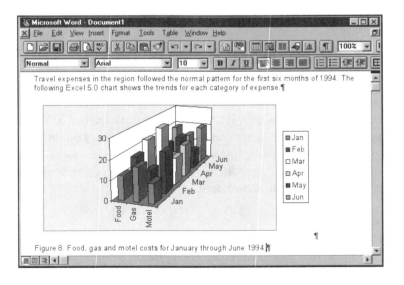

- Applications that use Microsoft's Open Database Connectivity 2.0 application programming interface (ODBC 2.0 API) get a speed increase from the new 32-bit version. Like OLE 2+, ODBC 2.0 was designed as a 32-bit product. Applications that access client-server databases run noticeably faster, especially when returning a large amount of data. (Tests were made only against Microsoft SQL Server for Windows NT 4.21a and Sybase System 10 because Microsoft supplied the only 32-bit driver for SQL Server when this book was written. The Microsoft driver also works with Sybase System 10, but does not support Sybase System 10's new features.) Figure 6.2 shows the ODBC 2.0 Administrator application displaying the setup of an SQL Server data source. Microsoft has announced that the next version of Visual Basic will create 16- and 32-bit applications, so it's a good bet that a 32-bit version of the Jet Database engine will accompany the retail release of an updated edition of Visual Basic.

▶ See Chapter 16, "Using Windows 95 Clients with Existing Networks"

Introducing Windows 95

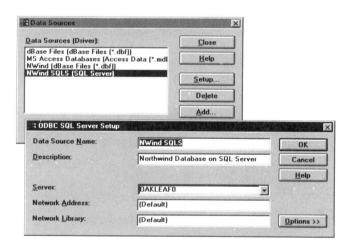

Fig. 6.2
The ODBC 2.0 Administrator application displaying the setup for an SQL Server data source.

Preemptive Multitasking

Multitasking is the Windows feature that lets you run more than one application at a time. Microsoft Windows has supported multitasking from its earliest version, Windows 1.1, released in November 1985. Win16 applications use a process called cooperative multitasking; the application running in the foreground (on top of other application windows) periodically yields its preferential status to other applications running in the background. Yielding control allows the other applications to continue with whatever activities were started before the foreground process commenced. In many cases, applications can't or won't yield frequently; in this case, an hourglass appears, other applications are "locked out," and you can't make another application active by pressing Alt+Tab or Ctrl+Esc. For example, the "locked out" condition occurs while Win16 database applications read from or write to disk drives or while Win16 apps that use ODBC 1.0 are obtaining information from a client-server database.

Properly written Win32 applications exploit the preemptive multitasking features of Windows 95. Preemptive multitasking is orchestrated by the Windows 95 operating system; if one Win32 application needs an operating system or hardware resource in use by another application, the requesting application can choose to wait for the resource to become free or proceed with other activities until the resource becomes available. Windows 95 manages the allocation of resources, providing an "equal-opportunity environment" for all running applications. For example, you can play digital video from a CD-ROM, print a large Word 6.0 document file and save it to your fixed disk, plus download files from CompuServe or the Internet—all at the same time. Although Windows 3.1+ FAX and communication applications commonly run in background mode, pre-emptive multitasking makes the communication operation run much more smoothly.

Unfortunately, preemptive multitasking isn't available to Win16 applications in Windows 95; the design goal of running Windows 95 within 4M of RAM precludes pre-emptive multitasking for Win16 applications. Win16 applications share a common block of RAM called an address space; pre-emptive multitasking requires that each application have its own protected address space. Thus, you'll also hear Win32 applications referred to as protected-mode programs. Windows NT 3.5 optionally runs Win16 applications in protected mode; however, Windows NT 3.5 requires a minimum of 12M of RAM but runs best with 16M or more.

Multithreaded

Up to this point, the discussion of Win32 has dealt primarily with applications: shrink-wrapped software that runs under Windows or special-purpose programs you create or are created for you with Visual Basic, Visual C++, or other programming languages compatible with Windows. From Windows 95's viewpoint as an operating system, applications are processes. You'll be hearing a lot more about processes, threads, multitasking, and multithreading when Windows 95 hits the retail shelves. Thus, you should be at least familiar with terms that are essential to full 32-bitness. For starters, a Win32 process has the following components:

- An executable program, which provides the instructions (code) and built-in data needed to launch the application. Executable Windows applications carry an EXE file extension. Many 32-bit executable files include 32 in their file names.

- System resources that the operating system—in this case, Windows 95—can allocate to the executing process. System resources include connections to the keyboard, video display, disk drives, communication and printer ports, and other hardware. System resources also include software components, such as semaphores, which control the allocation of resources to processes.

- A protected address space that's allocated to the process in virtual memory and which no other process can use. Virtual memory is a representation of physical memory, including both RAM and space in Windows 95's swap file if insufficient RAM is available to the process. The protected address space appears to the process as a contiguous collection of addresses, regardless of how the physical memory is scattered among locations in RAM and on disk.

- A minimum of one thread of execution, commonly called a thread. A thread is simply a clearly identifiable task within a process. An example of a task is when a database front-end application requests a set of records for a customer from a back-end database server. The process tells the thread what records are wanted, and the thread presents the data from the records to the process. While the preceding thread is executing, another thread can be sending payroll records to the database. Windows 95 manages execution of the threads for all the processes running on your computer.

Threaded applications are required to take maximum advantage of Windows 95's multitasking environment. A single-processor operating system can run only one thread of execution at a time; Windows NT supports multiprocessing, but Windows 95 doesn't. (The term *multiprocessing* means a process that creates two or more threads that can execute in parallel; multithreading means a process that can create more than one thread of execution.) A multithreading, multitasking operating system such as Windows 95, however, appears to be executing more than one process at a time; Windows 95 accomplishes this by a sleight-of-hand method that depends on a single high-speed Intel-compatible processor to execute the following subtasks:

1. Windows 95 detects a new thread spawned (created) by a process.

2. Windows 95 runs the thread, unless execution of the thread is interrupted by an external event, such as waiting for the availability of a system resource. Availability of system resources is determined by a set of semaphores that, when raised, indicate the resource isn't available. Lowering the semaphore allows another thread access to the resource.

3. If execution of the thread is interrupted, Windows 95 saves the context of the thread. The context of a thread consists of an unique identifier of the thread and information about the state of the thread when interrupted.

4. Windows 95 then loads the next thread's context if another thread is pending, and executes the thread from the point at which that thread was interrupted if its execution was halted.

Figure 6.3 is a diagram showing the steps of the preceding list. Steps 3 and 4 provide the primary benefit of preemptive multitasking, maximizing the execution of simultaneous processes in which one or more threads are interrupted. Execution of steps 3 and 4 is called context switching; a lot of context switching goes on when you use OLE Automation to program other application's objects. To take real advantage of Windows 95's multitasking, Win32 applications must be designed from the outset for threaded operation.

> **Note**
>
> Multithreaded applications can take advantage of Windows NT 3.5's multiprocessing capability, running threads on the processor that has the lowest workload. (Windows 95 doesn't support multiprocessing.) Windows NT 3.5 offers symmetric multiprocessing (SMP), which means that all the processors on the motherboard are treated as equals. Asymmetric multiprocessing, used by IBM's OS/2 2.1, devotes one microprocessor to the operating system and runs application processes on the other microprocessor(s). SMP is considerably more efficient than the asymmetric method.

Availability of Fully Win32-Compliant Applications

It's unlikely that you'll find first 32-bit upgrades to Win16 productivity applications taking full advantage of Windows 95's multithreading capabilities. Converting an existing Win16 application to a Win32 application that provides threads to a multitasking environment is a major undertaking.

Applications such as Excel 5.0 and Word 6.0, often called mega apps, contain hundreds of thousands of lines of convoluted legacy programming code that defies unsnarling to provide fully threaded operation.

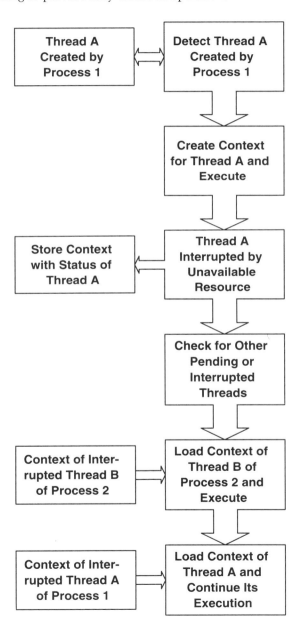

I

Introducing Windows 95

Fig. 6.3
A diagram of threaded multitasking with one thread interrupted by an unavailable resource.

> **Note**
>
> You can run Win32 applications under 16-bit Windows 3.1+ if the applications are designed to accommodate the Win32s standards. Win32s is part of the Win32 software developer's kit (SDK) that includes a number of redistributable (freely licensed) files that software publishers can include with their Win32 products to allow them to run under Windows 3.1+. Software publishers now face the problem of needing to distribute two versions of each 32-bit application: one for Windows 3.1+ running Win32s, and one for Windows 95 and Windows NT 3.5 that supports the full Win32 API.

According to an article subtitled, "Requirements for the New Windows Logo," by Tammy Steele in the July 1994 issue of *Microsoft Developer Network News*, the basic requirements to apply the "Designed for Microsoft Windows 95" logo to applications, language compilers, development tools, and utilities will be as follows:

1. The software must be a Win32 executable file that complies with the Portable Executable (PE) format used by Windows 95 and Windows NT.

2. The software must have the Windows 95 look and feel, as defined in Microsoft's UI Design Guide 4.0.

3. The software must run successfully under Windows 95 and Windows NT 3.5. Software that uses Windows 95-specific features must "degrade gracefully" under Windows NT 3.5, and *vice-versa*.

4. The application must support long file names. Windows NT 3.1 supported long file names only if you used the Windows NT file system (NTFS). Windows NT 3.5, like Windows 95, also supports long file names under the conventional DOS file allocation table (FAT) file system.

There are a variety of other requirements, including support for OLE 2+ and some minor exemptions, for specific classes of Windows-compatible software products. However, there's no requirement or even a suggestion that logo-bearing Win32 applications support threaded processes. (Doing so, in all likelihood, would prevent Microsoft from applying the logo to its current crop of of sidegraded applications.) You may have to read the fine print or call the publisher to determine whether a product supports threads; you aren't likely to find "Does not support multithreading" in the feature list on the shrink-wrapped box.

It's clear, however, that Microsoft is leveraging the potentially huge Windows 95 market to increase the number of applications available for Windows NT, thus giving Windows NT 3.5 Workstation a major desirability boost. A brief report in the Aug. 8, 1994, issue of *PC Week* magazine reported that software publishers must comply with the preceding standards to apply the newly designed "Designed for Microsoft Windows 95" logo to their products after April 30, 1995. *PC Week* also reported that Microsoft would cease licensing the current Windows-compatible logo design on Sept. 30, 1994.

Many Windows software publishers, which Microsoft calls independent software vendors (ISVs), have groused about the proposed logo licensing schedule. The complaints arose because C and C++ compilers needed to create full-scale Win32 products, such as Microsoft Visual C++ 2.0, were still in the beta stage, together with the two qualifying operating systems, when Microsoft made the licensing announcement. (Visual C++ 2.0 had been released for a couple of months when this book was written.) It remains to be seen whether Microsoft sticks to its licensing guns or relents to ISVs' requests for more time to sell current products with the former Windows 3.1+ logo.

Note

One of the side effects of the ISVs' rush to comply with Microsoft's licensing requirements will likely be a further delay in the availability of the 32-bit software required to take advantage of Apple Computer's Power Mac and System 7.5 and IBM's forthcoming PowerPC product line. When this book was written, Apple Computer had sold only about 300,000 Power Macs and IBM's PowerPC products were primarily in the hands of potential software developers. Mercury Research, in a sales forecast of Intel-compatible and PowerPC-based computers quoted in the Aug. 15, 1994, issue of *Business Week* magazine, projected that only about 10 to 15 million PowerPC-based systems would be shipped in 1999 vs. 100 million Intel-compatible PCs. (Mercury's projection for the Intel products is identical to that of Andy Grove, Intel's president, quoted in the first chapter of this book.) What sensible ISV is going to give PowerPCs the priority, when there are likely to be 10 million Windows 95 users by the end of 1995? (According to the Mercury projection, there won't be 10 million PowerPCs in use until about mid-1998.)

Part II

Exploring Windows 95's Multimedia Features

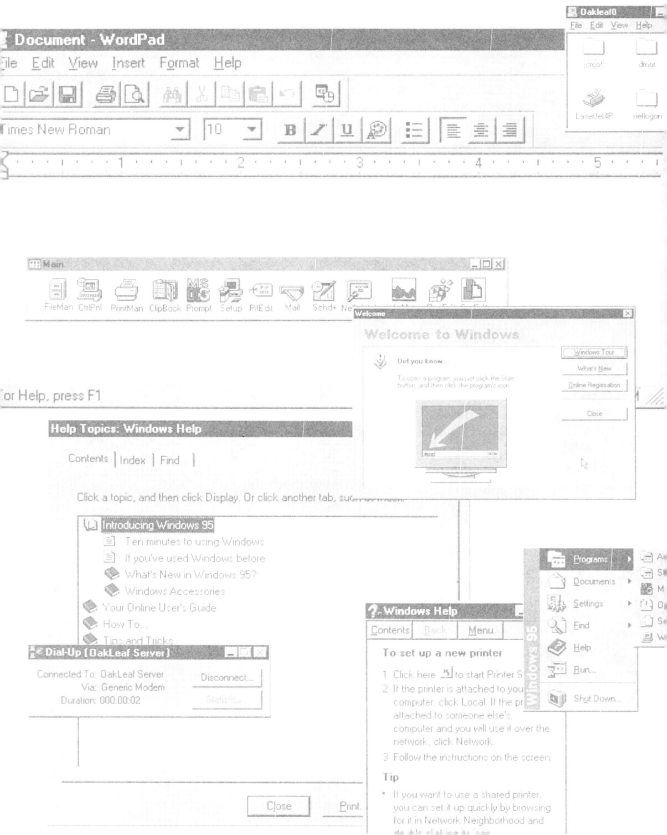

Document - WordPad

File   Edit   View   Insert   Format   Help

Times New Roman   10   **B** *I* U

Oakleaf0

File   Edit   View   Help

[croot]   droot

LaserJet4P   netlogon

Main

FileMan   CtrlPnl   PrintMan   ClipBook   Prompt   Setup   PifEdit   Mail   Schd+   Network

or Help, press F1

Welcome

Welcome to Windows

Did you know...

To open a program, you just click the Start button, and then click the program's icon.

Windows Tour

What's New

Online Registration

Close

Help Topics: Windows Help

Contents | Index | Find |

Click a topic, and then click Display. Or click another tab, such as Index.

Introducing Windows 95
  Ten minutes to using Windows
  If you've used Windows before
  What's New in Windows 95?
  Windows Accessories
  Your Online User's Guide
  How To...
  Tips and Tricks

Dial-Up (OakLeaf Server)

Connected To: OakLeaf Server
Via: Generic Modem
Duration: 000:00:02

Disconnect...

Statistics

Windows Help

Contents | Back | Menu

To set up a new printer

1 Click here to start Printer S

2 If the printer is attached to you computer. click Local. If the pr attached to someone else's computer and you will use it over the network, click Network.

3 Follow the instructions on the screen.

Tip

* If you want to use a shared printer, you can set it up quickly by browsing for it in Network Neighborhood and double clicking its icon.

Programs
Documents
Settings
Find
Help
Run...
Shut Down...

Close   Print

Chapter 7

Interacting with Windows 95 Multimedia

It happens every year: Computer pundits predict that next January 1 will signal "the year of multimedia," the year that multimedia really takes off. The Windows 95 convergence described in Chapter 1—lower-cost and higher-performance PC hardware combined with a new, easy-to-use 32-bit operating system optimized for multimedia—is likely to finally cause these perennial predictions to come true. The home PC market drives multimedia sales, and the advent of the "information appliance" means big bucks for multimedia publishers. The natural reluctance of information systems managers to change PC operating systems and environments may slow the adoption of Windows 95 in the corporate arena, but it'll be full speed ahead for Windows 95 in the consumer marketplace because of Windows 95's new, easy-to-use multimedia features.

There's convergence in the capital markets, too. Wall Street and the venture capitalists have caught multimedia fever. Several 1994 IPOs (Initial Public Offerings) of stock for entertainment-related multimedia firms were wildly oversubscribed and more than doubled their offering price the first day of issue. Bill Gates says Microsoft is investing more than $100 million per year in its consumer-oriented Microsoft Home product line and into the interactive multimedia information superhighways described in this chapter. Investor perception of Windows 95's potential impact on the home PC market has greatly increased the infusion of venture capital into multimedia startups.

Multimedia is a difficult subject to define precisely. Bill Gates opened his address at the Lehman Brothers Multimedia Technology Conference, held at the end of April 1994, with this observation: "The great thing about the term 'multimedia' is that it's so broad you can talk about almost anything you're interested in and it fits into this topic." Both Gates and his partner during the early years of Microsoft, Paul Allen, have personal investments in multimedia firms: Continuum Productions Corporation and Starwave Corporation, respectively. *Business Week* reported in a July 25, 1994, article titled, "Seattle: A Multimedia Kind of Town," that Allen also owns a piece of Lone Wolf Productions, a company developing networked audio systems for multimedia. For the purposes of this book, interactive multimedia is a combination of animated graphics and synchronized sound reproduced by a PC under the control of the computer's user.

This chapter starts out with a short summary of what's new with Windows 95 in the multimedia department and then goes on to discuss subjects that relate to the aggregate of Windows 95's multimedia features: Microsoft's Consumer Products division and its Microsoft Home product line, interactive multimedia on the Internet and The Microsoft Network, and the future of multimedia distribution by cable and satellite.

What's New in Windows 95 for Multimedia Buffs and Developers

Microsoft is emphasizing the Windows 95 multimedia feature set because of the importance to the growth of the consumer PC market of better multimedia capabilities at the operating system level. The four chapters that follow provide detailed descriptions of the new multimedia-related features incorporated in Windows 95, but here's an up-front summary:

- *Plug and Play support for multimedia devices,* such as audio adapter cards, SCSI and IDE CD-ROM drives, and video overlay devices that play analog video. Based on the historical problems associated with adding sound cards to PCs under DOS and Windows 3.1+, Plug and Play will have more significance to multimedia and computer game addicts than to any other category of PC user. Plug and Play is covered in Chapter 2, so the following chapters include only peripheral comments on Plug and Play.

- *Better performance of CD-ROMs* that use Windows 95's new 32-bit CD file system (CDFS), which is modeled on Windows 95's 32-bit fixed-disk file system.

- *AutoPlay of CD-ROMs* automatically launches the CD-ROM's viewer application when you close the door on the CD-ROM drive. Windows 95 looks for a file called AUTORUN.INF in the CD-ROM's root directory.

If the file is present, Windows 95 follows the AUTORUN.INF script to run a game or other CD-ROM-based application. Microsoft calls this feature "Spin and Grin."

■ *More effective compression of digital audio files* comes about with two new software audio codecs (coders-decoders) for Windows 95 that use ADPCM techniques. Microsoft has licensed the TrueSpeech compression process for voice recording and playback from DSP Group, Inc. DSP stands for digital signal processing, a subject you'll be hearing a lot about in 1995. A special codec for music that provides about 2:1 to 4:1 compression without noticeable loss of fidelity also is included with Windows 95.

■ *Improved MIDI performance* is brought about by Windows 95's new Polymessage MIDI feature that allows fast transmission of complex MIDI messages with very little processor overhead. This is especially important for users who make use of message-intensive MIDI exotica, such as polyphonic aftertouch.

■ *Music while you work.* Playing grunge rock audio CD tracks in the background while filling in your Excel worksheet is a reality with Windows 95's new audio CD player that takes full advantage of 32-bit multitasking. If you have one of Pioneer's CD-ROM changers, you can hide the audio CD at the bottom of the stack, so the boss won't find it.

■ *Built-in support for digital video,* including a variety of software video compression codecs that support the most important video file formats. Previously, you had to install Microsoft's Video for Windows 1.1, a stand-alone application, to watch and listen to digital video. Windows 95's upgraded Media Control Interface (MCI) now provides remote control for VCRs and other video devices that comply with Sony's VISCA standard. (You'll need a video overlay card, however, to watch analog video from VCRs and laser disc players on your PC.) Hardware MPEG decompression, which requires a special adapter card, lets you play the new 75-minute, full-screen digital CD Video disks.

■ *A new display control interface (DCI),* developed jointly by Microsoft and Intel, takes full advantage of the capabilities of today's VLB and PCI sophisticated display adapter cards. The new DCI is aimed at further improving digital video performance and offers built-in chroma keying and other special effects. Plus, DCI accepts professional YUV-encoded (chrominance-hue-luminance) video signals, in addition to conventional RGB (red-green-blue) color data. (Chapter 10, "Watching *Real* Digital Video," explains these terms.)

II

Exploring Multimedia

■ *Faster play of computer games with the WinG API.* The PC game business has been dominated by DOS titles because Windows 3.1+'s graphic device interface (GDI) slows redrawing of the display. The new WinG (Windows Game) application programming interface lets game publishers create 32-bit titles for Windows 95 that rival the performance of DOS-based products.

Windows 95's new control center for multimedia devices is the Properties for Multimedia sheet that you open by double-clicking the Multimedia icon in the Control Panel. The Advanced page lists the multimedia device drivers that come with Windows 95, plus other Microsoft or third-party drivers that you install from floppy disk (see fig. 7.1). Windows 95's complement of Media Control Interface (MCI) drivers includes:

■ *CD Audio Device* for listening to standard audio CDs

■ *MIDI Sequencer Device* for playing and recording MIDI music files

■ *Motion Video Device* for digital video recording and playback using Intel Indeo, SuperMac Cinepac, Microsoft, and third-party video codecs

■ *PIONEER LaserDisk Device* for controlling playback of analog video laser discs through a video overlay card

Fig. 7.1
The Advanced page of Windows 95's Properties for Multimedia sheet, the control center for media components.

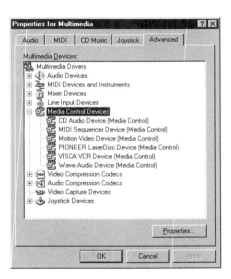

■ *VISCA VCR Device* for controlling VCRs and other video devices that use the Sony VISCA protocol

- *Wave Audio Device* for playing and recording digitized sound in .WAV files, with or without compression by Microsoft, TrueSpeech, or third-party codecs

Multimedia hardware suppliers usually provide their own 32-bit drivers for their implementation of a specific device. Use of each of Windows 95's built-in device drivers is described in the following four chapters.

The Multimedia PC Spec the Second Time Around

One of the major impediments to growth in pre-1994 Windows multimedia markets was the first version of the Multimedia PC specification (MPC 1.0) conceived by Microsoft and brought into the world by the Multimedia PC Marketing Council in 1991. Marketing types, not multimedia professionals, spearheaded development of the MPC 1.0 spec; the goal was to establish a minimum specification for a multimedia computer that would retail for less than $2,000 in 1991. A 12 MHz 80286 with 2M of RAM, a 16-color VGA display, a 30M fixed disk, a CD-ROM drive, and an 8-bit monaural sound card qualified as a "Multimedia PC," which could proudly bear the MPC 1.0 logo. A PC with such a configuration could barely run Windows and was woefully short of the horsepower needed to run professional multimedia titles, such as those available for the Apple Macintosh computers of the era. Macintosh users read the MPC 1.0 spec and laughed; early MPCs were no match for multimedia-enabled Macs. (Even the lowest-priced Macintosh computers, however, were about twice as expensive as MPC-compliant, no-name clone computers at the time.) The MPC 1.0 spec's minimums were upgraded later to require a 16 MHz 80386SX processor, but even this change didn't solve the performance problems.

The Multimedia PC Marketing Council wised up the second time around; the current MPC specification, released in May 1993, provides two qualification levels. Level 1 conformance requires meeting the upgraded MPC 1.0 spec, while Level 2 compliance makes MPCs meet the more realistic minimum specification shown in table 7.1. Level 2 compliance also was targeted at the $2,000 retail price limit when the new MPC spec was written. The street prices of PCs, however, are dropping faster than the MPC Marketing Council can issue new specifications or add levels to the existing MPC spec. When this book was written, you could buy a PCI-bus 486DX2/66 computer with 8M of RAM and a 128K cache, a PCI video accelerator card with 1M of RAM,

▶ See Chapter 8, "Using CD-ROM Drives with Windows 95," Chapter 9, "Playing and Recording Hi-Fi Sound and Music," and Chapter 10, "Watching *Real* Digital Video"

a 540M fixed disk drive, a double-speed CD-ROM drive, and a Sound Blaster-compatible audio adapter card for about $2,000. For an additional $100 to $300, you can upgrade from the Sound Blaster's simple FM MIDI (Musical Instrument Digital Interface) synthesizer to a wave-table synthesizer that uses digitally recorded sounds of musical instruments (called samples) stored in ROM.

Table 7.1   Minimum Hardware Requirements to Meet the MPC Level 2 Specification

Device	Minimum Requirement
CPU	Intel 80486SX or equivalent, 25 MHz.
RAM	4M.
Fixed disk	160M capacity.
CD-ROM drive	Double-speed drive with a minimum data transfer rate of 300K per second and a seek time of 400 milliseconds (ms) or less, providing CD-DA (Yellow Book digital audio) and CD Audio (analog or Red Book audio) outputs, and supporting CD-XA (Extended Architecture) and Photo CD multisession formats. The drive must consume less than 60 percent of the processor cycles when delivering data at the maximum rate.
Digital audio	8-bit and 16-bit stereo recording and playback capability at sample rates of 11.025, 22.05, and 44.1 KHz with less than 10 percent consumption of processor cycles.
Audio mixer	Three inputs: CD-DA, CD Audio, and MIDI synthesizer, with volume control for each input.
Synthesizer	General MIDI-compliant polyphonic synthesizer with nine melodic timbres on MIDI channels 1-9 and up to eight simultaneous percussion voices on MIDI channel 10.
Video display	640 x 480 pixels with 16-bit color (64K colors).

Tip

The "MPC2" logo that adorns PCs equipped with CD-ROMs and sound cards doesn't mean that the system is optimized for use with Windows 95. Some 1994-model sound cards have demonstrated compatibility problems with beta versions of Windows 95. In addition to the "MPC2" logo, look for multimedia products that carry the "Designed for Windows 95" logo. The Windows 95 logo assures you that the product includes Plug and Play features, 32-bit drivers, and applications that have been tested with both Windows 95 and Windows NT 3.5.

Bill Gates prophesied in his Lehman Brothers address that the average PC configuration in 1995 will be "16 megabyte Pentium machines that have CD-ROM drives, audio, 400 meg hard disk—an extremely capable machine." Although a Pentium computer with a triple- or quad-speed CD-ROM drive and an audio adapter card with sampled sounds is the ideal platform for multimedia, an 80486DX2/66 PC is satisfactory for all but demanding video applications. Triple-speed CD-ROM drives will be the multimedia standard by early 1995. Users of commercial TV production software will likely opt for Windows NT 3.5 as the operating system rather than Windows 95. The two most important elements of a multimedia PC are disk space and video display quality. As mentioned in Chapter 2, "Making Hardware Plug and Play," digital audio and video consume large amounts of disk space. A video display unit with 0.28mm or smaller dot pitch is a necessity for quality graphic reproduction; if you can afford the extra $400 cost, invest in a 17-inch multisynchronous display. Local bus (PCI or VLB) graphic adapter cards are essential for full-screen digital video. Although most multimedia CD-ROM titles are designed for 640- by 480-pixel VGA display mode, you'll find 600- by 800-pixel SVGA (SuperVGA) mode better suits everyday use of Windows 95. It takes a 17-inch monitor to make the standard 8-point Arial font used for Windows 95's system text easily readable in SVGA mode. Also, multimedia graphics and full-screen digital video is much more impressive on a 17-inch rather than a 14- or 15-inch display in standard VGA mode.

II

Exploring Multimedia

Tip

One of the problems that faces prospective home PC users is the fear that their PC will quickly become obsolete. Rapid advances in PC technology and declining retail prices give apparent credence to the conundrum: "The best time to buy a PC is tomorrow." Spending a few hundred dollars more up front to purchase a 90MHz Pentium PC with a PCI bus is the best insurance against short-term obsolescence. Consumers appear to be following this advice; Intel reports that Pentium PCs have a substantially larger percentage of the home PC than the business PC market.

Windows 95 and Microsoft's Consumer Products Division

Microsoft's Consumer Products Division, headed by Patty Stonesifer, markets the new "Microsoft Home" product line and produces an eclectic collection of "edutainment," CD-ROM titles for children and adults. (Book and CD-ROM publishers refer to their products as *titles*. CD-ROM authors and firms that license material, such as books and movies, to CD-ROM publishers are called *content providers*.) The Consumer Products Division also markets Microsoft Flight Simulator (a DOS game), Microsoft applications for the small-office home-office (SOHO) market (Works, Money, and Publisher), Microsoft Mouse, and a variety of accessory products.

The Microsoft Home Product Line

When this book was written, 15 Microsoft titles were carrying the MPC logo. In addition to licensing the use of the MPC logo for MPC-conforming computers, the MPC Marketing Council also licenses the logo to CD-ROM publishers as well as multimedia upgrade kit and sound card suppliers. *Microsoft Encarta*, a multimedia encyclopedia, is the featured member of Microsoft's "multimedia library," which also includes *Microsoft Cinemania '94, Bookshelf, Art Gallery, Dinosaurs, Isaac Asimov's The Ultimate Robot*, and three CD-ROMs featuring major works by Beethoven, Stravinsky, and Mozart. Figure 7.2 shows the opening window of *Microsoft Encarta, 1994 Edition*, running under Windows 95, and figure 7.3 illustrates a typical topic of the encyclopedia, one that provides example musical clips. *Microsoft Musical Instruments* combines detailed photographs of a variety of instruments together with 1,500 individual sound samples, plus examples of several musical styles. *Microsoft Complete Baseball* was released in early 1994. Each title is also available in a version for the Apple Macintosh. According to Ms. Stonesifer, Microsoft plans to have more than 100 titles in production by early 1995. (Patty Stonesifer was director of marketing of Que Corporation before she moved to Microsoft's multimedia group.)

Fig. 7.2
The opening window of *Microsoft Encarta, 1994 Edition,* displaying Encarta Highlights.

Fig. 7.3
Encarta's Afro-American Music topic, which offers four sample sound clips.

In the aggregate, CD-ROM reviewers give the Microsoft Home product line highest marks for both quality of content and visual appeal. *Encarta* is Microsoft's bid to unseat *Compton's Interactive Encyclopedia,* published by Compton's New Media (now a division of the (Chicago) Tribune Company), as the most popular multimedia encyclopedia. *Compton's Interactive Encyclopedia* is included by many suppliers as a bonus product with their CD-ROM drives or multimedia upgrade kits; *Encarta,* on the other hand, is sold primarily through retail channels. When you run *Encarta* under Windows 95, the video segments run more smoothly and Encarta opens windows with more "snap," due primarily to Windows 95's new 32-bit CDFS file and disk access, plus its improved TrueType font rasterizer and faster handling of bit-mapped graphics. Videos, such as the example shown in figure 7.4, appear in 1/4-display format (320×240 pixels), rather than Video for Windows 1.0's 160×120 pixel oversized postage-stamp dimensions. Frame rates in *Encarta* 1994's AVI (audio-video interleaved format) videos are slowed to accommodate playback by Windows 3.1.

Just as movies have trailers, *Encarta* has a catalog that advertises other members of the growing family of Microsoft Home CD-ROMs (see fig. 7.5). In his Lehman Brothers address, Bill Gates stated, "[W]e'll be coming out with a new title every week in the years ahead." Gates also says he expects the Consumer Products group to be the firm's largest division by 1997, so it's not surprising to find advertisements included in Microsoft's edutainment products. Microsoft now shows Office 4.3 in the credit segment of the PBS programs it sponsors, but the company has heavily advertised its Home product line on cable TV. You can expect many advertisements for Windows 95 to include screen shots of *Encarta, Cinemania '94,* and *Microsoft Complete Baseball.* The Microsoft Network will make dialing into Microsoft's on-line "Baseball Daily" update service for *Complete Baseball* users as easy as double-clicking an icon. *Complete Baseball* is the answer to baseball fans who need their daily fix, despite the premature end of the 1994 Major League season.

Fig. 7.4
Playing a video clip from *Microsoft Encarta, 1994 Edition,* under Windows 95.

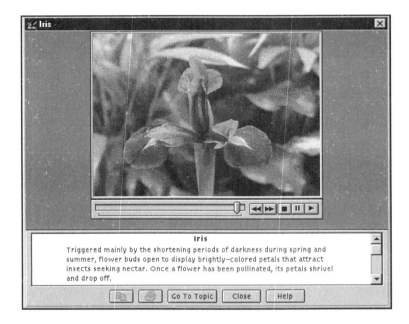

Today's CD-ROMS as Grist for Tomorrow's Infobahn Mill

▶ See Chapter 14, "Hooking Up to the Internet"

The information superhighway, no matter how it's implemented, ultimately will devour multimedia content. Telephone companies and cable-TV service providers are making deals with Hollywood movie moguls and anyone else they can find to create content for pay-per-view services on tomorrow's infobahn. There is a persistent rumor in the entertainment industry that Bill Gates & Company intends to purchase, invest in, or form a joint venture with a major film studio. Entertainment-on-demand will create an enormous market for TV and film producers, especially those who are able to create engaging interactive multimedia productions.

CD-ROMs represent today's most efficient and practical method of delivering interactive multimedia content. Thus, the collective content of the thousands of CD-ROMs now in production ultimately will end up on the infobahn, providing on-demand access. Even the present-day Internet offers opportunities for electronic publishing. A story titled *"Britannica on the Internet"* in the August/September 1994 issue of *CD-ROM Multimedia* magazine, a Canadian publication, announced that the 32 volumes of the *Encyclopedia Britannica,* containing more than 44 million words and over 23,000 illustrations, will be distributed to libraries and universities on the Internet. Britannica will use a special version of the most popular graphical front-end for the Internet, Mosaic, modified by WAIS, Inc. to provide the hypertext links that will make the vast amount of information in *EB* easily accessible.

Fig. 7.5
The opening window of the Microsoft Home multimedia CD-ROM catalog.

II

Exploring Multimedia

Note

Microsoft says there won't be a version of Mosaic included with Windows 95, but there are plenty of software publishers to fill the gap. According to Bill Miller, director of marketing for Microsoft's Online Services group, quoted in the December, 1994 issue of *Windows Watcher* newsletter, The Microsoft Network won't offer a Mosaic-style browser until late 1995." Fortunately, the freeware version of Mosaic, demonstrated in Chapter 14, "Hooking Up to the Internet," is a 32-bit Windows application that runs well under Windows 95 and Windows NT. Mosaic is available over the Internet at no charge.

▶ See Chapter 13, "Joining The Microsoft Network"

You'll probably see major CD-ROM publishers place their content on the Internet, following EB's lead. According to Bill Gates, "These [Microsoft] titles really move us to the information highway because, although today you have to go and buy a CD and put it into the drive to look at the information, when your PC is connected up, all those compact discs will be available up on the server." The first place you're likely to find online versions of Microsoft Home titles, however, is on The Microsoft Network. *Information & Interactive Services Report* for Oct. 21, 1994, quoted Bill Gates during his appearance at the Networked Economy conference in Washington, D.C.: "Gates described [The Microsoft Network as] a service that would capitalize on Microsoft's current crop of CD-ROM applications, allowing users to dial up data from its *Encarta* encyclopedia, for instance."

Delivering Interactive Multimedia over the Wire and on the Airwaves

▶ See Chapter 12, "Connecting to the Outside World"

Like computers built to the MPC 1.0 specification, modem dialup from Windows 95 at today's 14,400 bps is adequate for text-based products, such as encyclopedias, with simple line drawings or small four-color illustrations. However, modem dialup is far too slow for interactive multimedia applications. Even 128-Kbps ISDN lines throttle the flow of video data to a rate of about 10 percent of yesterday's 150-Kbps single-speed CD-ROM drives. ISDN is, however, adequate for video conferencing, which lets users share data and see images of participants' video displays. Microsoft's Bill Gates and Intel's Andy Grove share an optimistic view of the future of teleconferencing. The incorporation of ISDN connectivity in Windows 95 through the Telephony API (TAPI) attests to Microsoft's faith in this middle-band telecommunications medium. Figure 7.6 shows Version 1.6 of Intel's ProShare teleconferencing application in use. According to an article in the Aug. 8, 1994, issue of *PC Week* magazine, Intel plans to abandon the low-end commodity modem market (except for its successful SatisFAXtion fax modem) to "focus its efforts on next-generation voice/data/video modems that support its ProShare videoconferencing system." Teleconferencing is just one of the new technologies that will make telecommuting with Windows 95 a commonplace practice.

Fig. 7.6
Teleconferencing
with Intel ProShare
(courtesy of Intel
Corp.)

II

Exploring Multimedia

Delivering interactive multimedia on demand requires high-bandwidth communication channels, such as those used by television broadcasters. Cable TV distributors, regional Bell operating companies (usually called RBOCs or Baby Bells, also telcos), long-distance carriers (AT&T, MCI, Sprint, and others), cellular telephone service providers, and satellite communication consortiums are trying to grab a slice of the interactive (and non-interactive) on-demand multimedia pie. Achieving high bandwidth over the wire requires coaxial cables or fiber-optic connections; satellite transmission appears to be the best bet for connection via the "luminiferous ether." Announcements of new joint ventures between content owners, primarily movie studios and would-be infobahn distributors, appear almost every week.

Microsoft and Bill Gates aren't taking the chance of missing the on-demand multimedia boat; they're betting on both sides of the high-bandwidth telecommunications business. According to a story in the March 7, 1994, issue of *Television Digest,* TCI Cable Management Corporation and Microsoft plan to conduct a joint test of interactive, on-demand cable TV service in Seattle and

Denver. The test will use the TCI networks and Microsoft's Windows NT-based digital video server product, code-named *Tiger*, now in the development stage. A trial phase limited to Microsoft employees was slated to begin in late 1994, with expansion in 1995 to individual customers in Seattle and Denver. Besides Windows 95, Microsoft is developing the operating system for TV-top boxes that handle the conversion from digital to conventional analog TV. Bill Gates devoted much of his keynote address to the November 1994 COMDEX computer exposition, "Information at Your Fingertips—2005," to interactive cable TV entertainment systems. There's been no formal announcement, but the chances are good that a direct digital cable-TV connection to Windows 95 is in the works. Microsoft also has a joint venture with Nippon Telephone and Telegraph (NTT), Japan's state-owned telephone monopoly, and Mtel, who's a nationwide U.S. provider of paging and wireless data services. Bill Gates and Paul Allen also are investors in Mtel. No doubt you'll be able to page your acquaintances from Windows 95's Exchange client in the near future, plus receive and send wireless e-mail with Windows 95's Exchange client. Widespread availability of cabled interactive multimedia, however, isn't likely to occur until the 21st century. In the short term, it may be a small satellite dish, described near the end of Chapter 13, "Joining The Microsoft Network," that brings interactive multimedia to the affluent home PC user.

Chapter 8

Using CD-ROM Drives
with Windows 95

Having a CD-ROM drive in your PC is no longer a status symbol; it's a necessity. CD-ROM drives are rapidly displacing the 5 1/4-inch floppy disk drives that were *de rigeur* for yesterday's PCs. By mid-1995, experts estimate that about 80 percent of new PCs will ship to North American users with CD-ROM drives pre-installed. It's a safe bet that 100 percent of the PCs sold to the home market in 1995 will include a CD-ROM drive; only the most pecunious business PC purchasers are likely to omit this essential hardware item. By mid-1994, increased production volume and intensive competition between CD-ROM drive manufacturers reduced the street price of double-speed drives below $200, and triple-speed or even quad-speed drives should be heading toward the $200 mark by the time you read this book.

Understanding CD-ROM Buzzwords

The CD-ROM, a member of the laser disc family, was invented by Philips N.V., a Dutch conglomerate that got its start making carbon-filament light bulbs in the early 1890s and ultimately became the largest manufacturer of TV sets in the world. The first laser discs appeared in 1974 in the form of 12-inch LaserVision discs used for recording motion pictures, primarily competing with the videotape medium. The audio CD in the 120mm Compact Disc format, jointly developed by Philips and Sony Corporation of Japan, revolutionized the music world in 1982 by providing unprecedented reproduction fidelity unattainable with cassette tapes (the Philips Compact Cassette format) or vinyl LPs. In 1983, Philips and Sony adapted the CD-DA (Compact Disc-Digital Audio) format to store computer data, primarily in text formats. Philips and Sony are major manufacturers of CD-ROM drives.

Figure 8.1 shows a Philips LMS CM207 double-speed CD-ROM drive; the CM207 is a Plug and Play device with an enhanced IDE interface that complies with the IDE/ATAPI standard described in Chapter 2, "Making Hardware Plug and Play." Like most of today's moderately priced CD-ROM drives, the CM207 does not use a CD-ROM carrier (caddy); instead, the drive has a motorized tray in which you place the CD-ROM.

Fig. 8.1
The Philips CM207 double-speed CD-ROM drive (courtesy of Philips LMS, a Philips Electronics North American Co.).

Reading a CD-ROM Drive Spec Sheet

Intense competition in the CD-ROM drive business is forcing manufacturers to upgrade their products on very short cycles. The "specifications subject to change without notice" clause on manufacturers' CD-ROM drive data sheets means what it says, but in the case of CD-ROM drives, the change is likely to be for the better. Following are the most important elements of the CD-ROM drive specs:

■ *Data transfer rate*. The rate at which a CD-ROM drive transfers data is determined by how fast the drive's spindle turns the CD-ROM disc. Single-speed drives deliver about 150K per second, double-speed (2x) drives have a data rate of 300K per second, and so forth. Even the fastest quad-speed (4x) CD-ROM drives, with a data rate of 600K per second, don't come close to the 2M to 5M per second rate of today's fixed disk drives. By the time you read this book, triple-speed CD-ROM drives (450K per second) are likely to be the standard for multimedia PCs.

■ *Average access time*. The average time it takes a CD-ROM to move the optical read head to the desired track (called seeking) is determined by the head-positioning mechanism. Average access time is not related to spindle speed and data transfer rate. The average access time of today's CD-ROM drives is between 0.3 and 0.4 seconds. (Today's fixed disk drives have access times of 8 to 12 milliseconds, about 35 times faster than a typical CD-ROM drive.) Average access time is not as important as data transfer rate, but the difference between 0.3 and 0.4 seconds is noticeable with many multimedia titles.

- *Buffer capacity.* Data buffering improves the data transfer rate for sequentially accessed tracks by storing CD-ROM data in advance of a request for the data by your computer. The standard buffer size for moderately priced CD-ROM drives is 64K. A 256K or larger buffer provides significantly better performance, especially with hi-fi sound and digital video tracks. Windows 95's CD-ROM data caching, however, makes buffer size less important than for earlier versions of Windows.

- *Interface.* The three CD-ROM drive interfaces are SCSI, proprietary, and IDE. The SCSI interface is the most universal of the three but is also the most costly for manufacturers to implement. A proprietary interface requires that you dedicate a valuable expansion slot in your computer to a single CD-ROM drive, unless your audio adapter card includes a proprietary CD-ROM interface. (Creative Laboratories and Advanced Gravis, for example, supply sound cards that support Sony, Mitsumi, and Panasonic proprietary interfaces.) The IDE interface, which shares a simple IDE adapter card with your fixed disk and floppy disk drives, is likely to become the standard interface for moderately priced drives by early 1995.

- *Disc loading.* Traditionally, high-quality CD-ROM drives have required a carrier (caddy) into which you place the CD-ROM and then insert into the CD-ROM drive. Caddies protect the CD-ROM; if you exchange members of a set of favorite CD-ROMs, storing frequently used CD-ROMs in caddies prevents inadvertent damage. The trend, however, is toward caddyless CD-ROM drives that have a retractable tray on which you place a bare CD-ROM, similar to audio CD players. Caddyless operation is more convenient for most users. Drives with an automatic, motorized tray usually are more reliable and convenient than those with the manual, spring-loaded type.

- *CD-DA (analog) audio outputs.* As mentioned earlier in the chapter, most (but not all) CD-ROM drives include audio outputs. Analog audio is available from a front-panel stereo mini-jack for headphones and usually from a rear-panel 3-pin or 4-pin connector for a cable that leads to a similar connector on your audio adapter card. If you're interested in

II

Exploring Multimedia

taking advantage of CD-DA audio and Windows 95's built-in CD-ROM player, make sure that the CD-ROM drive you buy has a rear-panel audio connector. Otherwise, you must loop a mini-plug jumper from the headphone jack to the line-input (or, with an attenuating cable, to the microphone input) connector of your sound card to hear or record Red Book audio tracks.

> **Tip**
>
> If you're upgrading your computer for multimedia, make sure that the CD-ROM drive you buy includes at least CD-ROM XA (extended architecture) mode 2, form 1 capability. If the drive specification states that it's compatible with Photo CD multisession discs, this indicates that the drive supports the CD-ROM XA format. Almost all double-speed and faster CD-ROMs are CD-ROM XA capable, but some bargain-priced CD-ROM drive advertisements don't mention CD-ROM XA or are described as "CD-ROM XA-ready" by their suppliers, meaning that you'll need to purchase an upgrade kit to provide CD-ROM XA-capability. If your CD-ROM drive doesn't have CD-ROM XA compatibility, you won't be able to read multisession Photo CDs or White Book video discs. Some CD-ROM drivers provide a feature that lets you read single-session Photo CDs on older, single-speed CD-ROM drives.

Colored Books: The First CD-ROM Standards

Subsequent to development of the compact disc, new data formats were developed to add graphics and sound to CD-ROMs and create interactive CDs. Each specification for these Philips-Sony formats was bound in covers of a specific hue. The four most popular Philips-Sony formats are:

- *Red Book* Audio, the standard for consumer CD-Digital Audio discs.

- *Yellow Book* CD-ROMs, a derivative of the Red Book format for storing PC files.

- *Green Book* CD-Interactive (CD-I) discs that use the CD-ROM XA format that interleaves sound and graphics tracks for better synchronization.

- *Orange Book* writable discs that let you record your own CD-ROMs, if you have the required equipment.

Virtually all CD-ROM drives today can read Yellow Book CD-ROMs that use the CD-ROM XA technology, derived from the Green Book format, that bridges the gap between CD-ROM and CD-I formats. Thus, you often hear the term *XA bridge discs* applied to CD-ROMs that take advantage of the interleaved file format of CD-I disks.

Newer CD-ROM File Formats

During the past few years, a variety of other CD-ROM file formats have emerged, many of which have fallen by the wayside. Following are the most important of today's CD-ROM formats developed by firms other than Philips and Sony:

- *Photo CD,* Eastman Kodak Corporation's proprietary format for photographic imaging, which can also accommodate digital audio.

- *Karaoke CD,* developed by JVC (Japan Victor Corporation) in 1992 to compete with Pioneer's laser disc karaoke players, which previously had enjoyed a virtual monopoly in Asian markets.

- *Video CD,* a joint JVC-Philips adaptation of the Karaoke CD format to provide motion control features equivalent to those found on a VCR, also called *White Book* video.

The primary impetus for adding CD-ROM XA capability to CD-ROM drives was the ability to read Kodak's multisession Photo CD format. Thus, Photo CDs might qualify as "Chartreuse Book" discs. Kodak's Photo CD formats are discussed in the next section. Video CD—not to be confused with CD-Video or CD-TV (an early Commodore proprietary format)—is one of the subjects covered by Chapter 10, "Watching *Real* Digital Video." The Yellow Book, Photo CD, and White Book CD-ROM formats are of greatest interest to users of Windows 95. Most, but not all, CD-ROM drives provide stereo analog audio outputs so that you can play Red Book audio for entertainment; some CD-ROMs, called *mixed media,* incorporate Yellow Book data and Red Book sound tracks on the same disc.

Kodak's Portfolio Format Brings Do-It-Yourself

Eastman Kodak Co. introduced the Photo CD format and TV-based Photo CD players in 1990. Kodak originally targeted its new format and players to the consumer market, with photofinishers lined up to transfer amateur shutter bugs' 35mm images on film to the Photo CD's high-resolution digital format at relatively low cost (about 60 cents per photo). The consumer market for Photo CDs did not live up to Kodak's expectation; however, professional photographers found the Photo CD to be the best thing since sliced bread. The Photo CD is the best way to archive valuable photographs because it eliminates the age-induced color changes that affect conventional photographic film. In addition, photographers' agents and stock photo agencies can distribute examples of a photographer's work on duplicated Photo CDs very inexpensively.

II

Exploring Multimedia

Kodak now provides a variety of Photo CD formats for consumer and commercial images, including the larger 2 1/4-by-2 1/4-inch, 4-by-5-inch, and even 8-by-10-inch formats preferred by professionals. However, none of these formats qualify for multimedia status because they don't support sound files. The new Kodak Portfolio Photo CD format lets you combine photos, slides created in presentation graphics applications (such as Microsoft PowerPoint), and digital audio recordings into a multimedia presentation (but without digital video or animation). What's more, you can have a service bureau create one or hundreds of Portfolio Photo CDs at a much lower cost than conventional CD-ROMs. The process goes like this:

1. Use Kodak's Arrange-It software to create a script that determines the sequence and duration of appearance of Photo CD and bit-mapped images created from your presentation graphics package.

2. Record the audio tracks in waveform audio (WAV) files by using your audio adapter card. (The Portfolio Photo CD service bureau converts the WAV files to Red Book audio files.)

3. Link the images and the sound files, and then add navigation features, called branches, to your production with menus. (Portfolio Photo CDs don't support buttons or other forms of navigation control.)

4. Send the Photo CD and the script file, image files, and sound files on disk to an authorized Portfolio Photo CD service bureau. The service bureau combines the files according to the script and delivers you a finished Photo CD disc that includes free player software. (Some 300+ locations of Sir Speedy and its Copies Now subsidiary are authorized Portfolio Photo CD service bureaus.)

Aside from low mastering costs, the advantage of do-it-yourself Photo CD Portfolio discs is that they are compatible with CD-ROM drives (both PC and Macintosh), CD-I players, some 3DO game devices, and Kodak's own stationary and portable Photo CD players. Figure 8.2 shows Kodak's Photo CD Player application displaying an image from a demonstration Portfolio Photo CD. The advantage of using Windows 95 to display the files for Portfolio Photo CDs is the much better performance you achieve with Windows 95's 32-bit CDFS file system.

> **Note**
>
> You need an audio cable between the audio output of your CD-ROM drive and the CD-ROM audio input of your sound card to hear the audio on Portfolio Photo CDs because the audio is recorded in Red Book (CD-DA) format. Using Red Book audio allows Portfolio Photo CD audio tracks to play back from a conventional audio CD player, as well as Kodak Photo CD players that connect to your TV set.

Fig. 8.2
Windows 95 running the Photo CD Player displaying an image from a Portfolio Photo CD (courtesy of Eastman Kodak Co.).

II

Exploring Multimedia

Windows 95 Bids Farewell to MSCDEX.EXE

Windows 95 provides a full 32-bit protected-mode CD-ROM file system (CDFS) of its own that replaces the 16-bit MSCDEX.EXE driver used with DOS and previous versions of Windows. MSCDEX.EXE (Microsoft Compact Disc extension) is a terminate-and-stay-resident (TSR) DOS application that translates the ISO-9660 CD file system to a format compatible with DOS. One advantage of CDFS over MSCDEX.EXE is that it does not use conventional DOS lower memory. Another benefit is that CDFS uses protected mode for reading CD-ROMs, while MSCDEX.EXE runs in real mode. CDFS is also faster than MSCDEX and has its own memory cache, similar to the cache for the 32-bit fixed disk driver (VFAT).

▶ See Chapter 23, "Setting Up and Managing Windows 95"

Users who buy a PC with Windows 95 and a pre-installed CD-ROM drive with Windows 95-style drivers don't need MSCDEX; it's not required to use CD-ROM drives for which Windows 95 drivers are available. Windows 95 identifies both conventional and Plug and Play SCSI and IDE CD-ROM drives during the startup process. If, for example, you add a Creative Labs Sound Blaster 16 SCSI card to a computer running Windows 95, Windows 95 recognizes the Adaptec SCSI controller chip when you restart the computer. If you add a CD-ROM drive with a proprietary interface to a computer running Windows 95, you probably won't have to use MSCDEX. Windows 95 comes with a variety of drivers for popular CD-ROM adapter cards, such as those used with Mitsumi, Sony, and Panasonic (Matsushita) drives (see fig. 8.3). Virtually all CD-ROM drive manufacturers will be supplying 32-bit virtual device drivers (VxDs) for their proprietary adapter cards by the time Microsoft releases Windows 95.

Fig. 8.3
Some of the drivers for proprietary CD-ROM adapter cards supplied with Windows 95.

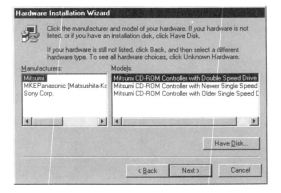

If you install Windows 95 over an existing Windows 3.1+ and/or DOS installation, and your AUTOEXEC.BAT file includes a MSCDEX.EXE entry, Windows 95 substitutes the new 32-bit CDFS-compatible driver for MSCDEX by changing the entry in AUTOEXEC.BAT to D:\WINDOWS 95\COMMAND\MSCDEX.EXE where D:\WINDOWS 95 is the directory that you installed Windows 95. To maintain compatibility with CD-ROM adapters that pre-date Windows 95 or don't have a Windows 95 driver, Windows 95's MSCDEX.EXE uses the existing driver for your CD-ROM drive specified in CONFIG.SYS. For example, the entries to make the Sound Blaster 16 SCSI's Adaptec SCSI interface and EZ-SCSI ASPI (Advanced SCSI Programming Interface) software play in real mode under Windows 95 are as follows:

```
rem [Sound Blaster and Adaptec SCSI Section of CONFIG.SYS]
DEVICE=C:\SB16\DRV\CTSB16.SYS /UNIT=0 /BLASTER=A:220 I:10 D:1 H:5
DEVICE=C:\SB16\DRV\CTMMSYS.SYS
DEVICE=C:\SCSI\ASPI2DOS.SYS /D /Z
DEVICE=C:\SCSI\ASPICD.SYS /D:ASPICD0
rem [Adaptec SCSI Section of AUTOEXEC.BAT]
D:\WINDOWS 95\MSCDEX.EXE /D:ASPICD0 /L:G /M:12
```

The Sound Blaster 16 SCSI's Adaptec SCSI controller is supported by Windows 95, so you should disable the preceding entries in your CONFIG.SYS and AUTOEXEC.BAT file by adding rem before each entry. (If you run into a problem with the Windows 95 driver, you can disable the Windows 95 VxD and delete the rems to return to real-mode operation.)

> **Note**
>
> Microsoft has announced that Windows 95 will be distributed on CD-ROM as well as on conventional 3 1/2-inch floppy disks. If Microsoft uses the same method for installing Windows 95 as for Windows NT 3.5, you'll receive one or two 5 1/4-inch and 3 1/2-inch boot floppy disks that will recognize most popular CD-ROM adapters. Otherwise, you'll need to have your CD-ROM operational under an earlier version of DOS and MSCDEX to run the setup program on the CD-ROM.

How Windows 95's CD-ROM Feature Set Will Affect Titles

Today's Windows CD-ROM titles that carry the MPC logo will run without any problems at all under Windows 95. Thus, there won't be a sea of change to Windows 95—only CD-ROM titles. As more PC users adopt Windows 95 as their operating system, however, title publishers will alter their CD-ROM products to take advantage of Windows 95's advanced multimedia features. Some of the improvements in CD-ROM titles you'll see in 1995 and beyond are as follows:

■ *Titles designed only for double-speed or faster CD-ROM drives.* By mid-1995, the majority of edutainment and game CD-ROMs will require double-speed CD-ROM drives. Video and animation titles played from single-speed drives will appear jerky, and audio will hiccup or fail to stay in sync with the action. Triple- and quad-speed drives will provide full-screen video with hi-fi audio reproduction.

■ *Multiple digital video files.* Medio Multimedia, Inc.'s titles, some of which are discussed in the following section, include both small (160-by-120-pixel, 1/16th-screen) and large (320-by-240-pixel, 1/4th-screen) AVI (audio-video interleaved) video clips. If you have a single-speed drive, you see the small version; double-speed or faster CD-ROM drives deliver the larger video image.

■ *Dual sound tracks.* The standard format for audio narration and musical background on most of today's CD-ROMs is 8-bit, 22.05 KHz mono and stereo because 8-bit sound cards (typified by Creative Labs' original Sound Blaster) represent a sizable percentage of the present audio adapter card population. As with digital video, CD-ROM publishers are likely to offer ADPCM-compressed 16-bit, 44.1 KHz CD-Audio quality sound as an option for Windows 95 users with 16-bit sound cards.

▶ See Chapter 10, "Watching *Real* Digital Video"

■ *Feature films playing on your computer.* Publishers of motion picture laser discs are gearing up to produce a flood of conventional Yellow Book and new MPEG White Book CD-ROMs from their laser disc library. According to a story titled, "Movies on PC Could Make This Stock Boffo," in the Aug. 1, 1994, issue *of Business Week*, Image Entertainment, Inc. plans to market its line of CD-ROM movies, which use the Apple QuickTime format, through video rental and music stores, as well as through PC suppliers. (You need an MPEG decompression adapter card or a VGA adapter card with on-board MPEG hardware decompression to display White Book movies. No additional hardware is required to play QuickTime movies.)

▶ See Chapter 11, "Taking Advantage of Windows 95's Games Features"

■ *More games for Windows.* DOS has dominated the CD-ROM PC game business because Windows 3.1+ slows painting the display, a process called *blitting*. Microsoft calls Windows 95's new WinG API (Windows Game application programming interface) a "very thin layer" between graphics data and your display. WinG is backward-compatible with Windows 3.1+, so you'll see a trend in 1995 toward DOS game publishers releasing Windows versions of their most popular products. By the end of 1995, it's likely that DOS and Windows games will be running neck-and-neck in the market.

> **Note**
>
> Microsoft's policies for licensing CD-ROM publishers to use the "Designed for Microsoft Windows 95" logo hadn't been published when this book was written. 32-bit features that specifically support Windows 95 and Windows NT are required for applications to carry the Windows 95-compatible logo. Thus, it's a good bet that CD-ROM title producers will also face the prospect of having to add WinG and other 32-bit features for Windows 95 and Windows NT to their product lines to apply the new Windows 95 logo that will replace the current Windows 3.1 logo by mid-1995.

Taking the Conservative Approach to Multimedia Publishing

Steve Podrachik, president and CEO of Medio Multimedia, Inc. of Redmond, Wash., is taking the conservative, look-see approach to adding Windows 95-specific features to his company's highly successful titles, such as *JFK Assassination,* a widely acclaimed documentary CD-ROM that combines text excerpted from reports and books with video clips, photos, and animated drawings. Another popular Medio title, *Jets,* provides details on 160 turbine-powered aircraft, including more than 500 photos, video clips of jet fighters in flight, biographies of the pilots who flew them, and animations that let you view the aircraft from any angle you choose.

According to Podrachik, there's such a variety of PCs claiming multimedia status that assuring compatibility of CD-ROMs with the user's hardware and PC setup is Medio's number one technical priority. He adds, "We exert a tremendous effort on making our setup and conformity-checking systems bulletproof."

Medio's attention to compatibility issues pays off; figure 8.4 shows Windows 95 running the opening screen of the first issue of *Medio Magazine,* a general-interest monthly publication on CD-ROM. The only detectable difference in playing *Medio Magazine* under Windows 95 as opposed to under Windows 3.1+ is that the playback of digital video clips is noticeably smoother, plus Windows 95 adds its look and feel to the dialogs that appear during the installation process.

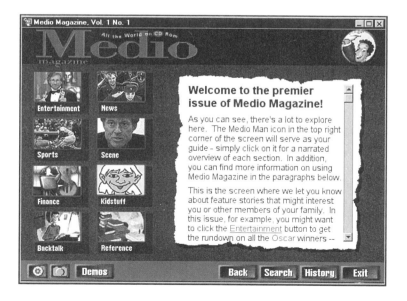

Fig. 8.4
Windows 95 displaying the opening screen of the first issue of *Medio Magazine.*

Although Windows 95 will help alleviate compatibility issues, Podrachik points out that Medio has to support the millions of PCs running Windows 3.1+ before Windows 95 becomes the ubiquitous Windows operating system. Medio's CD-ROM setup application checks your PC's settings, such as the number of colors of your VGA display, and then pops up a wizard similar to Windows 95's Hardware Installation Wizard to guide you step by step through the process for making needed changes. Several of Medio's titles are Visual Basic applications and use VBX (Visual Basic custom control) files. (Podrachik was a Visual Basic product manager for Microsoft before leaving in 1993 to start Medio.) For Visual Basic titles, the setup application checks the version of existing VBXs and automatically replaces obsolete VBXs with newer versions on the CD-ROM. The setup application also checks your computer's digital video performance; if performance is not up to par (indicated by too many skipped video frames), you have the option of displaying 1/8-screen instead of 1/4-screen video. It's this attention to detail, Podrachik says, that minimizes technical service calls and product returns.

Biting the Windows 95 Bullet

When you install most multimedia CD-ROMs, the setup program copies a multitude of files to the title's newly created subdirectory and, in most cases, to your \WINDOWS\SYSTEM directory, too. One or more of the files added to your fixed disk comprises a reader application, which is necessary to implement the interactive features of the CD-ROM. Titles that include digital video copy the run-time version of Video for Windows 1.1, which includes a 32-bit driver compatible with Windows 3.1+ for displaying AVI files, to your \WINDOWS\SYSTEM subdirectory. Reader applications, however, are likely to remain real-mode, 16-bit Windows programs for many months after Microsoft releases Windows 95.

The major problem now faced by multimedia title producers is the lack of 32-bit, protected-mode multimedia authoring tools and readers for Windows NT 3.5 and Windows 95. Several 32-bit applications for creating and playing Win32 multimedia titles were in the beta-test stage when this book was written. David Howe, product manager for Macromedia Director 4.0, one of the leading multimedia authoring tools, says Director will be one of the "first wave" products for Windows 95. The performance of 32-bit interactive multimedia titles is likely to be significantly better than the 16-bit variety, but it is doubtful if most edutainment title producers can recoup the programming cost involved in converting existing titles to 32-bit versions. (PC game publishers are an exception; Win32S and WinG are a necessity to deliver performance under Windows that can compete with high-speed, DOS-based games.)

Another unresolved issue is CD-ROM audio quality and the use of ADPCM compression to make high-fidelity background music and quality music clips fit on the CD-ROM. Windows for Workgroups 3.11 includes the Microsoft Sound Mapper 2.0 and the ADPCM Codec 2.0, but Windows 95's Audio Compression Manager and Wave Mapper supports a wider variety of the new codecs, including the IMA codec designed specifically for music. The dilemma facing multimedia title producers is the necessity to support Windows 3.1+ with conventional digital audio files and to take advantage of Windows 95's new codecs; this requires duplicate audio tracks.

► See Chapter 9, "Playing and Recording Hi-Fi Sound and Music"

Perhaps Microsoft Home will lead the way, after Windows 95 appears, with "spin and grin" 32-bit multimedia titles carrying the "Designed for Microsoft Windows 95" logo; only time will tell. Producers of titles for Apple Macintosh computers may have a leg up on their Windows competitors because all Macintosh multimedia applications are of the 32-bit variety. Thus, the first 32-bit Windows CD-ROMs may be Macintosh titles for System 7+ that are converted to 32-bit Windows applications. Regardless of the 16-bit/32-bit issues, you're likely to enjoy CD-ROM multimedia more running under Windows 95 than you did running under Windows 3.1+, if only because of the greatly improved CDFS and Windows 95's attractive user interface.

II

Exploring Multimedia

Chapter 9

Playing and Recording Hi-Fi Sound and Music

If it doesn't have high-fidelity sound and music, it isn't multimedia. Professional narration, on-the-scene live interviews, and quality background music will make the difference between winning and losing titles in the multimedia publishing business of 1995 and beyond. Windows 95's support for software decompression of 44.1 KHz, 16-bit digital audio makes it practical for publishers to include CD-Audio quality sound on multimedia CD-ROM titles, even titles designed for playback on single-speed CD-ROM drives. The new wave of low-cost PC sound cards with sampled sounds for synthesized music makes MIDI files come alive. Windows 95 brings more new and improved features to the audio side of computing than to any other component of the operating system. This chapter gives you a preview of what's in store for audiophiles and musicians, amateur and professional alike, in Windows 95.

Picking Up PC Audio Jargon

Like CD-ROM drive suppliers, the folks who bring you digital audio have added their own jargon to the technobabble of the PC world. Following are short definitions of some of the more important definitions of the terms used in PC sound recording and reproduction:

- *Analog audio* is one of the two common methods of recording and reproducing sound. Analog audio reproduces sound from grooves cut in records or from various magnetic fields on conventional audiotapes.

The phonograph cartridge or tape playback head generates a continuously varying voltage that's analogous to the sound waves of the original sound source. Audio CDs store sound in digital form, but two digital-to-analog converters (DACs) in the player change the output of audio CDs to a stereo analog signal for compatibility with most of today's home sound systems.

■ *Digital audio* uses a process called *sampling* to periodically measure the amplitude (loudness) of an analog sound signal (from a microphone, for instance) and to convert the sound to a series of digital bits. One analog-to-digital converter (ADC) is used for each stereo channel. The output of the two ADCs is in the form of 8-bit bytes that can be stored on a disk drive and processed by computers. Engineers call digital audio *pulse code modulation* (PCM); in Windows, digital audio is called *waveaudio* or *waveform audio* and is stored in the form of WAV files.

■ *Resolution* is the number of bits (discrete steps) that make up a single sample of analog sound. 8-bit samples provide only 256 volume steps; 16-bit samples have about 64,000 steps. Audio CDs use 16-bit resolution; 8-bit resolution is adequate for recording voice messages. Most of today's audio adapter cards offer a choice of 8-bit or 16-bit resolution.

■ *Sampling rate* is the number of analog-to-digital conversions per second, expressed in KHz (kilohertz, thousands of samples per second). The most common sampling rates are 11.025, 22.05, and 44.1 KHz. Audio CDs have a 44.1 KHz sampling rate, which can reproduce audio frequencies up to 22.05 KHz (1/2 the sampling rate). Playing or recording 16-bit (2-byte), 44.1 KHz stereo sound requires processing $2 \times 44,100 \times 2$ = 176,200 bytes per second. (Note that 176.2K per second exceeds the data rate of a single-speed CD-ROM drive, 150K per second.) Most audio adapter cards provide the three standard sampling rates; some offer 5.0125 KHz for voice notes. Most of today's multimedia CD-ROMs use 8-bit resolution at a 22.05 KHz sampling rate, which all sound boards can handle.

■ *Codec* is an abbreviation for (en)coder-decoder, a software algorithm (computational method) stored in your computer's RAM or implemented in a hardware chip that encodes (compresses) or decodes (decompresses) digital signal streams, such as those resulting from recording digital audio and video. *Symmetrical codecs* compress and decompress the signals in real time. Some complex encoding processes, such as MPEG video compression, can't be done in real time; MPEG is called an *asymmetrical codec*.

■ *ADPCM* is an abbreviation for adaptive-differential pulse code modulation, a method of compressing digital sound to reduce the amount of storage space occupied by digital audio files and the data rate required for reproduction. *Adaptive-differential* means that the algorithm used to compress the sound relies on the difference between succeeding sets of samples and adapts the computation to take into account the average amplitude of the sound. A variety of ADPCM algorithms is commonly used today. Figure 9.1 shows some of the ADPCM codecs that were included with an early beta version of Windows 95. The new Windows 95 Audio Compression Manager and the audio codecs supplied with Windows 95 are discussed in a later section in this chapter.

Fig. 9.1
The audio codecs supplied with Windows 95.

II

Exploring Multimedia

■ *MCI* is an abbreviation for Windows Media Control Interface, the part of Windows that deals with media objects, such as sound and video files, as well as media devices, which typically are sound cards, analog video overlay cards, VCRs, and laser disc players. MCI provides multimedia application developers a high-level scripting language that uses simple statements such as *open new type waveaudio alias capture*, which opens a WAV file buffer (temporary storage location) for recording. MCI also offers a variety of low-level media control functions for hard-core C/C++ programmers.

■ *MIDI* is an acronym for the Musical Instrument Digital Interface, a specification that defines how electronic musical devices (primarily keyboards and synthesizers of various types) are interconnected and the protocol used to transmit and receive messages that represent the frequency and duration of notes, as well as a multitude of other types of messages. MIDI is the undisputed standard of the electronic musical instrument industry. Windows has included MIDI features since the introduction of the multimedia version of Windows 3.0; the Windows 3.1+ MCI includes a full set of built-in MIDI functions, which are also present in Windows 95.

■ *General MIDI* (GM) is a standard for defining a common set of synthesized instruments and identification numbers (called *patch numbers*) for all manufacturers of MIDI synthesizers. The General MIDI standard was derived from Roland Corporation's General Synthesizer (GS) standard; Roland is a major Japanese manufacturer of MIDI devices with a sizable presence in North America. Before GM, if you created a MIDI file (which has a MID extension) for one synthesizer, playing the file back on another synthesizer often resulted in wholesale transformation of the work. The French horn part might have been played by a samisen or koto, and woodwind sections often turned into a chorus of guitars and string basses. Windows 95, like its Windows 3.1+ predecessors, supports the General MIDI standard, and you can use Windows 95's upgraded MIDI mapper to make non-GM devices adhere to the GM scheme. General MIDI can use from 10 to all 16 MIDI channels, assigning one melodic instrument to each channel except channel 10. Channel 10 is reserved for percussion instruments.

■ *MPU-401* is the model number of the first widely distributed MIDI adapter card for PCs, which was developed by Roland Corporation. The MPU-401 converts signals on your computer's bus directed to the card into MIDI messages and vice versa. Windows 95 includes a protected-mode MPU-401 driver for the adapter card, as well as other synthesizer cards that adhere to the Roland standard, such as Roland's original MT-32 (not GM-compliant) and the current SCC-1 Sound Canvas GS/GM card.

■ *Sequencers* record and play back MIDI messages, usually in the form of files in standard MIDI format (SMF) files carrying a MID extension. Many keyboard synthesizers (called *music workstations*) include sequencers implemented by hardware. A wide variety of sequencer and related applications are available for Windows. Windows 95 includes full support for type 0 and type 1 SMF files, and the new PolyMessage MIDI frees your computer's processor from overload on complex MIDI passages. Windows 95 supports long file names, so you can finally name your MIDI file Beethoven's Fifth Symphony instead of BEETH5TH.MID.

Specifying a Windows 95-Ready Audio Adapter Card

One of the problems with buying a preconfigured multimedia PC carrying the MPC2 logo is that you're likely to receive the lowest-cost audio adapter card available or get limited audio features built into the motherboard. A multimedia PC that meets only the Level 1 requirements of the Multimedia PC Specification 2.0 described in Chapter 7, "Interacting with Windows 95 Multimedia," isn't a satisfactory platform for the multimedia sound of 1995 and beyond. Even MPC Level 2 compliance doesn't guarantee your satisfaction with the quality of the sound emitted by an audio adapter card, especially if you have good ears or are musically inclined. The following sections describe what to look for when you're buying a Windows 95-ready sound card, in the approximate order of the subject's importance.

Plug and Play Sound Cards

Plug and Play installation of audio adapter cards probably will be the most important contribution of Windows 95 to the world of PC sound and music. If you've successfully installed a conventional audio adapter card in a PC, especially a networked PC with some extra specialized adapter cards, you deserve a "Qualified PC Technician" certificate. Finding unoccupied IRQs and I/O ports so your sound card doesn't disable another device in your PC requires the deductive powers of Agatha Christie's Hercule Poirot. The problem with Plug and Play sound cards is that you'll probably need a new PC (or motherboard) with Plug and Play BIOS and you aren't likely to find a wide variety of fully Plug and Play-compliant audio adapter cards when Microsoft releases Windows 95. Creative Labs promises to have jumperless Plug and Play-compliant Sound Blaster products on the retail shelves for the official release of Windows 95. No other sound board manufacturers contacted during the course of writing this book were willing to commit to release dates for Plug and Play-compatible products.

◀ See Chapter 2, "Making Hardware Plug and Play"

II

Exploring Multimedia

Media Vision's current series Pro Audio Spectrum (PAS) boards are *almost* Plug and Play compliant. According to Glen Gottlieb, Media Vision's product-line manager for sound and video, the firm had the foresight when it designed the original Pro Audio Spectrum products to eliminate the jumpers most other sound cards use for selecting IRQs and base I/O addresses. Media Vision PAS products use software to set the IRQs and I/O addresses and store these settings in on-board memory. (Only two jumpers appear on PAS boards that include a SCSI adapter; these jumpers are used to set the SCSI address, which you seldom need to change from the default values.) Windows 95 includes the drivers for the complete line of Media Vision products, ranging from the original 8-bit Thunder Board to the current 16-bit PAS series that offers optional 3-D sound and wavetable MIDI synthesis. Although current PAS cards technically aren't fully Plug and Play compliant, they behave as though they are. Windows 95 identifies the presence of a PAS board and automatically loads the proper driver, which in turn establishes non-conflicting settings for the card. If you want to buy a mainstream sound card today that's ready for Windows 95 in 1995, your best bet is one of the Media Vision boards.

> **Note**
>
> Even if the preconfigured multimedia PC you buy claims to have a Plug and Play BIOS or a flash BIOS that's Plug and Play-ready, there's no guarantee that the audio adapter card or the audio chips on the motherboard follow the Plug and Play rules. Make sure before you buy an MPC that you can remove or disable the drivers from within Windows 95 if you replace the sound card. If the sound chips are on the motherboard, be sure that you can disable the audio devices and add a sound card from within Windows 95, without the need to manipulate jumpers.

Wavetable vs. FM MIDI Synthesis

One of the most important distinctions between audio adapter cards is the method by which the card implements MIDI synthesis. The original Sound Blaster card and all the Sound Blaster cards that have followed it to date use a technique called *digital FM (frequency modulation)* synthesis to emulate musical instruments. FM synthesis was invented in the early 1980s by John Chowning, then a graduate student at Stanford University. Stanford granted Yamaha Corporation, the largest Japanese musical instrument manufacturer, an exclusive license to use FM synthesis. The first widely distributed professional synthesizer to use the FM technique was the famous Yamaha DX-7, which is still used by many professional musicians.

The original 8-bit Sound Blaster card used the Yamaha OPL-II chip set, a two-operator implementation that emitted very "thin" sound that lacked the rich overtones that distinguish one instrument from another. Later Sound Blaster and compatible cards use the OPL-III chip set, which has four operators and can produce more overtones. The OPL-III is quite similar in sound quality to the now-discontinued Yamaha DX-12 keyboard synthesizer and TX-81Z FM sound module.

The early 1990s witnessed a major shift by professional-grade MIDI synthesizers from FM and other constructive synthesis methods to the use of sampled sounds. These new MIDI synthesizers, called samplers, can record an instrument's sound and create a sample that's stored in RAM or on a disk.

A process called *looping* lets a relatively short-duration sample be repeated to play a sustained note. Other parameters, such as attack, sustain, and decay are applied to the looped sample to emulate the waveform envelope of the sampled instrument. Sample playback synthesizers, which don't include sample recording capability, use read-only memory (ROM) for sample storage and are considerably less expensive than professional-grade samplers.

> **Note**
>
> Technically speaking, devices that use sampling methods aren't synthesizers because the sounds are derived by recording the waveforms of the originating instruments. Devices that use digital FM and other constructive methods of creating sounds, such as Stanford University's new WaveGuide technology, are true synthesizers. *Sampling synthesizer* and *sample-playback synthesizer* (or *synth*), however, are universal terminology of the music business.

FM synthesis is *passé* in today's world of musical synthesis. Virtually all the background music for today's television and motion picture productions is synthesized, in whole or at least in part. Don't even consider buying a sound board that doesn't have sampled (also called *wavetable*) sounds built in or offer the capability to upgrade to sampled sound on an auxiliary printed circuit board (called a wavetable *daughtercard*). Before you buy an audio adapter card, listen carefully to the sampled sounds even if you don't buy the wavetable daughtercard with the sound board. All GM wavetable devices support the same collection of instruments, but there's a perceptible difference between the implementations of different manufacturers. Following are some qualitative observations on these differences:

II

Exploring Multimedia

- Creative Labs' 16-bit Sound Blaster card's AWE daughtercard implements the E-mu Proteus 1/XR's sample set in 4M of RAM. (The Proteus 1/XR is a MIDI sound module used by many professional musicians.) The E-mu sounds are relatively pure (dry) tones, and you may find them lacking the acoustic ambiance added by reverberation provided by a digital effects processor.

- The Roland SCC-1, SCD-10 daughtercard, and MPC-compliant RAP-10 Roland Audio Producer adapter cards use the 4M of samples of the Roland Sound Canvas modules. The Roland SCC-1 Sound Canvas board was the first popularly priced GM/GS audio adapter card and quickly became the standard to which all other wavetable cards are compared. The Roland cards have built-in reverberation and chorus effects that, at their default settings, create a "wet" sound that's more lifelike. (Reverb and chorus are echo effects created by adding delayed copies of the original waveform to the sound.) Several Windows MIDI sequencer applications—for example, Midisoft's Recording Session included with several sound boards—have "knobs" that let you adjust the depth (amount) of both effects. Roland's acoustic grand piano patch (sound or voice) is hard to beat. The SCC-1 works fine with Windows 95's built-in MPU-401 driver. The SCD-10 can be plugged into the Wave Blaster connector of all 16-bit Sound Blaster cards. The Roland SCD-13 provides a wider range of samples at a somewhat higher price.

- The Media Vision wavetable daughtercard provides 4M of samples from Korg's 03R/W GM synthesizer. Korg Corporation, like Roland, is a large Japanese electronics firm that produces performance-grade keyboard synthesizers and sound modules. Many Korg sounds, especially those instruments associated with rock and jazz tunes, have an "upbeat" feel, and Korg has always been noted for its professional-quality piano voices. Like the Roland cards, the Media Vision daughtercard offers adjustable reverberation and chorus effects. You also can upgrade a Sound Blaster 16 board that has a Wave Blaster connector to Korg sounds with the Media Vision daughtercard.

- The Advanced Gravis UltraSound card is unique because its samples are stored in RAM, not in ROM. You load the standard General MIDI samples into the UltraSound's 512K of memory during the computer's boot process. (You can increase the amount of RAM to 1M by adding a single chip.) This means that you can record your own sound samples, use the waveform audio file editor to modify the sample WAV files, load the edited file into the UltraSound, and then play it as an instrument. The off-the-shelf UltraSound card has 1/8 of the sample storage of most sound boards that use ROM, which limits the fidelity of the samples to the sound of the original instrument. However, the UltraSound card is priced competitively with cards that offer only FM synthesis, and creating your own samples can be fun. The UltraSound MAX comes with WinSoft SoundStation, Midisoft's Recording Studio, Howling Dog Software's Power Chords, and Turtle Beach's Wave Lite for Windows, plus DOS applications.

■ Turtle Beach Systems offers four sound cards, each of which uses the ICS WaveFront sampling technology. The Monterey board combines 16-bit, 44.1 KHz stereo digital audio recording and playback with the WaveFront MIDI sounds for full MPC-II Level 2 compliance. (The Monterey replaces Turtle Beach's widely acclaimed MultiSound board, which is no longer in production. The MultiSound used the E-mu Proteus 1/XR sample set, modified by Turtle Beach. The WaveFront samples aren't the same as those of the MultiSound.) Turtle Beach's Rio is a Wave Blaster-compatible daughtercard using the WaveFront samples. The Rio card includes a socket for a 0.5M, 1M, or 2M SIMM (Standard In-line Memory Module) that you can use to store your own sound samples. Maui is a plug-in card that adds wavetable synthesis to systems with sound cards that don't have a Wave Blaster connector. Tropez is a multipurpose board designed for PC game compatibility. In Fall 1994, Turtle Beach released the Monte Carlo, a low-cost, game-oriented sound card that uses the firm's new V-Synth technology to provide software-driven 32-voice polyphony with wavetable sounds. (You need an 80486 or better PC to make V-Synth synthesis work.)

II

Exploring Multimedia

Note

If you have a 16-bit Sound Blaster card or any other sound card with a Wave Blaster-compatible connector, the easiest and least costly way to add wavetable MIDI synthesis to your system is to buy a wavetable daughtercard. Simply plug the daughtercard into the Wave Blaster connector, and the wavetable sounds replace the FM sounds of the OPL-III. In most cases, you don't need to make any changes to the drivers for your sound card—it's all automatic.

Of the four wavetable daughtercards tested for writing this chapter, the Roland SCD-10 was the winner for sample quality and musical "presence." Evaluating waveform synthesis cards is a very subjective process, so you should compare the sounds yourself, if possible. Few retailers, however, provide the facilities for side-by-side comparison of sound card quality.

Sound Card Digital and Analog Audio Quality

Most 16-bit audio adapter cards provide high-quality sound from 16-bit, 44.1 KHz WAV files, but some exhibit higher fidelity reproduction than others. What you hear is the output of the card's digital-to-analog converter and line or speaker amplifier, together with any noise that's contributed by the card's circuitry and stray electromagnetic fields emanating from your computer's components. If the card's DAC isn't up to snuff or compromises are made in the output amplifier section, frequency response, total harmonic distortion, and signal-to-noise ratio suffer. Improper shielding of the analog sections of the board leads to induced noise; audible noise can be quite distracting. Many early sound cards, with the exception of Turtle Beach's MultiSound, were quite noisy and exhibited substantial harmonic distortion. Most of today's 16-bit sound cards come close to audio CD quality. As with wavetable synthesized sound, it's best to test the performance of a sound card's waveform audio recording and reproduction at the 44.1 KHz, 16-bit stereo setting before you buy it.

Note

The Roland RAP-10 sound card offers the unique capability of adding programmable reverberation and chorus effects when recording waveform audio files. The Roland Audio Tools software that accompanies the RAP-10 lets you create a new type of sound file, called *WaMI* (WaveAudio/MIDI), that combines waveform audio and MIDI signals in a single WAM file.

Sound Enhancement Systems

The two primary sound enhancement systems, which contribute a three-dimensional quality to your perception of sound, are Dolby Laboratories' Surround Sound and Sound Retrieval Systems' SRS 3-D sound circuitry. Surround Sound—now a common feature of high-end consumer audio equipment—requires additional speaker(s) placed behind the listener to achieve its 3-D effect. Advanced Gravis, for example, offers a Surround Sound option for its audio adapter cards. SRS, an offshoot of defense contractor Hughes Aircraft, has developed circuitry that uses a psychoacoustic method to create 3-D effects with a standard pair of stereo speakers or headphones. Media Vision offers SRS 3-D sound in its Premium 3-D sound card product line. Aside from the need for additional speakers, the primary advantage of the SRS method is that it doesn't require the special recording techniques needed to gain the full benefits of Surround Sound. According to Media Vision's Glen Gottlieb, SRS 3-D "makes any sound, including Surround Sound, better." Gottlieb says that double-blind tests conducted in shopping malls showed users preferred SRS 3-D sound for computer games by a margin of better than 2 to 1 compared to unenhanced sound.

Sound enhancement, like other digital effects, is a perceptive process and thus a matter of personal taste. Whether you like music "wet" or "dry," is strictly your choice. Most recorded music, especially of the rock variety, is mixed with a variety of depthy effects designed to add "presence" to the song. Sound enhancement simply adds to the presence; SRS 3-D is especially effective in adding lifelike realism to the soundtracks of computer games.

Digital Signal Processors

A new trend in sound cards is to use programmable *digital signal processors* (DSPs) to perform operations normally handled by your computer's micro-processor. DSPs are a special category of microprocessor devoted to handling streams of data, such as digital audio and video signals, modem communica-tion, and the like. Most audio adapter cards use dedicated DSPs that are pre-programmed by the manufacturer; the programs are stored in on-board ROM. Programmable DSPs, as defined in this book, use your computer's RAM or on-board RAM chips to store programs and data. The manufacturer, third-party software suppliers, and dedicated amateur programmers can write drivers to use the DSP for a variety of purposes. The most common applications for programmable DSPs are to emulate software codecs and to add digital effects, such as reverberation, to wavetable MIDI and digital audio sounds.

The Turtle Beach MultiSound board was the first PC sound card to offer a programmable DSP. The MultiSound's DSP is programmed by the Turtle Beach driver to provide hardware decompression of digital audio files com-pressed with the standard Microsoft ADPCM codec. As noted earlier in this chapter, the Advanced Gravis UltraSound and Turtle Beach Rio boards in-clude a programmable DSP that lets you create your own sound samples. Creative Labs offers the ASP (Advanced Signal Processing) option for Sound Blaster cards. You plug the ASP chip into a socket on the Sound Blaster 16 and gain hardware compression and decompression of waveform audio signals. Using the DSP instead of your computer's processor to handle the codec's job frees resources to handle other simultaneous operations, such as painting digital video on your display. You'll see a variety of new audio adapter cards that use programmable DSPs in 1995 and beyond.

▶ See Chapter 10, "Watching *Real* Digital Video"

According to a story titled, "Making the PC a Multimedia Speed Demon," in the March 28, 1994, issue of *Business Week*, Microsoft, IBM, AT&T, and other suppliers were developing a standard Windows application programming interface (API) for enabling programmable DSPs to work with Windows 95.

II

Exploring Multimedia

The forthcoming 32-bit DSP API is initially intended primarily to support DSPs used in modems and other communications-related devices that use Microsoft's Telephony API (TAPI). In all likelihood, sound card manufacturers ultimately will adopt the DSP API standards so that custom software written for one card's DSP will work with a card from another manufacturer. The DSP API probably won't be finished in time to be included with Windows 95, so DSP device suppliers will provide the required support software on their installation disks.

> **Note**
>
> You may not need a DSP adapter card for your Pentium PC when the "Intel building DSP functions into Pentium CPU" story that appeared Oct. 17, 1994, issue of *PC Week* magazine becomes fact. According to the story, Intel "has teamed up with developer Spectron Microsystems Inc., of Santa Barbara, Calif., to provide a version of Spectron's Spox DSP (digital-signal processor) operating environment for Pentium CPUs that will work with Microsoft Corp.'s Windows 95 and Windows 3.1. IA-Spox lets users perform signal processing functions directly on the CPU, rather than requiring them to install DSP-based add-in cards for digital video and audio capture and playback."

Using Windows 95's Audio Compression Manager and Wave Mapper

Windows 95's new Audio Compression Manager (ACM) makes playing back compressed audio files a snap. Figure 9.1 at the beginning of this chapter shows a list of the software audio codecs included with Windows 95. When you play a WAV digital audio file that was created with any standard codec, the ACM opens the appropriate codec driver automatically, creating a software decoding "layer" between the data in the file and the data sent to your audio adapter card via the card's assigned DMA channel. Without going into a discourse on the relative merits of each codec, following is a list of Windows 95's standard codecs:

- *IMA ADPCM CODEC* is designed for compressing 16-bit WAV files by up to a ratio of about 4 to 1 without significant loss of fidelity. The IMA codec is designed primarily for music. Figure 9.2 shows the property page for the IMA codec set for recording 16-bit samples at either 44.1 KHz (mono) or 22.05 KHz (stereo).

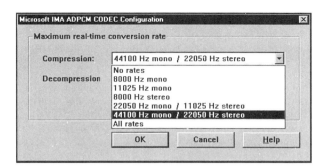

■ *ADPCM CODEC*, a general-purpose codec developed by Microsoft, is included primarily for backward compatibility with WAV files recorded in this format. The IMA and TrueSpeech codecs offer improved compression for music and voice data, respectively.

■ *GSM 6.10 Audio CODEC* compresses and decompresses files in accordance with the European Telecommunications Standards Institute's Group Special Mobile (ETSI-GSM) recommendation 6.10. GSM 6.10 is used primarily for cellular telephone communication.

■ *CCITT G.711 A-law and u-law CODEC* uses the Consultative Committee for International Telephone and Telegraph's G.711 algorithms for compressing speech. These codecs, sometimes called *companders* (compressors/expanders), also are widely used for telecommunication in North America.

■ *DSP Group TrueSpeech Software codec* is a highly efficient voice-only codec (called a *vocoder*, for voice encoder) that Microsoft licensed from the DSP Group, a Santa Clara, California, firm that specializes in vocoders. The TrueSpeech codec wasn't included in the early beta version of Windows 95 used to write this book. Thus, the name of the codec as it appears in the ACM's property page may differ from the name given here.

■ *Microsoft PCM Converter* alters the sample size (resolution) and playback (sampling) rate of conventional (uncompressed) WAV files. For example, this codec can convert a WAV file recorded in 16-bit, 44.1 KHz format to an 8-bit, 22.05 KHz file that the original 8-bit Sound Blaster cards can play. The ACM automatically invokes the PCM Converter codec when you open a WAV file with a sampling rate or resolution beyond the capabilities of your sound card.

If you have a sound card with a built-in hardware audio codec (a Sound Blaster16 ASP card, for example) or a card with a programmable DSP (such as the MultiSound), Windows 95's new wave mapper comes into play, making sure that the hardware rather than the software version of the codec is used. When you open a WAV file, the following steps occur:

1. The wave mapper checks to see whether the file is compressed. This compression format information is stored in the header section of the WAV file, before the waveform audio data.

2. If compression is used, the wave mapper next tests the capabilities of your sound card to see whether it supports the compression method directly.

3. If your sound card supports the file's compression method, the wave mapper sends the compressed data directly to the card.

4. If your card doesn't support the compression method, wave mapper causes ACM to search through the list of installed codecs that appear in the Audio Compression page of the Properties for Multimedia sheet to find the first compatible software codec. (You set the sequence of the search by clicking the Priorities button and setting the priority of each codec.)

5. If you don't have a hardware or software codec that supports the compression method, you get a `Can't play the file` error message.

Manufacturers of audio adapter cards with programmable DSPs can take advantage of the ACM, too. ACM drivers can be written to load individual sets of DSP software (called algorithms) stored in ROM on the card or in the DSP chip itself to support a variety of codecs. The advantage of ACM drivers is that you can choose the codec you want by altering the priorities in the Audio Compression page's list.

Making Sound Cards Play with Windows 95

▶ See Chapter 23, "Setting Up and Managing Windows 95"

When this book was written, built-in 32-bit protected-mode waveform audio and MIDI drivers were included only for Creative Labs and Media Vision products, plus the original Ad Lib card (the granddaddy of all FM synthesis cards). When you install Windows 95 over an existing copy of Windows 3.1+

with operating sound card(s), Windows 95's Setup program retains the entries required to use your sound card's existing DOS and Windows 3.1+ drivers in CONFIG.SYS and environmental variable entries (such as SET statements) in AUTOEXEC.BAT. Even if Windows 95 has built-in drivers for your sound cards, the Setup application installs the real-mode (16-bit) drivers; this process results in a high probability that your sound card will work when you first start Windows 95. It's very reassuring to hear your sound card play TADA.WAV when the setup application reboots Windows 95. The two sections that follow describe how 16-bit real-mode and 32-bit protected-mode audio drivers work with Windows 95.

Using Real-Mode Audio Drivers with Windows 95

If you've pre-installed your sound card(s) under Windows 3.1+, the 16-bit real-mode drivers for most cards work fine under Windows 95. For example, upgrading an 80386DX33 system (used primarily for musical composition with a fairly elaborate home MIDI studio) from Windows for Workgroups 3.11 to Windows 95 proceeded without a hitch. Windows 95 detected the Turtle Beach MultiSound and the Roland SCC-1 sound cards and then automatically installed the proper drivers for each card. The Roland SCC-1 Sound Canvas card uses Windows 95's built-in protected-mode MPU-401 driver, and the MultiSound runs under the version 2.0 real-mode drivers supplied by Turtle Beach, originally installed under WfWg 3.11. Figure 9.3 shows the MultiSound Hardware and Driver Setup dialog for the version 2.0 drivers opened from the MIDI page of the Properties for Multimedia sheet. After you install a card that uses real-mode drivers, you must assign a MIDI instrument to the card using the MIDI pane of the Properties for Multimedia sheet (see fig. 9.4). Both figures 9.3 and 9.4 are from the M6 (Beta 1) version of Windows 95; it is likely that significant changes will be made to MIDI setup operations in Windows 95 beta versions subsequent to M7 (Beta 2).

II

Exploring Multimedia

Caution

Before you run version 2.0 of the Turtle Beach diagnostic application, turn your speaker volume down because you may hear an alarming screech during most of the testing process. Despite the distracting noise, the MultiSound diagnostic application completed its tests without a hitch.

Fig. 9.3
The real-mode
MultiSound
Hardware and
Driver Setup dialog
with the Windows
95 look.

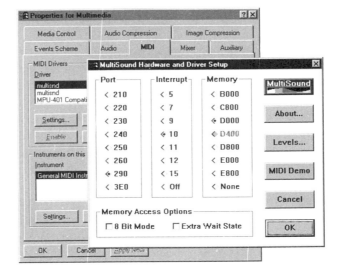

Fig. 9.4
Assigning the
General MIDI
instrument set to
the MultiSound
device.

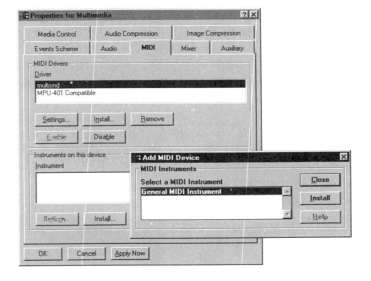

Real-mode drivers don't allow sound cards to take advantage of Windows 95's new features, such as preemptive multitasking, 32-bit operation, and PolyMessage MIDI. However, until you replace your audio applications, such as MIDI sequencers, with 32-bit versions designed to support Windows 95, you won't observe major improvements in performance. Playback of a complex MIDI composition for the Roland SCC-1 card having simultaneous pitch bends on multiple channels, appeared to be improved by use of the built-in 32-bit MPU-401 driver. Under Windows 3.1+ running on an 80386DX33 computer, this piece exhibited noticeable MIDI stutter (perceptible hiccups during playback).

> **Note**
>
> You'll most likely be able to install real-mode drivers for most sound cards from Windows 95's DOS prompt because Windows 95 retains the CONFIG.SYS, AUTOEXEC.BAT, WIN.INI, and SYSTEM.INI files for backward compatibility with Windows 3.1+. Installing the real-mode drivers for the Media Vision Pro 3-D sound card under a beta version of Windows 95 succeeded on one of the computers used to write this book. Suppliers of sound cards whose drivers aren't included with Windows 95 may need to provide a modified setup application, pending completion of writing and testing 32-bit protected-mode drivers for their products. If you plan on buying a card from one of these manufacturers, verify (preferably by demonstration) that the setup application works under Windows 95 before buying the card.

Installing Sound Cards with the Hardware Installation Wizard

If you have any of the Creative Labs' Sound Blaster cards or one of Media Vision's Pro Audio Spectrum or Thunder Board series, you can use the Hardware Installation Wizard (HIW for short) to set up the built-in protected-mode drivers for your sound board. If you're a Microsoft Access user or you've created pivot tables or graphs with Excel 5.0, you're already acquainted with Microsoft's new Wizards that automatically guide you step-by-step through a linear process. When you double-click Control Panel's Hardware icon, the introductory HIW dialog box appears (see fig. 9.5). Click the Next button, and the HIW asks whether you've installed the adapter card. If you click Yes and then the Next button, the HIW tries to detect all the adapter cards installed in your computer and the IRQ, DMA, and base I/O address settings the cards use (see fig. 9.6).

> **Note**
>
> You don't need to use the Hardware Installation Wizard for Plug and Play sound cards. Your computer's Plug and Play BIOS and the Plug and Play circuitry on the sound card handle all the installation details for you. The process described in this section applies only to non-Plug and Play sound cards.

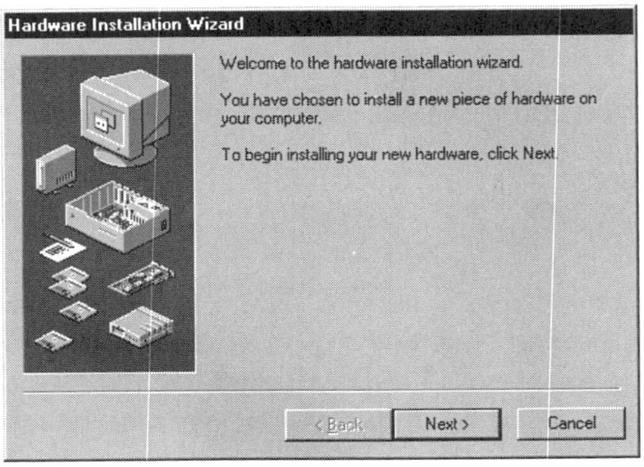

Fig. 9.5
The opening
dialog box of
the Hardware
Installation
Wizard.

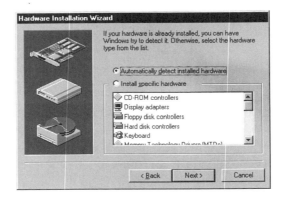

Fig. 9.6
The Hardware
Installation dialog
box that lets you
choose between
automatic
detection and
manual installa-
tion of drivers.

Depending on the number of adapter cards installed, the Hardware Installation Wizard may take a minute or two to perform the detection process. If
the HIW thinks the IRQ, DMA, or base I/O address settings of the cards conflict, it notifies you that the card will be installed in the disabled state. The
next step is to install the drivers from the appropriate Windows 95 floppy
disk or from the CD-ROM drive (see fig. 9.7). If an interrupt, I/O address, or
DMA channel conflicts with another adapter card, you see the dialog shown
in figure 9.8. Clicking the Start Conflict Troubleshooter button opens an
interactive help window that takes you through the troubleshooting process.

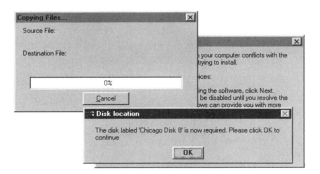

Fig. 9.7
Installing the
built-in protected-
mode driver for
the Sound Blaster
16 card.

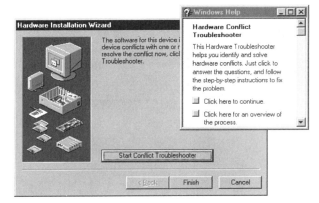

Fig. 9.8
The dialog that
opens when a
device conflict
occurs and you
click the Start
Conflict Trouble-
shooter button.

II

Exploring Multimedia

If the HIW installs your audio adapter card in the disabled state, you must activate the card by double-clicking Control Panel's System icon to display the Properties for System sheet and then click the Device Manager tab to display the list of devices installed in your computer, as shown in figure 9.9. (If you use the help system, the Properties for System properties sheet appears when you click the Click Here to Continue shown in figure 9.8.) Click the entry for the driver to select it, then click the Properties button to display the properties sheet for the driver and display the Resources page (see fig. 9.10). The two instances of the Creative Labs Sound Blaster 16 driver were used to generate the device conflict shown in preceding figure 9.8.

Fig. 9.9
The Device Manager displaying the driver for Sound Blaster 16 cards and compatible devices.

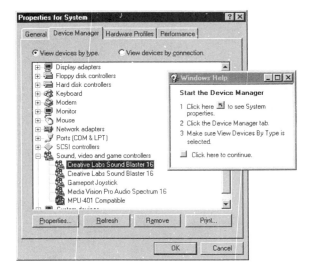

Fig. 9.10
The Resources page of the Properties for Creative Labs Sound Blaster 16 sheet with conflicts shown in the Conflicting Device List.

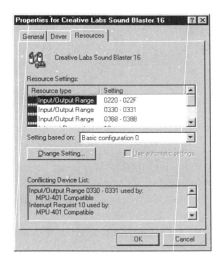

Finally, resolve the conflict by clicking the Change Settings button of the Resources page of the driver properties sheet to display the Resources page and click the Manual Based On option button to display the Edit Input/Output Range dialog. Change the value of the Input/Output range in the Value text box with the spin buttons to a non-conflicting setting, as shown in figure 9.11. You then click the OK button, close the properties sheet, and reboot your computer to make the newly assigned driver settings take effect.

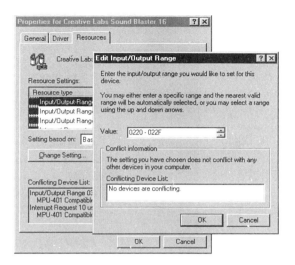

Fig. 9.11
Resolving an I/O
Range device
conflict with the
Edit Input/Output
Range dialog.

II

Exploring Multimedia

Caution

Windows 95 doesn't allow 16-bit real-mode and 32-bit protected-mode drivers
to coexist for a single device. If you install the protected-mode drivers with real-
mode sound card drivers in place, you must manually edit your AUTOEXEC.BAT,
CONFIG.SYS, and SYSTEM.INI files to remove the references to the real-mode drivers
and then reboot your computer. Real mode drivers are installed if you update to
Windows 95 a Windows 3.1+ system with a sound card or if you install a sound card
that isn't "Designed for Windows 95" under Windows 95.

Note

If the supplier of your non-Plug and Play sound card provides Windows 95 protected-
mode drivers, you use the Hardware Installation Wizard to install the drivers. Just
place the setup floppy disk in a drive and click the Have Disk button when it appears.
The supplier's setup application installs the drivers and guides you through the setup
process.

Running Audio Applications under Windows 95

Windows 95 includes two simple applets designed to play digital audio and other multimedia files and adds a built-in audio volume control with mixing capabilities. Fortunately, Windows 95 demonstrates excellent compatibility with existing 16-bit, third-party digital audio, and MIDI applications. Windows 95 has a new MIDI mapper and its own CD Player applet, neither of which were included in the early beta version used to write this book. The final sections of this chapter briefly describe Windows 95's built-in digital audio and media applications and using third-party sound applications under Windows 95.

Using Windows 95's Sound Recorder, Media Player, and Mixer

The 32-bit Sound Recorder (SOUNDREC.EXE) and Media Player (MPLAYER.EXE) applets supplied with Windows 95 are almost identical to their Windows 3.1+ ancestors. You can use Sound Recorder to record and play back digital audio files, with or without ADPCM compression, using real-mode or protected-mode sound card drivers. When you open a new file for recording with Sound Recorder's File New command, Windows 95 opens the Sound Selection dialog (see fig. 9.12). You can select one of three standard quality formats (CD, Radio, or Telephone) from the Name combo box. Alternatively, you can choose your own codec from the Format (driver) combo box and then select one of the compressed formats supported by the codec from the Attributes combo box, as illustrated by the lower Sound Selection dialog in figure 9.12. If you don't want to compress your audio file, the PCM Converter lets you choose the sampling rate and resolution for Windows conventional waveform audio format.

If you have protected-mode drivers for your sound card, Sound Recorder and Media Player let you play MIDI and digital audio files simultaneously (see fig. 9.13). Figure 9.14 shows the minimal version of Windows 95's built-in mixer applet (SNDVOL32.EXE) at the top left. Pressing Alt+E or choosing Expanded View from the control box menu (at the left edge of the title bar) opens the full version of the playback mixer, Volume Control (see fig. 9.14, top right). Pressing Alt+R or choosing Recording View from the control box menu adapts the mixer for recording from standard sound sources (see fig. 9.14, bottom).

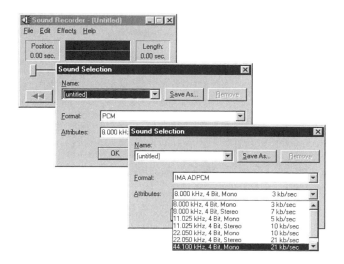

Fig. 9.12
Selecting a standard or custom audio compression format with Windows 95's Sound Recorder applet.

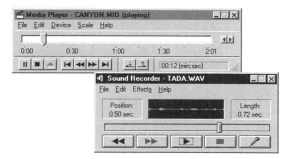

Fig. 9.13
Simultaneous playback of a MIDI file with Media Player and a digital audio file with Sound Recorder.

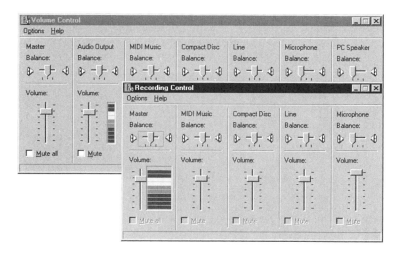

Fig. 9.14
Windows 95's mixer applets: Volume Control for playback and Recording Control for recording digital audio.

II

Exploring Multimedia

> **Note**
>
> Most playback, editing, and other 16-bit applets supplied with your sound card will work with the card's real-mode drivers but aren't likely to be operable with Windows 95's protected-mode drivers. To use the new "Designed for Microsoft Windows 95" logo after March 31, 1995, applications must be supplied in 32-bit protected-mode versions that are compatible with Windows 95's protected-mode drivers.

Running Your 16-Bit MIDI Applications under Windows 95

◄ See Chapter 5, "Running Your Current Applications under Windows 95"

► See Chapter 23, "Setting Up and Managing Windows 95"

Most of today's MIDI sequencer applications seem to get along fine with Windows 95. Several Windows sequencer and musical construction applications—including Midisoft Studio, Cakewalk, Master Tracks Pro, Cubase, Band-in-a-Box, and SuperJAM!—were installed on the computer before it was upgraded from Windows for Workgroups 3.11 to Windows 95. Each operated as they did under WfWg 3.11, playing MIDI files through the MultiSound and the SCC-1 cards. Recording tracks from a Fatar System 90 88-key MIDI keyboard connected to the MIDI IN port of the MultiSound card proceeded without incident in tests made using each of the three sequencers. Windows 95, of course, lends its look to all your 16-bit Windows programs, including Windows 95's version of Program Manager. (ProgMan doesn't appear by default when you first run Windows 95 unless you install Windows 95 over an existing version of Windows 3.1+. If you use the dual-boot installation method, you have to add Program Manager to your Windows 95 desktop from My Computer or Explorer.) Figure 9.15 shows the program groups that Windows 95's setup application created automatically from the original WfWg 3.11 installation. Figure 9.16 illustrates the appearance of Midisoft Studio 3.1 playing in Windows 95, and figure 9.17 shows SuperJAM! playing its demonstration MIDI file.

Fig. 9.15
Windows 95's
Program Manager
sporting program
groups inherited
from Windows
3.1+.

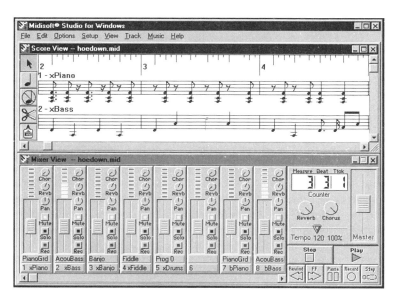

Fig. 9.16
The Windows 95
look added to
Midisoft Studio
3.1.

II

Exploring Multimedia

Fig. 9.17
SuperJAM!
running under
Windows 95.

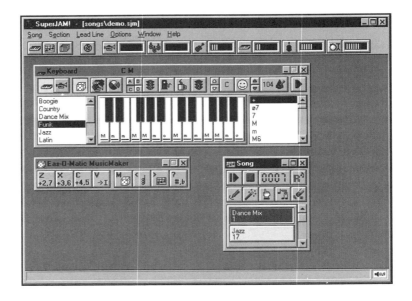

Playing Audio CDs with Windows 95

Windows 95 includes a CD Player applet that lets you play music during your
computer activities. You launch the CD Player, like other Windows 95 multimedia applets, from the Start.Accessories.Multimedia menu. CD Player's window, which resembles that of the CD player applets supplied with sound
cards, includes a toolbar and the standard VCR-like playback controls (see
fig. 9.18.) Clicking the playlist button of the toolbar or choosing Disc.Playlist
opens the Disc Settings dialog shown in figure 9.19. You can enter the artist's
name(s), album title, and track names in the dialog's text and list boxes. The
M7 version used to write this book, however, did not allow you to save and
load your playlist entries as a file. This oversight is likely to be corrected in
the final version of Windows 95; if not, there are plenty of CD player applets
which provide this feature.

Fig. 9.18
Windows 95's CD-
Player applet.

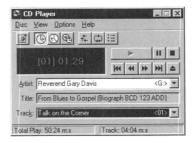

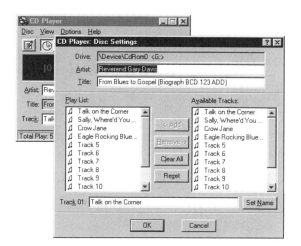

Fig. 9.19
Adding artist, title, and track information in CD Player's Disc Settings dialog.

Note

The M7 (Beta 2) release of Windows 95, which was used to write this book, appears to be missing some MIDI features that are likely to be included with later beta versions and the retail release of Windows 95. Basic waveform audio and MIDI functions performed statisfactorily with Sound Blaster 16 and Pro Audio Spectrum adapter cards using the Creative Labs and Media Vision drivers. There was no supplemental information on M7's MIDI implementation included in Microsoft's Resource Kit documentation for Beta 2. Advanced waveform audio and MIDI functions are among the most difficult to implement within an operating system because of the wide variety of audio adapter cards and MIDI devices that these features must support. Thus, you can expect continuing improvements to Windows 95's audio department until Microsoft releases the retail version of Windows 95.

Chapter 10

Watching *Real* Digital Video

Digital video has been the nemesis of PC hardware manufacturers, software suppliers, and CD-ROM title publishers. Microsoft's early Video for Windows 1.0 brought "dancing postage stamps" (160- by 120-pixel, 1/16-screen windows) to your PC's display. Now, 32-bit Video for Windows 1.1, which is built into Windows 95, brings you 320- by 240-pixel 1/4-screen "dancing credit cards," if you have a double-speed or better CD-ROM drive. (If you don't have a double-speed drive, the credit cards stumble rather than dance.) Credit card-sized images clearly are an improvement over the postage-stamp variety, but they're no substitute for a 30-inch or larger television set when it comes to playing interactive video games or even passively watching TV. PC users want full-screen, full-motion, interactive video; the problem is that pumping that kind of video data down your PC's bus takes a *lot* of horsepower.

PC users ultimately get what they want. Surprisingly, dancing credit cards add real zest to multimedia titles when used as illustrative examples rather than for their intrinsic entertainment value. Thus, Windows 95's implementation of Video for Windows 1.1 still has its place in the scheme of video things. For knock-'em-dead PC games and compelling entertainment videos, however, you'll need to add a moderate-cost MPEG-1 adapter card to your PC. Even a single-speed, 150K per second CD-ROM drive can play full-screen MPEG video, but a double-speed or better drive gives enhanced performance. MPEG video and White Book CD-ROMs are where it's at in today's digital video world, and MPEG's where it's likely to stay, even into the HDTV world of the (very) late 1990s. Thus, this chapter devotes much of its coverage to MPEG video.

A multimedia PC's place is in the home. Business uses of multimedia, although still promising, never achieved the status promised by the media soothsayers of the early 1990s. While this book was being written, Microsoft abandoned manufacturing its Microsoft Sound System audio adapter card, a product that was aimed squarely at business users. (The Microsoft card wasn't MPC-compliant and didn't include MIDI features.) The sidebar story, "A Pentium PC in Every Pot," in the July 25, 1994, issue of *Business Week* quoted Richard B. Pierce, Intel Corporation's multimedia marketing director, as saying that "about half of Pentium computer purchases are made through retail channels, indicating a strong consumer demand." As Pentium prices drop, it's likely you'll find a far larger percentage of Pentium-based PCs in homes than in offices and factories. As the *Business Week* story noted, "Home multimedia applications featuring sound and animation can require more computer horsepower than word processing and other office chores."

Combine a Pentium PC running Windows 95 and a triple- or quad-speed CD-ROM drive with an MPEG decompression board, and you've got a PC-video powerhouse that's not likely to be obsolete by the time you finish paying for it. Intel reportedly is planning to produce a Pentium processor with on-chip video decompression circuitry; when it's ready, you're likely to be able to simply plug such a processor into the PC's existing Pentium socket. This chapter, however, is primarily devoted to describing the new world of digital video running on the high-performance home "information appliance" that's available today. The fact that digital video is taking off at the same time that Microsoft is introducing Windows 95 isn't serendipity; it's just another part of the media convergence discussed in Chapter 1, "Building the 'Information Appliance' of the 1990s." Analog video buffs and home video producers get some Windows 95 goodies, too; Windows 95's new analog video overlay features are discussed at the end of this chapter.

Wading through PC Video Terminology

The introduction to this chapter uses terms such as *MPEG* and *analog video overlay* as though they were part of everyday English. If you're a video expert, you might want to skip this section that defines the terminology that you need to know to understand the significance of Windows 95's new multimedia features. For those who aren't video gurus, here's the lowdown:

- ■ *Analog video* is the present worldwide standard for television broadcasting, VCRs, and video laser discs. A varying voltage, corresponding to the brightness (luminance) of the image, creates the basic black-and-white TV signal. Color information (chrominance) is added to the luminance information to create a composite color signal; monochrome TV sets simply ignore the chrominance part of the composite signal. North America's NTSC (National Television Standards Committee) format delivers approximately 30 video frames per second. PAL and SECAM standards, which are used outside North America, deliver 25 frames per second. Each frame (one image) is made up of two interlaced fields; interlacing (displaying alternating lines of video in each field) reduces the apparent flicker of the image. Full-motion video is defined as the capability to deliver (or emulate) 30 frames per second to your PC.

■ *VHS* and *S-VHS* are the two most common analog video recording formats for VCRs. S-VHS (Super VHS, also called S-video) significantly improves video image quality, compared with VHS, by separating the luminance and chrominance data into two signals called S-video. Sony's Hi8 (8mm) format uses a similar technique and offers picture quality slightly better than the S-VHS format, along with a stereo digital audio sound track for dubbing, in addition to a stereo analog FM sound track. High-end TV sets and monitors offer S-video inputs.

■ *Video overlay*, also called video-in-a-window or ViW, is a method of displaying conventional analog video on your PC. Video overlay adapter cards, such as Creative Labs' Video Blaster, accept analog TV data from VCRs, laser disc and CD-I players, and TV sets; some even include all-channel TV tuners. The adapter card converts the analog signals to the digital RGB (red, green, and blue) data streams required to create images on your PC's display. Video overlay boards also can capture still images from the video stream and save the images in various file formats. Most video overlay adapter cards require an internal connection to your video display adapter card. Video overlay cards deliver full-motion video, but you need a VCR or other analog video source device to use them.

■ *ViSCA* (Video System Control Architecture) is a protocol developed by Sony Corporation for controlling VCRs and other analog video devices from the serial (COM) port of your PC. Microsoft adopted the ViSCA protocol for the new MCI VCR command set that makes its first appearance in Windows 95. ViSCA now is implemented only in Sony semi-professional ("prosumer") product lines; with the advent of Windows 95, you can expect Sony and other VCR manufacturers to add ViSCA control features to their high-end consumer products. Windows 95, like Windows 3.1+, also includes an MCI driver for Pioneer laser disc players that have a wired remote control feature. Descriptions of ViSCA and other features of Windows 95 related to analog video appear at the end of this chapter.

- *Digital video* records analog TV data in the form of computer-compatible streams of bits that can be stored on fixed-disk drives and CD-ROMs. The process of digitizing TV signals is similar in principal to the method of recording digital sound described in the preceding chapter. Digital video signals require drastic compression before your PC can even *hope* to process the data; video compression codecs are discussed in detail in this chapter.

- *HDTV* (high-definition television) will use digital video transmission methods to achieve unprecedented picture quality by the end of the 20th century. (Japan's present HDTV standard is analog video.) HDTV uses a new 16:9 wide-screen format that replaces today's 3:2 (768 x 486 or 720 x 480, CCIR 601) broadcast TV aspect ratio, which is similar to the 4:3 (640 by 480) aspect ratio of PC video display units. (You don't see the full 3:2 aspect ratio on your TV set because a process called overscanning cuts off the right and left edges of the image to prevent vertical black bands from appearing on the screen.)

- *AVI* (Audio-Video Interleaved) is the Microsoft standard codec and file format for digital video files. AVI files use adjacent CD-ROM tracks to hold digital and audio data streams so that slower CD-ROM drives can deliver sound synchronized with the video images. A variety of codecs that support the AVI file format are included with Windows 95.

- *MPEG* (Motion Picture Experts Group) is an international standard codec for compressing digital video data to the extent that up to 75 minutes of full-screen, full-motion audio and video signals fit on a conventional CD-ROM. This is no small feat and MPEG is a *very* complex codec; thus, hardware-assisted playback, in the form of an MPEG-1 adapter card (or a video display card with an on-board MPEG-1 decoder chip) is required to obtain satisfactory performance with MPEG. MPEG-2 is an even more complex video codec that can achieve broadcast-quality digital video standards with acceptable compression ratios.

- *Motion JPEG* (Joint Photographic Experts Group) is an alternative standard codec that applies compression methods originally developed for still images to digital video signals. Motion JPEG is not as efficient a compression method as MPEG, and this codec is of interest primarily to specialists in the graphic arts field. Motion JPEG requires a hardware codec; the majority of Motion JPEG boards are priced in the $2,000 range.

The terms in the preceding list are described in the context of Windows 95 in the balance of this chapter.

Understanding Video Compression Codecs

Compression of digital video data is an absolute necessity. It takes about 5M to store 1 second of uncompressed digitized color video; thus, a standard 640M CD-ROM could store only about 2.2 minutes of uncompressed video, not including sound. There's no way a CD-ROM can deliver 5M per second of data to your PC; even if this were possible, your PC's internal bus couldn't handle the data. Thus, various digital video compression methods, implemented by software-based and hardware (adapter card) codecs, have evolved over the past few years.

Figure 10.1 displays a list of the codecs included with the M7 (Beta 2) version of Windows 95. The Windows 95 codecs are the same 32-bit codecs included with Microsoft Video for Windows 1.1; these codecs give about the same performance under Windows 3.1+, Windows NT 3.5, and Windows 95. The sections that follow describe these codecs, as well as other hardware and software codecs that are expected to be released for computers running Windows 95.

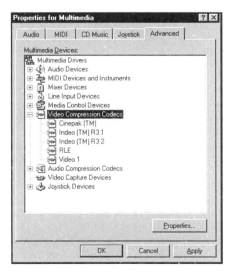

Fig. 10.1

The Advanced page of the Properties for Multimedia sheet displaying the video codecs supplied with Windows 95.

II

Exploring Multimedia

Symmetrical Codecs

Symmetrical codecs, also called *interframe* codecs, encode (compress) and decode (expand) video data at about the same speed. Thus, symmetrical codecs provide real-time capture and playback of small (320×240-pixel, 1/4-display) video images. The capture and playback rate, measured in frames per second (fps), depends on the capability of your hardware. Indeo, Video 1, and QuickTime codecs can achieve 30 fps on 80486DX2/66 computers with local bus video adapter cards. Intel uses the Indeo codec for its video-conferencing applications. Figure 10.2 is a simplified block diagram of the video recording and playback process using symmetrical codecs. During the recording process, a video capture card such as Creative Labs' Video Blaster provides the analog-to-digital conversion (ADC) for the video signal, while a sound card performs ADC services for the audio stream. The video and audio codecs compress both data streams, which are merged into an interleaved file on fixed disk. (Some codecs don't compress the audio data; thus, the audio codec appears in gray in figure 10.2.) During playback, a de-interleaving process separates the two streams. The video display adapter card handles the digital-to-analog conversion (DAC) chore, and the audio adapter card provides similar services for sound.

Fig. 10.2
A simplified block diagram showing digital video processing with symmetrical codecs.

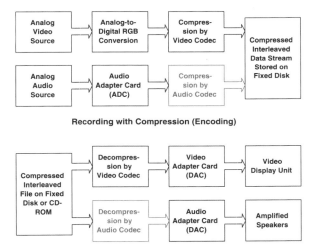

Following is a brief description of the symmetrical codecs included with Windows 95, plus Apple Computer's QuickTime, which is included because of QuickTime's prevalence in the Macintosh world and Image Entertainment, Inc.'s new dual-media titles for Macintosh and Windows computers due out in late 1994, or early 1995.

■ *Indeo* is a codec developed by Intel Corporation. Indeo has gone through several iterations, as evidenced by the three versions of Indeo included with Windows 95. The early versions provided about the same performance as Microsoft's original AVI codec. The latest version (3.2) gives about the same performance as Supermac's Cinepak, but compression is faster. Cinepak is one of the two codecs described in the following section. Intel supplies a moderately priced video-capture adapter card that provides built-in hardware compression for real-time video image capture and compression using the Indeo codec.

■ *RLE* (run-length encoding) is a simple codec primarily used for compressing still bit-mapped images, such as splash screens (the window that temporarily appears when you launch Windows 95 and applications). RLE works well for simple animations of line art, such as a dynamic bar chart, but is inadequate for digital video.

■ *Video 1* is a codec developed by Microsoft that is efficient (has low CPU overhead) and provides full-motion video of moderate quality, together with adequate (but not CD-quality) sound reproduction. Medio Multimedia, Inc.'s CD-ROM titles use the Microsoft Video 1 codec. Medio includes the run-time version (player) of Video for Windows 1.1 on each CD-ROM for compatibility with Windows 3.1+. Figure 10.3 shows one of the 320 by 240 video sequences on Medio's *World Beat* CD-ROM playing under Windows 95.

Fig. 10.3
A Video 1 sequence of African pop music from Medio Multimedia's *World Beat* CD-ROM.

■ *QuickTime* is the standard codec for Apple Macintosh computers. The recently released QuickTime Version 2.0 provides somewhat better performance than Microsoft Video 1 does and allows inclusion of MIDI messages, together with the audio and video data streams. You need Apple's QuickTime for Windows application to play QuickTime movies on PCs. Apple had just released QuickTime 2.0 for Windows when this book was written.

According to Michael North, president of North Communications, Inc., Apple's QuickTime codec provides the best performance on the 4 million to 6 million multimedia-capable Apple Macintosh and IBM-compatible PCs that comprise today's North American home PC market. North Communications is a leading supplier of interactive multimedia kiosks for customers such as the state of California, the Social Security Administration, and the Internal Revenue Service. Image Entertainment, the subject of the article, "Movies on PC Could Make This Stock Boffo," in the Aug. 1, 1994, issue of *Business Week* (mentioned in Chapter 8), was an early equity investor in North Communications, and North's firm provides marketing and technical consulting services to Image Entertainment. According to North, Image Entertainment's titles deliver 1/4-screen video on 25 MHz 80386 PCs and Apple Macintosh computers equipped with double-speed CD-ROM drives, and full-screen video is practical with Pentium computers. The Image Entertainment titles come with the Macintosh and Windows versions of QuickTime, so all you need is a sound card to play them on a PC. (Recent Macintosh computers, which North estimates comprise about 33 to 50 percent of present home PCs, have 8-bit stereo sound built in.) North doesn't use the symmetrical encoding feature of QuickTime; instead, the firm uses Sony's Betacam component video as the source, compresses the analog video to a 150K per second MPEG-1 data stream, and then uses a software conversion utility to convert the MPEG data, stored on optical discs, to the QuickTime format. This process lets North optimize the 256-color palette of the QuickTime format for maximum color fidelity on a scene-by-scene basis. As MPEG capability becomes common in PCs, Image Entertainment can quickly re-release its titles in White Book video format.

If you want to create your own digital video sequences, you need at least a simple hardware video-capture card (called a frame-grabber) such as Creative Labs' Video Blaster, or a combination capture-compression board, such as the Smart Video Recorder board manufactured by Intel. There are many other manufacturers of video-capture boards, which range in cost from about $300 to more than $2,000; the cost depends on the codec(s) the board supports, the board's capability to record full-screen, full-motion video, and other features implemented by the board. Matrox Electronic Systems Limited's Marvel II Professional Multimedia Controller was the most versatile video board available when this book was written. With all options installed, this $1,195 PCI adapter card provides digital video capture in Microsoft AVI format, MPEG playback, analog video overlay, a Windows graphic accelerator, and NTSC video output for VCRs (see fig. 10.4). Janet Matey, Matrox's marketing manager for video production, says Matrox is "betting heavily on the PCI bus for its future video product lines." Matrox plans to have a Plug and Play version of the Marvel II ready when Windows 95 goes retail.

Fig. 10.4

The fully loaded version of the PCI-bus Matrox Marvel II Professional Multimedia Controller.

Asymmetrical Codecs and Windows 95

Unlike the preceding codecs, which are capable of real-time digital video image capture from an analog video source, asymmetrical or interframe codecs use off-line compression methods. Off-line compression requires a professional-grade VCR (often called a VTR for videotape recorder) or a laser disc player that sends one analog video frame at a time to the compressing codec. Asymmetrical compression codecs spend a lot of time comparing successive frames of the video sequence, eliminating duplicate information so only the changes from frame to frame need be stored. Intraframe compression can reduce the video data rate by a factor of 100 or more, depending on the size and quality needed for the compressed digital video sequence. In addition to eliminating duplicate data, asymmetrical codecs also sacrifice some color fidelity for improved compression ratios. The human eye is much more sensitive to brightness than to color, so some chrominance information can be discarded to allow more luminance data in the compressed stream.

Note

Technically, the term *codec* doesn't apply to asymmetrical methods of encoding and decoding video or audio data. Codecs are, by definition, bi-directional—that is, decoding is precisely the reverse (retrograde) process of encoding. Codec, however, is now commonly used to describe any type of compression and decompression method pair.

Following are brief descriptions of the most popular asymmetrical video codecs:

- *Cinepak* is an asymmetrical codec originally developed by Supermac Technologies and licensed by Microsoft from SuperMatch. Cinepak provides the highest quality images and the frame rates of all the software-only codecs. To achieve this quality, however, takes very long compression times; 12 to 16 hours to compress 10 minutes of finished video is typical. Cinepak is used by CD-ROM publishers for Windows and Macintosh titles. Microsoft Home used the Cinepak codec to produce its *Cinemania '94* and *Dinosaurs* titles.

- *DVI* (Digital Video Interactive) is an Intel codec that can deliver full-screen, full-motion video. Encoding DVI requires a major-scale investment in a super-computer, and you need an adapter card to play back DVI-encoded video. DVI was adopted early on by IBM and other firms for use in multimedia kiosks and high-quality video presentations. DVI has not acquired a significant presence in the Windows multimedia market but is an important factor in IBM's OS/2 multimedia product line.

- *MPEG* is called an "open" codec because MPEG is defined by an international standard, ISO 11172-1, under the aegis of the International Standards Organization, a United Nations agency headquartered in Geneva. MPEG-1, the CD-ROM codec, is limited to the 150K per second data rate supported by single-speed CD-ROM drives. (TV broadcasters use megabits per second, corresponding to MHz, to measure data rate; the maximum playback rate of MPEG-1 is 1.2 MHz.) MPEG-2, in the development stage when this book was written, is a video compression method for TV broadcasters and allows higher data rates. The Hughes DirectTV satellites, SBS-1 and SBS-2, have MPEG-2 capability, and MPEG-2 decoders are built into the RCA/Thomson set-top boxes that connect to a small satellite dish. It's very likely that MPEG-2 will be part of the forthcoming digital HDTV standard. ISO 11172-1 specifies video and audio compression methods.

MPEG-1 was designed for continuous display of video images and doesn't incorporate VCR features, such as pause, rewind, fast-forward, and seeking to a particular frame or video sequence. Thus, "to-the-spec" MPEG doesn't qualify as an interactive multimedia format. Chris Kitze, president of Aris Multimedia Entertainment, Inc., started the Open MPEG Council in 1993 and put together a group of more than 40 of the leading multimedia firms, including Microsoft, to encourage standards for MPEG compliance by MPEG software and hardware suppliers. Aris is the publisher of MPC Wizard 2.0, a diagnostic CD-ROM for Windows multimedia, and a series of more than 20 Media Clip CD-ROMs that provide still images, video clips, and text background information on a variety of themes. As a result of the Open MPEG Council's efforts, Microsoft has added MpegVideo as a new type of video device to the Windows 95 MCI's DV (digital video) command set to provide VCR-like capabilities for MPEG-encoded titles played under Windows.

> **Note**
>
> If you want to learn more about the new MpegVideo device, download MCIMPG.ZIP from Library 4 of the Windows Multimedia forum (GO WINMM) of CompuServe. MCIMPG.ZIP includes Microsoft Word and text versions of the preliminary specifications for the MCI command set applicable to the MpegVideo device.

Unlike MPEG, Cinepak and DVI are proprietary codecs. Because of its costly encoding process, DVI will likely fall by the wayside as MPEG takes over the hardware-assisted digital video world. (DVI stands a better chance of survival in the Windows 95 PC market if Intel decides to base its future Pentium decoder on DVI instead of MPEG, but embedding a proprietary codec in the processor is a rather risky proposition.) Cinepak is likely to remain a player in the software digital video codec market because you don't need to invest in an adapter card to play back high-quality Cinepak-encoded images. It doesn't hurt business to have your codec included with Windows 95, either.

MPEG Cards and White Book Video Titles

Clearly, the most exciting event in the digital video business is the emergence of MPEG-encoded White Book CD-ROMs in the fall of 1994. Says Greg Jones, vice president of marketing for Sigma Designs, Inc. of Fremont, California, the leading manufacturer of low-cost MPEG hardware playback cards, "We're getting more than 20 calls per week from prospective publishers of White Book CD-ROM titles wanting to know more about our RealMagic product line." The primary advantage of distributing full-screen video on CD-ROMs is that the cost of duplicating, packaging, and shipping CD-ROMs is substantially less than that for VHS videotape versions. The primary limiting factor is that White Book CD-ROMs can hold only 74 minutes of video and audio. Thus, longer films require two CD-ROMs.

As mentioned in the brief definition of MPEG at the beginning of this chapter, you need an adapter card with an MPEG-1 decoder chip to play back

MPEG video and audio. Until recently, MPEG adapter cards sold for about $1,000 and thus had a very limited market. Now you can buy an MPEG-1 adapter card for less than $300, and support for MpegVideo devices in Windows 95 makes the investment worthwhile. "We at Sigma Designs are thrilled about Windows 95," says Greg Jones. "Our RealMagic MPEG playback card depends heavily on the computer's bus, so Plug and Play makes the installation process virtually transparent to the user." According to Jones, Sigma Designs has had a preliminary version of Plug and Play in the company's jumperless MPEG cards since introducing the product line in late 1993. Sigma Designs makes the under-$300 RealMagic Lite board that uses your present sound card for audio; the RealMagic board, selling for about $50 more, includes its own Sound Blaster-compatible audio playback system. Sigma Designs also supplies a CD-ROM upgrade kit that includes a RealMagic board and a double-speed drive. Figure 10.5 shows Windows 95 playing a scene from from the MPEG version of Crystal Dynamics' PC game, The Horde,included with the RealMagic MPEG-1 adapter cards. (Sigma Designs was in the process of changing the name of its MPEG product line from ReelMagic to RealMagic when this book was written.)

Fig. 10.5
Sigma Designs'
RealMagic CD
player showing a
scene from the
MPEG version of
Crystal Dynamics'
The Horde.

Julien Nguyen, Sigma Designs' chief technical officer, says Windows 95's Plug and Play features for video-related adapter cards is "a giant step in the right direction. Our Windows 95 drivers will take full advantage of the multitasking features of Windows [95], and we're promoting the WinG API to eliminate game developers' dependence on DOS. MPEG and WinG enable incredible entertainment titles. There's no conflict between WinG and MPEG; in fact, they complement one another." Nguyen's group wrote the microcode for Sigma Designs' customized version of C-Cube Microsystems, Inc.'s (Milpitas, California) CL-450 MPEG decoder chip. According to John Reno, product marketing manager for C-Cube, "The RealMagic board created the market, but firms like VideoLogic, RasterOps, Matrox, and TrueVision also have MPEG cards in the works." Reno says the CL-450 is the "universal MPEG chip" that's also used in stand-alone MPEG players, such as the 3DO and Atari Jaguar TV-top boxes. Reno expects all the manufacturers of audio CD players ultimately to enter the MPEG player market. By the time Windows 95 ships, C-Cube's successor to the CL-450, the CL-480 combining audio and video decoding on a single chip, will further reduce system cost.

By the time you read this book, entertainment industry watchers project that there will be more that 1,000 White Book CD-ROM titles, and a few thousand more titles of widely varying quality will fill retailers' shelves by the end of 1995. According to *Business Week*, Image Entertainment now distributes more than 5,000 laser disc movie titles in North America, including pictures from Walt Disney, Orion Pictures, Playboy Home Video, and Turner Home Entertainment. The article cites "talk" that Image Entertainment plans to release *The Terminator*, *Dances with Wolves*, *The Silence of the Lambs*, and *RoboCop* as some the firm's first QuickTime releases before the end of 1994. Michael North estimates that only about 500,000 PCs now are equipped to handle MPEG, so distributing QuickTime versions makes sense for today's market. North hedged his QuickTime bet, however, by creating MPEG-1 digital video masters during the QuickTime conversion process. When the MPEG revolution arrives and hardware suppliers and title producers standardize on one version of MPEG, Image Entertainment will be ready with an arsenal of White Book video CD titles from Orion and other filmmakers. Metromedia owns a major stake in Orion Pictures, Image Entertainment, and North Communications; they're all part of the same corporate family. Cross-ownership is another example of convergence in the electronic entertainment industry.

An alternative to playing White Book video titles on your PC is to buy a dedicated TV-top box. If Philips' experience with the low sales of dedicated CDi (CD-Interactive, formerly CD-I) players is any guide, dedicated Video CD players aren't going to disappear quickly from retailers' shelves. Although several TV-top MPEG players in the $500 range are expected on the market by the end of 1994, you'll be able to buy a double- or triple-speed CD-ROM and MPEG-1 card for your PC at about the same price. The PC offers interactivity, while most set-top boxes simply play the discs. Thus, it's likely that the "information appliance" will be the leading purveyor of White Book

II

Exploring Multimedia

video entertainment until the infobahn pipes on-demand MPEG through your cable connection or to your home satellite dish.

> **Note**
>
> When this book was written, DirecTV used the MPEG-1 protocol for transmission of digital TV programming to the DirecTV 18-inch satellite dishes and set-top boxes manufactured in Mexico by Thompson Consumer Products under the RCA trademark. By the end of 1995, DirecTV and the coowner of the Hughes DBS-1 and DBS-2 satellites, US Satellite Broadcasting (USSB), expect to have 2 million or more North American subscribers. DirecTV is scheduled to change to MPEG-2 encoding in early 1995. MPEG-2 is a much more sophisticated encoding technique than MPEG-1 and will make more channels available on the two existing satellites. Hughes expects to launch another satellite, DBS-3, in Spring 1995. This satellite also will be capable of transmitting digital data, including interactive multimedia content, to PCs. Chapter 13, "Joining the Microsoft Network," gives you further detail on the potential use of DSBS-3 to deliver interactive multimedia content to home PCs.

Processing Analog Video on Your Windows 95 PC

Although digital video gets the most attention in today's consumer arena, there's plenty of life left in analog video on the PC after Windows 95. There are roughly 75 million VCRs in North America, and desktop TV publishing (DTTV) with PCs has been gaining ground on the traditional desktop print publishing (DTP) business. The capital investment required to set up for DTTV was about 10 times the cost of a personal laser printer in late 1994 because you need at least two video playback and recording devices with wired remote control. But the cost to set up DTTV is far less than acquiring the equipment needed for conventional commercial-quality video editing. The widespread deployment of PCs running Windows 95, with its built-in support for remote control of VCRs and LaserDisc players, is likely to bring down the cost of remotely controllable video devices from the $1,000 and up "prosumer" price range to less than $500 by mid- to late-1995. The following sections describe the adapter cards required for processing analog video and Windows 95's new support for DTTV.

What You Need to Play and Record Analog Video

You need a video overlay adapter card to play analog video in a Windows 95 window. The video overlay card includes the analog-to-digital needed to convert the NTSC video signal to the RGB signals your computer's video display unit expects. Most video overlay cards use your existing video adapter card to process the video signal. If you want to use your computer's graphics capabilities to add still images and titles to your videotape productions, you also need a video output card that merges the PC graphics with the NTSC analog video signal by a process called *chroma-keying*. Chroma-keying replaces the area of a specified color in the video stream with your computer image. The Matrox Marvel II card, discussed earlier in the chapter, provides all these capabilities and includes the video display circuitry on a single PCI-bus card.

Note

The RealMagic MPEG boards, described earlier in this chapter, replace a solid block of magenta in the RealMagic demonstration player's window with MPEG video using the chroma-key process. That's how the firm's logo is overlaid on each demonstration video clip.

To create your own professional-appearing videotapes, you also need VCRs (or laser disc players) that can seek to a specific beginning video frame and then play a video sequence of a specified duration that's recorded on the master tape. This means that your camcorder must be capable of recording a time-code on the videotape. Professional equipment uses the SMPTE (Society of Motion Picture and Television Engineers) time-code; Sony's Hi8 camcorders and VCRs use a simplified version of SMPTE called RC (rewritable consumer). While one VCR (A) is playing a sequence, a second VCR (B) uses the time-code to seek the next sequence to be recorded on the master tape. This process, called *A-B roll editing*, is where Windows 95's built-in VCR commands come into play.

The VCR Command Set of Windows 95's Media

The VCR device of the MCI implements Sony's ViSCA protocol for video devices, which is closely related to the MIDI standard for electronic musical instruments. ViSCA uses one of the serial (COM) ports of your computer to connect to the ViSCA In port of the first of up to 8 ViSCA-compatible devices. Additional devices are connected by cables from one device's ViSCA Out port to the next one's ViSCA In port. Each device is automatically assigned its own ID number based on its position in the "daisy chain." At the time this book was written, only three ViSCA-compatible devices were in distribution: Sony's VCD-1000 Vdeck, a Hi8 VCR; Vbox, a device that adapts other consumer control protocols (LANC or Control-L and Control-S) to ViSCA; and the XV-D1000 Digital Special Effects Generator. Figure 10.6 shows a typical Vdeck and Vbox setup for creating Hi8 tapes. The Vdeck has an internal video switcher that accepts inputs from 1 S-video and 2 NTSC sources (you can fade between the sources) and an audio switcher with 2 line-level inputs and a microphone input.

Fig. 10.6

A diagram showing ViSCA connections between a PC and Sony Vdeck and Vbox devices.

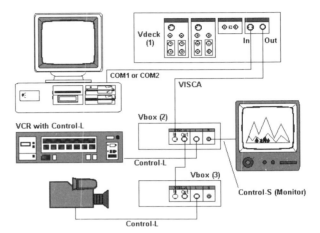

Figure 10.7 shows the Properties for the ViSCA VCR Device (Media Control) sheet that opens from Windows 95's Properties for Multimedia sheet. The MCI ViSCA Configuration dialog appears when you select the ViSCA VCR Device item and click the Properties button, then click the Settings button of the ViSCA properties sheet. You can assign the ViSCA device to one of four COM ports. (COM4 is the most common because your mouse is likely to occupy COM1, and COM2—which shares IRQ3 with COM4—usually is devoted to an internal fax modem.) You specify the number of VCRs connected to the ViSCA chain so that each VCR can be identified as data source and destination; alternatively, you can let the Windows 95 ViSCA driver detect the VCRs or Vbox devices in the ViSCA chain.

To run your ViSCA-compatible video editing setup, you need a video editing application that can use the ViSCA drivers. At the time this book was written, only a few commercial ViSCA-compatible Windows 3.1+ applications were available for A-B roll editing. Adobe Premier 4.0 for Windows, as an example, supports ViSCA devices, as does the editing application that accompanies FAST Electronics' Video Machine adapter card. Lenel Systems, Inc., of Pittsford, New York, one of the pioneers in developing ViSCA-compatible applications, offers OLE 2-compatible ViSCA applications and an OLE 2 ViSCA custom control (OCX) for use with Access 2.0, the next release of Visual Basic, and other Windows applications that can act as containers for

OCX objects. When Windows 95 is released, you can expect most suppliers of conventional and non-linear video editing systems, such as Matrox Personal Producer, to add ViSCA features to their new 32-bit Windows applications for analog video production.

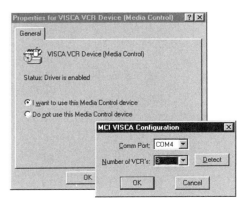

Fig. 10.7
Setting up a serial port to control ViSCA devices in the Properties for ViSCA VCR Device (Media Control) sheet.

Chapter 11

Taking Advantage of Windows 95's Game Features

This chapter takes a quick look at the promise that Windows 95 holds for game enthusiasts and game developers alike. Windows 95's multimedia features provide a leg up for many game developers, as well as ensure that future generations of games will continue to have new and exciting features for players. Also, Windows 95 supports Microsoft's special library of 32-bit high-speed graphics routines developed especially to support games in Windows.

This chapter starts by discussing how Windows 95's comprehensive multimedia capabilities enhance game performance and features and then discusses the high-speed graphics capabilities provided by the optional WinG graphics library. Finally, this chapter looks at how multiplayer games can tap into Windows 95's inherent network and telephony capabilities.

The Increasing Market for Windows-Based Games

So far, according to statistics published by Microsoft, games are the only remaining software products where sales for DOS-based software exceed sales for Windows-based software. The reasons for this situation are fairly clear, as shown in the following:

- The capability of producing high-speed scrolling graphics and animation—a required feature for arcade-type games and for most interactive action or role-playing adventure games—is essentially non-existent in

Windows 3.1+. In DOS, the game is the only application running, and it can take direct control of the video display, throwing images onto the screen fast enough to emulate real-time events.

■ To provide music, sound effects, or digitized speech—and to keep the sounds correctly synchronized with game events—the game application usually needs to take direct control of the system's sound components, conflicting with Windows control of sound components.

■ Most software game publishers can't count on their customers having the additional, optional Windows software components necessary to support advanced sound or video technologies that they might incorporate in a game. As a result, game publishers include their own internal or external drivers with the game, requiring the game to operate from DOS.

Because of these factors, DOS has remained the primary platform for game software. This situation, however, is likely to change rapidly over the next year or so, for a variety of reasons.

Apart from the simple fact that many hobbyist computer owners bought a computer with Windows ready to run precisely so that they wouldn't have to fool around with DOS and are now breathing heavily down the necks of software developers for easy-to-install and easy-to-run games, the anticipated rapid growth of the Windows game market will be fueled by three factors:

■ Increased support for interactive high-speed animation in Windows through the WinG additions. (WinG is discussed later in this chapter.)

■ Increased internal support in Windows 95 for multimedia adjuncts to interactive games, such as music, video clips, digitized speech, and so on.

■ The fact that many large-scale developers with projects initially conceived or developed for interactive television are piping their products into the interactive CD-ROM market. As reported in the May 2, 1994, issue of *Business Week* magazine, many developers regard the interactive PC game market as a practice forum to determine which types of content will be a hit when interactive television becomes a reality.

Many of Windows 95's new features will encourage game developers to create recreational software for Windows 95, and will actually provide indirect economic incentives for them to do so. Mostly, developing games for Windows 95 requires less development overhead than does developing games for DOS because games developed for Windows 95 can take advantage of Windows 95's advanced memory management (no 640K limit), built-in multimedia features, and hardware support (no need for game developers to create their own device drivers).

Note

Another incentive for game developers is the likelihood of increased consumer satis-faction (hence increased repeat sales) with products developed for Windows 95. Technical features in Windows 95, such as improved memory management, built-in multimedia support, and so on, translate into happier customers. People who just spent $60 (a typical price) for a computer game are likely to feel justifiably frustrated and/or cheated to discover that their new game won't run because there isn't enough conventional memory available on their computer, or that they can't hear music or speech in the game because the game doesn't come with the specific device driver for their sound card. (Memory problems are especially common with DOS-based game software—almost every game manual has a section explaining how to load device drivers into upper memory via CONFIG.SYS to make more conven-tional memory free for the game.) Solving game installation problems usually means the would-be game-player must make changes to CONFIG.SYS, wait to obtain spe-cial device drivers by mail, incur additional expense obtaining device drivers via modem, or experience some other unhappy delay. Even Microsoft has learned that product installation must remain carefree—consumers who have unhappy installation experiences seldom (if ever again) view that particular product favorably, no matter how good the software is once it gets running.

Installing Windows 95-based game software should also be much easier than installing DOS-based games. Because of Windows 95's device-independent architecture, there's no need for you or the game's installation program to add device drivers or TSRs to CONFIG.SYS or AUTOEXEC.BAT—the applica-tion will instead use Windows 95's device drivers. Since most technical sup-port calls for software of any type tend to revolve around installation and changes to CONFIG.SYS and AUTOEXEC.BAT, Windows 95 game software should find rapid acceptance with consumers.

Finally, Windows 95 game developers who use Windows 95's inherent capa-bilities to support their games' multimedia and graphics features can justifi-ably offload technical support issues to other vendors. If a Windows 95-based game component (such as sound or video) doesn't work correctly, the game developer isn't at fault (provided the game developer really has used Win-dows 95's virtual device driver interfaces). Technical support issues then be-come the responsibility of Microsoft or the specific hardware manufacturer.

◄ See Chapter 7, "Interacting with Windows 95 Multimedia"

The remaining sections of this chapter describe some of the benefits for game developers and consumers in Windows 95.

Inherent Game Support in Windows 95

Windows 95 has many features that, although not specifically designed to support interactive games, provide useful and powerful resources for game developers. Windows 95 features that inherently support game development and play take advantage of current improvements in hardware and software technology.

Software Enhancements Affecting Game Play and Development

The following list summarizes some of Windows 95's software features that support or enhance game development and play:

- "Hot-switching" of video modes is available. (Video mode refers to the current number of colors and screen resolution your display adapter and monitor are using; standard VGA video mode, for example, uses 16 colors and a screen resolution of 640 ×480 pixels.) With the right kind of installed hardware, Windows 95 can change video modes dynamically, without having to restart Windows 95. This means that a game program can switch to a suitable video mode on its own, without requiring you to make any specific alterations in Windows 95's display settings before starting the game. (This also means the game can restore the video mode in effect when it started, leaving your usual work environment clean and unchanged.)

- Windows 95 provides off-screen video buffering, a hardware-level capability not available in Windows 3.1+. Off-screen video buffering allows an application to assemble a graphic picture "behind the scenes," where the time required to paint the picture isn't as noticeable to you. Once the picture is assembled, it's then rapidly displayed so that, as far as you can tell, the picture appears instantaneously. Combined with the WinG features described later in this chapter, off-screen video buffering helps increase the apparent speeds of graphics and animation in the Windows 95 environment.

- Because Windows 95 provides device-independent color palettes, games written for Windows 95 will have a more consistent appearance on different video cards and display monitors. This will probably increase customer satisfaction, since what they see on-screen will more closely match illustrations on the game's box and what they see on their friends' computers—except for differences related to monitor gamma. (Monitor gamma is the term for how differences in the manufacture and performance of individual monitors affect the consistency with which colors are reproduced on different monitors.)

■ Because OLE is built into the Windows 95 operating system, game developers can include OLE functionality in their games easily.

This last item—adding OLE capabilities to games—has interesting ramifications for game players. Already, many game publishers produce modular or semi-modular games. For example, Origin Systems (producers of the popular Ultima role-playing games) has several games now in distribution that use modular components. In modular games, you typically buy a base game package and then buy optional game modules that provide things such as digitized speech or additional adventure scenarios that expand the base game.

Adding OLE functionality to a game will make it easier for users and developers to create and use expandable, modular games. As another example, some game developers produce a series of games that allow you to transfer your role-playing character to each successive game in the series. Frequently, you need an external utility program or special game module to transfer a character's attributes from one game in the series to another. With OLE drag-and-drop, the game player might simply drag the character from one game to another. If game manufacturers are willing to go along, OLE might allow you to share player characters among games from different publishers. Games might similarly share monsters, non-player characters (such as innkeepers, armorers, and street beggars), weapons technologies, or essentially any other game object among several different games from the same or different publishers. Who knows?—future game companies may specialize in developing buildings, landscapes, and "local color" characters for sale as development kits for other game companies.

The success of add-in editors that allow users to create their own dungeon levels, monsters, and other game elements for the DOS-based shareware DOOM game testifies to the popularity and desirability of user-customizable games. OLE functionality in a game might permit a much greater degree of user-customization for various game products.

II

Exploring Multimedia

Finally, OLE capabilities lend themselves to the creation of multiplayer games by making it possible to embed a game (or set of game moves) into mail or other documents to send to another player. Imagine playing chess (or any game played with alternate turns) by electronic mail: make your move, drop the entire chessboard into a message to send to your friend, and then receive the same board back containing your opponent's latest move.

Improved Hardware Device Management

Windows 95's complete support for Plug and Play hardware may indirectly stimulate game sales by making it easier for you to upgrade your system with sound cards, CD-ROM players, joysticks, or other devices that enhance game play, or make game play possible. If you feel more confident about making your own hardware upgrades, the theory goes, the dollars that you formerly spent for a technician's time may instead go into additional recreational software purchases. Also, because Windows 95 makes it easier to install new hardware devices (and for game software to use the installed hardware), it's less likely that installation problems will ruin your experience with your new purchases. Most users will be more satisfied with their purchases and, consequently, be more inclined to buy more games or game-related hardware.

Apart from Plug and Play, Windows 95's device-independent support for CD-ROM drives, sound cards, video displays, digital video, networking, modems, and joysticks, mice, and other pointing devices can only reduce the amount of time to bring new games to market and increase the playability of new game products. Developing games rapidly makes it easier for publishers to keep prices low; device independence also means more reliable games, and games that are more likely to use all the sound, video, network, or other hardware in your computer.

◀ See Chapter 2, "Making Hardware Plug and Play"

One notable trend in PC game software is the increasing tendency of game publishers to increase the realism of their games by including action video clips or by incorporating animation sequences based on video recordings of real actors. Windows 95's inherent support for video recording and playback supports this gaming trend.

Better Sound Quality and Improved Event Synchronization

Good sound quality in games simply increases player satisfaction—in fact, spiffy music and complex sound effects are now considered essential game features by many players. Games that use only the PC speaker for sounds are increasingly spurned as inadequate—regardless of the quality of graphics, animation, or other game features.

Windows 95's increased support for high-fidelity sound and music fits right in with game development and play. Threaded multitasking in Windows 95's operating system allows game developers to create games with separate threads to play music, providing a more seamless aspect to the game. By programming a separate thread to play music, game programs can avoid the "stalled" silences that occur in many contemporary games whenever software loads data (say, for a new scene or dungeon level) from disk.

◀ See Chapter 9, "Playing and Recording Hi-Fi Sound and Music"

Incidentally, game developers can also use this multithread capability to avoid the blank screens that occur in many games during scene changes—one thread loads the new data, while another thread continues with animation and screen updates, while yet another thread plays music or sound effects.

▶ See Chapter 22, "Understanding Windows 95's Operating System Architecture"

As mentioned earlier in this chapter, synchronization of sound effects with events in the game is very important. Correct synchronization of sounds with user input and on-screen events (such as a sword strike, explosion, or the splash of a character falling into a pool of water) is essential to a game's realism and playability. Games with poor sound synchronization are regarded as clunky by most players, and their satisfaction with such games is quite low. Games with poorly synchronized or no sound aren't likely to generate repeat sales for a game producer—customers will go for one that provides games with more auditory glitz.

The synchronization of user input with resulting action in the game is equally important, if not more so, than sound synchronization. Games that have a noticeable delay between your selection of an action and the result of that action on-screen really aren't playable—especially in role-playing action games that purport to simulate real-time events. Windows 95's scheduling and event-control options for multithread programs allow all game events, especially user input, to be coupled closely to their corresponding visual or auditory events.

WinG: High-Powered Graphics for Windows

Although not directly a part of Windows 95, the WinG library of graphics routines is available in 16-bit and 32-bit options, making it fully compatible with Windows 95's 32-bit system. WinG (an abbreviation for Win Games and pronounced win-jee) is a dynamic link library (DLL) that provides a group of fast screen-painting routines to Windows game developers (and developers of any other software applications that require extremely high-speed graphics).

To stimulate Windows game development, Microsoft provides the WinG library DLLs to software developers at no charge and allows the developers to redistribute the run-time components of WinG without a royalty fee. Only applications originally programmed to use the WinG DLL can make use of the high-speed graphics routines that it contains; all other applications use the standard graphics routines.

The graphics routines in WinG produce animation speeds and responsiveness that are usually found only in DOS-based game applications. WinG routines are optimized specifically to support all the graphic colors and screen resolution options that Windows 95 supports. Before WinG, games programmed for DOS achieved their high speed simply by taking over the video hardware and writing the graphics data directly to the video card's RAM. Windows 3.1+, which rightly generalizes operations performed on the video screen by requiring programs to write data on-screen through the GDI (graphics device interface), specifically prohibits the kind of direct writing needed for acceptable graphics speed.

Figure 11.1 shows an animated graphics screen from a shareware Windows 3.1+ graphics game. Notice that the animated figures in the game (the several tanks visible at the center and left of the game window) are rendered in a very simple fashion. Notice the corresponding simplicity of the terrain scenery visible in the game window. Most Windows 3.1+ graphics games are similarly plain and unadorned visually. Windows 3.1+ graphics games just can't produce high detail or use a large variety of colors without becoming unreasonably slow. This isn't to say that the programmers for various Windows games have done a bad job—it's just that they quickly run into the speed limitations of the Windows 3.1+ graphics capability.

WinG, however, provides game programmers with a device-independent bit map (DIB) to draw graphic images on. Programs draw their graphics images on the DIB and then use WinG routines to shove the image rapidly onto the display area, very much like the way current DOS-based programs place their graphics on-screen.

Figures 11.2 and 11.3 show two different game windows from a Windows version of the popular DOS-based shareware game, DOOM. (This version, now under development, isn't yet available.) This game, called WinDOOM, uses the 32-bit WinG routines. Animation speeds and action are comparable to those in the DOS version of the game.

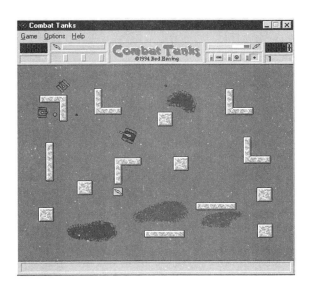

Fig. 11.1
Windows 3.1+ games tend to have simplistic graphics because of limitations in the Windows 3.1+ graphics capability.

Fig. 11.2
WinDOOM uses the WinG library to provide real-time animation and screen updating with smoothness and responsiveness to user actions.

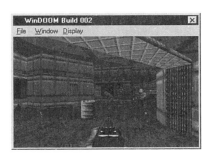

Fig. 11.3
Another frame from WinDOOM. The WinDOOM game window (shown at its default size) is the same size as the standard AVI window.

WinG and Windows 95 together create a game development environment that should make it easier to create full multimedia games that rival or exceed the speed of their DOS-based compatriots.

Playing with Someone besides the Computer

Even devoted PC game players will admit occasionally that they miss human interaction in games that can be played only with or against the computer. Many computer gamers want to play with or against other human players— either for hand-to-hand combat in action arcade games or for a team spirit in role-playing adventures.

Let's face it: If you have a good chess program, the outcome of games you play against the computer is much more predictable than the outcome of games you play against another human being. Even simulation games involving random numbers to determine certain events can end up being boring—once you develop a winning strategy, you can always beat the computer. A human opponent, on the other hand, will surprise you often, keeping games more interesting and lively.

▶ See Chapter 17, "Creating Workgroups with Windows 95's Peer-to-Peer Networking"

Windows 95's built-in network and modem support make it possible for game programmers to create multiplayer games easily. Because Windows 95 provides a uniform API for telephony and network connections, programmers can easily make game programs interact over network or telephone connections, making multiplayer games available to people in physically remote locations, whether that means across the office or across the world.

▶ See Chapter 12, "Connecting to the Outside World"

A new modem technology called VoiceView (expected to be shipped with almost every new modem sometime in 1995) allows the modem to share a voice and data call on the same line. Players will be able to speak to each other directly, while periodically allowing their modems to exchange data necessary for game play. This arrangement makes multiplayer games accessible to people who don't want the expense or effort of adding additional phone lines to their homes just to play interactive games occasionally.

To prove the feasibility of network and modem games, Microsoft includes a couple of simple multiplayer games, Rumor, with Windows 95. Hearts, originally supplied with Windows for Workgroups, is a computer version of the card game by the same name. One player on the network sets up as the dealer, and the other players connect to that dealer. Each player's computer displays the cards that are visible to all players, as well as the cards in that player's own hand. Figure 11.4 shows the dealer's screen for a game of Hearts.

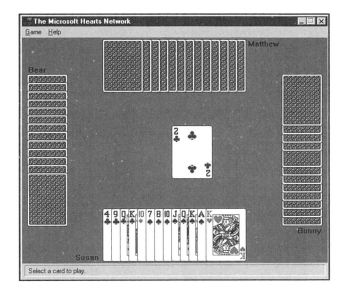

Fig. 11.4
The Hearts card game connects network users to a dealer. All computers display the same common face-up cards, plus one player's private hand.

The Rumor game simply displays a message bar on-screen. Various players post anonymous "rumors" onto the network—all computers that are running connected to the same game of Rumor receive the posted "rumors."

Although these multiplayer games may not seem very exciting, multiplayer, interactive action, and role-playing adventure games for Windows 95 are just around the corner. Since the DOS version of DOOM already includes network and modem player support, it's reasonable to assume that the finished WinDOOM game also will allow modem and network play.

Part III

Telecomputing with Windows 95

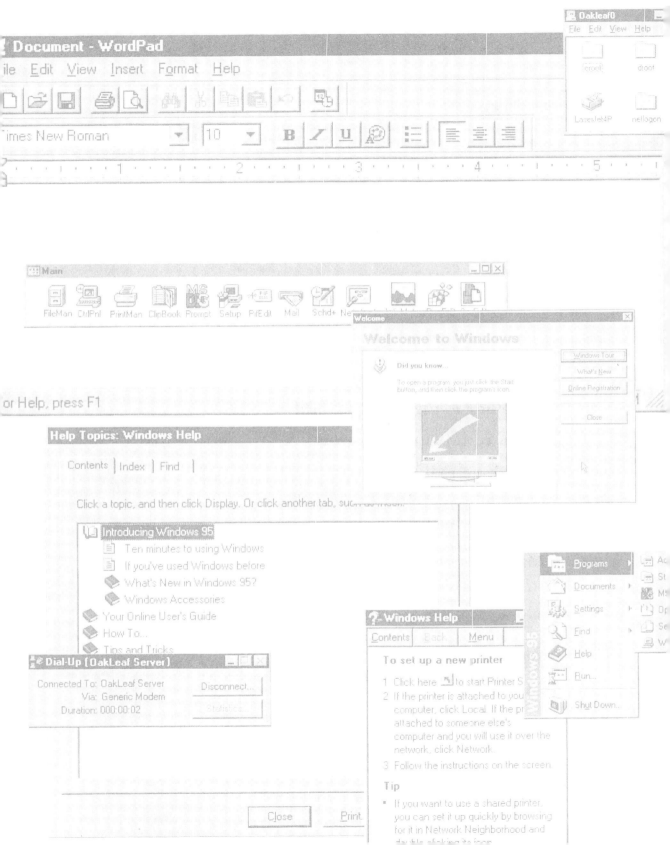

Chapter 12

Connecting to the Outside World

Windows 95's enhanced telecommunication capabilities rank with Plug and Play, improved networking, and upgraded multimedia capabilities as the most important new features that Windows 95 brings to Windows. Windows 95 is the first operating system to take full advantage of the basic features of Microsoft's TAPI (Telephony Application Programming Interface). This chapter describes Windows 95's 32-bit communications architecture, TAPI, and the Integrated Services Digital Network, more commonly called ISDN.

Windows 95's New 32-Bit Communications Architecture

Figure 12.1 is a diagram of the layers of APIs and drivers between Windows communications applications, such as the HyperTerminal applet included with Windows 95, and modems. (The arrows in figure 12.1 show data flow in the transmission direction only.) In addition to conventional modems, independent hardware vendors (IHVs) can plug their own 32-bit communications drivers and device drivers into Windows 95's COMM structure. Figure 12.1 shows IHV drivers for an internal ISDN board; however, Windows 95 can handle a variety of simultaneously installed communications devices, such as voice mail boards, PBX boards, and the like.

Fig. 12.1

A diagram of
Windows 95's 32-
bit and 16-bit
communications
architectures.

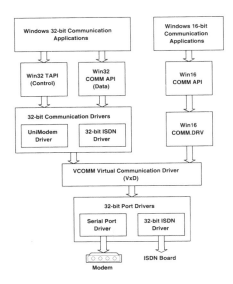

The most important of the new communications features of Windows 95 are
as follows:

■ The VCOMM virtual communications driver is Windows 95's new
32-bit layer to supply protected-mode services to applications that use
serial ports, parallel ports, or internal modems for communications.
VCOMM loads communications device drivers into memory only
when needed by applications, thus minimizing resource consumption.
VCOMM also is responsible for handling Plug and Play configuration
and installation of communications devices.

■ Applications call the Telephony API (TAPI) to control modem operations such as dialing, answering, or hanging up a phone line. TAPI—
the subject of the next section—provides a standard set of modem
services that all communications devices can use.

■ UniModem, Windows 95's new modem driver, is the layer that provides
services for data and fax modems, plus voice/data switching operations
for the new breed of fax modems you'll see in 1995. UniModem
handles specialized modem protocols through mini-drivers written by
the modem's manufacturer. Windows 95 includes a variety of modem
mini-drivers; however, the Generic mini-driver handles almost all
Hayes-compatible modems correctly.

■ 32-bit preemptive multitasking lets new Windows communications
applications handle much higher communications rates than the

monolithic, real-mode COMM drivers supplied with Windows 3.1+, which were limited to about 14,400 bps or less on slower computer systems. Many suppliers of high-speed modems wrote their own COMM drivers to replace Microsoft's version; this won't be necessary for most high-speed modems running under Windows 95.

Windows 95 provides modem connections for existing 16-bit Windows communications applications through modified versions of the 16-bit Windows 3.1+ COMM API and COMM.DRV that now communicate with VCOMM instead of directly with the modem or serial port. Third-party 16-bit communications drivers, however, communicate directly with the serial port.

Understanding the Telephony API

The Telephony API is a member of Microsoft's Windows Open Systems Architecture (WOSA) family. As noted elsewhere in this book, WOSA includes a variety of APIs, primarily for communication with databases (Open Database Connectivity or ODBC API), mainframes (Microsoft SNA Server), and providers of financial data (Real-Time Financials API, WOSA XRT). Basic TAPI delivers the following services:

■ *Windows interface to telephone features.* Today's telephone desk sets provide features such as call forwarding, call parking, speed dialing, and conference calling. According to Microsoft's Toby Nixon, chief architect for TAPI, most people typically use only one or two of the most basic features because they can't remember (or never learned) how to use the more sophisticated functions. Using a Windows interface to the telephone lets you set up a conference call simply by clicking the names of the conferees in a list box. Plus, you substitute a low-cost adapter card for the expensive desk set. (The handset hangs on the side of your monitor.)

■ *PC management of voice communication.* Windows lets your PC handle incoming telephone calls and can automatically control which calls reach you if caller identification is implemented. You can set up your system so that important calls are forwarded automatically to a different location. TAPI provides a streams interface to make integrating voice mail with other messaging services easy; Windows 95's new ADPCM voice compression methods make storing voice mail messages on your fixed disk practical. Thus, you can read e-mail and listen to voice mail from Windows 95's Exchange client. By the time Windows

III

Telecomputing

95 is released, a variety of moderately priced, TAPI-compliant PC adapter cards will be available at your local computer store.

- *Easy access to the telephone network.* Basic TAPI's modem control features let applications implement autodialing functions using a standard API. It's likely that every personal information manager (PIM) released in 1995 will include TAPI dialing capability.

TAPI is extensible; thus, third-party ISVs and IHVs can add features not supported by basic TAPI. TAPI specifies the following two interfaces and two devices:

- *Telephony API,* which is a set of function calls to the TAPI DLL (dynamic link library). Basic TAPI provides only call completion and termination services.

- *Telephony Service Provider Interface (TSPI),* which lets manufacturers of telephone devices and switches, such as conventional PBXs (private branch exchanges), write a standard set of drivers for their equipment.

- *Phone device,* which represents a standard telephone handset with a receiver and transmitter, plus a Touch-Tone (DTMF, dual-tone, multiple-frequency) dialing pad. The phone device can be implemented on an adapter card into which you plug a handset or a headset.

- *Line device,* which is any connection to the switched telephone network or a leased line. Line devices can connect to POTS (plain old telephone services), ISDN, and T1 lines, or any other type of network switch. A line device and phone device can be combined on a single adapter card. A line device also can be an internal or external voice/data modem under the control of VCOMM and the serial port driver.

> **Note**
>
> Voysys Corp. of Fremont, Calif., was one of the first suppliers to announce a moderately priced line device for automated PC voice response systems. According to the article, "The Smooth Operator on the Other End May Be a PC," in the Sept. 26, 1994, issue of *Business Week,* "VoysAccess software lets callers locate and hear, in a computer-synthesized voice, information managed by programs such as FoxPro, dBASE, and Visual Basic." Voysys released its first VoysAccess development kits for Microsoft FoxPro in November 1994. Kits that support Access MDB and dBASE .DBF databases are scheduled for release in January 1995.

Figure 12.2 is a simplified block diagram that shows the relationship among TAPI, TSPI, a phone device, and a line device. You can have as many individual phone and line devices as will fit in your computer's available expansion slots.

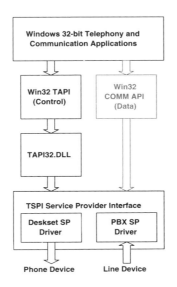

Fig. 12.2
A block diagram showing the relationship of TAPI, TSPI, and telephony devices.

Setting Up a Modem for Use by Windows 95

When you install Windows 95 on a PC with a modem, the Setup program detects the COM port to which the modem is connected and identifies the manufacturer and model of the modem. If the Windows 95 distribution floppy disks include a mini-port driver for your modem, Setup automatically completes the installation for you. If your PC doesn't have a modem when you install Windows 95 or you change the make or model of your modem, you must run Windows 95's modem installation procedure.

You install new modems by double-clicking Control Panel's Add New Hardware icon to launch the Hardware Installation Wizard (HIW). Figure 12.3 shows the second dialog of the HIW with the Modem hardware type selected. When you click the Next button, the Install New Modem dialog advises you to turn the modem power switch on, if you have an external modem, and close any open communications applications before proceeding with the modem detection process (see fig. 12.4). When you click the Next button, the HIW checks your computer's COM ports for the presence of a modem. If a modem is found, the HIW issues a query to the modem to determine its make and model, as shown in figure 12.5.

> **Tip**
>
> You can elect to have the Hardware Installation Wizard detect all of the devices installed in your computer by choosing the Automatically Detect Installed Hardware option (see fig. 12.3). The automatic detection process for all devices can take several minutes. It's much faster to select the type of hardware you want to install from the Install Specific Hardware list box. Detecting a modem requires only a few seconds.

Fig. 12.3
The Hardware Installation Wizard's hardware type selection dialog.

Fig. 12.4
The first dialog box of the Install New Modem wizard.

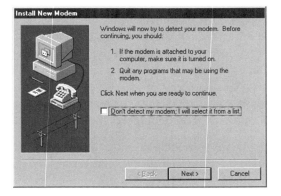

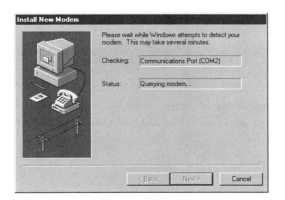

Fig. 12.5
The modem
detection dialog in
the Install New
Modem process.

If Windows 95 can determine the make and model of the modem and has a
32-bit mini-port driver for the modem supplied by the manufacturer, you'll
be prompted to insert the appropriate Windows 95 distribution floppy disk.
Otherwise, your modem will be detected as a Generic Modem, as shown in
figure 12.6. The majority of Hayes-compatible V.32/V.32bis/V.42bis fax/
modems operate satisfactorily with the Generic Modem driver. (An internal
Zoltrix V.42bis 14.4 kbps fax/modem is installed in the computer used to
write this book.) If you have a modem with special features that require a
device-specific driver, click the Change button to select the proper driver
from the list of the modem drivers supplied with Windows 95. If the driver
for your modem isn't on the list, you'll need to install the 32-bit driver from
the manufacturer's setup diskette. When you click the Next button of the
Verify Modem dialog, the final Install New Modem dialog appears as shown
in figure 12.7.

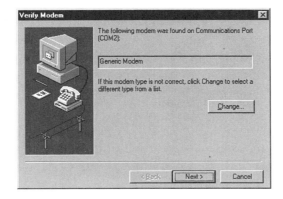

Fig. 12.6
The Verify Modem
dialog box that
indicates the type
of modem
detected.

III

Telecomputing

Fig. 12.7
The final dialog
box of the Install
New Modem
process indicating
a successful
installation.

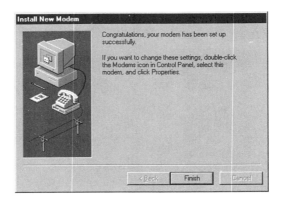

To change the settings for your modem, double-click Control Panel's Modems icon to open the Properties for *ModemName* Modem sheet. You can change the COM port and maximum speed for the modem in the General page, as shown in figure 12.8. Setting the modem speed to a rate higher than the modem's maximum speed is recommended; the 38,800 bps setting works well for most internal modems. The Connection page, shown in figure 12.9, lets you set the default connection preferences (data bits, parity, and stop bits) for your modem. Most bulletin boards use an 8N1 connection, 8 data bits, no parity, and 1 stop bit. CompuServe uses a 7E1 connection, 7 data bits, even parity, and 1 stop bit. Clicking the Advanced button of the Connection properties page displays the Advanced Connection Settings dialog. In most cases, you can accept the dialog's default values. If you have difficulty connecting to an online service, tick the Record a Log File check box to create a MODEMLOG.TXT file in your \WIN95 directory that contains an entry for each step in the connection process. Typical MODEMLOG.TXT entries for a successful connection to The Microsoft Network and a subsequent logoff appear as follows:

```
12-05-1994 18:55:48  - Generic Modem in use.
12-05-1994 18:55:48  - Modem type: Generic Modem
12-05-1994 18:55:48  - Modem inf path: MDMGEN.INF
12-05-1994 18:55:48  - Modem inf section: Gen
12-05-1994 18:55:48  - 38400,N,8,1
12-05-1994 18:55:48  - 38400,N,8,1
12-05-1994 18:55:48  - Initializing modem.
12-05-1994 18:55:48  - Send: AT<cr>
12-05-1994 18:55:49  - Recv: <cr><lf>OK<cr><lf>
12-05-1994 18:55:49  - Interpreted response: Ok
12-05-1994 18:55:49  - Send: ATE0V1<cr>
12-05-1994 18:55:49  - Recv: <cr><lf>OK<cr><lf>
12-05-1994 18:55:49  - Interpreted response: Ok
12-05-1994 18:55:49  - Send: AT<cr>
12-05-1994 18:55:49  - Recv: <cr><lf>OK<cr><lf>
12-05-1994 18:55:49  - Interpreted response: Ok
12-05-1994 18:55:49  - Dialing '8363844'.
```

```
12-05-1994 18:55:49  - Send: ATDT8363844<cr>
12-05-1994 18:56:13  - Recv: <cr>
12-05-1994 18:56:13  - Interpreted response: Informative
12-05-1994 18:56:13  - Recv: <lf>
12-05-1994 18:56:13  - Interpreted response: Informative
12-05-1994 18:56:13  - Recv: CONNECT 14400/ARQ
12-05-1994 18:56:13  - Interpreted response: Connect
12-05-1994 18:56:13  - Connection established at 14400bps.
12-05-1994 18:56:13  - Error-control activated.
12-05-1994 18:56:13  - No data compression.
12-05-1994 18:56:13  - 38400,N,8,1
12-05-1994 18:58:39  - Hanging up the modem.
12-05-1994 18:58:39  - Hardware hangup by lowering DTR.
12-05-1994 18:58:39  - Session Statistics:
12-05-1994 18:58:39  -                Reads : 2237 bytes
12-05-1994 18:58:39  -                Writes: 2224 bytes
12-05-1994 18:58:39  - Generic Modem closed.
```

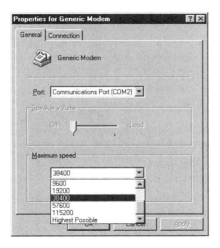

Fig. 12.8
Setting the COM port and maximum speed of your modem in the General properties page.

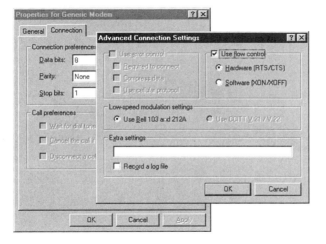

Fig. 12.9
The modem Connection properties page and Advanced Connection Setting dialog box.

III

Telecomputing

> **Note**
>
> If you change the modem installed in your computer, open the Properties for
> *ModemName* Modem sheet, click the name of the modem in the list box, then click
> the Remove button to remove the driver for the old modem before running the
> Install New Modem process for your new modem.

Communicating with Online Services and Bulletin Boards

When you have a modem installed and set up under Windows 95, you can
use Windows 95's 32-bit HyperTerminal applet or most current 16-bit Windows communications applications to communicate with on-line services
such as CompuServe, America Online, or Delphi, as well as electronic bulletin
board services (BBSs). The next two sections describe how communications
applications work with Windows 95.

Using the HyperTerminal Applet

Hilgraeve, Inc. adapted its commercial HyperTerminal application for
Windows 95, and Microsoft licensed a less-than-full-featured version of
HyperTerminal for distribution with Windows 95. HyperTerminal is the
best bet for testing your new modem installation. When you first launch
HyperTerminal, the Connection Description dialog appears. You enter a
name for the connection, choose an icon to represent the connection
(see fig. 12.10), and then click OK to open the Phone Number properties
sheet, shown in figure 12.11, to set up the connection.

Fig. 12.10
Identifying a new
HyperTerminal
connection.

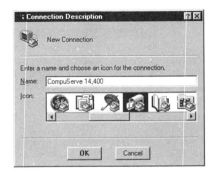

Fig. 12.11
Setting up the properties for a HyperTerminal connection.

When you click OK in the Phone Number properties sheet, HyperTerminal displays the Dial dialog (see fig. 12.12). Clicking OK initiates the dialing process, which uses the Connect dialog to monitor call progress (see fig. 12.13). HyperTerminal uses TAPI to initiate the call and monitor the status during the connection process.

Fig. 12.12
HyperTerminal's Dial dialog box.

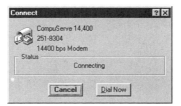

Fig. 12.13
Connecting to CompuServe with HyperTerminal.

III

Telecomputing

Once you connect to the CompuServe network, indicated by the appearance of Connected in the status bar (see fig. 12.14), you press Ctrl+C to connect to CompuServe services. HyperTerminal's Auto Detect feature sets the 7E1 (7 data bits, even parity, and one stop bit) serial protocol required for CompuServe. (Most BBSs use 8N1 protocol: 8 data bits, no parity, and one stop bit.) You enter your user ID and password to log on. Figure 12.15 shows CompuServe's opening menu. When you log off and close HyperTerminal, you're prompted to save your session (connection) data. When you restart HyperTerminal and click the open folder icon, your saved connection appears in the Select Session File dialog (see fig. 12.16).

Fig. 12.14
Logging on to CompuServe Information Services.

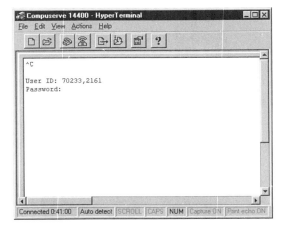

Fig. 12.15
CompuServe's opening menu in HyperTerminal.

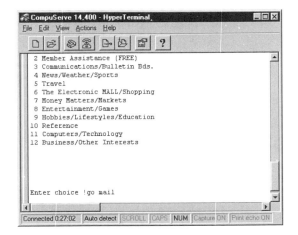

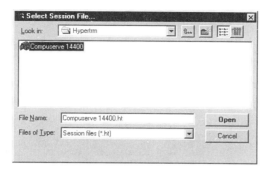

Fig. 12.16
Opening a saved Hyper-Terminal session (connection).

Using Other Windows Communications Applications with Windows 95

Other than HyperTerminal, most likely there will not be many 32-bit versions of popular communications applications available when Windows 95 reaches the retail shelves. Most of today's popular 16-bit communications applications will, however, work with Windows 95. Figure 12.17 shows the CompuServe Information Manager (WinCIM) running under Windows 95. (You can download WinCIM from CompuServe for a nominal charge, which CompuServe rebates in the form of free connect time.)

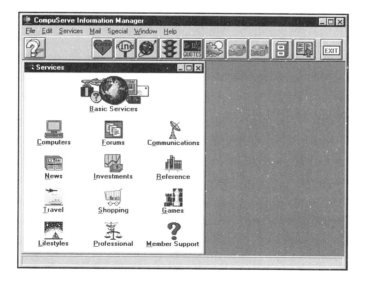

Fig. 12.17
CompuServe's 16-bit Information Manager running under Windows 95.

III

Telecomputing

Windows communications applications that were written for Windows 3.0 and haven't been updated to take advantage of the improved communications drivers included with Windows 3.1 won't work with Windows 95. If you try to launch such an application, you receive a message similar to that in figure 12.18. In this case, you need to obtain an updated 16-bit version of your communications software or wait for the 32-bit upgrade to appear.

Fig. 12.18
The message indicating that a communications application isn't compatible with Windows 95.

Taking Advantage of ISDN

This book makes numerous references to the use of high-speed Integrated Services Digital Network (ISDN) lines, primarily in the realm of multimedia, telecommuting, and teleconferencing. If you're planning to use Windows 95's remote access services (RAS) or need to transfer large document or graphics files between several locations, ISDN is the way to go because it can speed the transfer of data between PCs by about a factor of 10, compared with today's mix of 9,600 bps and 14,400 bps modems. Although the telcos—primarily the regional Bell operating companies, also known as RBOCs or Baby Bells—now don't offer ISDN lines in all their respective territories, most telcos offer ISDN in major metropolitan areas. (When this book was written, however, there were reports of difficulty in obtaining ISDN services in some of the boroughs of New York City.)

Telco subscribers in California are lucky because Pacific Bell, a subsidiary of Pacific Telesis (Pacific Telephone before divestiture in 1984 and now a holding company), offers ISDN service in most areas of California and plans to complete a $1 billion plan to provide full ISDN broadband service to all of California by 1997. What's even better is that PacBell's tariff for a home or business ISDN line carries only a $15 monthly surcharge over the standard line rate (D-channel packet service costs an extra $4 per month). Pacific Bell plans to install four ISDN lines in each of California's 7,400 schools, libraries, and community colleges by 1996; Pacific Bell will waive installation charges and provide the first year's service at no charge. Some, but not all, of the other Baby Bells are planning similar programs to get ISDN off the ground and connected to everyone's PC.

> **Note**
>
> If Pacific Bell's proposed tariffs go into effect on Jan. 1, 1995, an ISDN line will cost less per month than for the two conventional telco lines required to provide dedicated voice and data lines. Basic-rate ISDN (BRI) lets you conduct up to three simultaneous voice or data conversations on a single line to the central office. Thus, you can use a single ISDN line to provide a conventional voice line, a dedicated fax line, and a dedicated modem line, and still use it for high-speed ISDN communication.

"The value that ISDN holds right now is that ISDN is an established standard the PC world is starting to rally behind," says Kathie Blankenship, Pacific Bell's former executive director of Product Marketing-Data Services (now retired). "The question is, are you going to have to wait for optical fiber and ATM (asynchronous transfer mode), staying in dark ages with a conventional modem? Or are you going to take an intermediate step up with ISDN? It took 15 years for color television to achieve a 50 percent adoption rate; cellular phones were introduced in about 1984, but people now are just getting around to putting them in their kids' cars. The hope for early adoption of ISDN is integration of ISDN services with the computer's operating system."

> **Note**
>
> Pacific Bell has published a 60-page booklet, *ISDN: A User's Guide to Services, Applications and Resources in California*. Even if you don't live in California, you'll find the booklet a useful guide to ISDN services in North America and applications in which ISDN has proven especially cost-effective. The booklet also includes a list of ISDN-related hardware suppliers. Call Pacific Bell at 510-823-7543 to request a copy.

The ease of installing a new modem in a computer running Windows 95 makes ISDN almost a part of the computer's operating system. Windows 95's TAPI makes the ISDN modem available to any communications or telephony application. It may take a while for PC manufacturers and packagers to include the special ISDN modem, NT-1 (network termination device), and power supply required to implement ISDN in a home or business environment. In the meantime, a variety of adapter card manufacturers and Internet service providers have teamed up to offer high-speed ISDN connection to the Internet. Performance Systems International, Inc. (PSI, 800-827-7482) provides a complete Internet kit, including a low-cost ISDN modem adapter card, to access the Internet via ISDN. PSI's adapter card requires you to buy the NT-1 and power supply separately.

▶ See Chapter 14, "Hooking Up to the Internet"

III

Telecomputing

> **Tip**
>
> Before you buy an ISDN modem, make sure the service provider guarantees compatibility with the device. Conversely, if you already have an ISDN modem installed, you need to confirm that the Internet service provider you choose supports your particular modem. Not all ISDN modems can talk to each other, at least at present.

Digiboard's (800-344-4273) new DataFire ISDN modem includes the NT-1 and the power supply, which can cost up to $300 if bought separately. According to Julie Thometz, Digiboard's product marketing manager for remote access, the board carries a $595 list price and is expected to have a street price between $300 and $400. Thometz says that many buyers of ISDN modems have been disappointed to find that they needed $300 worth of additional equipment to connect the modem to a telco ISDN line. The DataFire modem provides full 128 Kbps access in locations that provide full broadband (64 Kbps per channel, not 56 Kbps per channel) ISDN service.

Chapter 13

Joining The Microsoft Network

The Microsoft Network (MSN), formerly code-named Marvel, is Microsoft's new online information service, which is fully integrated into the Windows 95 user interface. The MSN client in Windows 95 brings unprecedented simplicity to the initial sign-on process for MSN; thus, the majority of Windows 95 users whose computers have modems undoubtedly will give MSN a trial run. MSN is likely to be the primary source of Microsoft's Product Support Services (PSS) for Windows 95 and ultimately for all other Microsoft products, so Windows 95 users will have a strong incentive to subscribe to MSN. Some observers forecast that MSN ultimately will be a more significant development than Windows 95 itself. As this chapter illustrates, the prediction is quite likely to be proved correct.

The official announcement of Microsoft Network at the November, 1995 COMDEX computer exhibition in Las Vegas, evoked a maelstrom of controversy centering on the issue of whether including the MSN client with Windows 95 constitutes "unfair competition." According to Peter Friedman, general manager of Apple Online services, Apple Computer intends to bundle its eWorld front-end with every Macintosh computer shipped by mid-1995, the time Windows 95 is expected to be released. Thus, Microsoft is not alone in its plans to provide an integrated online service with its operating system(s).

When this book was written, the commercial online information utilities, CompuServe, America Online, The Prodigy Service, GEnie, Delphi, and others, had a combined total of about 5 million subscribers. It is a reasonably sure bet that by the end of 1995, MSN will have at least 5 million Windows 95 subscribers. Regardless of the final determination of the "fairness" issue, MSN is likely to be the winner in the subscriber-numbers sweepstakes.

Whether MSN's subscribers generate monthly revenues for Microsoft and its third-party MSN content providers that are greater than those of the competing online services remains to be seen. According to the Nov. 15, 1994 issue of the *Newsbytes News Network*, Microsoft's Bill Gates said at COMDEX: "Currently, less than 10 percent of the users who get on a service stay on. The existing services are too slow, too complicated, and offer no unique content."

When this book was written, both the Windows 95 client and the Windows NT "back-end" of MSN were in the early beta testing stage. The messaging (MSN e-mail), bulletin boards (BBSs, similar in concept to CompuServe's forums), and interactive chat features of MSN were in place and operational. Beta users were able to upload and download files as attachments to e-mail messages. Internet e-mail and "live feeds" of Internet Usenet newsgroup messages were promised, but not yet implemented. According to Microsoft representatives, many functions of MSN, such as a World-Wide Web browser, are not expected to be introduced until late 1995. To date, none of the announced content planned for MSN is "unique" and none of its currently operational features are appreciably faster or simpler than those of competing online services. Bear in mind, however, that MSN was still in its infancy during early 1995. You can expect Microsoft to employ innovative new technology and acquire exciting content for MSN. The question in early 1995 was: "When?"

One of the major concerns of online *aficianados* is monthly and hourly connection charges, plus big-time surcharges for "premium" services. Bill Gates didn't add "... and too expensive" to his preceding three reasons why only 10 percent of subscribers remain committed to an online service, but Microsoft is well known for its aggressive pricing policies. When this book was written, Microsoft refused to be pinned down to specific pricing for MSN, opting for an official "we'll be competitive or better" stance. The December, 1994 issue of the *Windows Watcher* newsletter quotes Russ Siegelman, Microsoft's general manager of the Online Services group: "[MSN] must be very inexpensive relative to competitive services." Industry bets are on a $4 to $6 monthly rate for basic services, including several hours of connection time, and a very low hourly charge thereafter. Third-party content providers, the subject of a section later in this chapter, undoubtedly will surcharge their services, unless the content is advertising-related or is devoted to retail transactions.

> **Note**
>
> You're likely to see the acronym MOS in MSN's viewer windows and as a suffix to some MSN user IDs (also called aliases or handles). MOS is an abbreviation for Microsoft Online Services, the organization within Microsoft responsible for developing and supporting MSN, as well as providing and arranging for its content.

Bill Gates launched Microsoft's now-famous "Information at Your Fingertips" slogan at a 1990 COMDEX show. Four years later, Microsoft commenced its $100-million TV and print advertising campaign for the new "Where do you want to go today?" theme. Microsoft is betting millions of development and advertising dollars that you'll want to go to The Microsoft Network every day to get your online information. This chapter provides the details on today's MSN and attempts to project the future of MSN, letting you make your own odds on the outcome of Microsoft's online bet.

Understanding the Concept and Structure of MSN

The Microsoft Network is a dial-up client-server messaging system. Dial-up means that you connect to the network by a modem and the switched telephone network, at least for the time being, instead of by means of a network interface card (NIC) and Ethernet cabling. For those few readers not familiar with the concept of client-server computing, following is a brief list of the ways in which client-server methodology differs from conventional computing techniques, with emphasis on online information services:

- Mainframes and minicomputers traditionally have used "dumb terminals" to provide users access to computer applications and databases. A dumb terminal (typified by the IBM 3270 mainframe terminal) simply displays messages sent from the computer and returns text you type to the computer for processing. When you use a communications application like Windows 95's HyperTerm to connect to an online information service such as CompuServe, you are running in dumb terminal mode. CompuServe's mainframe is doing all the work; your computer simply displays the messages.

- Client-server computing divides the workload between a client workstation (called the front-end) and an operating system that runs an application to display the user interface and to perform many other tasks locally. Thus, the client off-loads much of the work normally required of the mainframe or minicomputer and reduces demands on the communication link with the back-end computer. The back-end computer's primary activity is supplying data to and accepting data from the client workstations. The client application is responsible for processing the data into information that is understandable to the user. In most cases, the client application is designed for a single specific use, such as entering invoices or displaying sales figures.

■ Client-server computing most commonly is associated with databases. Online information services basically are very large databases containing text messages, files for downloading to subscribers' computers, and the text of a variety of documents for which subscribers can search by attributes, such as keywords, and then read online. (Online services call collections of such documents "databases," but such documents are more closely related to a set of indexed messages within the master database.) Most online services require that you formulate your query to return desired information, other than e-mail messages directed to your mailbox, while connected to the service. Client-server systems let you formulate queries off-line, connect to the server and retrieve the data, then review the information off-line. A category of third-party PC applications, called *off line readers*, provides this feature for messages.

■ Applications that add a graphical front-end to an existing character-based online information system, such as CompuServe's WinCIM (CompuServe Information Manager for Windows), are not true client applications. WinCIM-equipped PCs still appear as a dumb terminal to CompuServe's computers. The Prodigy Service, however, qualifies by the preceding definition as a client-server system because the client application translates data sent in North American Presentation Level Standard (NAPLS protocol) by Prodigy's computer into vector-based graphics on your display. (You currently cannot access Prodigy in character-based, dumb-terminal mode.) Prodigy expects to change from the NAPLS protocol to the Internet-standard Hypertext Markup Language (HTML) in 1995.

There are additional subtle distinctions between the client-server methodology employed by MSN and the conventional character-mode operation of most online services, including the Internet. Many of these distinctions are explained later in this chapter. The upshot of the preceding list is that conventional online services must accommodate a variety of personal computers and operating systems, even dumb terminals. Thus, with the exception of Prodigy and eWorld, such services are locked into conventional computing mode. MSN, on the other hand, is designed specifically for use with Windows 95 and its MSN client. This lets Microsoft optimize its client-server online system to a degree that CompuServe, America Online, GEnie, and Delphi are not likely to be able to match in the near future. Some of these MSN optimization methods are described in the sections that follow.

The Microsoft Network Client

The Microsoft Network client differs substantially from front-end applications offered by other online services. The most obvious difference is the close integration of MSN front-end functions with Windows 95's Explorer and the Exchange messaging system. The name change of M6's Info Center to M7's Exchange is quite significant: MSN represents a preview of the client side of Microsoft Exchange Server, which Microsoft expects to release in mid-1995 as an update to its BackOffice client-server product suite. Microsoft Exchange Server is a client-server messaging system designed to replace the present MS Mail 3.2 system. MS Mail 3.2, like most other popular PC-oriented e-mail products, is based on conventional file-sharing technology. Microsoft Exchange Server is targeted squarely at Lotus Notes, which presently dominates the messaging and document interchange elements of workgroup computing. Many of the features of the Microsoft Exchange client, described at the June 1994 Microsoft Exchange Conference in Seattle, such as the ability to apply a variety of formats to message text, appear in Windows 95's MSN client. Figure 13.1 shows Windows 95's Exchange client displaying a list of messages received from MSN users; the design of Windows 95's Exchange Inbox is indistinguishable from that of the client for Microsoft Exchange Server shown in Microsoft's white paper, "The Client: Electronic Mail & Information Sharing," published in November 1994.

Microsoft's ability to unify the front-end and back-end of MSN allows data communication between the client and server to be compressed, and files and messages can be stored in compressed form on Microsoft's servers. Microsoft has not disclosed its compression algorithm (Apple's eWorld uses Aladdin Systems' Stuffit) but whatever the method MSN employs, it's certainly effective. Messages with large attachments, such as lengthy Word 6.0 documents, are transmitted in the background in a matter of seconds. You no longer need to use separate file compression utilities, such as PKWare's PKZIP.EXE, to minimize message or file upload and download times.

III

Telecomputing

Fig. 13.1
The Inbox window of Windows 95's Exchange client showing messages received from MSN.

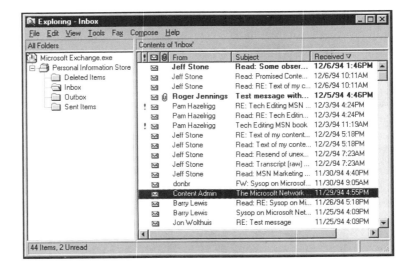

Note

MSN uses a method called *progressive rendering* to speed delivery of MSN's bitmapped graphic images to your display. Progressive rendering causes images to be drawn on your display in a series of passes; each pass increases the clarity of the image. According to Microsoft, the method is more sophisticated than simply transmitting alternate pixels. Aside from the interesting special effect progressive rendering creates, users perceive the process as faster graphics transmission because the first pass usually produces a discernible image.

Another feature of MSN that serious users will appreciate is the ability to maintain several concurrent MSN sessions over a single modem connection. Most Windows communication applications provide cooperative multitasking features, allowing you to perform other Windows activities while downloading a large file. MSN provides an additional capability: Multitasking the communication channel. As an example, you can download large files to your computer while continuing to send and receive text in two or more individual Chat sessions. Data packets sent to and from the MSN server carry a session handle in the packet header that directs the returned data to the appropriate window.

The MSN client also includes a number of small-but-useful features that help dispel some of the new-user mysteries of online communication. The taskbar button for MSN, shared with the rightmost time-of-day button, includes the following features, each of which is illustrated by figure 13.2:

- The speaker icon lets you right-click to display a slider that controls the sound volume of the signal alerting you to the arrival of incoming mail.

- A modem icon with tiny lights represents the data transmit (Tx) and receive (Rx) light-emitting diodes (LEDs) of external modems. As you send and receive data, the tiny lights blink, indicating that your connection to MSN is active. When you place the mouse pointer on the modem icon, a tooltip displays the sizes of the last files or messages sent and received.

- The MSN icon indicates that you are connected to MSN, and the tooltip confirms this connection. Clicking the MSN icon with the right mouse button displays a shortcut menu offering a number of choices, including Sign Out to log off The Microsoft Network.

- The Go To Service dialog box appears when you choose **G**o To from the MSN shortcut menu. If you know the code name of a bulletin board or other MSN service to enter, you can open the service's initial window. (This feature is similar to CompuServe's GO *FORUMNAME* command and Prodigy's Jump Word.)

- An envelope icon appears when you've received e-mail or when you're sending a message. A tooltip confirms that you've received mail.

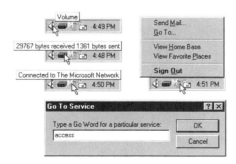

Fig. 13.2
Tooltips, the shortcut menu, and the Go To Service Dialog displayed by MSN icons in the right taskbar button.

III

Telecomputing

The Server Side of The Microsoft Network

For "competitive reasons," Microsoft had not revealed details of the design of the server side of MSN when this book was written. The following list, gathered from trade publications and other sources, provides some insight into the scope of Microsoft's investment in the back-end of MSN and how the service works:

- Approximately 200 Intel-based servers running Windows NT 3.5 are connected to MSN's network backbone in Redmond, WA. At least one of the servers reportedly has 1G of RAM installed. (That's a thousand megabytes of RAM, not fixed disk space.)

- Digital Equipment Corp. (DEC) will manage the infrastructure of the MSN network under a five-year contract with Microsoft. DEC has been a major proponent of Windows NT and announced the development of clustering software for Windows NT Server in late 1994. (Clustering software allows a group of servers to share the computing load.) DEC undoubtedly hopes to provide MOS with high-powered AXP servers based on its 64-bit Alpha RISC processor.

- An additional Microsoft facility, located in Colorado, provides backup service in case of catastrophic failure of the Redmond system. Data is replicated (copied) from Redmond to the Colorado site. Built-in replication services are provided by Microsoft Exchange Server and Microsoft SQL 95, the forthcoming version of Microsoft SQL Server.

- Microsoft SQL Server for Windows NT handles subscriber information, billing, and other clerical chores. It is likely (but not confirmed) that e-mail and bulletin board messages are processed by a beta version of Microsoft Exchange Server.

- Microsoft has contracted with AT&T's InterSpan Information Access Service, Sprint Corp., and Canada's Unitel Communications Inc. for North American telecommunication services, and with British Telecom's Global Network Service (GNS) for the European and Asia-Pacific regions except Australia. Microsoft's joint venture with national telecommunications provider Telstra Corp., On Australia Pty. Ltd., provides services down under. 9,600-bps nodes will be the most common until the carriers update more locations to 14,400-bps or 28,800-bps capacity. (2,400-bps modems won't give adequate performance with MSN, especially when receiving graphic images.) When this book was written, ISDN connections to MSN were not available to beta testers.

Note

Bill Gates and Paul Allen, cofounders of Microsoft, and Microsoft Corp. itself have made large investments in Destineer Corp., an 80-percent-owned subsidiary of Mobil Technologies Communication Corp. (Mtel), which has a Personal Communications Services (PCS) license to operate a two-way nationwide wireless network. According to a Dec. 9, 1994 story from the *NewsBytes News Network,* after the transactions involved in the acquisition by Mtel of 100 percent of the shares of Destineer Corp. are completed, and Gates, Allen, and Microsoft exchange their Destineer shares for Mtel stock, the Mtel network will allow a PC or PDA (personal digital assistant) to connect to MSN without relying on a hardwired connection to the preceding carriers' nodes.

Microsoft clearly intends MSN to be a showcase to provide the capabilities of the principal components of 1995's BackOffice suite: Windows NT 3.5 Server, SQL 95, and Exchange Server. The technical success of MSN, regardless of its immediate commercial profitability, will demonstrate whether the BackOffice components are ready for enterprise-wide, prime-time duty. All indications during late 1994 beta testing point to MSN's technical success, but a million or two subscribers, logged on to MSN simultaneously, ultimately will tell the tale.

Garnering Third-Party Content for MSN

At the fall 1994 COMDEX show, Bill Gates was quoted as saying, "We will not measure ourselves on content, but instead will focus on unique developments and technology." (*Newsbytes News Network*, Nov. 15, 1994.) Microsoft will provide the infrastructure for "basic services," such as e-mail, bulletin boards and chat sessions, Usenet news groups, plus the content for Microsoft-oriented activities, like technical support for Windows 95, Microsoft Office, and other software products. Count on Microsoft to advertise its Home Products CD-ROMs on MSN with online demos, possibly with online versions of Encarta, Cinemania, and other top sellers. Whether Microsoft can entice more than 10 percent of the Windows 95 users who sign on to MSN to subscribe on a regular basis, however, ultimately will depend on the quantity and quality of content provided by others.

Microsoft plans to lure third-party content providers to MSN by offering them a bigger piece of the online action. Today's major online services keep 80 percent or more of the revenues generated by third-party content; according to industry sources, Microsoft will pass 50 percent or more of the surcharge revenue on to the content provider. The content provider can elect to

III

Telecomputing

bill the subscriber directly or have Microsoft tack the charge on a credit card. Some content providers will charge a monthly or hourly access fee, others will elect to bill on a "pay-per-view" basis. There weren't any surcharged "extended" MSN services when this book was written (MSN was free for Windows 95 M7 beta testers), but MOS's Content Administration group was busy wooing prospective third-party content providers. It remains to be seen how many of the competition's major content providers plight their troth to MSN.

Development Tools for MSN Content

Bringing third-party content providers into the MSN fold requires a suite of development tools to create files compatible with MSN's infrastructure. When this book was written, the tool set for MSN, code-named "Blackbird," was still in the development stage. According to the Dec., 1994 issue of the *Windows Watcher* newsletter, Bill Miller, director of marketing for MOS, says that Microsoft Word will be the vehicle for MSN document creation and Visual Basic will be used to create forms and lay out documents for presentation with the MSN client.

It's a good bet that MediaView, Microsoft's new replacement for Multimedia Viewer 2.0, also will play an important role in creating third-party content documents for MSN. If you're a subscriber to the Microsoft Developer Network, the newest MSDN CD-ROMs use MediaView with a custom front-end. (Unlike Multimedia Viewer, MediaView does not have its own graphic front-end; you must create your own front-end with Visual Basic or C/C++.) MediaView provides the indexed full-text search engine that's needed by providers of news stories, magazine articles, entire books, and similar text-heavy content. Full-text search lets you find multiple instances of one or more keywords in the body of articles and books. MediaView, which uses Microsoft's rich text format (RTF) as the source for compiled viewable documents, is closely related to the new Windows 95 help system.

Connecting to The Microsoft Network

Before you can connect to MSN, you must install Microsoft Exchange and The Microsoft Network. The M7 (beta 2) version of Windows 95 used to write this book requires that you specify Custom Setup in order to install Exchange. It's likely that the Standard Setup program for the retail version of Windows 95 will detect if your computer has a modem and, if it does, ask if you want to try MSN. If you answer "No" and later want to connect to MSN, double-click Control Panel's Add/Remove Programs Icon, select the Windows Setup properties page, and mark The Microsoft Network item in the Components list box, as shown in figure 13.3. When you click OK, you'll be asked to insert the Windows 95 CD-ROM or the appropriate distribution diskette(s).

Fig. 13.3
Installing The Microsoft Network client application subsequent to your initial Windows 95 installation.

After you install the MSN client, you must create a Microsoft Exchange profile (or modify your existing Exchange profile) to add MSN to the Available Information Services. Double-clicking the Microsoft Exchange Profiles icon in Control Panel opens the properties sheet. You click Add to create a new profile or Edit to alter an existing profile, then select the Services page and click Add to open the Add Service to Profile dialog. Double-clicking the Microsoft Online Services item in the Available Information Services list box adds MSN to your Exchange profile, as shown in figure 13.4.

> **Caution**
>
> If you've installed Microsoft At Work Fax as an information service of the Exchange profile that includes MSN, make sure that you've set the Autoanswer feature off before you attempt to sign up for an MSN account. In the M7 beta version of Windows 95, Autoanswer prevents the MSN client from dialing the MSN server. (This may change in the retail release of Windows 95.) The "E-Mail" section, which follows later in this chapter, describes how to set up multiple profiles and choose the profile to use when you launch Exchange or use MSN e-mail.

III

Telecomputing

Fig. 13.4
Adding The
Microsoft Network
to your Exchange
Profile.

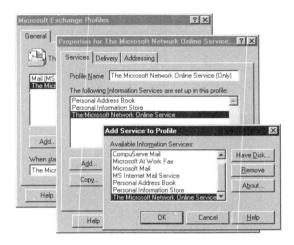

After you install the MSN client and add MSN to your Exchange profile, you then sign up for MSN. Microsoft has made the MSN sign-up process quick and easy. Choosing Start.Programs.Accessories.Sign Up for The Microsoft Network opens the first dialog box of the MSN Signup Wizard shown in figure 13.5. Microsoft doesn't refer to the series of dialog boxes used to obtain an MSN account as a "wizard," but the process is similar to that employed to accomplish sequential tasks by other wizards incorporated in Windows 95 and members of the Microsoft Office suite. Clicking OK opens a dialog box, illustrated by figure 13.6, in which you enter your area code and prefix of the telephone number you'll use for MSN. Clicking Dial in the next dialog box calls MSN's toll-free number and downloads to your computer a list of the local access numbers for MSN's telecommunication carriers, billing, and pricing information; then the Wizard disconnects from MSN.

Fig. 13.5
The first step in
the sign-up
process for MSN.

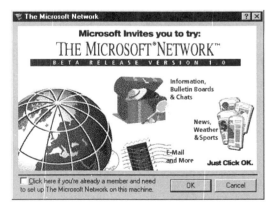

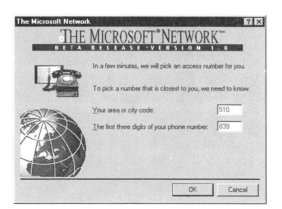

Fig. 13.6
Entering the area code and prefix of your modem's telephone number.

You conduct the next three steps of the sign-up process, shown in the dialog box in figure 13.7, off line. Clicking the Tell us your name and address button displays the entry dialog box for the personal information required for your MSN account, as illustrated by figure 13.8. (To preserve your privacy, MSN allows other subscribers to view only your name, city, and country.) Windows 95 beta testers aren't charged for using MSN, so the Next select a way to pay button is checked in the M7 beta release. In the final version of MSN, you'll be able to pay with major credit cards and probably by direct debit from your checking account. Finally, you must read and agree to the Membership Terms of Usage, the first part of which appears in figure 13.9. After you've completed these three steps, the Price and Support Information dialog box appears, as shown in figure 13.10. Undoubtedly, the final version of MSN will have substantially more pricing and support information than what appears in figure 13.10.

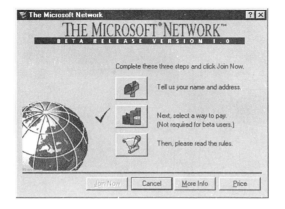

Fig. 13.7
The three steps required to sign up for MSN.

Fig. 13.8
Providing personal
information for
your MSN
account.

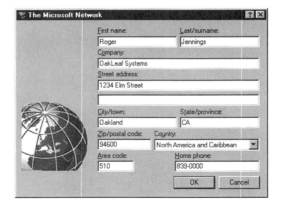

Fig. 13.9
Reading the
Membership
Terms of Usage
for MSN.

Fig. 13.10
The M7 beta
version of the Price
and User Support
dialog.

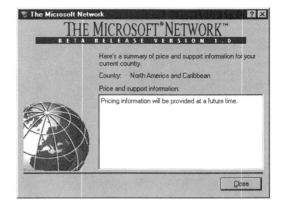

After the preliminaries are over, you're asked to select a Primary and Backup local access number (also called a node) for the MSN telecommunication carrier in your local dialing area. Clicking the Change button for the Primary number opens the Choose an Access Number in Your Area dialog box. You pick your country and state or region from the two drop-down lists, and city in the list box shown in figure 13.11. Then you repeat the process for a Backup number. When you're done, your Access Number dialog appears, as shown in figure 13.12.

> ### Note
>
> Figure 13.12 shows a 9,600-bps Primary node and a 2,400-bps Backup node for Oakland, CA. This Primary node has unadvertised 14,400 bps capability. (Many of the carriers currently are updating their nodes from 9,600 bps to 14,400 bps or even 28,800 bps.) Microsoft considers 2,400 bps service inadequate for MSN, so you might want to select a 9,600 bps (or higher) node in a surrounding city for the Backup number. As an example, Oakland, CA (510 area code) has toll-free access to San Francisco (415 area code), so the San Francisco node makes an ideal Backup.

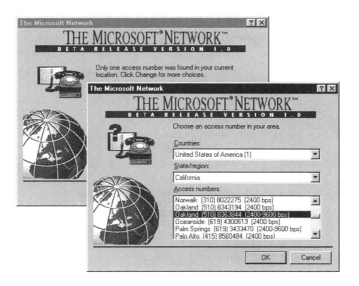

Fig. 13.11
Selecting a Primary or Backup local access number for MSN.

III

Telecomputing

When you've completed the off-line sign-up chores, the Calling dialog box of figure 13.13 appears. Clicking on Dial connects you to MSN by using the Primary node. (If the Primary node is busy or out of service, the MSN client automatically attempts to dial the Backup node.) When you connect to MSN, a dialog appears requesting that you enter a Member ID and Password, as illustrated by figure 13.14. Your Member ID may not contain spaces, but you can substitute underscores to make your Member ID more readable. Once you've sent your Member ID and Password to MSN by clicking OK, the Welcome to The Microsoft Network dialog appears as shown in figure 13.15. After you've read the tips, you're a member of The Microsoft Network and the MSN icon appears on your desktop.

Fig. 13.12
Primary and
Backup numbers
for Oakland, CA
nodes.

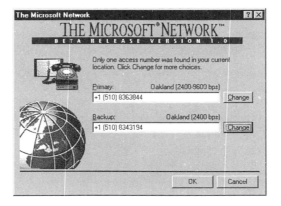

> ### Note
>
> Although the M7 beta of MSN lets you use an alias (also called a handle) for your account, it appears to be the consensus of active MSN users that using your real name as your Member ID better conforms to the unwritten rules of MSN "netiquette." If your name (or alias) has already been assigned to another subscriber, MSN will notify you and you must enter a different Member ID. Adding an underscore after your last name usually works.

Fig. 13.13
Dialing into MSN
with your Primary
or Backup access
number.

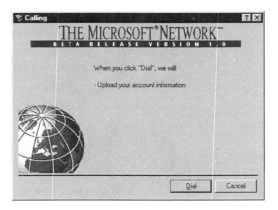

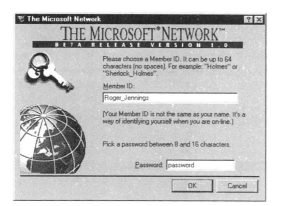

Fig. 13.14
Entering the
Member ID and
Password for your
MSN account.

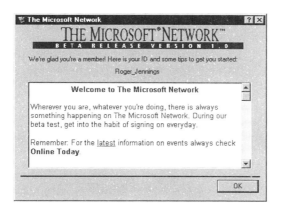

Fig. 13.15
Reading the
Welcome to The
Microsoft Network
message.

After your initial sign-up session, double-click The Microsoft Network desktop
icon to initiate your connection to MSN with the sign-on. Your Member ID
automatically appears in the Sign In text box, but you must enter your Password manually. (Mark the Remember My Password check box to eliminate
the need to enter your password during subsequent sign-in operations.)
When you click the Connect button of the Sign In dialog box, the MSN client
dials the Primary access number, as illustrated by figure 13.16. When you
connect to the local node, MSN verifies your Member ID and Password, as
shown in figure 13.17. After your account is verified, the Sign In dialog box
disappears and, shortly thereafter, the opening MSN window appears.

III

Telecomputing

> **Note**
>
> The sign-up and connection processes for MSN described in the preceding text and figures was valid for the M7 beta version used to write this book. The procedure in the "Preview" beta and final versions of MSN undoubtedly will differ somewhat from that described here. The primary differences, however, are likely to be related to billing methods and the appearance of individual dialog boxes.

Fig. 13.16
Dialing MSN with your Member ID and a saved Password.

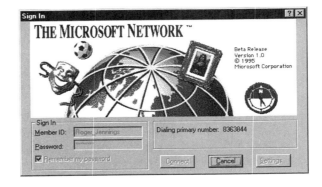

Fig. 13.17
Verifying your Member ID and Password after connecting to the MSN server.

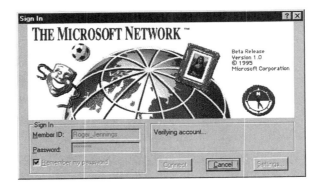

Navigating The Microsoft Network

After you connect to MSN and your account is verified, the opening window (called the MSN *Front Page*) appears, as shown in figure 13.17. The six icons associated with primary categories of services provided by MSN are hot-spots; a single click on the associated icon displays the following:

- *On-Line Today* opens the MSN Today window that describes four of what Microsoft considers the most significant current events on MSN. Clicking the Calendar of Events or MSN Today Archive icons leads to another window; clicking Today's TidByte displays a pop-up window with the definition of a computer term.

- *E-Mail* launches the Microsoft Exchange client, then checks for pending MSN mail. If you have messages waiting on MSN, they are automatically downloaded to the Inbox of your Personal Message Store and then are deleted from the MSN server.

- *Favorite Places* opens a window in which you create shortcuts to services that you use most often. When you first sign in to MSN, your Favorite Places window is empty.

- *Categories* displays a window with icons representing the first level of basic services provided by MSN. Extended services, when available, also are likely to be represented by one or more icons in the Categories window.

- *Headlines* was not implemented in the M7 beta version of MSN, but is likely to lead to a choice of products offered by newswire services. The Orientation window of Member Services states that MSN will provide news, weather, sports, and financial information.

- *Member Services* opens a window that leads to descriptions of the information services provided by MSN, conduct rules, and a Netiquette BBS that provides advice for new users (often called *newbies*) of online systems.

The following sections describe the service categories of the preceding list in greater detail.

> **Note**
>
> To prevent a proliferation of cascaded windows as you navigate through MSN, choose **V**iew **O**ptions and select the Browse Folders by Using a Single Window option in the Folder property page.

MSN Today

Always make MSN Today your first stop when you connect to The Microsoft Network. MSN Today provides brief highlights of important events taking place on MSN, such as moderated discussion (chat) sessions with MOS

III

Telecomputing

program and product managers, authors, and other online experts. MOS Content Administration usually posts transcripts of moderated chat sessions the day after the session occurs; transcript availability is announced in MSN today, as shown in figure 13.19. (The "Moderated Chat Sessions" section, later in this chapter, describes how MSN uses Windows 95's multitasking features to manage the question-and-answer process.) Newly added information services are announced on MSN Today. Also, descriptions of new features implemented by MSN are likely to appear as the system matures. MSN takes advantage of shortcuts, similar to those of the Windows 95 desktop, to take you directly to the information service whose icon you click.

Fig. 13.18
The Front Page of The Microsoft Network.

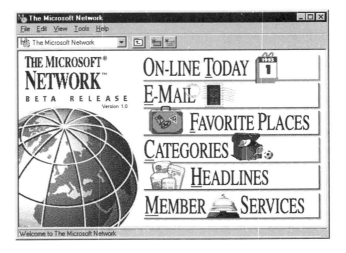

> **Note**
>
> One of the more interesting navigational features of MSN is the ability to include shortcuts to a specific BBS or information service within a message posted in a BBS or in your e-mail. Read the message, click the shortcut enclosure, and the window specified by the shortcut icon opens.

MSN Today offers two additional useful features: MSN Today Archive, and Calendar of Events. The MSN Today Archive maintains a list of the past six days' items that appeared in the MSN Today window, as illustrated by figure 13.20. The Calendar of Events lists recurring activities, such as weekly informal chat sessions conducted by members of special-interest BBSs. Figure 13.21 shows just a few of the scheduled chat sessions in early December, 1994. The "Victorian Cocktail Hour," sponsored by MOS Content

Administration, is a forum for MSN beta testers to provide suggestions for the future content of MSN. The "Cocktail Hour" was a very lively place during the M7 beta program.

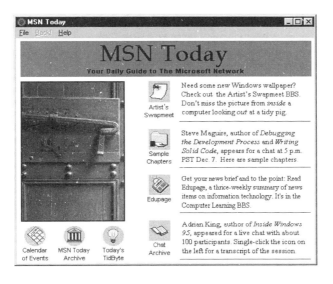

Fig. 13.19
The MSN Today window for November 30, 1994.

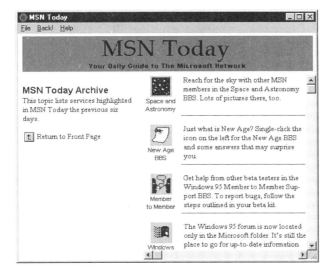

Fig. 13.20
The MSN Today Archive for Nov. 30, 1994.

III

Telecomputing

E-Mail

If you're already using Microsoft Mail 3.2+ or another e-mail system with Windows 95, you'll find MSN e-mail operations to be virtually indistinguishable from networked e-mail usage. This similarity is consistent with

Microsoft's description of the Exchange client: "The Universal Inbox." Chapter 18, "Messaging with Windows 95's Exchange Client," describes in detail Windows 95's e-mail features, so this section discusses only the minor differences you see when you send or receive MSN e-mail.

Fig. 13.21
A few of the MSN weekly chat sessions scheduled in December 1994.

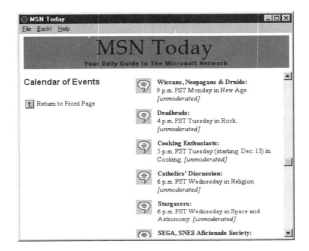

You can set the properties of MSN e-mail independently of other e-mail service providers included in your Exchange Profile. Figure 13.22 shows the Services properties page for MSN e-mail. Ticking the Download at Startup check box causes the MSN client to automatically download in the background pending messages from MSN when you connect. If you have a slow connection or only want to check to see how much mail you have, you can choose to Use Remote Preview, which only transfers the message headers to your computer. Double-clicking an individual header entry in your Inbox downloads the content of the previewed message.

The Delivery properties page, shown in figure 13.23, lets you set the priorities for sending your mail. (Delivery priorities are significant only if you originate a substantial amount of mail.) You can determine which address book to use first when sending mail with the Exchange client. If you select The Microsoft Network or one of the regional choices for MSN subscribers (see figure 13.24, which limits MSN addresses to North American subscribers) as the first address book to use, clicking the To button of Exchange's Compose window automatically initiates a connection to MSN and displays the MSN address list.

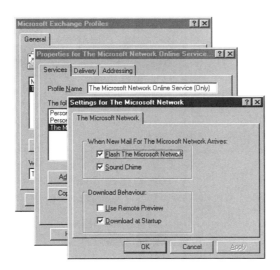

Fig. 13.22
Setting the properties for the MSN Information Service.

Fig. 13.23
Setting e-mail delivery priorities with multiple message service providers for an Exchange Profile.

If you're a heavy-duty e-mail and fax user, you may want to establish multiple Exchange Profiles. To choose the appropriate profile when you first launch the Exchange client, you choose **T**ools, **O**ptions for Microsoft Exchange from Exchange's menu and select the General properties page. (See figure 13.25.) Select the Choose Profile to Open option in the At Startup frame to display a drop-down list of Exchange Profiles when Exchange opens. Alternatively, you can select a default profile to use every time you launch Exchange.

III

Telecomputing

Fig. 13.24
Selecting the initial
address book,
destination for
personal addresses,
and address
verification
sequence.

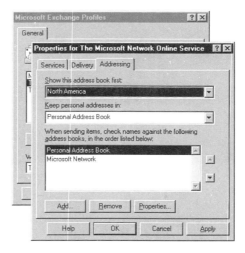

Fig. 13.25
Setting General
properties for the
Exchange client.

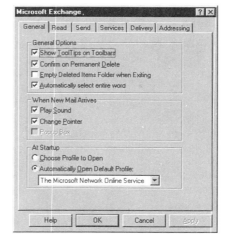

E-mail messages you receive from MSN, including Internet mail, appear in your Inbox list as shown in figure 13.26. Explorer displays the senders' first and last names, rather than their MSN aliases, in the From column. Double-clicking the Inbox item displays the message, as shown in figure 13.27. The "MSN" To address sends a message to all MSN subscribers. (In the M7 beta version of MSN, individual subscribers could address broadcast messages to "MSN" but this dubious feature is likely to be removed from future versions of the MSN client.)

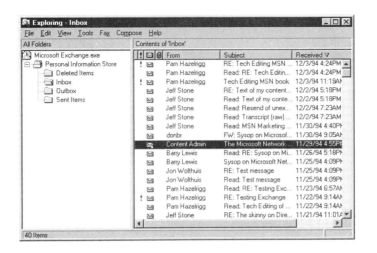

Fig. 13.26
Exchange's Inbox
filled with MSN
e-mail message
headers.

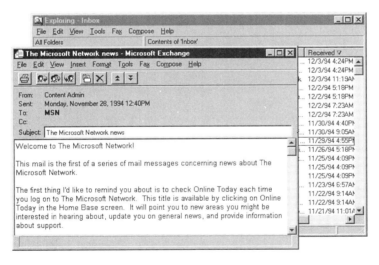

Fig. 13.27
Exchange display-
ing a broadcast
message from
MSN's Content
Administrator.

III

Telecomputing

Sending e-mail messages to MSN subscribers is almost identical to the process
used for networked e-mail systems. MSN has a unique feature, however, that
lets you select the desired recipient from the current subscriber list. When
you click the To button, the Select Names dialog box appears, as shown in
figure 13.28, with the first 12 MSN subscriber names in alphabetic sequence
for the region you select from the drop-down list. You type the first few characters of the recipient you are seeking into the Type Name text box; almost
immediately, subscribers whose names begin with the characters you type
appear in the list box. To verify that you've selected the correct recipient, you
click the Properties button to display the properties sheet for the subscriber,

as shown in figure 13.29. MSN completes the General Properties page from information you provided during the sign-up process. The Personal and Professional properties pages for MSN subscribers were empty and not editable in the M7 beta version of MSN, but you may be able to provide this information as an option in later versions.

Fig. 13.28
Choosing the region from which to select an MSN subscriber name.

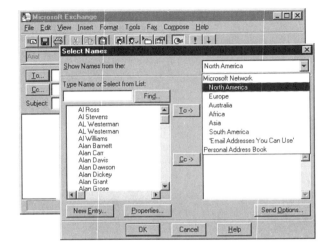

Fig. 13.29
Displaying the General properties page for a selected MSN subscriber.

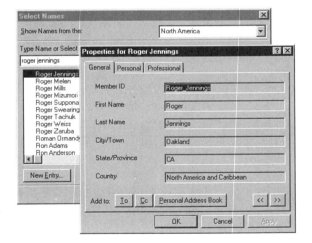

Favorite Places

Most graphical front-ends for online services provide a method of quickly navigating to features of the service you use most frequently. MSN is no exception; the Favorite Places window holds icons representing shortcuts to those BBSs, Chat sessions, and other MSN services. Figure 13.30 shows the author's Favorite Places window for the services available in late 1994. To add a service to the Favorite Places window, select the service and click the right mouse button, then select Favorite Places from the shortcut menu. Alternatively, you can click the toolbar button with the heart symbol to add the service to Favorite Places. (See figure 13.31 in the next section.)

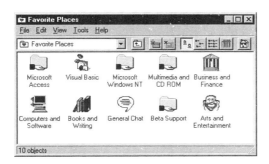

Fig. 13.30
A few of the author's favorite places in MSN.

Categories

Categories of MSN services represent the top of the hierarchy for the bulletin boards, chat sessions, and other information services provided by MSN and its third-party content providers. In this respect, the structure of MSN's services resembles a conventional hierarchy of directories and subdirectories of a fixed disk drive. Figure 13.31 shows the basic information categories available from MSN in late 1994, equivalent to the root directory. By the time the retail version of MSN is released, it's likely that Microsoft will add additional basic categories, such as News and Weather.

> **Note**
>
> The Microsoft Knowledge Base (MSKB) is a database containing articles relating to Microsoft's retail products. The MSKB database also is available on CompuServe (GO MSKB). The MSKB articles offer tips, describe known bugs, and provide workarounds for known problems. The M7 version of MSN displays all Knowledge Base articles for the selected product. It is likely that future versions of MSN will provide a keyword search facility to locate specific Knowledge Base articles.

When you double-click a category icon or folder, the next level of folders appears. As an example, double-clicking the Computers and Software icon leads you to the window from which you can select the Software folder. The Software window provides folders for Microsoft and other firms participating

III

Telecomputing

in MSN. Opening the Microsoft window displays folders for individual Microsoft applications and operating systems, plus direct access to Microsoft Knowledge Base articles for all Microsoft products.

Fig. 13.31

The basic categories of information services available on MSN in late 1994.

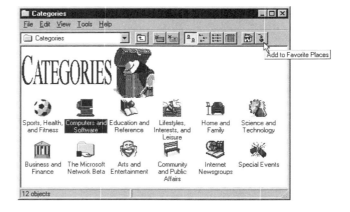

Fig. 13.32

A partial list of the Knowledge Base articles about Microsoft Access.

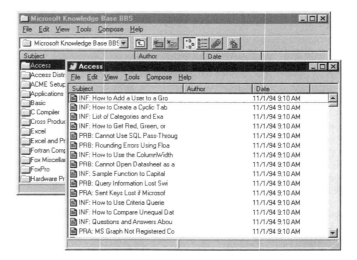

There was no third-party content on MSN when this book was written; however, the Business and Finance category gave hints of services to come. Figure 13.34 shows the selections available in the Business and Finance folder as of late 1994. Clicking the Kiosk icon opens a window that describes the services available. You can return to MSN's Front Page (also called the Home Base) by clicking the toolbar button with the house symbol. Figure 13.35 shows corporate information to be supplied in the future by Reference Press; when this book was written, there was no content behind the Reference Press icons.

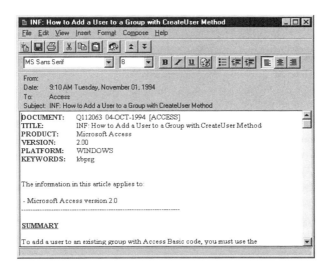

Fig. 13.33
Part of a Knowledge Base article about Microsoft Access.

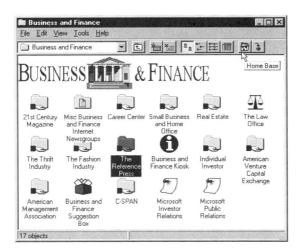

Fig. 13.34
Services available in the Business and Finance folder.

Member Services

The Member Services category provides information on how to use MSN, MSN's Rules of Conduct, and suggested *netiquette* (guidelines for getting along well with other MSN subscribers). Figure 13.36 shows Bill Gates' welcoming message to new MSN subscribers and figure 13.37 shows one of the windows of the New Member Orientation sequence.

III

Telecomputing

Fig. 13.35
Some prospective
corporate informa-
tion services to be
provided by
Reference Press.

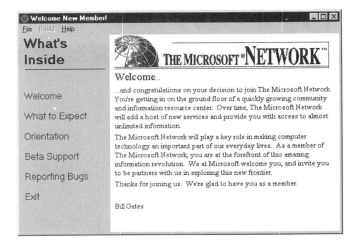

Fig. 13.36
Bill Gates' welcom-
ing message to new
MSN users.

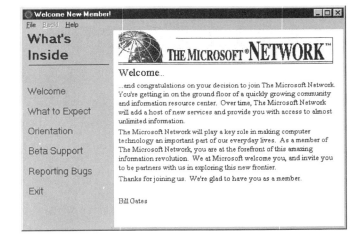

Chatting on The Microsoft Network

The ability to communicate with other subscribers in real-time, called chat-
ting, is a major revenue producer for commercial online services. Prodigy,
for instance, attributes its slower subscriber growth, in comparison with
CompuServe and America Online, to the service's previous lack of chat
capability. The *NewsBytes News Network* for Dec. 6, 1994, quotes Brian Ek,
Prodigy's director of communications, as saying: "In only 90 days after the
inauguration of our chat lines, we have recorded more than a half a million

hours of billable chat time per month." The Internet Relay Chat (IRC) also is one of the most popular features of the Internet. MSN offers two types of chat sessions, informal and moderated, which are described in the sections that follow.

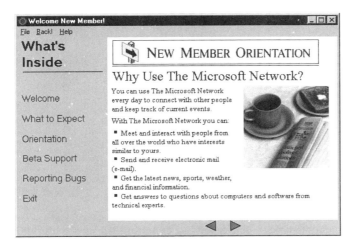

Fig. 13.37
Reasons for using MSN, one of a series of windows in the Orientation sequence for new MSN users.

Informal Chat Sessions

By far the most popular chat sessions on all online services are informal discussions between subscribers having similar interests. Most MSN information categories have a dedicated *CategoryName* Chat icon. Figure 13.21, earlier in this chapter, shows only a few of the scheduled chat sessions (also called *rooms*) devoted to specific interest areas. Members of conversations in special-interest chat sessions are expected to "speak" to the category's topic. The General Chat in the MSN Beta folder, which was the most active of all chat rooms in late 1994, is a gathering place for an eclectic group of MSN beta testers and representatives of Microsoft's Online Services group. Figure 13.38 shows a typical General Chat session on the subject of MSN's content and user interface. The aliases (User IDs) of participating members are listed in the box (called the tray) to the right of figure 13.38. Future versions of MSN will display the General property sheet for the member when you right-click an entry in the tray. Boldface text indicates the entrance and exit of members of the conversation. You can turn this feature off in the properties sheet you access with the **V**iew, **O**ptions menu choice; most users leave this feature on so they can say "hello" as new people join the session.

III

Telecomputing

Fig. 13.38
An informal
conversation
in the General
Chat room.

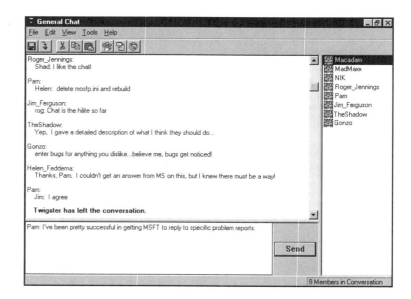

To join the conversation, you type your contribution in the text box below the main chat window, then press Enter or click the Send button to transmit your text. The entry text box includes a wordwrap feature that allows sending multiple lines of text. (The M7 version of MSN has a limit of 255 characters per transmission; this limit may increase in future versions.) The text you send is prefaced with your MSN alias, as shown in figure 13.38. Once sent, MSN clears your entry text box for your next contribution.

Moderated Chat Sessions

MSN's moderated chat sessions resemble CompuServe's moderated conferences, such as the bi-weekly Macmillan Computer Publishing conference held in the PHCP forum. Figure 13.39 shows part of a Microsoft "Special Event" conducted with Adrian King, the author of Microsoft Press's *Inside Windows 95*, as the guest in late November, 1994. Babbage Auditorium is located on Microsoft's Redmond campus. At one point, more than 100 members had joined the Special Event, which kept the SysOp (System Operator, also called the Host) and the Assistant quite busy sorting and passing member's questions to King.

Moderated chat sessions take full advantage of MSN's multitasking communication capability described earlier in this chapter, making the process of asking questions and receiving answers much simpler than methods used by other online services. In a moderated chat session, you open two simultaneous chat sessions; one to post questions (Ask Questions Here) and the other

(Babbage Auditorium) to see both the questions to and the answers given by featured guests. (See figure 13.40.) The SysOp and one or more Assistants maintain order by copying members' questions to the clipboard, then pasting the questions to the text box of the main session (after the guest has answered the preceding question). In a moderated session, you can't transmit text to the main chat window.

Fig. 13.39
Part of a Microsoft-sponsored moderated chat session conducted with Adrian King as the guest.

Anticipating the Future of MSN

The increasing percentage of PCs devoted to domestic "edutainment" activities will force commercial online information services to rethink their content strategy for 1995 and beyond. Microsoft's online competitors are scrambling to provide new and improved Internet services. Simply providing connectivity to the Internet will not suffice; most home PC neophytes will be intimidated by the scope of the information available, not to mention the unfettered profanity and explicit sexual content of many popular Usenet "news groups." Interactive multimedia features—multiplayer games complete with sound effects and music, plus on-demand video clips of news and sports highlights—are what's likely to draw today's couch potatoes to an online information service in 1995 and beyond.

Microsoft has made many promises for the final version of MSN, not the least of which is "rich multimedia content and services" heralded by the Microsoft press releases and white paper that accompanied MSN's fall 1994 COMDEX

III

Telecomputing

announcement. Static graphics and the occasional sound byte does not qualify as "rich multimedia content." Information & Interactive Services Report for Oct. 21, 1994 quotes Bill Gates as describing MSN as "a service that would capitalize on Microsoft's current crop of CD-ROM applications, allowing users to dial up data from its Encarta encyclopedia, for instance," at the Networked Economy conference in Washington DC. Gates also said in his "Information At Your Fingertips - 2005" COMDEX keynote address:

> "It's this kind of experimentation of what's popular, how should it be presented, getting the tools out there, that's going to get us to the critical mass of information that makes people want to have electronic access everywhere they go every day. The impact of this is quite substantial. It's not just movies on demand. People think of it that way and they mislead themselves. Because that alone would not be enough to justify this investment. People think of it as computing but I think that also misleads us because it's not really about computing. If it's about any one thing it's about communications. Taking today's phone system to a new level where we not only have video but we have the intelligence in the system to help us locate things, to follow links, to store the information so we can get at it when we want to. The kind of electronic commerce that will go on here of picking real estate, finding a professional that you want to work with, allowing people with expertise even if they want to stay at home most of the time to offer that expertise and work through the screen, it's really very, very different than anything that's happened before."

Fig. 13.40
The two simultaneous chat sessions used for Special Events.

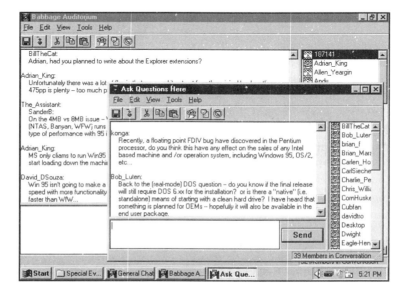

Taking today's phone system to a new level, in which transmission of full-screen, full-motion video becomes practical, is a monumental undertaking for the RBOCs as well as their erstwhile cable competitors. As discussed in Chapter 10, "Watching *Real* Digital Video," providing on-demand video of acceptable quality, or even hi-fi sound and music, requires communication bandwidths not economically available from today's switched telephone network. ISDN is a step in the right direction, but few home PC users will be satisfied with the video quality ISDN is capable of delivering. Without interactive multimedia features, most home PC owners who initially log in to MSN will join the 90 percent or more of the online users who let their subscriptions lapse after the initial novelty wears off.

If MSN is to fulfill its promise of "rich multimedia content" in the twentieth century, it appears that Microsoft has the following two options to obtain the necessary transmission bandwidth until the telcos take "today's phone system to a new level":

- Contract with cable TV providers having digital distribution capability who are willing to devote a channel to MSN. You'll need cable TV service, plus a special cablemodem, similar to a network interface card, in your PC. The problems with this option are that digital cable service is now only in the early testing stages and each cable consortium may elect to use different transmission methods and cablemodems. It's likely to be the turn of the century before digital cable TV gains widespread availability in the U.S.

- Acquire one or more channels, called transponders, on a direct-broadcast satellite (DBS). The advantage of this approach is that Microsoft, rather than cable TV distributors, can control MSN's transmission system. (Federal Communications Commission regulations require that broadcasters own a share of the DBS satellite.) You'll need to purchase a small satellite receive-only dish, such as that used by GM Hughes Electronics' DirecTV service, and mount it on your roof or a south-facing balcony to receive the satellite signal.

The Associated Press reported on Dec. 21, 1994 that Tele-Communications, Inc. (TCI) had acquired a 20 percent interest in MSN for $125 million of TCI common stock. (TCI's 20 percent purchase establishes a value of $625 million for 100 percent of MSN, a substantial amount for an online service that's in the early beta stage.) According to the AP story, the agreement with TCI's Technology Ventures unit will supply MSN with technical expertise for

III

Telecomputing

developing services that can be carried by cable TV. Russell Siegelman, General Manager of MSN, is quoted in the story as saying MSN "could have a cable option as early as 1996, [but it is] too early to know what additional services might be offered." The most obvious advantage of cable TV distribution is the ability to transmit digital audio and video signals in real time to MSN subscribers, using techniques similar to those planned for interactive, on-demand television entertainment. Microsoft's Windows NT-based video server operating system, code-named *Tiger*, is likely to play an important role in distributing MSN content to subscribers when MCI's regional cable distributors add an "MSN Channel" to your set-top box.

> **Note**
>
> The Microsoft/TCI partnership was preceded by a November 1994 announcement of the formation of a joint venture between Sprint, TCI, Comcast Corporation, and Cox Cable to bundle cable TV, local and long-distance telephone services, and wireless communications into a single package for homes and businesses. As mentioned earlier in this chapter, Sprint is one of MSN's primary telephone carriers. Once the joint-venture has its digital telephony technology in place, many MSN subscribers are likely to be able to communicate to and from MSN over their upgraded cable TV connection.

Microsoft is rumored to be hedging its TCI bet by looking to a Direct Broadcast Satellite (DBS) for wideband delivery of MSN content. (Both of the transmission methods currently are designed to use a relatively slow-speed backchannel, such as a 9,600-bps modem connection, to send data from your PC to MSN.) DirecTV and Thomson Consumer Products, which manufactures the satellite dish and set-top box under the RCA logo for the DirecTV service, are spending millions of advertising dollars in an attempt to lure viewers from cable to satellite TV service. Industry experts expect DirecTV to have one million subscribers by mid-1995 and to achieve a subscription rate of about two million per year thereafter. By mid-1995, Thomson and Sony will share the DirecTV hardware market, so equipment cost is likely to fall below the present $700 to $1,000 retail price range. According to the Nov. 30, 1994 issue of the *Satellite Business News* newsletter:

> "Microsoft and DirecTV are in talks involving a wide variety of cooperative and joint ventures. The talks center on Microsoft using DirecTV's DBS satellites to deliver several types of data and specialized video services. DirecTV's planned launch of a third satellite [DBS-3] early next year will allow the company to start focusing on delivery of such services.

"Talk has also circulated of Microsoft leasing or buying transponders on DBS-3 and possibly investing in DirecTV, according to two industry sources.

"Among the specific applications being discussed with Microsoft's Advanced Technology Group," the sources said, "is satellite-to-home delivery of the company's recently announced Microsoft Network. ...Also under discussion," the sources said, "is some sort of commercial data delivery service that would essentially allow large amounts of digital information to be downloaded to computers from a central location or several locations....

"Microsoft is also interested in using DirecTV to deliver its recently launched Microsoft TV network to its own offices, its employees' homes, and other locations. Microsoft cofounder Bill Gates "is particularly interested in the potential uses of DirecTV and its smaller TVRO [television receive only] antenna to deliver data and video services and in DBS's many potential consumer applications."

Taking advantage of DirecTV to downlink Microsoft TV is preferable to the present transmission system, which uses the Galaxy 7 satellite and requires a conventional (and relatively expensive) TVRO dish for reception. DirecTV also is preferable to DirecPC, a Hughes Network Systems satellite data offering. DirecTV's upfront cost is lower, DirecPC is dedicated to data (no NTSC video output connector is provided), and DirecPC uses a larger (24-inch) dish. DirecPC promises Internet-by-satellite and multimedia services in spring, 1995, and IBM plans to deliver software to retailers via DirecPC. Both DirecTV and DirecPC use an adapter card to make the connection between the high-speed data port of the RCA/Thomson set-top box and the PC or to the satellite dish in the case of DirecPC.

> **Note**
>
> You can obtain further information on Microsoft TV from the MSTV Forum on CompuServe and learn more about DBS satellite systems and the TV programming they offer in the Consumer Electronics Video Forum (GO CEVIDEO). If you don't have a C-band or Ku-band satellite dish that can pick up Galaxy 7, you can purchase videotapes of Bill Gates' COMDEX keynote speed and bi-weekly MSTV programs from MobilTape Co., Inc. at 800-369-5718.

III

Telecomputing

The preceding discussion of wideband transmission methods for MSN is speculative. Microsoft had made no official announcement of its plans for wideband distribution of MSN content when this book was written, beyond the sketchy information included in the TCI announcement. It's clear, however, that 9,600-bps or 14,400-bps delivery of "rich multimedia content" won't satisfy the expectations of the majority of Windows 95 users when signing up for The Microsoft Network. Making MSN where everyone wants to go every day for online information and entertainment clearly requires "unique developments and technology," not only in MSN's content but also in its delivery.

Chapter 14

Hooking Up to the Internet

Connectivity is one of the computer industry's hot topics for the '90s. Connecting computers to networks and on-line services—the so-called information superhighway—has received a great deal of attention in both computer-related and nontechnical media. Windows 95's designers included a tremendous variety of connectivity features in Windows 95, ranging from various built-in networking capabilities to all the tools needed to connect your computer to the Internet—even connecting your local network to the Internet.

▶ See Part IV, "Networking Windows 95"

This chapter describes the Windows 95 features that make it easy for you to connect to the Internet. This chapter begins with a quick overview of the Internet itself and the basic ways of establishing connections to the Internet. The chapter describes the TCP/IP (Transport Control Protocol/Internet Protocol) feature in Windows 95 and how to establish a SLIP (Serial Line Interface Protocol) or PPP (Point-to-Point Protocol) connection using TCP/IP and the various Internet connectivity applications supplied with Windows 95. This chapter concludes with a brief discussion of using the National Center for Supercomputer Applications' (NCSA) Mosaic program to access the Internet from Windows 95.

Internet Fundamentals

Many computer users and professionals believe that the information superhighway isn't a thing of the future, but that it's already here in the form of the Internet. The plethora of information, special interest group (SIG) forums, and e-mail services now available on the Internet support this idea. Certainly, demand for Internet connections has increased significantly during the past year. The demand for Internet access is reflected by the increased number of computer systems providing access to the Internet. The Aug. 22, 1994, issue of *Time* magazine reports that, so far in 1994, the number of computer systems providing access to the Internet has increased 81 percent. Many on-line services such as CompuServe, Prodigy, and America Online have recently added or expanded their connections to the Internet's mail and other services.

> **Note**
>
> The topics of the Internet's history, how computers on the Internet interact with each other, and many other features of the Internet are beyond the scope of this chapter. Several excellent books have been written about the Internet and about using the Internet. You may want to read *Using the Internet*, Special Edition, published by Que Corporation, for detailed information about obtaining an Internet service provider, finding information on the Internet, and legal issues related to using the Internet.

What Is the Internet?

The Internet was originally created in the mid-1960s as an informal offshoot of various federal government research programs. Researchers working at various university and government laboratories needed a convenient way to exchange research data and communications. This need first resulted in the connection of several computers into two different wide area networks known as the DARPAnet (Defense Advanced Research Projects Agency). ARPAnet and DARPAnet were later connected together, and other institutions and agencies were added to the network system now known as the Internet.

Over the ensuing years, the Internet has grown steadily so that it now includes almost every major university in the United States, many different federal and state government agencies, and many private businesses. The Internet isn't restricted by national boundaries: educational and governmental institutions all over the world are connected to the Internet.

No one owns the Internet, nor is the Internet subject to any single governing or controlling agency. Rather, the various institutions that are part of the Internet own their own computers and administer whatever policies on their computers they consider prudent or desirable. Individual agencies or corporations choose to make their computers available as part of the Internet because of the mutual benefits involved—by connecting to the Internet, you gain access to a truly stunning array of information, communication, and other resources. Internet users form a community governed primarily by the personal values and ethics of its individual members—a governing ethic that science fiction writer Robert Heinlein once described as "rational anarchy."

Why TCP/IP?

Although the Internet isn't ruled by any single governing body, the various members of the Internet have agreed on standards for the communications protocols used to connect the Internet's computers together (a necessity for making such a complex network function at all). Computers attached to the Internet use dialup or leased telecommunications lines to establish the physical link between various computers on the Internet. To make sure that each computer on the Internet can "understand" commands or requests sent to it, the TCP/IP (Transmission Control Protocol/Internet Protocol) network communication standard was developed.

TCP/IP provides a standardized method for two computers to communicate over a real-time serial connection, whether the connection is a dialup modem connection or a leased land-line connection. The TCP/IP software contains all the instructions necessary for computers on the Internet to transfer data back and forth—just like the network drivers for your local network allow the computers in your office to exchange data (the Internet computers are just farther away). Windows 95 includes a built-in TCP/IP network protocol driver, which makes it easy to get hooked up to the Internet; with Windows 3.1+, you have to load a variety of TSR programs and other device drivers to get the TCP/IP connectivity built into Windows 95.

What You Need to Connect to the Internet

To use Windows 95 to connect your computer or local network to the Internet, you need the following minimal equipment and software:

- A modem
- An Internet service provider
- Windows 95's Dial-Up Networking and TCP/IP software installed

To make browsing the Internet more congenial, you'll probably also want to use a program such as Mosaic, which provides a graphic user interface for the Internet's resources; otherwise, you'll need to learn how to use some UNIX or VAX/VMS operating system commands (most computers on the Internet are UNIX or VAX mainframes or local networks of UNIX workstations such as the Sun Apollo).

III

Telecomputing

An account with an Internet service provider is probably the most difficult item to obtain—and that isn't really hard. (The Internet *service provider* sells you access to the Internet—typically via a computer system owned by the service provider, to which you connect with a phone line—for a monthly and/or hourly fee.) Many different directories of Internet service providers have been published. Que's *Using the Internet*, Special Edition, contains a listing of several different Internet providers; you can also find Internet provider services listed in the classified advertisements in many computer magazines.

When you select an Internet service provider, make sure that the provider can give you the type of services you need. To use Windows 95's Dial-Up Networking and TCP/IP software, you'll need an Internet service provider that can give you either a SLIP or PPP account—SLIP/PPP accounts are different from the standard dialup account.

Types of Internet Connections

You can connect to the Internet essentially in two ways. The first—and simplest—way is through a dialup connection. The second but more versatile method is to establish a SLIP (Serial Line Interface Protocol) or PPP (Point-to-Point Protocol) connection.

Dialup Connections

A dialup connection to the Internet isn't substantially different from using your modem to communicate with any BBS (bulletin board service) or other on-line service (such as CompuServe, Prodigy, and America Online).

◀ See Chapter 12, "Connecting to the Outside World"

In a dialup Internet connection, you use any telecommunications program (and your modem, of course) to call the Internet service provider. When you connect to the Internet service provider, your computer is attached to the computer at the service provider as though it's just another terminal on that computer—any programs or utilities that you use must be located on the remote computer. Figure 14.1 shows a dialup session to the NetCom Internet provider, using Windows 95's HyperTerminal.

Fig. 14.1
Dialup Internet connections allow you to connect your computer as a terminal to the service provider's computer system.

SLIP/PPP Connections

By using a SLIP or PPP connection, you can actually make your computer a part of the Internet. When you connect to your Internet service provider with a SLIP or PPP connection, your computer (and, optionally, your entire network) becomes part of the Internet. Using a SLIP/PPP account offers advantages over a dialup connection. Because you're actually part of the Internet for as long as you maintain the connection, you can transfer files directly to and from your computer, execute programs locally or on other computers in the Internet, and generally enjoy a more powerful and flexible relationship with various Internet services.

Note

Because SLIP and PPP fulfill the same purpose and operate much the same, you'll frequently see the two abbreviations together: SLIP/PPP. You should make certain that your Internet service provider can give you a SLIP/PPP account if you want to use Windows 95's TCP/IP drivers to make your computer or LAN become a part of the Internet.

The next section describes how to get Windows 95 set up for a SLIP/PPP connection to the Internet.

III

Telecomputing

Using Windows 95's SLIP/PPP Connection

To use a SLIP/PPP connection, you must first install the Dial-Up Networking software, configure Windows 95's network protocol and adapter drivers, and then create a connection in the Dial-Up Networking folder accessed through the Start Programs Accessories menu on your computer. After going through this setup process, you're ready to connect your computer to the Internet.

Setting Up TCP/IP and SLIP/PPP

When you connect to the Internet through a SLIP/PPP connection, you're actually attaching your computer to the Internet as a member of the Internet network, not as a terminal. Logically, then, you must configure Windows 95 for use with SLIP/PPP by making changes in your computer's network configuration in the Control Panel.

Windows 95, like most operating systems that include networking features, divides its network capabilities into several different layers. For a SLIP/PPP Internet connection, you need to install two different layers of software: the Dial-Up adapter driver and the TCP/IP protocol driver. Figure 14.2 shows the opened Network applet in the Windows 95 Control Panel. Notice the Microsoft TCP/IP protocol (the highlighted item in the list), and the Dial-Up adapter (at the top of the list). The Dial-Up adapter provides the layer of software that controls your modem and handles the actual SLIP/PPP connection; the TCP/IP protocol provides the layer of software that handles communications with other computers on the Internet.

Fig. 14.2
You must install the Dial-Up adapter and the TCP/IP protocol driver in the Network applet of Control Panel to create a SLIP/PPP Internet connection.

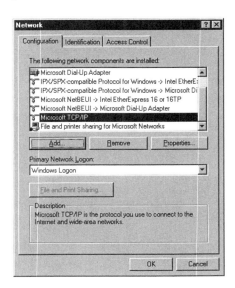

You should already have an Internet SLIP/PPP account before you try to install or set up TCP/IP for use with SLIP/PPP, because you'll need the following information from the Internet service provider:

■ *Your IP (Internet Protocol) address.* This is a code number that designates your address on the Internet. For example, the author's IP address at CRL (an Internet service provider) is 165.113.241.150.

■ *Your IP subnet mask.* The subnet mask is an additional code number that further identifies your Internet address.

■ *Your login name.* This is the name by which you're known on the Internet.

■ *Your login password.*

■ *The gateway IP address.* This is a code number, similar to your IP address, that specifies the address of the gateway. (A *gateway* is the computer system that provides your attachment to the Internet.)

■ *Your host name and domain name.* The *host name* is the name of the computer through which you connect to the Internet, while the *domain name* is the name of the part of the Internet to which you connect. The Internet is divided into domains, such as cities and states, that allow e-mail and other file transfers to be routed to the correct destination. Domains often contain other domains. Most universities, for example, belong to the edu domain; specific universities form smaller domains within the edu domain. Internet users at the University of Colorado are in a domain named colorado. The domain name for the University of Colorado, then, is colorado.edu. (Internet domain addresses are read from right to left.) If a specific computer at the University of Colorado has the host name rintintin, the combined host and domain name is rintintin.colorado.edu.

■ *Your DNS server IP address.* The DNS (Domain Name Server) is the computer that serves your particular domain in the Internet; its IP address is a code number like the other IP addresses already discussed.

To set up and configure Windows 95 for TCP/IP and SLIP/PPP use, you must first make sure that the optional Dial-Up Networking software is installed. (If you didn't install the Dial-Up Networking software when you installed Windows 95, you can install it at any time by using the Add New Programs applet in the Control Panel.) If the Dial-Up Networking software is installed, it will appear as a folder menu choice on the Accessories submenu of the Start Programs menu.

III

Telecomputing

After ensuring the presence of the Dial-Up Networking software, you'll need to perform these procedures with the Network component of Control Panel:

- Install the Dial-Up adapter, if it isn't already present. Use the Add button in the Network applet's Configuration sheet (see fig. 14.2) to add network adapters and protocols.

- Install the Microsoft TCP/IP protocol driver.

- Set up the TCP/IP parameters. Enter the necessary information on the various pages for the TCP/IP driver's properties sheet—you'll need to enter your IP address and subnet mask in the IP Address page and the Gateway IP address in the Gateway page. Be sure to disable the WINS resolution on the WINS Configuration page and enable DNS on the DNS Configuration page (you'll also need to enter your host and domain names and the DNS server on this page).

- Use the properties sheet for the Dial-Up adapter driver, and bind the TCP/IP protocol driver to the Dial-Up adapter. Figure 14.3 shows the Bindings page of a properly configured Dial-Up adapter driver.

Fig. 14.3
You must bind the Dial-Up Adapter to the TCP/IP protocol to make it possible to connect to Internet with SLIP/PPP.

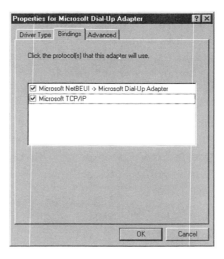

■ Use the Make New Connection wizard in the Dial-Up Networking folder
to create a new dial-up (also called *remote access*) connection to your
Internet service provider. (You can access the Dial-Up Networking
folder through the Start Programs Accessories menu.) Figure 14.4 shows
the second step of the Make New Connection wizard. When you create
your remote access connection, be sure to configure the modem as well
(use the Configure button in the Create a New Connection dialog).
When you configure your modem, use the Options properties page to
avoid displaying a terminal window—you don't need it for your SLIP/
PPP Internet connection, and it will complicate the connection process.
Figure 14.5 shows the Options page for a modem properly configured
for a SLIP/PPP Internet connection.

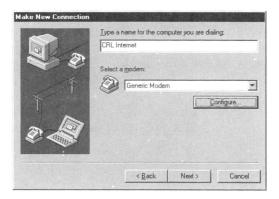

Fig. 14.4
Create a new
remote access
connection to your
Internet service
provider to
connect to the
Internet via SLIP/
PPP and TCP/IP.

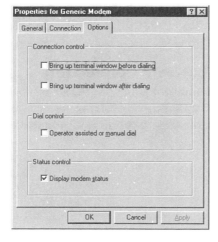

Fig. 14.5
Don't use a
terminal window
for your SLIP/PPP
Internet connec-
tion.

III

Telecomputing

> **Note**
>
> The modem property settings that you make for your Dial-Up Networking connection affect only connections made with that particular Dial-Up Networking connection—other modem properties for other connections remain unchanged.

After you create your remote access connection, Windows 95 adds a new icon to the Dial-Up Networking folder for the new connection. Figure 14.6 shows the icon in the Remote Access folder that resulted from creating a new connection for the CRL Internet provider. (The Make New Connection icon starts the Make New Connection wizard; the icon for the new CRL Internet connection is named CRL Internet.)

Fig. 14.6
Windows 95 keeps all your remote access connections in the Dial-Up Networking folder, accessible through the Start Programs Accessories menu.

As a final step, check the properties for the new dial-up connection you just created, and make sure that the server type is set to either SLIP: Unix Connection, or to PPP: Windows 95, Windows NT 3.5, Internet. (You can access the properties sheets for a dial-up connection by right-clicking on the dial-up connection's icon; change the server type by clicking the Server Type button in the property sheet.)

Making Your SLIP/PPP Connection

Once you've installed and configured the TCP/IP protocol driver, the Dial-Up adapter driver, created a Dial-Up Networking connection, and selected the correct server type for the dial-up connection, you're ready to connect to the Internet.

To make the connection, simply double-click the remote access connection icon. Windows 95 displays the Connect To dialog, asking for your user name and password (see fig. 14.7).

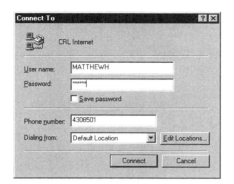

Fig. 14.7
Before dialing the
Dial-Up Network-
ing number,
Windows 95 asks
you to provide
your user name
and password.

Note

When Windows 95 asks for your user name, it really wants you to enter what many
Internet service providers refer to as the *router login*. This is the login name for your
Internet router.

When you click the Connect button, Windows 95 dials the number for your
Internet provider and connects you. If everything goes well, you'll see a dialog similar to the one shown in figure 14.8, showing you the name of the
remote access connection in use, the status of the connection, the method
used to establish the connection, and the length of time you've been connected. Choose the Disconnect button to end the connection.

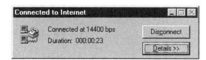

Fig. 14.8
Windows 95
displays a dialog
box that lets you
keep track of the
status and duration
of your remote
access connection.

Sometimes, the Internet gateway that you're connecting to won't be able to
get all the information it needs to complete the connection from your remote
access connection. In this case, you may see a dialog asking you for your user
name, password, and domain name. Fill in the requested information (remember that your user name is your router login) and click OK to complete
the connection.

III

Telecomputing

Windows 95's Internet Utilities

Establishing a SLIP/PPP connection to the Internet is just the first step. When you connect to a BBS, on-line service (such as CIS or Prodigy), or dialup Internet account, you use a modem program, such as HyperTerminal, to make the connection. The modem program makes your computer appear as a terminal connected to the system you've called.

When you connect to the Internet through SLIP/PPP and TCP/IP, you become part of the Internet—your computer is just another computer on the network. You still need a separate application program to view information, issue commands, and transfer files over your network connection.

Windows 95 includes versions of the three basic and essential communication programs required to access the Internet through a SLIP/PPP and TCP/IP connection: PING, FTP, and TELNET. Windows 95 installs these utilities in its home directory. Figure 14.9 shows an Internet Access folder (created by the user, not Windows 95) with Shortcut icons to each of Windows 95's Internet utility programs. Each Internet utility is described in the next few sections.

Fig. 14.9
An Internet Access folder with Shortcut icons.

Using PING

The PING utility is the most basic and essential tool for connecting with the Internet. PING gets its name because it fulfills essentially the same purpose as a sonar or radar ping—you use PING to verify the existence of particular domains in the Internet or determine the names and number of intermediate computers between you and some particular domain.

> **Note**
>
> Remember, you must first make your connection to the Internet before you can use the utility programs described here.

The PING utility included with Windows 95 is actually a DOS application rather than a Windows application. If you execute PING at a DOS command line by itself, it displays a help screen explaining its options and command syntax. To use PING, you execute PING with an Internet domain or server name as a command-line argument.

Figure 14.10 shows the PING window after pinging the `crl.com` domain (CRL is an Internet service provider). Use PING to verify that your SLIP/PPP connection to the Internet is working correctly and that systems you might try to reach actually exist.

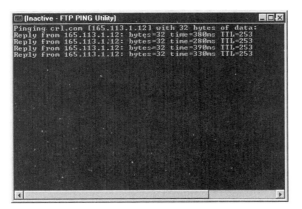

Fig. 14.10
Use PING to verify that your Internet connection is working or to get information about the existence of various Internet domains.

Using FTP

The next most basic Internet utility is FTP (File Transfer Protocol). FTP is a program that allows you to transfer ASCII or binary files to or from your computer. FTP also provides a couple of commands to get information about files, such as directory listings, file sizes, and whether a file is text or binary.

To use FTP, you must first establish your Internet connection, and then start the FTP program. The most important FTP commands you should know are summarized as follows (the parts of the commands in italic represent information that you must supply):

- open ftp.*domain_server_name*   This command opens access to a particular domain in the Internet. Figure 14.11 shows an FTP session; notice the `open` command at the top of the screen, followed by the name for Microsoft's Internet domain. The `ftp.` prefix is required; it tells the other computer to use FTP to communicate with you.

III

Telecomputing

Fig. 14.11

Opening an
FTP session to
microsoft.com,
Microsoft's
Internet domain.

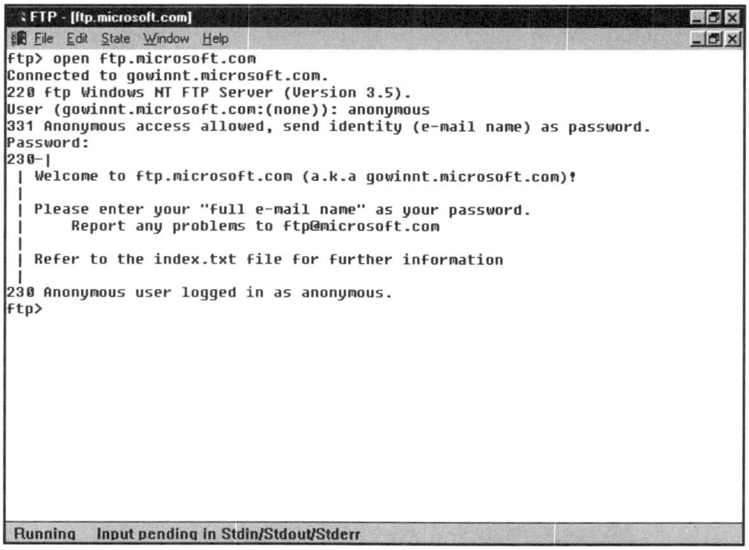

- ls and dir   These two commands have similar functions: to show a
  listing of the files and directories on the computer to which your FTP
  session is now connected. ls provides a quick listing; dir provides more
  details.

- get *filename*   The get command causes FTP to retrieve the file specified by a particular file name; the retrieved file is stored in the current
  disk and directory on your computer. When you use this command,
  remember that Internet systems usually run on the UNIX operating
  system, which is case-sensitive. On the Internet, the file name README
  isn't the same as readme.

- disconnect   This command ends a particular FTP communication with
  a particular Internet domain server. You must disconnect from one
  server before you can connect to another. It's also good manners to
  disconnect before hanging up the phone or otherwise terminating your
  Internet connection.

Using TELNET

You may still be wondering how you get to use the Internet as though you
had a terminal connected to it. The final utility supplied with Windows 95,
TELNET, solves this problem. Like the other Internet utilities, you must first
use Dial-Up Networking to connect to the Internet through your SLIP/PPP

connection. You can then use TELNET to operate other computers on the network (provided you have a logon name and password for those computers) as though you have a terminal connected to those computers.

Note

To issue commands on another Internet computer, you must know the correct operating system commands for that computer. Most of the computers on the Internet use UNIX or VAX/VMS as their operating system, so you'll need to acquire a rudimentary knowledge of some UNIX commands and operations. You may want to read *Introduction to UNIX*, Second Edition, published by Que Corporation, to learn about the UNIX operating system and its commands.

The first time you use TELNET with a particular Internet domain server, you must configure TELNET for that remote computer. The Connect Remote System command opens the Connect dialog (see fig. 14.12); enter the requested information and click Connect to make TELNET aware of that remote system.

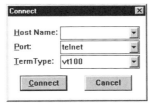

Fig. 14.12
First configure TELNET for connection with a particular remote host computer on the Internet.

You may also need to use the Terminal Preferences command to select the correct terminal type for the remote host computer to which you want to connect. Figure 14.13 shows the Terminal Preferences dialog for setting terminal preferences.

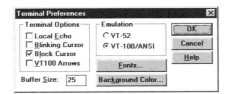

Fig. 14.13
You may need to set terminal preferences so you can communicate successfully with the remote Internet host.

III

Telecomputing

To actually make a connection with TELNET, use the Connection menu and select any remote connection you've previously configured. TELNET displays a window similar to the one shown in figure 14.14, which shows a user logging on to a remote host on the Internet.

Fig. 14.14
Once you connect to the remote host with TELNET, you must log on and issue operating system commands as though you're using a terminal connected to the remote host computer.

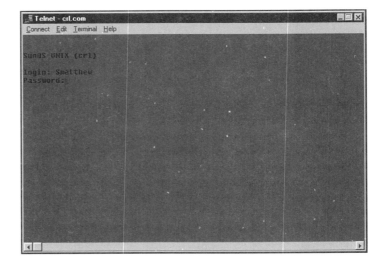

To end a TELNET session, simply use the `logoff` or `logout` command (depending on the host system to which you're connected) to disconnect from the remote host. TELNET displays a dialog indicating that you've disconnected from the remote host. You can then exit TELNET as you would any other application.

Third-Party Internet Tools: Mosaic and Gopher

Although Windows 95 doesn't include a Mosaic or Gopher program, you can easily obtain these programs—usually at no charge and in Windows-compatible versions—from various sources. Both programs can make using the Internet much easier.

Mosaic is an application that creates a graphic user interface for the Internet. Figure 14.15 shows the title screen for the NCSA Mosaic program. This version of Mosaic was obtained from the Internet forum on CIS information services; it's licensed at no charge to private individuals, but business users must obtain a specific license.

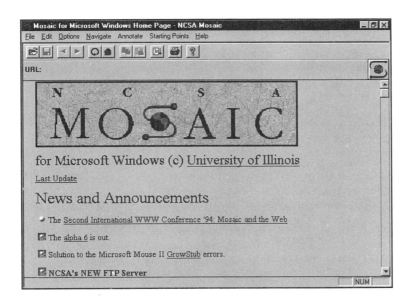

Fig. 14.15
The NCSA Mosaic program provides a way to find and view information on the Internet using a graphic user interface.

Notice that NCSA Mosaic provides a toolbar, complete Windows-style menus, scroll bars, and other features associated with a Windows-style user interface. Mosaic really makes the Internet seem much more like a part of your own computer. You can use Mosaic to search for and view documents on the Internet that contain text, multimedia sound, video, and still graphics.

> **Note**
>
> Although NCSA Mosaic runs in standard VGA resolution (640×480), it requires 256 colors. NCSA Mosaic won't run in 16-color VGA mode. Make sure that your display adapter and monitor are set for 256-color mode before starting Mosaic.

Gopher programs get their names for a couple of reasons: they help you burrow through the Internet, and they help you "go fer" things. Figure 14.16 shows the opening menu for the Gopher module in the NCSA Mosaic application. Essentially, the Gopher menu is a directory of available computers, directories, and files. Items that show up on the Gopher menu may represent items anywhere on the Internet. For example, the `All the Gopher Servers in the World` choice in figure 14.16 literally provides you with a listing of every Internet computer in the world that supports Gopher requests.

III

Telecomputing

Fig. 14.16

Use a gopher
program to locate
items through a
tree-type directory
of topics.

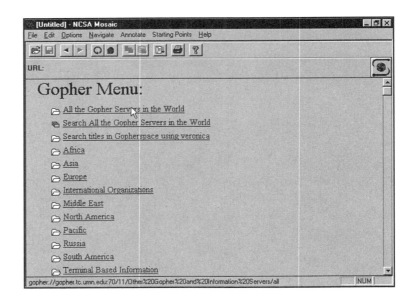

Chapter 15

Faxing with Microsoft At Work Fax

Transmission and reception of documents by fax are rapidly becoming as common as using first-class mail. Today, you can buy a reliable class 1/2 14,400 bps faxmodem adapter card for less than $80. PCMCIA faxmodems for laptop computers now sell for about twice the price of the standard ISA bus version, but intense competition is expected to lower street prices of PCMCIA devices.

Adding a faxmodem to your computer is substantially less costly than buying a dedicated fax machine, and Windows makes programming fax transmissions a breeze. The only limitation of computer faxing is that you need a scanner to fax paper documents. You can buy a monochrome hand scanner complete with the necessary scanning software for about $150. Most computer faxes, however, originate from documents created within Windows.

Windows 95 includes a spiffed-up version of the Microsoft At Work Fax (abbreviated AWFax or MAWFax) application that's included with Windows for Workgroups 3.11. AWFax integrates the transmission and reception of faxes within Exchange client, treating faxes simply as another form of e-mail. Thus, it's no longer necessary to install the fax software that comes with your faxmodem or buy a third-party package, such as Delrina's WinFax Pro. AWFax, however, provides only basic fax services; you can expect firms such as Delrina to produce fax applications for Windows 95 with an expanded feature set, including document management capabilities. This chapter describes how AWFax is installed on a Windows 95 computer and how it manages sending, receiving, and storing of fax documents.

Note

The version of AWFax used to write this chapter is the beta version included with beta 2 (M7) of Windows 95. Some of the features of this version of AWFax, such as sending faxes without opening the Exchange client, weren't operable. Thus, some of the figures in this chapter may differ from those you'll see in the retail version of Windows 95 that includes AWFax.

Understanding the Basics of Fax Transmission

World War II saw the first facsimile transmission of large numbers of documents over the switched telephone network. After the war, facsimiles continued to be used for peacetime purposes, such as transmitting weather maps to the FAA's Flight Service Stations and airline dispatchers. It wasn't until the late 1980s that fax machines became common outside Japan and Europe; by the mid-1990s, just about every firm in North America had a fax machine or computer-based fax installation that could transmit at 9,600 bps or better. High-speed faxing (9,600 bps or 14,400 bps) of a one- or two-page document costs the same or less than sending the document by first-class mail.

Conventional fax transmission involves a rasterizing process, also called rendering, similar to that used for creating television images. The primary differences from TV are that faxes ordinarily are black and white, the signal is a stream of digital bits (rather than a TV analog signal), and the bit stream isn't interlaced. A major improvement in fax transmission speed is provided by compression of the bit-mapped image; large areas of white space require only a few bytes to transmit.

The standards for fax transmission and the compression schemes for fax data are issued by the Consultative Committee for International Telephone and Telegraph (CCITT), which also governs the protocols used for high-speed modem data transfer. Thus, you'll see faxmodems identified by the CCITT specification numbers: V.29, V.27ter, and V.21 channel 2 for faxing and V.32, V.32bis, and V.42bis for data. CCITT also specifies groups and classes of faxes; almost all faxes today fall into Group III, which can transmit at 9,600 bps or higher.

AWFax lets you use Group III, Class 1 faxmodems to transmit faxes in the form of binary data rather than as a rasterized bit stream. Binary transmission is a non-standard transmission format "on top" of the CCITT T.50 transmission protocol, which provides much faster transmission of binary documents from files. Setting up for AWFax binary transmission is described in the next section.

> **Note**
>
> If you're buying a faxmodem, make sure that the device supports 14,400 bps fax and data transmission and Group III, Class 1 features. Many 9,600 bps faxmodems provide only a 2,400 bps data modem; such faxmodems are obsolete. If the modem supports only Class 2 or is a CAS modem, you can't use binary fax transmission mode to send documents to other AWFax users, which can be several times faster than conventional Group III rasterized transmission.

Installing Microsoft At Work Fax

Using At Work Fax requires that you install the AWFax service provider as an Information Service in your default messaging profile, usually My Mail. Figure 15.1 shows the Microsoft Exchange Profiles dialog that opens when you double-click Control Panel's icon of the same name. Clicking the Properties button opens the Properties for My Mail sheet (see fig. 15.2).

> **Note**
>
> You must have previously installed and set up the Exchange client before you can install AWFax. If you don't use the Customize option of Windows 95's Setup application to install the Exchange client and Microsoft Mail 3.1 services, you need to install Microsoft Mail manually.

▶ See Chapter 18, "Messaging with Windows 95's Exchange Client"

III

Telecomputing

Fig. 15.1
The Microsoft Exchange Profiles dialog with Windows 95's default profile, My Mail.

Fig. 15.2

The Properties for My Mail sheet showing Windows 95's standard Information Services.

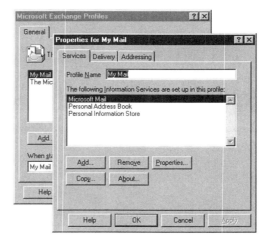

Clicking the Add button opens the Add Service to Profile dialog box (see fig. 15.3). You select the Microsoft At Work Fax entry and then click the OK button. When you close the Add Service to Profile dialog, a warning message similar to that in figure 15.4 appears to let you know that you need to enter information to set up your AWFax system. The sections that follow describe how you set the properties for your AWFax installation.

Fig. 15.3

Adding Microsoft At Work Fax from the Add Service to Profile dialog.

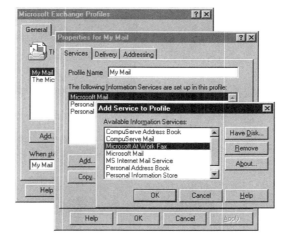

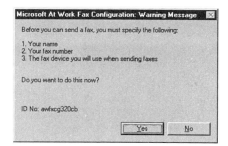

Fig. 15.4
The message that
advises you to
provide informa-
tion about your
faxmodem.

Setting Basic At Work Fax Properties

The Properties for Microsoft At Work Fax sheet opens when you click the
Yes button of the Warning Message (see preceding fig. 15.4) with the default
entries for the Basic page (see fig. 15.5). The Editable, if possible option button (selected by default) lets you send faxes in binary mode to other users of
AWFax. You also set the time to send faxes and select the cover page you
want in the Message page.

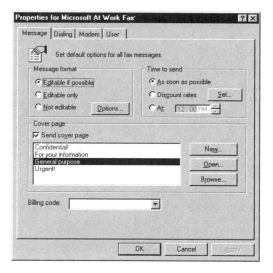

Fig. 15.5
The Message page
of the Properties
for Microsoft At
Work Fax sheet.

> **Note**
>
> The Editable, if possible selection queries the receiving fax to determine whether it supports the Microsoft binary fax protocol. If so, the data is transmitted as a series of bytes. If you choose the Editable option button, you won't be able to send your fax to a conventional Class III fax machine. Selecting the Not Editable option button sends conventional faxes, even to AWFax recipients.

Clicking the Options button of the Message page of the Properties for Microsoft At Work Fax sheet opens the Message Format dialog, where you can specify the paper size and orientation for non-editable (rasterized) faxes (see fig. 15.6). You also can specify the image quality. If you don't mark the Must Send All Attachments check box, Class III fax recipients won't be able to see documents you attach to your fax. The Message page of the Properties for Microsoft At Work Fax sheet also lets you defer sending faxes. Figure 15.7 shows the Set Cheap Rates dialog with the default times when cheap rates begin and end.

Fig. 15.6

Setting the rasterized fax paper size, orientation, attachment rendering, and image quality options.

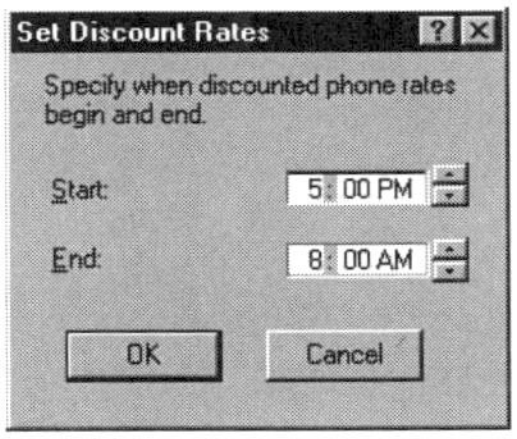

Fig. 15.7

Setting the time that cheap telephone rates begin and end.

Using the At Work Fax Cover Page Editor

AWFax includes a full-featured cover page editor that lets you create your own cover page from scratch or use one of the four example cover pages, listed in the Cover Page list box of preceding figure 15.5, as a template. Figure 15.8 shows the General Purpose cover page in the process of customization. The Confidential example cover page appears in figure 15.9.

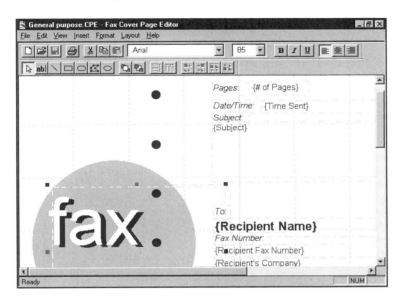

Fig. 15.8
Customizing Windows 95's General Purpose fax cover page.

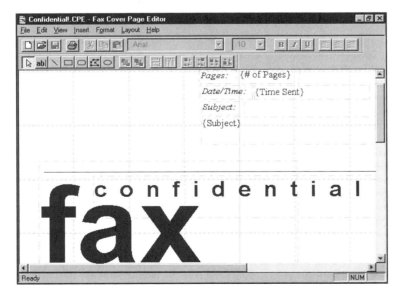

Fig. 15.9
The Confidential example fax cover page in the Cover Page Editor.

III

Telecomputing

Setting Fax Properties

◀ See Chapter 12, "Connecting to the Outside World"

In addition to creating your cover page, you need to provide AWFax with the information to fill in the cover page blanks. The User page of the Properties for Microsoft At Work Fax sheet, shown in figure 15.10, lets you enter your sender name and fax number, plus a variety of other optional information. You also must connect AWFax to a modem using the Modem page of the Properties for Microsoft At Work Fax sheet (see fig. 15.11). You need to set only the name of your faxmodem, assuming that you've already set up the modem for data communication. The Modem page also lets you determine whether to share your faxmodem with members of your workgroup.

Fig. 15.10
Entering data for the sending fax station that appears in your fax cover sheet.

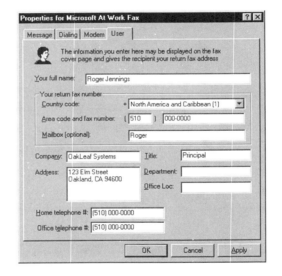

▶ See Chapter 20, "Using Windows 95's Dial-Up Networking"

Note

You can have only one autoanswer device per modem. Thus, if you want to make your computer available for dial-up networking (also called remote access services or RAS), you must turn off the fax autoanswer feature (and vice versa).

The Connection page of the Properties for Microsoft At Work Fax sheet sets retry and dialing options (see fig. 15.12). In the majority of cases, the defaults are satisfactory. Clicking the Dialing Properties lets you specify your computer's location so that the dialing prefix and area code correspond to your current telephone connection.

Fig. 15.11
Setting up the faxmodem configuration for AWFax.

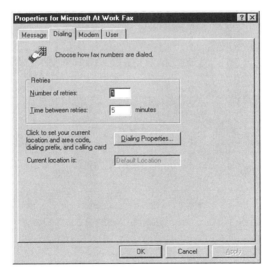

Fig. 15.12
Setting connection, log, and dialing options in the Advanced page of the Properties for Microsoft At Work Fax sheet.

III

Telecomputing

Creating Fax Address Entries

Before you send a fax, you should create one or more address entries in the Postoffice Address List (if you have Microsoft Mail administrative privileges) or in your Personal Address Book. Figure 15.13 shows the opening dialog of the New Fax Wizard that appears when you choose Compose New Fax from Exchange's Fax menu. Clicking the New Name button opens the Properties for New Fax dialog that lets you add a fax address to your Personal Address Book. Figure 15.14 shows the Fax page of the Properties for New Fax sheet in which you set the recipient's name and fax number.

Fig. 15.13
Using the New Fax Wizard to add a fax address to your Personal Address Book.

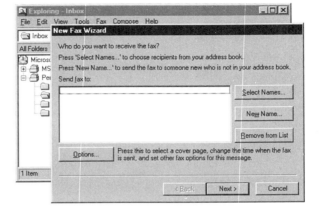

Fig. 15.14
Entering the recipient's name and fax number for the new Personal Address Book entry.

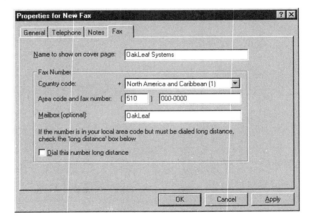

Note

You can send a fax to a recipient that isn't listed in one of the address lists by entering **FAX:fax_number** in the To text box of the message.

Sending and Receiving Faxes

After you've created your address book entry for the recipient, you send a fax in the same manner as sending an e-mail message: open Exchange client and click the Compose toolbar button, or choose New Message from the Compose menu to display the message composition window. Clicking the To button displays the Select Names dialog of the address list that you previously selected from the Show Names drop-down list (see fig. 15.15). You add the message text and include attachments if you want (see fig. 15.16). Clicking the Send button of the toolbar or choosing Send from the File menu starts the fax transmission process.

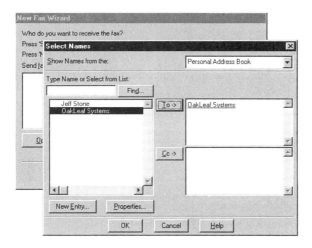

Fig. 15.15
Choosing a name of a fax recipient from your Personal Address Book.

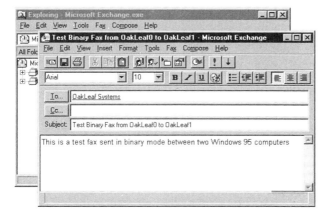

Fig. 15.16
Entering the text of a fax.

III

Telecomputing

At the receiving end, the Task Bar button for AWFax monitors the status of your modem. When receiving a fax, you see four messages: Initializing Modem, Negotiating, Receiving n Bytes, and, finally, Receive Successful. When you open your Inbox folder, the received fax appears in the list (see fig. 15.17). Double-clicking the entry displays the binary fax exactly as it was sent, as shown in figure 15.18. (Compare fig. 15.18 with fig. 15.16.)

Fig. 15.17

An Inbox entry for a newly received binary fax.

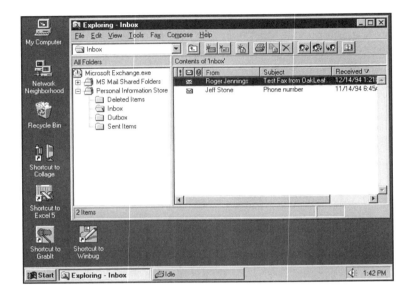

Fig. 15.18

Displaying the binary fax received by AWFax.

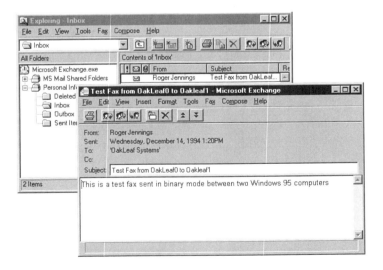

If you transmit a rasterized fax to a Windows 95 computer or receive a Class III fax from a fax machine, the recipient's Inbox entry and fax message appear (see fig. 15.19). Double-clicking the FAX2.AWD icon displays the rasterized fax in Windows 95's Fax Viewer (see fig. 15.20).

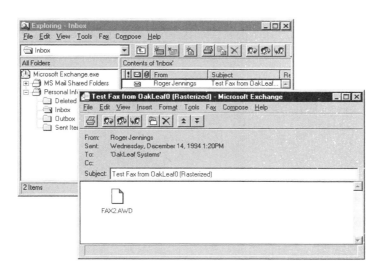

Fig. 15.19
A conventional, rasterized fax received in the Inbox.

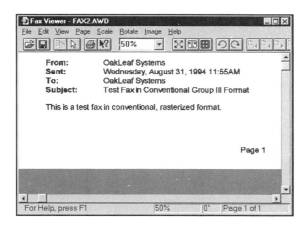

Fig. 15.20
Displaying a conventional fax with Windows 95's Fax Viewer.

Note

If you've used the AWFax feature of Windows for Workgroups 3.11, you'll find that Windows 95's methods of handling fax transmission and reception are quite similar. The differences between WfWg's and Windows 95's implementations of AWFax relate primarily to the user interface and not to fax transmission methodology.

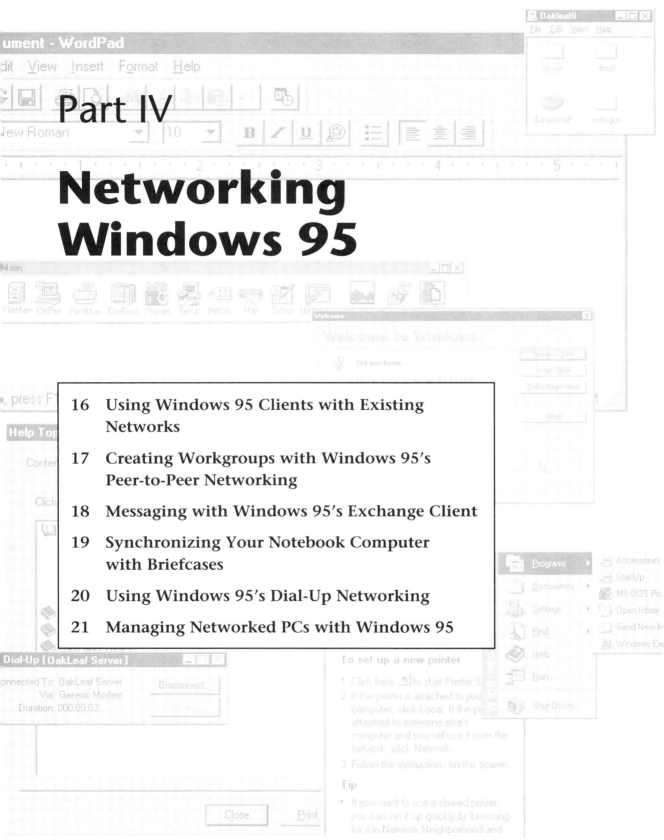

Part IV

Networking Windows 95

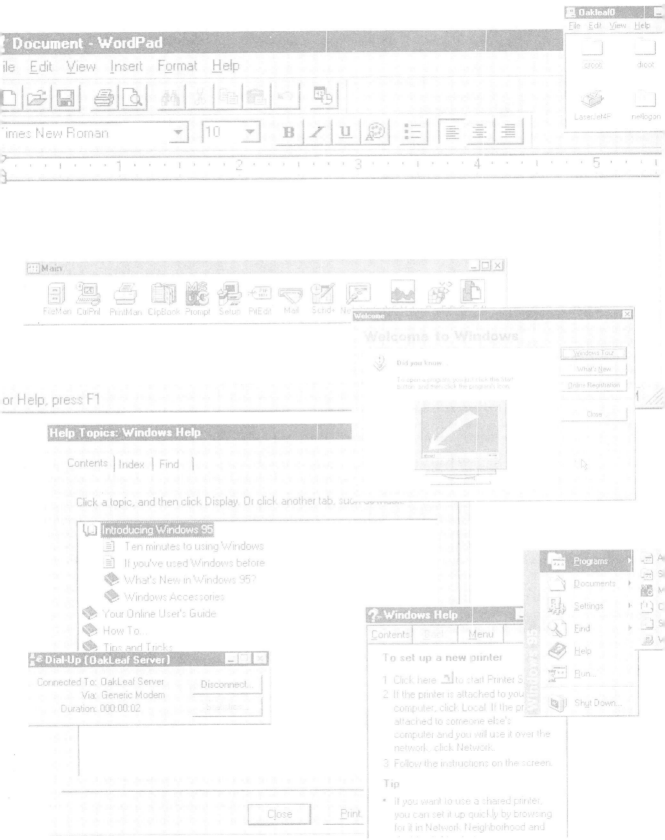

Chapter 16

Using Windows 95 Clients with Existing Networks

Microsoft designed Windows 95 from the ground up for local and wide area networking; Windows 95, together with Windows 3.5 Workstation, truly qualify for the term *universal client*. As noted in Chapter 1, "Building the 'Information Appliance' of the 1990s," PC industry market research firms predicted that about 60 percent of all PCs would be connected in local area networks by the end of 1994. Although the percentage of networked PCs will likely decrease as the consumer market for "information appliances" grows, the number of networked PCs is likely to increase dramatically in 1995 and beyond. It's not uncommon to find home computer users setting up a simple, two-computer peer-to-peer network so the kids can share files on their parents' computers. It's likely that set-top cable boxes and home satellite TV tuner/descramblers will send digital TV images over the same wires or cable that now interconnect PCs.

Most PCs running Windows 95 initially will connect to existing networks. Probably the existing network operating system (NOS) will be Novell NetWare 3+ or 4+, because Novell has more than 60 percent of the current NOS market. PCs in large corporate settings will likely be connected to UNIX-based (TCP/IP) networks, while small firms will use Windows 95's built-in peer-to-peer networking system that can comfortably handle 20 to 50 interconnected PCs, which share files, printers, backup tape drives, and other devices.

This chapter describes the features of Windows 95 that make connecting PCs to existing networks simpler and cheaper; the next chapter shows you how to hook up your own peer-to-peer, Windows 95-only network.

Swallowing a Small Dose of Network Terminology

It's terminology time again, so here's another section that network-conversant PC power users can skip. Windows 95 may provide the first opportunity for many PC users to connect to a network, so following are some of the terms networking *naïfs* need to know to understand Windows 95's new built-in networking features:

◀ See Chapter 14, "Hooking Up to the Internet"

■ *Servers* are computers dedicated to sharing files, running applications remotely, processing requests for information from databases, and providing connectivity to common peripheral devices such as CD-ROM changers, printers, and modems. The three major categories of servers are *file servers*, *application servers*, and *database servers*. Application and database servers usually run on high-performance 80486DX or, preferably, Pentium computers. Database servers are the foundation of today's client-server computing environment. Older, slower computers often are relegated to file-sharing and peripheral-sharing duties. (In peer-to-peer networks, an individual workgroup computer can act as both a server and a client.)

■ *Clients*, often called *workstations*, are PCs that take advantage of the services provided by application and database servers. Windows 95 is intended as the operating system for client PCs and includes the local (requester or redirector) software required to connect to Novell and Microsoft Windows networks, as well as to networks using the TCP/IP protocol. Additional software (PC-NFS, SunSelect's Network File Server, or the equivalent) is required to share files stored on a UNIX server, but you can download files over TCP/IP by using Windows 95's built-in FTP (File Transfer Protocol) command-line application. FTP primarily is used for downloading files from Internet host (server) computers. Publishers of network operating systems that don't operate with Windows 95's built-in drivers supply their own version of the required client drivers.

■ *Network interface cards* (NICs) are adapter cards that make the connection between the PC's bus and the network cabling. NICs for client PCs now sell for $100 or less, and many PCs now include the NIC circuitry on the motherboard. Most networks in use today use the EtherNet cards with conventional telephone wiring (twisted pair, called 10BASE-T) leading to a hub that usually can connect from 4 to 16 computers to one another. Hubs are interconnected to create larger networks. For smaller networks, thin coaxial cable (10BASE2) is used to interconnect PCs and servers. IBM's Token Ring network is a more expensive contender in the NIC business. NICs designed for servers provide better performance than those for PCs and are substantially more expensive.

- *Network operating systems* (NOSs) reside on the server and are the operating system for the server itself. Novell NetWare is the prevalent NOS, but UNIX (which has built-in multiuser and networking features) and Windows NT 3.5 Server are contenders in the NOS market. The NOS provides network security, controlling access to the network by user ID and password. The NOS lets you share applications from the server and gives you access to specific directories of files that are shared by the server. The NOS also is responsible for sharing peripherals, such as printers, CD-ROM drives, and modems.

- *Network protocols* are the methods by which clients and servers communicate on the network. Novell IPX (InterPacket Exchange) is the most common network protocol today, so Windows 95 installs the IPX protocol as the default when it detects an NIC. TCP/IP is the protocol used by local and wide area UNIX networks, including the Internet. The Microsoft Windows network (and IBM's LAN Server network) uses the NetBEUI (Network BIOS Extended User Interface) protocol, which is the default protocol for Windows 95, Windows for Workgroups, and Windows NT networks. A common feature of all network protocols is that the protocol sends and receives blocks of data, called *packets*, that are addressed to a particular server or client; protocols differ primarily in the way they handle network addresses. Windows 95 now allows a single client PC to use multiple protocols simultaneously. The PC that this chapter was written with uses IPX, TCP/IP, and NetBEUI protocols.

- *Bridges* make connections between networks that use different transmission methods and/or network protocols. You need a bridge, for example, to connect a Novell network to a TCP/IP network. Windows 95 offers an alternative to a bridge for individual users; you can install multiple adapter cards in your client PC, one for each type of network.

◀ See Chapter 14, "Hooking Up to the Internet"

- *Routers* are used in wide area networks (WANs) to send packets of data from a local area network (LAN) in one location to a LAN in another location. Routers are also used to connect host servers to the Internet.

The router is responsible for making sure that messages addressed to *you@yourfirm*.com or to *134.186.63.8* (two means of specifying a particular PC on TCP/IP networks) get to the right location.

■ *Gateways* connect PC-based LANs and WANs to minicomputers and mainframes. Gateways, also called *middleware*, are commonly used to provide PC network access to mainframe databases, such as IBM's DB2. Information Builders, Inc. (IBI) and Micro Decisionware, a subsidiary of database system supplier Sybase, Inc., are two of the major middleware suppliers for IBM mainframes.

Checking Out the New Networking Features in Windows 95

Before Windows 95 came along, you needed to load 16-bit real-mode, DOS-based network drivers and related programs by entries in your CONFIG.SYS and AUTOEXEC.BAT files to use network protocols other than NetBEUI under Windows. The drivers and programs required to allow the client PC to connect to the Novell or Microsoft Network servers consume about 140K of conventional memory. Adding TCP/IP connectivity to Windows for Workgroups 3.11 required another big chunk of conventional memory. Thus, you ended up needing a memory manager—such as the one included in DOS 6+ or provided by Quarterdeck's QEMM application—that loaded as many drivers as possible into high memory to free enough conventional memory to run Windows 3.1+ effectively. Complex CONFIG.SYS and AUTOEXEC.BAT files create nightmares for networked PC users and are the abomination of corporate PC support personnel.

If you're connecting to a Novell NetWare or Microsoft Windows network with Windows 95, you can say good-bye to 16-bit real-mode network drivers and convoluted CONFIG.SYS and AUTOEXEC.BAT files. Following is a list of some of the other advantages of using Windows 95's new 32-bit networking clients:

■ *Plug and Play installation of network cards.* When you put a Plug and Play network card into a PC with Plug and Play BIOS, the I/O address and interrupts are set to avoid conflicts with other Plug and Play cards and legacy devices, and Windows 95 automatically loads the driver for the card. If you insert a PCMCIA NIC in your Plug and Play notebook PC, the NIC's driver is located automatically and you're connected immediately to the network. When you unplug the NIC or disconnect the network cable, you no longer need to reboot your notebook. (Most—but not all—present-day notebook computers require a reboot when you pull the PCMCIA NIC.)

■ *Easy access to network resources.* The My Computer window displays all local disk drives and network file resources to which you are now connected. Network Neighborhood displays additional network resources available for connection. You can use a shared network printer as easily as though it was connected to LPT1 of your client computer.

▶ See Chapter 17, "Creating Workgroups with Windows 95's Peer-to-Peer Networking"

■ *Simultaneous multiple networks and protocols.* Windows 3.1+ supported only a single NOS and adapter card. Windows 95 lets you install multiple NOSs and more than one NIC, if necessary. This way, you can run the Microsoft Windows Network (NetBEUI), Novell NetWare (IPX/SPX), and TCP/IP client protocols simultaneously. For example, you can share files on a NetWare server with workgroup members connected via the Windows Network and connect to a remote Internet host with PPP (Point-to-Point Protocol) and TCP/IP at the same time. If you have SunSelect's PC-NFS installed, you can share files on UNIX servers with others who don't have PC-NFS installed.

■ *Single logons for multiple networks and password-protected documents.* Network administrators can set up user accounts on servers so that Windows 95 clients can log on to multiple networks and gain access to all network resources that the user is entitled to with a single user name and password. Windows 95's Master Key services allow a user with the appropriate logon password to open password-protected documents without having to enter the password manually. (Applications must be written to support Windows 95's Master Key services to make this feature work.)

■ *Long file names and UNC server connections.* If your server(s) support long file names, you can use the long file names under Windows 95. Both Windows NT 3.5 Server and Novell NetWare support long file names if the server is configured to do so. With Windows 95, you don't need to map shared server file resources to a local drive designation letter; you use the UNC (Universal Naming Convention) to specify a shared file resource. With Windows 95, you can enter **dir \\servername\sharename** at the command line to obtain a list of files and subdirectories in the shared directory.

▶ See Chapter 21, "Managing Networked PCs with Windows 95"

■ *Built-in administrative systems for networked PCs.* Windows 95 includes a variety of built-in administrative tools for managing Windows 95 networks. Many of these tools are similar to those supplied with Windows for Workgroups 3.11, including Net Watcher, which allows local and remote management of connections to Windows 95 peer-to-peer network services. Windows 95 also includes the Cheyenne ARCServe and Arcada Backup agents, both of which let NetWare and Windows NT 3.5 Server remotely back up files on Windows 95 clients' fixed disks.

- *Faster network operations.* Windows 95's client networking services are implemented as Windows Virtual Device Drivers (VxDs). VxDs are 32-bit protected-mode drivers; thus, they consume no conventional memory.

- *Increased client-side reliability.* Windows 95 allocates blocks of memory to its protected-mode VxDs, minimizing the chance of network drivers being "stepped on" by running applications. This makes Windows 95's network VxDs more reliable than 16-bit real-mode drivers by eliminating memory conflicts. Windows 95 handles resource allocation for network card interrupts, which eliminates the potential for client-side crashes that occasionally occur with real-mode drivers.

- *Improved security for peer-to-peer operations.* If you're running Microsoft Windows NT 3.5 Server or Microsoft LAN Manager with domain services, you can use domain-level security for sharing files and other resources.

Windows 95 provides full support only for Microsoft Windows and Novell NetWare networks through built-in VxDs, but other major NOS suppliers have announced their intention to supply 32-bit networking VxDs for Windows 95. Artisoft (LANtastic), Banyan (VINES), Digital (DECNet), and SunSelect (PC-NFS) are expected to have their Windows 95 client VxDs ready when Windows 95 is released, or shortly thereafter. The built-in Windows network client is compatible with Microsoft Windows for Workgroups 3.1+, IBM LAN Server, DEC Pathworks, and AT&T Starlan and LAN Manager for UNIX networks.

> **Note**
>
> Windows 95's default network protocol is Novell's IPX/SPX, not Microsoft's Net-BEUI protocol for the Windows network. There are two reasons for making IPX/SPX the default: NetWare is by far the most popular NOS, and IPX/SPX is a *routable* protocol—NetBEUI isn't. A routable protocol is required for network connectivity between multiple LANs connected by routers. (Both IPX/SPX and TCP/IP are routable protocols.) Windows NT 3.5 Server includes IPX/SPX services (called an *IPX/SPX stack*), so a Windows NT 3.5 server can appear to a Windows 95 client as a NetWare server. You also can use TCP/IP as a single protocol to connect to NetWare, UNIX, and Windows NT 3.5 servers.

Setting Up a Windows 95 Network Client

▶ See Chapter 23, "Setting Up and Managing Windows 95"

Microsoft has devoted a substantial amount of development time to making the installation of Windows 95's network client services as simple as possible. The following three sections describe how Windows 95 sets up its client networking services in three scenarios: installing Windows 95 over an existing networked version of Windows 3.1+, installing Windows 95 for dual-boot with DOS, and adding a network card after installing Windows 95.

Setting Up Windows 95 over an Existing Windows 3.1 Network Installation

When you install Windows 95 over an existing Windows 3.1+ installation that provides network client services, the Windows 95 Setup program reads your existing WIN.INI and SYSTEM.INI files to determine the type of network services now in use. If you're on a NetWare or Windows network, the Setup program makes the changes to WIN.INI and SYSTEM.INI required to load the new VxDs. If you're using a NOS that isn't supported by the two built-in clients, such as the Artisoft LANtastic network, the existing 16-bit real-mode drivers are used. It's up to NOS suppliers to provide upgraded protected-mode VxDs for their networks, either on distribution floppy disk(s) or an electronic bulletin board or information utility, such as CompuServe.

Setup doesn't remove the entries in CONFIG.SYS and AUTOEXEC.BAT to load the real-mode drivers. If Setup finds the Windows network's NET START instruction in AUTOEXEC.BAT, it changes the line to call `C:\WINBOOT\netstart.bat`. NETSTART.BAT contains the single line, `C:\WINBOOT\net start %1` to run Windows 95's 32-bit version of NET.EXE instead of the 16-bit version that remains in your \WINDOWS directory. Depending on the type of network in use, you might be asked to provide information that Setup can't find in WIN.INI or SYSTEM.INI. When the Setup process completes, Windows 95 displays a logon dialog typical of that shown in figure 16.1, the Enter Network Password dialog for a Windows NT 3.5 Server domain. If you enter the wrong network user name or password, Windows 95 opens the local logon dialog shown in figure 16.2. A network client installation of Windows 95 maintains its own local password list, so you don't have to enter your domain password each time you use a shared resource.

Network drive mapping is preserved from your prior Windows 3.1+ installation. After you log on to the network, Windows 95 flashes the Restoring Network Connections dialog for each network file share mapped to a local drive letter and for each networked printer you share. If you didn't successfully log on to the network in the opening Enter Network Password dialog, a different version of the Enter Network Password dialog appears, as shown in figure 16.3, giving you a second chance to enter a valid password and save the password in the local password list. (You can't, however, change your user name at this point.) If you succeed in mapping the drive, your My Computer window displays the appropriate network drive icons; Croot on 'Oakleaf0' (H:) and Droot on 'Oakleaf0' (I:) are examples of Windows 95's mapped network share icons (see fig. 16.4). If you can't log on to the network at this point, the mapped drives don't appear (see fig. 16.5). (Previous beta versions superimposed the international "No" symbol over the network share icon for the failed connection).

Fig. 16.1
Logging on to a Windows network that uses a Windows NT 3.5 Server.

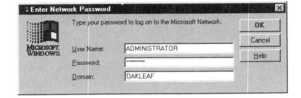

Fig. 16.2
Logging on to Windows 95 locally after a failed network logon attempt.

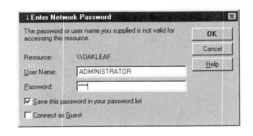

Fig. 16.3
Mapping a network drive to a local drive letter after a failed or canceled network logon.

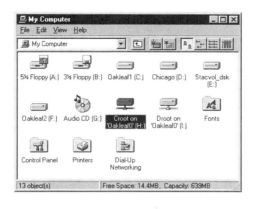

Fig. 16.4
My Computer
displaying net-
worked shares
mapped to local
drives H and I.

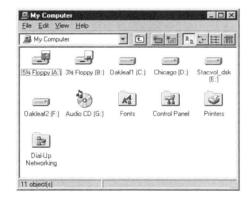

Fig. 16.5
The server share
icons disappear if
you can't connect
to the network.

Setting Up Windows 95 Networking in a New or Dual-Boot Installation

If you install Windows 95 in a dual-boot configuration to preserve your existing versions of DOS and Windows, the Setup program automatically detects
your network interface card and registers its I/O address and interrupt (IRQ)
number in Windows 95's Registry. In the unlikely event that Setup can't
identify your NIC, a dialog appears to let you choose a built-in driver for a
supported card, similar to that shown in the next section when you install a
new network card. If Windows 95 doesn't have a built-in driver for your NIC,
you'll need to install the real-mode or, if available, protected-mode VxD
driver from the setup floppy disk supplied by the card's manufacturer.

After setting up the driver for your NIC and completing the Setup process,
you reboot Windows to activate the driver. Windows 95 automatically
installs the client services for the Windows and Novell networks, plus the
protocol drivers for NetBEUI and IPX/SPX required to make the network
connection. In a dual-boot or new installation, you need to enter your user

▶ See Chapter 23,
"Setting Up
and Managing
Windows 95,"
and Chapter
24, "Replacing
WIN.INI,
SYSTEM.INI,
and REG.DAT
with Registry"

name, password, and domain name, if you're using the Windows Network, in the Enter Network Password dialog. Figure 16.6 shows the Enter Network Password dialog for a NetWare 3.1+ server resource.

Fig. 16.6

The Enter Network Password dialog to map a Novell 3.1 network resource to a local drive.

The process of mapping a Windows network drive to a local drive designator is similar to that used by Windows for Workgroups 3.1+'s File Manager. You click the Map Drive icon (see fig. 16.7) to display the Connect Network Drive dialog. After you enter the UNC path to the server share and optionally mark the Reconnect at Setup check box, click the OK button; My Computer automatically displays the folders (directories) and files of the new share (see fig. 16.8).

Fig. 16.7

Mapping a server share to a local drive designator letter.

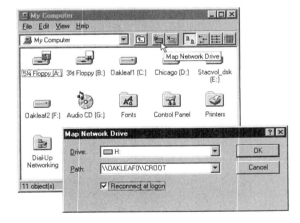

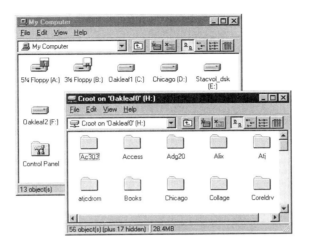

Fig. 16.8
A new window
opened by My
Computer after
connecting a
network file share.

Installing a Network Interface Card after Installing Windows 95

Many PC users without an existing network will install Windows 95 on their computers, and then add a network interface card when setting up a new client-server or peer-to-peer network. If you turn off your computer and in-stall one of the new Plug and Play NICs in a computer with Plug and Play BIOS, Windows 95 recognizes its appearance and automatically installs the required VxD for the card when you turn the power on. You'll be asked for an installation floppy disk if Windows 95 doesn't have a built-in driver for the card.

If you don't have Plug and Play BIOS, you need to make Windows 95 aware of the new card by opening Control Panel and double-clicking the New De-vice icon to open the Hardware Installation Wizard (HIW). You can choose to install the NIC driver with the HIW before or after you plug in the new card; installing the driver first lets you check to see whether the factory defaults for the base I/O address and IRQ level are free. Figure 16.9 shows the second dialog of the HIW, where you select the type of device you plan to install—in this case, a network adapter card. Clicking the Next button displays the Select Device dialog, which provides a list of network adapter card manufacturers whose products Windows 95 recognizes. When you make a selection in the Manufacturers list box, the supported products of the manufacturer appear in the Models list box (see fig. 16.10). You select the model of your card and then click the Next button.

Fig. 16.9
Specifying the type
of new device to
install with the
Hardware Installa-
tion Wizard.

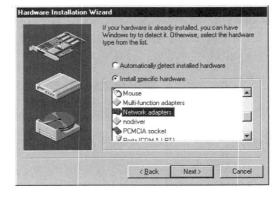

Fig. 16.10
Selecting the
manufacture
and model of
your NIC.

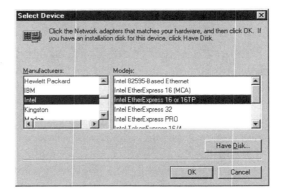

The HIW proposes to install the NIC with default values chosen by the NIC's
manufacturer, as shown in figure 16.11. You cannot alter the default values at
this point. When you click the Next button, the HIW checks to see whether a
conflict exists between the manufacturer's default I/O base address and IRQ
level. If a conflict exists, you must launch the Network properties sheet from
Control panel, select your NIC from the list of network devices, then click the
Properties button to display the properties sheet for your NIC. You select the
Resources page, which shows settings with conflicts preceded by an asterisk
(*). Figure 16.12 shows a conflict between the Interrupt (IRQ) 4 default value
and an existing adapter card. (IRQ 4 is used for the COM1 serial port in almost all PC systems.) In this case, you use the spinners of the IRQ text box to
choose an IRQ value that isn't preceded by an asterisk. IRQ 5 or IRQ 9, which
is the same as (cascaded with) IRQ 2, is a likely candidate for the NIC on most
computers.

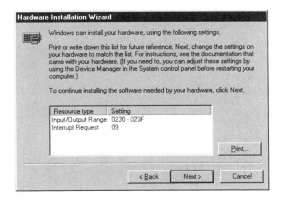

Fig. 16.11
The New Device Installation Wizard's dialog that proposes to install an NIC with the manufacturer's suggested default values.

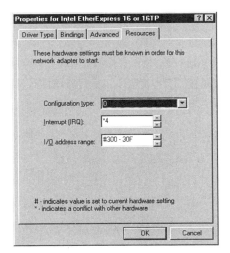

Fig. 16.12
The Resources page of Network's properties sheet for Intel Ether Express 16 NICs displaying a conflicting interrupt request (IRQ) value.

The Hardware Installation Wizard's comment, "If you need to, you can adjust these settings by using the Device Manager in the System control panel before restarting your computer" is incorrect. Figure 16.13 shows the System properties sheet with the Network Adapters item expanded. Clicking the Properties button displays the System properties sheet for the Intel EtherExpress 16, as illustrated by figure 16.14. This properties sheet does *not* allow you to change the card's settings. You must open the properties page for the NIC from Control Panel's Networks icon as described in the preceding paragraph.

Fig. 16.13
The Properties for System sheet with the Network Adapter card line expanded.

Fig. 16.14
The System properties sheet for the Intel EtherExpress 16 NICs.

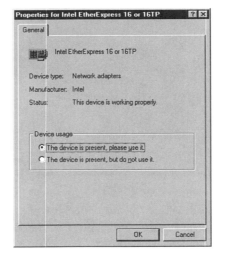

> **Tip**
>
> If you install a driver for your NIC with settings that conflict with the base I/O address or IRQ level of an existing adapter card, Windows 95 will likely hang during the startup process. If you reboot your computer and then restart Windows 95, the Fail-Safe Boot message appears and offers you the choice of not installing the driver that caused the system to hang—in this case, NET.EXE. You then pick a non-conflicting setting, run the NIC's software to reset the NIC to the corresponding values, and reboot your computer.

Configuring Network Client Services

The default network installation that includes both the Novell NetWare and Microsoft Windows networks satisfies the vast majority of networked PC users' needs. However, you need to identify your computer by name to most networks if you set up Windows 95 in dual-boot mode or added an NIC after installing Windows 95. Double-clicking Control Panel's Network icon opens the Network properties sheet; figure 16.15 shows the Identification page where you enter your computer's name and, if you plan to share files with others in a workgroup, the name of the workgroup. (The description entry is optional and isn't used by the network.) If you plan to share files with others and want to take advantage of the additional security offered by limiting users to those persons who have accounts on a Windows NT 3.5 network domain, click the User-Level Security option button and specify the domain controller where the users have accounts (see fig. 16.16). On current Novell networks, user-level security supports the NetWare bindery.

As noted earlier in this chapter, Windows 95 automatically installs the VxDs necessary to use Microsoft Windows and Novell Networks simultaneously. The Configuration page of the Network properties sheet lets you add or delete client services, drivers for adapter cards and remote access services, network protocols, and one of two network services that let you share files with other network users. Figure 16.17 shows the default network components for an installation of the Windows 95 network client, dial-up networking, and the Microsoft TCP/IP protocol stack.

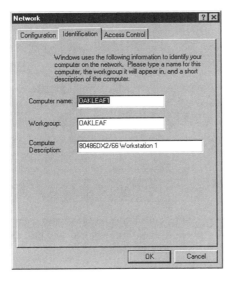

Fig. 16.15
Identifying your computer by name to other users on the network.

Fig. 16.16
Specifying user-level security for directories you share with other members of workgroups.

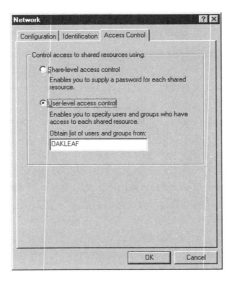

Fig. 16.17
The Configuration page of Windows 95's Network properties sheet, which lists installed network components.

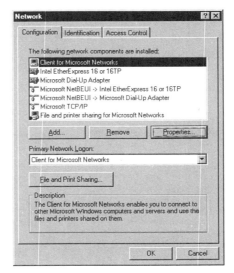

Tip

If you don't use a Novell network, it's a good idea to remove the Novell network VxD from the installed network components list. You may find that an unused Novell network VxD slows other network operations.

When you select a network component in the list box, clicking the Properties button displays the properties sheet for the component. Figure 16.18 shows the Microsoft Network Client properties sheet that lets you log on with your password verified by an existing Windows NT 3.5 Server domain. You also can specify either Quick or Verified connection of network shares. In most cases, the default Quick connection is the best choice.

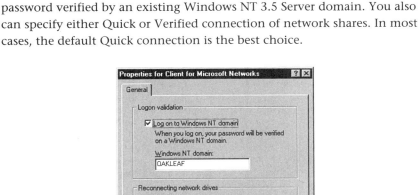

Fig. 16.18
Windows 95's
Microsoft Network
Client properties
sheet.

IV

Networking Windows 95

Figure 16.19 shows the properties sheet for the Intel EtherExpress 16 EtherNet NIC. The Bindings page displays the network protocols to which the NIC is bound (that is, which the NIC uses). Windows 95 supports multiple NICs in your PC. The functions of the other three pages of the NIC properties sheet (not shown here) are as follows:

- The Driver Type page lets you choose between protected-mode and real-mode drivers.

- The Resources page, shown in figure 16.12 earlier in the chapter, lets you set the I/O Base Address and Interrupt (IRQ) values to correspond to those you previously established by using the NIC manufacturer's setup application.

- The Advanced page lets you alter the operating characteristics of the NIC. The appearance of this page depends on the make and model of the NIC installed in your computer.

Fig. 16.19
The Bindings page of the properties sheet for an Intel EtherExpress 16 EtherNet NIC using the Microsoft Network (NetBEUI) and TCP/IP protocols.

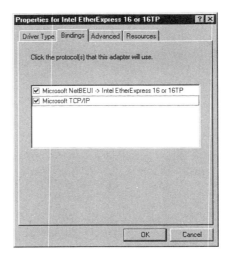

It's seldom necessary to change the default settings in the preceding three pages.

◄ See Chapter 14, "Hooking Up to the Internet"

► See Chapter 20, "Using Windows 95's Dial-Up Networking"

Figure 16.20 shows the Configuration page of the Network properties sheet with the Novel NetWare 4.1 client added to the list of installed network components. You choose in the Primary Network Logon combo box the network you want to use to validate your password, run logon scripts, and perform any other network startup services. If you are using NetWare, you ordinarily would select the NetWare client as the primary (default) network. Unless you're using a Unix (TCP/IP) network or a network that's not supported by Windows 95's built-in networking VxDs, the default Client for Microsoft Networks is the correct choice. The Microsoft Network client supports Windows NT 3.5 Server networks, plus Windows NT 3.5 Workstation, Windows for Workgroups 3.11, and Windows 95 peer-to-peer networking.

> **Caution**
>
> The preceding figures and descriptions of Windows 95 network client setup and configuration operations were valid for the M7 beta version of Windows 95 used in writing this book. Although continuous use of the networking features of the beta software over several months demonstrated that the networking elements of Windows 95 were quite stable, many changes occurred in the logon procedure and properties pages between the M5 and M7 beta versions. Microsoft may choose to alter the user interface or the networking feature set in subsequent beta versions and the retail version of Windows 95.

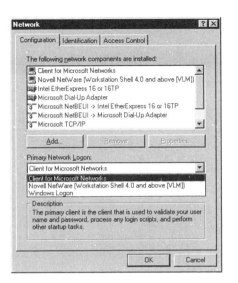

Fig. 16.20
Setting the primary (default) network protocol in the Network Configuration properties page.

Roaming the Network Neighborhood

Just as My Computer lets you browse the directories and files on your local disk drives, the Network Neighborhood window lets you browse network file resources, regardless of their location or the type of network that the file resource resides on. Network Neighborhood takes advantage of Windows 95's UNC (Universal Naming Convention) method of specifying network shares with the *servername**sharename* command-line syntax. Windows 95 lets you display the files and directories of a server share in a window. As an example, choosing Run from the Start menu and entering **oakleaf0****croot** in the Command Line text box of the Run dialog opens a window displaying the directories and files of the root directory of the OAKLEAF0 server. As mentioned earlier in the chapter, UNC syntax eliminates the need to assign a local drive designator letter to each server share you use.

▶ See Chapter 21, "Managing Networked PCs with Windows 95"

When you open Network Neighborhood, folders representing all network servers that you're connected to appear, including any peer-to-peer servers in your workgroup, and your computer. Figure 16.21 shows a simple network with one Windows NT 3.5 server (\\OAKLEAF0) and a single workstation (\\OAKLEAF1) on which this chapter was written. The server shares the root directories of both its physical disks plus \\OAKLEAF\NETLOGON, which is required for clients to log on to Windows NT 3.5 Server. If you're using Windows 95 on a large network, it's likely that the network administrator will set up your most commonly used network shares so that they appear when you open Network Neighborhood. To display all the network resources available in your domain, you double-click the Entire Network icon. In a simple networking environment, the shares are identical to the folders that appear in the main Network Neighborhood window.

Fig. 16.21
Using Network Neighborhood to browse network resources.

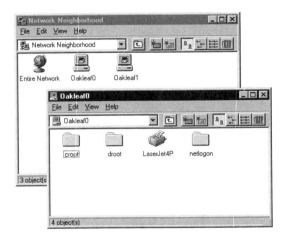

The advantage to using Network Neighborhood to browse the network and run applications from the network is the lack of the local logical disk drive designator. If you use one or more server shares regularly, you can add a desktop Shortcut to the share by dragging the folder from Network Neighborhood's window to the desktop. The Shortcut uses UNC rather than a local drive designator to open a window showing the content of the share. The process is identical to executing *servername**sharename* in the Run dialog.

Understanding Windows 95's Client Networking Architecture

Microsoft's primary objectives for the design of Windows 95's networking architecture were twofold: make setting up the client side and attaching to the network transparent to the user, and provide seamless connectivity to existing NetWare and Windows networks. (*Transparent* and *seamless* are marketing jargon for *easy* and *simple*.) Tests conducted during the writing of this book demonstrate that Microsoft's networking software developers achieved the preceding objectives. Dual-boot and Windows for Workgroups 3.11 upgrade installations provided immediate network connectivity on reboot after the Setup process. The WfWg 3.11 upgrade installation automatically connected the server shares used by the former WfWg client; it was only necessary to map the shares to local drives for the dual-boot installation.

For most Windows 95 network client users, the knowledge that they can effortlessly connect to and browse the network will satisfy their curiosity about Windows 95's networking architecture. For the more technically inclined, figure 16.22 is a simplified block diagram of the Windows 95 networking components, generally called the *network* or *protocol stack*, that make the connection between your computer's NIC and a Windows application running under Windows 95.

Following is a brief description of the elements that comprise the Windows 95 networking system, from the bottom up:

- *Device Driver Interface (DDI).* This layer handles the connection between the hardware NIC and the first standard layer in the stack. NIC manufacturers supply the VxD for each of their cards. DDI VxDs for popular NICs are included on the Windows 95 distribution floppy disks. Windows 95 supports NDIS (Microsoft's Network Device Interface Specification) Version 2.0 and the newer Version 3.1. Support for NetWare NICs that require ODI (open data-link interface) drivers is also included.

- *Transport Protocol (TP).* This layer processes the data packets received from or transmitted to the DDI. Only packets destined for a particular client pass through the TP layer. The TP layer also handles transmission errors, requesting resend of or resending packets that contain bad data as the result, for instance, of noise on the network cabling.

■ *Transport Programming Interface (TPI)*. The TPI provides a standardized method of handling packets from different transport protocols. Applications that don't require (or provide their own) file services can connect to the stack at the TPI layer. The Windows Sockets 1.1 interface, which Windows 95 supports for both IPX/SPX and TCP/IP protocols, is the layer at which Internet-oriented applications, such as TELNET, connect to the stack.

■ *Redirectors*. Redirectors are responsible for mapping network file resources to local drive letters; your computer redirects requests to open a network file from the local drive to the network drive. Other NOS suppliers can provide installable 32-bit redirectors.

■ *Installable File System (IFS)*. The IFS manager is responsible for arbitrating between the types of file systems in use: VFAT, CDFS, or one of the redirectors. The IFS manager also processes long file names, converting them if necessary, for servers that don't support long file names.

■ *Network Providers (NPs)*. The network providers constitute the client side of the NOS. Microsoft wrote both the NetWare and the 16-bit and 32-bit versions of the Windows NPs. Banyan, DEC, SunSelect, and other NOS suppliers will supply their own NP layer.

■ *Application (Programming) Interface (API)*. The Win32 Winnet and Print APIs consist of a standard set of functions that Windows applications call to invoke network services, such as opening and closing network files and printing to local or shared printers. These APIs are backwardly compatible with 16-bit Windows calls, so existing 16-bit applications can take full advantage of Windows 95's networking services.

Although the Windows 95 networking stack consists of many layers, Microsoft's developers have written the components to provide better performance than with a monolithic (non-stacked) networking system. The advantage to Windows 95's stacked structure is that third-party NOS suppliers can write their components to a known standard. Drivers and other networking components for Windows 95 also work with Windows NT 3.5 Workstation.

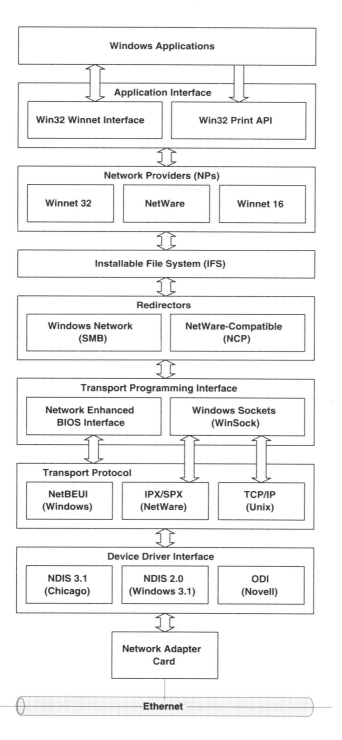

Fig. 16.22
A simplified block diagram of Windows 95's networking components.

Chapter 17

Creating Workgroups with Windows 95's Peer-to-Peer Networking

Windows 95's built-in networking features let small firms and users of more than one computer at home link their PCs easily and at very low cost. Peer-to-peer networks can also be used to create workgroups within a network that uses a dedicated server computer. Workgroup members can share files and other local peripheral devices with one another on an *ad hoc* basis without relying on the central server. Workgroup computing adds flexibility to the centrally administrated, structured networks of large organizations. Creating semi-autonomous, self-administered workgroup structures is one of the techniques recommended to implement business process reengineering.

As noted in Chapter 16, "Using Windows 95 Clients with Existing Networks," Microsoft designed Windows 95 to make setting up a network an almost trivial job. This chapter is devoted primarily to setting up small peer-to-peer networks of PCs running Windows 95 or a mixture of Windows 95 and Windows for Workgroups 3.1+. Most of the techniques described here, however, are equally applicable to setting up Windows 95-based workgroups running under a network with dedicated file servers.

Understanding Peer-to-Peer Networks

During the early history of the PC, peer-to-peer networking was the most common method of sharing files and peripheral components. IBM's PC LAN software, developed in cooperation with Microsoft, was one of the first peer-to-peer networking systems. PC LAN was easy to install and administer, so firms didn't need to hire a network manager to keep the system running. As the number of PCs on these networks grew into the hundreds, however, performance quickly deteriorated. To overcome the file-sharing bottleneck, organizations installed high-performance dedicated file servers, which also could act as application servers. Novell was one of the first firms to supply a true network operating system (NOS) that ran on a dedicated server. Novell also supplies a peer-to-peer NOS, NetWare Lite.

In a peer-to-peer network, any computer can share harddisk directories and printers with any other PC that it's connected to. Most peer-to-peer network software, including Windows 95, lets you share CD-ROM drives and some (not Windows 95) provide modem-sharing capabilities. The principal limitations of peer-to-peer networks are:

- The maximum number of PCs on a peer-to-peer network is anywhere from about 10 to 30, depending on the amount of network traffic.

- It's not practical to use peer-to-peer PCs as application servers (application servers let others run Windows and applications from the server, rather than from a local fixed disk). Peer-to-peer networks are designed only for sharing resources, such as multiuser database files and laser printers.

- The performance of applications running on PCs that act as servers in a peer-to-peer network deteriorates when the PCs' resources are used by others. You can control the degree of performance degradation by giving a higher priority to local activities at the expense of slower network file access and printing.

What's great about a peer-to-peer network—besides its low startup cost—is how easy it is to convert a peer-to-peer network to a full-scale, dedicated-server network when the need arises. For example, you can install Windows NT 3.5 Server from a CD-ROM in less than 30 minutes and then copy the shared files from the peer-to-peer servers to directories on the dedicated server. (Windows 95 PCs recognize the server as soon as you turn it on.) If you're not too worried about security, you can use share-level (password) access to server directories (shares). With 25 or so PCs on-line, it might take less than a day to complete the upgrade.

Choosing the Cabling for a Peer-to-Peer Network

EtherNet is by far the most common method of implementing PC networks, primarily because of its simple cabling and the low cost of EtherNet NICs (network interface cards). As mentioned in Chapter 16, you can buy standard 16-bit EtherNet NICs, such as the Intel EtherExpress 16, for about $100. The most important decision is the type of network cabling to use. Following are your choices:

- *Thin EtherNet* (10BASE2, also called *thinnet*) uses coaxial cable (coax) and BNC connectors (the same as the cabling used for cable TV installation) to interconnect NICs. You plug a BNC tee connector into each NIC and string coax between the PCs. A terminator is plugged into the open BNC tee connection at each end of the system to prevent reflections, just as SCSI cabling requires a terminator at each end. Repeaters are required if the cables are longer than 200 meters.

- *10BASE-T* cabling uses telephone-type wiring (called an *unshielded twisted pair*) to connect NICs to a distribution box, called a *hub* or *concentrator*. A single hub commonly serves 8, 12, or 16 PCs within a 10- to 20-meter radius. Conventional telephone-like extension cables with RJ-45 connectors are used for the local cabling. Hubs are connected by two twisted pairs. (Shielded twisted pair is also used.)

If you're planning to connect only from two through five PCs that are reasonably close together, thin EtherNet is the way to go because you don't need to buy a $200 to $300 10BASE-T hub. (The computers used to write this book are connected by thin EtherNet cabling.) If your PCs are distributed over a wider area, 10BASE-T is the best bet because twisted-pair cabling is less expensive than coax on a per-foot basis.

> **Tip**
>
> Decide on the cabling method before you buy your NICs. Most low-cost NICs have either a BNC or an RJ-45 connector, not both. If you start with thin EtherNet but plan to expand your network later, spend a bit more to buy NICs with both BNC and RJ-45 connectors.

Setting Up Peer-to-Peer NetworkFile Shares

Chapter 16 describes how to install an NIC and set it up for use in Windows 95 networking. Once you have your NICs and cabling installed, you can start sharing directories or even entire hard disk drives with other PCs on the network. The sections that follow describe the sequence of establishing shared peer-to-peer file resources.

Identifying Your Workgroup Computer

The first step in the process is to identify your PC to other network users by assigning it a name and creating a named workgroup. You use the Identification page of Control Panel's Network properties sheet to assign a computer name, workgroup name, and a description of your computer (see fig. 17.1). Only other members of the workgroup named in the Identification page can share your PC's resources.

Fig. 17.1
Identify your computer to other members of the workgroup on the Identification page of the Network properties sheet.

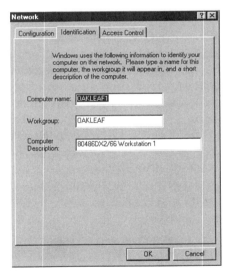

Establishing Workgroup Security

By default, Windows 95 establishes share-level security for peer-to-peer network shares. Share-level security means that you assign a password to each shared resource. When workgroup members want to use a shared resource, they must have entered a unique computer name and the name of the workgroup in which the resource share was created. The first time the members use the share, they are asked for the password. If they mark the Save

Password check box, the password is cached (saved) on their local computer, eliminating the need to enter the password when reconnecting to the share.

One complaint lodged by network administrators against Windows for Workgroups 3.1 was the lack of user-level security. User-level security requires that a user's account be authenticated by a network server, a feature that was incorporated into Windows for Workgroups 3.11. If you're connected to a Windows NT or Microsoft LAN Manager domain or have access to a NetWare 3.1+ bindery or NetWare 4.0+ NDS (Network Directory Service), you can employ user-level security to gain tighter control over who can access your peer-to-peer shares. Figure 17.2 shows the Security page of the Network properties sheet with the default share-level security specified. To implement domain authentication, you click the User-Level Security option button and enter the domain name in the text box. Windows 95 authenticates each workgroup member with the domain before allowing the member access to peer-to-peer shares.

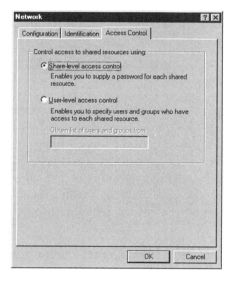

Fig. 17.2
Choosing between share-level and user-level security under an existing Windows NT, LAN Manager, or NetWare network.

Creating the Workgroup File Share

The final step in the process is to set up the workgroup shares. As noted earlier in the chapter, you can share specific subdirectories or make your entire fixed disk(s) accessible by sharing its root directory. To create a directory share, you click the directory folder in My Computer to select it and then right-click the folder to display the shortcut menu. Choosing Properties displays the properties sheet for the directory. Click the Shared As option button of the Sharing page to enable sharing of the directory (see fig. 17.3). The name of the directory defaults to the directory name, but you can substitute another name if you want. You also can add an optional description of the share.

Fig. 17.3
Enabling sharing of a directory from My Computer.

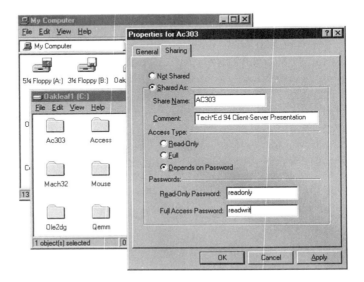

▶ See Chapter 21, "Managing Networked PCs with Windows 95"

You can choose to give users read-only or read-write (full) permission for all the files in the directory by clicking either the Read-Only or Full option button and then entering a password in the single enabled text box. (If you don't enter a password, everyone on the network who knows the workgroup name has access to your share.) Alternatively, you can give some members read-only access and others read-write access by clicking the Depends on Password option button. In this case, you enter different passwords in the two text boxes (refer to fig. 17.3).

You also can create file shares from Explorer using the same method as from My Computer. Figure 17.4 shows how you share your entire C drive for read-only access. Once you have created your shares, they appear in other members' Network Neighborhood window (see fig. 17.5). The c$ and d$ folders are administrative shares created when you allow remote administration of a Windows 95 computer.

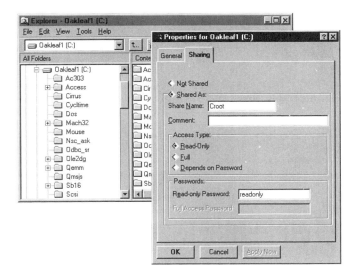

Fig. 17.4
Creating a read-only share of drive C from Explorer.

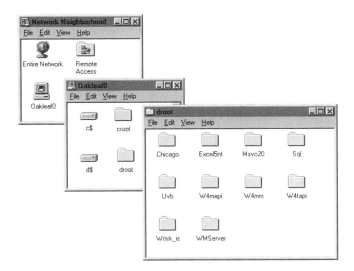

Fig. 17.5
Workgroup shares as they appear to users in Network Neighborhood.

> **Note**
>
> Although the figures of this chapter and Chapter 16 show shared root directories of multiple hard disk drives, this is an uncommon practice for conventional workgroups, especially if you allow read-write access to the share. As a rule, you set up a new directory for the workgroup and move or copy the files you want to share into the new workgroup directory. When you share a conventional CD-ROM drive, it's the normal practice to share its root directory. (If you do share a root directory, use a share name such as JaneRoot or JaneRoot, rather than simply C or CRoot, so users know to which computer they're connected.)

Setting Up and Sharing Your Printer with Other Users

One of the most common network operations is printing to a shared laser printer. Firms can save substantial money by placing shared printers in central locations; this is especially true of expensive color laser printers, where one printer may serve an entire firm. The following sections describe how you set up a Windows 95 printer share for a Hewlett-Packard LaserJet 4P. Setting up and sharing other types of laser printers follow a similar course.

Sharing a New Local Printer with the Workgroup

When you install a new printer that supports Plug and Play—such as the Hewlett-Packard LaserJet 4 series—on a Windows 95 computer, the Windows 95 operating system detects the new device (even without Plug and Play BIOS installed). The New Device Found dialog box appears to give you the option to use the printer driver supplied with Windows 95 (if available), install the driver from floppy disk(s) supplied by the printer's manufacturer, or don't use the device.

Once you've installed the printer, you need to create a printer share so others can use the printer. Right-clicking the printer's icon in the Printers window opens the shortcut menu; selecting Properties displays the properties sheet for the printer. The Sharing page for the printer lets you assign a share name, optional description, and optional password for the printer share (see fig. 17.6).

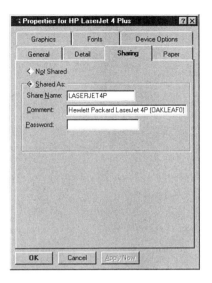

Fig. 17.6
Creating a printer
share.

> **Note**
>
> It's common practice not to password-protect conventional laser printers.
> Passwords often are assigned, however, to color laser printers because of the cost of
> consumables, such as paper and dye- or wax-transfer supplies, which may total as
> much as $3 per copy.

Using a Shared Printer under Windows 95

When you install Windows 95, the Setup application printer pseudo-wizard
leads you through the process of adding the driver required for your printer.
If you've already set up a network printer, all you need to do is provide the
UNC (Universal Naming Convention) address of the printer on the network,
*SERVERNAME**PRINTERNAME*. When installing a network, it's a common practice
to acquire a higher-performance printer with greater paper tray capacity to
accommodate more users. Some printers can connect directly to the network
through a self-contained EtherNet NIC, in which case the printer isn't connected to the parallel or serial port of a PC.

You connect to a newly shared network printer by opening the Printers window from the Start menu or by double-clicking Control Panel's Printers icon
and then clicking the Add Printer button to display the opening dialog box
of the Add Printer Wizard (APW), shown in figure 17.7. Clicking Next
displays the second APW dialog box, where you specify a network printer

(see fig. 17.8). In the third dialog box, shown in figure 17.9, you type the UNC network name of the printer. You can click the Browse button to open the Network Neighborhood window, find the networked printer you want to use, and click OK to enter the UNC sharename of the printer.

Fig. 17.7
The opening window of the Printer Wizard.

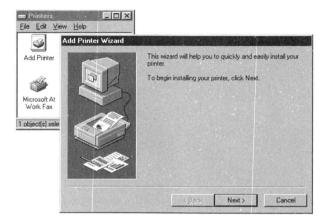

Fig. 17.8
Specifying a network instead of a local printer.

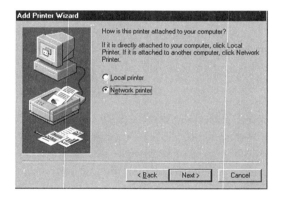

Each computer that uses the shared printer must have the appropriate driver installed before making the connection. If your printer isn't Plug and Play-enabled, you pick the printer manufacturer and model in the list boxes of the Select Device dialog that displays the printer drivers supplied with Windows 95 (see fig. 17.10). If your printer isn't listed, click the Have Disk button to install the drivers from the manufacturer's floppy disk(s). You'll need to have your distribution disks for Windows 95 or the CD-ROM available (or access to a copy of Windows 95 on the network) to install a Windows 95 driver (see fig. 17.11).

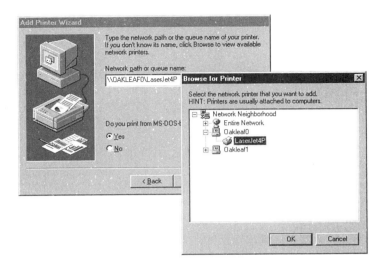

Fig. 17.9
Browsing for the network location and name of the shared printer.

Note

The Hewlett-Packard LaserJet 4P and other current H-P LaserJet printers conform to the Plug and Play printer standard. The Add Printer Wizard automatically detects the make and model of Plug and Play printers and leads you through five additional dialogs to assign the printer to one of your LPT (line printer) ports and install the driver for your printer. The Select Device dialog only appears if the Add Printer Wizard can't detect the make and model of your printer.

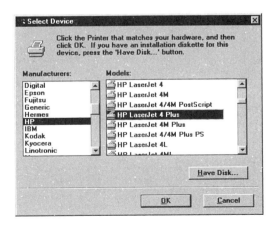

Fig. 17.10
Selecting the manufacturer and model of the network printer.

Fig. 17.11

Installing the printer driver from the Windows 95 distribution disks.

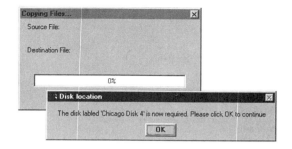

Once you've installed the driver software, the network printer appears, along with any local printers you've previously set up, in the Printers Folder. Right-clicking and choosing Properties displays the properties sheet for the printer (see fig. 17.12). The Detail page lets you open the Spool Settings dialog box to set the print-vs.-application priority and include a separator page for your print jobs, if you want (see fig. 17.13). Figure 17.14 shows the Graphics page that lets you set options for printing bit maps and vector graphic images.

Fig. 17.12

The General page of the printer's properties sheet.

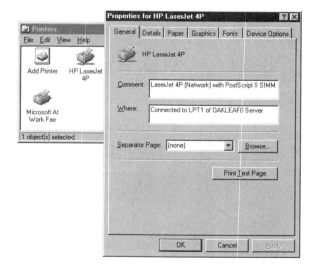

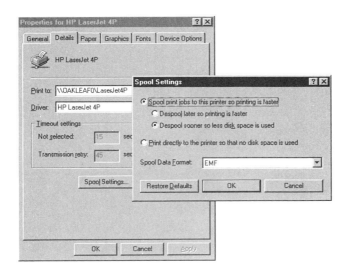

Fig. 17.13
The Detail page of the printer's properties sheet.

Fig. 17.14
Setting options for printing bit maps and vector graphics on the Graphics page.

Note

The options—such as resolution, dithering, and density—that you set in the printer properties sheet affect only your print jobs, not print jobs submitted to the printer by others.

Chapter 18

Messaging with Windows 95's Exchange Client

The most rapidly growing segment of the computer software industry is electronic mail applications. An estimated 15 million electronic mail (e-mail) boxes were in operation in North America in 1993, and industry experts look for e-mail growth rates of from 40 percent to 50 percent in 1995. Much of the reason for the hyperexpansion of e-mail user counts is the Internet, but corporate e-mail growth is expanding apace. Lotus Development Corporation's cc:Mail, which originally was the industry leader, now is running neck-and-neck with Microsoft Mail 3+ with about 5 million seats each.

Windows 95's general-purpose information client (code-named *Capone* in the first Windows 95 beta) is implemented by the Microsoft Exchange client, called *Exchange* in this chapter. Exchange gathers access to all of Windows 95's mail-related (messaging) services into a single location and provides each service with a consistent user interface based on the Explorer. Windows 95 includes built-in support for two services: Microsoft Mail 3+ and faxing with Microsoft At Work Fax. At Work Fax (usually abbreviated AWfax or MAWfax) and one of the members of the Microsoft At Work product line designed for automating office machines are the subjects of Chapter 15, "Faxing with Microsoft At Work Fax." Windows for Workgroups 3.11 (WfWg) offers both e-mail and fax services, but the WfWg version of Microsoft Mail 3+ is enhanced considerably in Windows 95. Windows 95 also is ready for installation of the Microsoft Mail 4.0 client that's expected to be released, together with the Microsoft Exchange e-mail and groupware server, in mid-1995. Microsoft Exchange Server is a component of Microsoft's new BackOffice suite of client-server products. A brief description of BackOffice and Exchange Server appears at the end of this chapter.

> **Note**
>
> The Schedule+ 1.0 group appointment scheduling and task management (to-do list) application, which is included with WfWg 3.1+, isn't supplied with Windows 95. Some of the stand-alone features of Schedule+ 1.0 are incorporated in Windows 95's WinPad applet. A 32-bit, protected-mode version of Schedule+ is expected to be released after Windows 95, probably in conjunction with 16-bit and 32-bit versions of the Microsoft Mail 4.0 client, and Exchange Server. In keeping with Microsoft's new product-numbering scheme, the new version of Mail (called Mail 4.0 in this chapter) and of Schedule+ may be called Microsoft Mail 95 and Schedule+ 95.

This chapter describes Microsoft's Messaging Application Programming Interface (MAPI), shows how Windows 95 implements Microsoft's new Extended MAPI, and examines a third-party mail service provider for sending and receiving CompuServe Mail.

Integrating Messaging with Windows 95 Computing

Most e-mail systems in North America today use simple network file sharing to maintain user lists (postoffices), store messages, and provide other e-mail-related services to client computers. Until Microsoft released Windows for Workgroups 3.1, you bought a license for an e-mail supervisory program, such as Microsoft Mail 3.2 or Lotus cc:Mail, and then bought additional licenses for workstations that used the mail system, usually in batches of 10 or 100. E-mail software suppliers generate much more revenue from client than from server licenses.

WfWg 3.1+ changed the complexion of the e-mail software business by including the basic Microsoft Mail client software with Windows. Not only was the client software built-in, but also WfWg 3.1+ let you set up your own workgroup mail system so you didn't need to buy the server-side software. When Bill Gates told attendees at the Electronic Messaging Association's conference in June 1994 that Windows 95 would include the basic e-mail client and file-shared postoffice features with the operating system, he was greeted by stunned silence. E-mail marketing managers saw their 1995+ e-mail sales projections flying out the window. Microsoft expects to make its messaging money by selling the enhanced version of the Microsoft Mail 4.0

client software to messaging power users running either Windows 95 or Windows 3.1+. To take full advantage of MS Mail 4.0, large organizations also will need to license the Microsoft Exchange Server.

Understanding the Messaging API

Microsoft's Messaging Application Programming Interface (MAPI) is the heart of the Windows e-mail system. MAPI is a member of the Windows Open Services Architecture (WOSA) that includes a variety of Microsoft products designed to provide Windows connectivity to telephones (Telephony API or TAPI), databases (Open Database Connectivity or ODBC), mainframes (Microsoft SNA Server), stock market service providers (Real-Time Financials, WOSA/XRT), and the like. Microsoft Mail for PC Networks 3+ and the WfWg 3.1+ implementation of MS Mail 3+ use 16-bit Simple MAPI. Windows 95 installs the 32-bit version of Microsoft's Messaging API, called Extended MAPI or MAPI 1.0, which also is included with Windows NT 3.5. Both the simple and extended versions of MAPI provide common services, such as sending documents by e-mail and handling routing lists, to all messaging-aware applications. All current versions of Microsoft productivity applications, such as Excel 5.0 and Word 6.0, include the capability to send documents from the applications as attachments to MS Mail messages. Lotus applications include similar features for integration with cc:Mail and Lotus Notes.

> ### Note
>
> Messaging-aware applications that use Simple MAPI, such as the 16-bit versions of Microsoft Excel 5.0 and Word 6.0, cannot send mail directly when run under Windows 95. The Send and Routing Slip choices of the File menu of these applications do not appear. To use the built-in messaging features of these products, you'll need the new Windows 95 upgrades to the 32-bit versions of Microsoft productivity applications, expected to be available on or shortly after the release date of Windows 95. As a temporary workaround, you can copy documents to the clipboard and paste them into Exchange messages.

Microsoft's implementation of DOS and Windows e-mail, now MS Mail 3.2 for PC Networks, includes a front end (the MS Mail user interface or UI) and a back end (the MS Mail Service Provider or SP). The front end is used to compose and read messages, and to manipulate address lists for e-mail, fax, and other types of messages. The back end connects to local or network MS Mail postoffice(s) where user addresses and messages are stored. Simple MAPI provides the "glue" between front-end and back-end elements and offers standard UI components. UI components include address-list manipulation windows, a message composition and display form, and a window to process incoming and outgoing messages. Third-party developers can create their own specialized front-end and back-end service providers for MAPI. MAPI also provides built-in support for the Lotus-sponsored VIM (Vendor-Independent Messaging) API, which is the backbone of cc:Mail. Figure 18.1 is a simplified diagram of MAPI illustrating a client e-mail setup with three service providers.

Fig. 18.1

A simplified block diagram of MAPI-based messaging with multiple service providers.

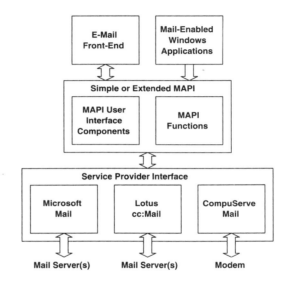

Note

A related messaging interface, called the Common Mail Calls (CMC) API, implements the same functions as MAPI under a variety of operating systems. Versions of the CMC API are available for DOS/Windows, Windows NT, OS/2, and various flavors of UNIX. Developers can choose either CMC or MAPI to implement basic e-mail functions in applications, but CMC is recommended for cross-platform compatibility.

Extended MAPI and Information Stores

Extended MAPI adds a variety of new features to Simple MAPI. The most evident member of the new feature set is the capability to select the type family (font) for outbound messages. Figure 18.2 shows a Windows 95 message formatted in the ransom-note style, using three exotic TrueType fonts. Extended MAPI adds the concept of an *information store* to the basic messaging services of Simple MAPI. An information store is a folder that can contain a variety of types of information, not just messages and faxes stored in DOS file format. As an example, messages and other objects in the information store can be records in a client-server messaging database, such as that used by the forthcoming Microsoft Exchange Server. Files created by applications, such as Microsoft Excel 5.0, that use the object linking and embedding (OLE) 2.0 compound document storage format, can also be included in information stores. Voice-mail messages created by TAPI-compliant applications also can go into the information store. (Microsoft is reported to be developing a TAPI voice-mail messaging system, code-named *Tazz*.) Extended MAPI lets developers create electronic forms (e-forms) with fill-in fields. The blank e-form is stored on the server and is shared by all the e-form's users; thus, the message needs to contain only the data entered in the e-form's fields. E-forms are integral components of collaborative workflow applications.

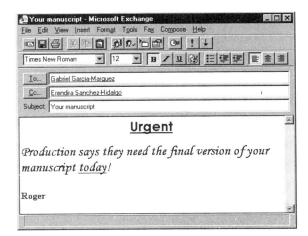

Fig. 18.2
A Microsoft Mail message using three type families and a variety of font sizes.

> **Note**
>
> The built-in e-form capability of Extended MAPI is similar to that provided by the Microsoft Electronic Forms Designer (MEF) 1.0, an extension to Visual Basic 3.0. Forms created with MEF 1.0 are compatible with Extended MAPI and MS Mail 4.0. To take full advantage of Extended MAPI's e-form features, however, you'll need to use Microsoft Exchange and its new e-form development tools.

Future versions of Windows productivity applications are expected to be *messaging-enabled*. A messaging-enabled application takes advantage of the added e-mail features of Extended MAPI. By mid-1995, Microsoft is expected to release an OLE Automation "wrapper" for Extended MAPI, called *OLE/Messaging*. OLE/Messaging will let OLE 2 client applications handle messaging operations with OLE Automation, a much simpler programming method than calling the MAPI functions directly. Schedule+ will gain a similar OLE Automation wrapper called *OLE/Scheduling*.

Setting Up Windows 95's Exchange

The method you choose to install Windows 95 determines the process by which you set up Exchange to handle e-mail and other messaging operations. The four sections that follow describe how the Windows 95 Setup program upgrades existing MS Mail 3+ installations, what you need to do to connect to an existing MS Mail postoffice, how to create a new workgroup postoffice, and how to establish multiple messaging profiles.

Upgrading from MS Mail 3+ or Windows for Workgroups Mail

If you install Windows 95 over an existing Windows 3.1+ directory and you now are using MS Mail 3+, Exchange reads your MSMAIL.INI file to determine the location of your MS Mail for PC Networks or workgroup postoffice. Your postoffice address list, personal address book, and fax mailing lists automatically appear in Exchange's implementation of the Microsoft Mail 3+ UI. (Windows 95 creates MSMAIL.PST for you, but Exchange's message store is not compatible with Microsoft Mail 3.2's MMF files.) Setup makes most of the Windows 3.1+ to Windows 95 upgrade process for Microsoft Mail transparent.

When you open Exchange, the only item that appears in the message list is Microsoft Personal Information Store (PST). Double-clicking the PST entry displays the familiar MS Mail choices of Deleted Items, In Box, Out Box, and Sent Mail. Figure 18.3 shows Exchange displaying a message previously sent via the CompuServe Mail service provider. Figure 18.4 illustrates the fictitious Postoffice Address List used to write this chapter. The e-mail feature set of Exchange is nearly identical to that of MS Mail 3.2, so MS Mail 3+ users will find it easy to adapt to Exchange's new look and feel.

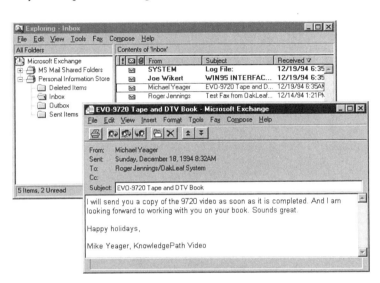

Fig. 18.3

Windows 95's adaptation of the MS Mail 3+ user interface for reading messages.

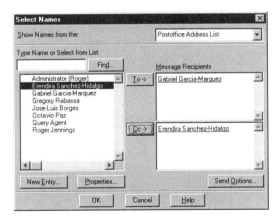

Fig. 18.4

A fictitious workgroup mail Postoffice Address List created with Windows for Workgroups 3.11.

Connecting to an Existing Postoffice with a Dual-Boot System

When you install Windows 95 in the dual-boot mode, the setup application doesn't detect that you have Microsoft Mail installed. Exchange needs to know your mailbox name and the location of your MS Mail for PC Networks or workgroup postoffice. The Microsoft Exchange Setup Wizard takes you though each of the following steps to attach the Exchange client to an existing MS Mail postoffice:

1. Launch Microsoft Exchange Profiles from Control Panel, then click the Add button to open the first dialog box of the Microsoft Exchange Setup Wizard (MESW) shown in figure 18.5. Select the information services you want to use in the list box, then click the Next button.

Fig. 18.5
Choosing the information services to include in your new Microsoft Exchange Profile.

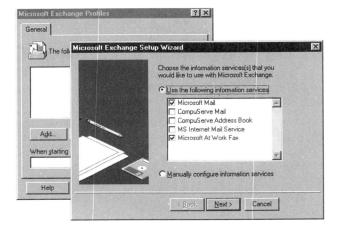

2. Enter a name for your profile in the second MESW dialog box as shown in figure 18.6, then click the Next button.

Fig. 18.6
Assigning a name to your new Microsoft Exchange Profile.

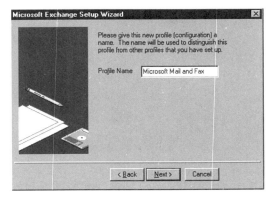

3. Enter the UNC (Uniform Naming Convention) path to the network server share in which your Microsoft Mail postoffice is located in the third MESW dialog box, as shown in figure 18.7, then click the Next button.

Fig. 18.7
Entering the network path to the existing Microsoft Mail 3+ postoffice.

4. Select your mailbox "friendly" name from the list box of the fifth MESW dialog box, shown in figure 18.8, and click the Next button.

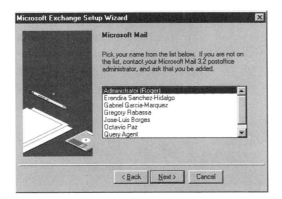

Fig. 18.8
Selecting your name from the existing Microsoft Mail 3+ Postoffice Address List.

5. Type your password in the sixth MESW dialog box (see fig. 18.9) and click the Next button.

Fig. 18.9
Entering the
password for your
Microsoft Mail 3+
mailbox.

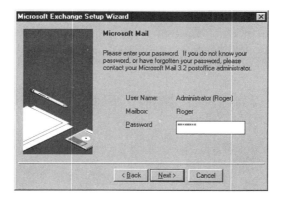

6. If you included Microsoft At Work Fax as an information service, the seventh dialog box, shown in figure 18.10, appears. If you have previously installed your faxmodem, the name of your modem appears in the list box. (See Chapter 12, "Connecting to the Outside World," for details about setting up your modem, and Chapter 15, "Faxing with Microsoft At Work Fax," for instructions on using the service). Click the Setup button to review your faxmodem's settings, as illustrated by figure 18.11. Click OK to close the Fax Modem Settings dialog box, then click the Next button to display the second faxmodem dialog box. Your name, country code, and area code are entered automatically, as shown in figure 18.12. so enter your fax number and click the Next button.

Fig. 18.10
Selecting the
modem for use
with the Microsoft
At Work Fax
service.

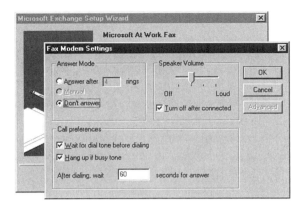

Fig. 18.11
Confirming or
changing the
settings for your
faxmodem.

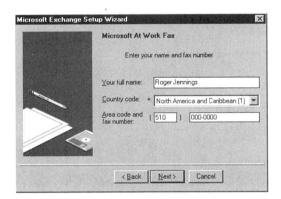

Fig. 18.12
Your name,
country code,
and area code
are entered
automatically.

7. The final dialog box confirms that you've completed the setup process.
When you click the Next button, your new Exchange Profile properties
sheet appears as shown in figure 18.13.

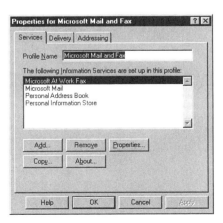

Fig. 18.13
The Properties for
Microsoft Mail and
Fax sheet created
by the preceding
steps.

Setting the Properties of Exchange Information Services

After you've added a profile to Exchange, you can change the default properties for e-mail operations, the MS Mail 3.2 postoffice location, and other e-mail settings. Figure 18.14 shows the Delivery page of the properties sheet for your new messaging profile that determines the name of the message store for incoming messages and the order of service providers for outgoing messages if you have more than one SP driver installed. The Addressing page, shown in figure 18.15, determines the default address book that appears when you choose Address Book from the Tools menu. The Addressing page also determines the order in which address lists are searched for e-mail name resolution.

Fig. 18.14
Selecting inbound and outbound message routing in the messaging profile properties sheet's Delivery page.

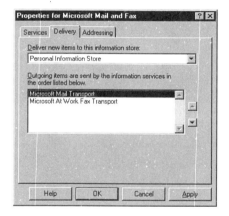

Fig. 18.15
The messaging profile properties sheet's Addressing page.

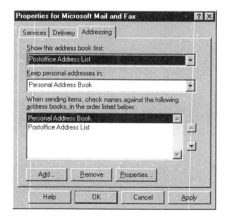

Selecting one of the items in the Information Services list, which includes any third-party service provider drivers you've added, and clicking the Properties button opens the properties sheet for the item. Figure 18.16 shows typical property settings for an MS Mail 3.2 workgroup postoffice displayed in the Connection page. If you've installed Windows 95's dial-up networking services, you can set up your notebook computer to retrieve your mail by establishing the appropriate settings in the Remote Configuration, Remote Session, RAS, and Log property pages. Chapter 20, "Using Windows 95's Dial-Up Networking," describes how to manage your mail through a modem connection. Alternatively, you can create messages off-line and then connect your notebook to the office network to send and receive your mail. Figure 18.17 shows Windows 95's default settings for sending and receiving Microsoft Mail messages in the Delivery page. The primary purpose of the Delivery page is to let you choose whether you want to be notified immediately when new high-priority mail arrives and how often you want the MS Mail 3.2 agent to check for all new mail, regardless of priority. Clicking the Address Types button opens the Address Types dialog to let you restrict sending mail to a particular set of the e-mail SP drivers installed on your computer.

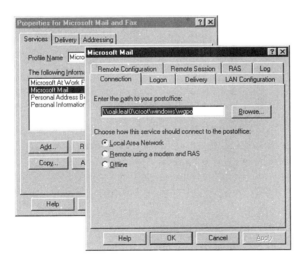

Fig. 18.16

Setting the type of connection and postoffice data in the Connection page of the Microsoft Mail service provider's properties sheet.

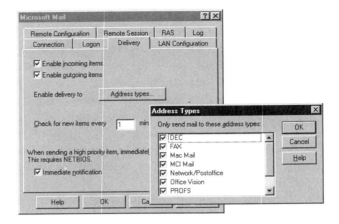

Fig. 18.17
Setting delivery
options in the
Delivery page of
the Microsoft Mail
properties sheet.

Administering a Microsoft Mail Postoffice

You can administer an existing Microsoft Mail postoffice or create a new
postoffice from your Windows 95 computer. The workgroup e-mail system
included with Windows 95 is identical to the full version of Microsoft Mail
Server 3.2, with the following exceptions:

- You can have only one postoffice to serve all members of the
  workgroup; Microsoft Mail Server lets you set up multiple postoffices.

- You cannot connect to other e-mail systems through Microsoft Mail
  gateways.

- Only one person can be designated as the postoffice administrator.

- The Exchange administrative tools are limited to adding and deleting
  e-mail users; support for systemwide groups and import or exporting
  of postoffice users is not provided.

The postoffice is a temporary message store. When you send a message to a
workgroup member, the message is stored in a postoffice file. When the recipient retrieves the message, the message is copied to the recipient's personal
message store (PST file) and then is deleted from the postoffice file. You do
not need a dedicated file server for a workgroup postoffice, because any computer can act as a server under Windows 95's peer-to-peer networking system.
If you have more than about 20 regular e-mail users, however, you'll gain
better performance if your post office is stored on a dedicated server that also
stores the workgroup's shared files.

To set up a new workgroup postoffice or administer an existing workgroup
postoffice, you double-click Control Panel's Microsoft Mail icon to display

the Microsoft Workgroup Postoffice Admin mini-wizard shown in figure 18.18. (Microsoft calls the Postoffice Admin feature a "utility," but it qualifies as a wizard because you are lead through the process in a series of steps.) You select whether you want to administer a new or existing postoffice, then click the Next button to display the second dialog box in which you enter the UNC path to the post office directory, as shown in figure 18.19.

Note

The conventional location for a workgroup postoffice is \WINDOWS\WGPO, Windows for Workgroups 3.1+'s default location. Before you begin the postoffice administration process, you should establish a server share for the existing postoffice directory or create a new shared directory for a new postoffice. Windows 95's UNC paths for network servers eliminates the need to map a drive to postoffice directory.

Fig. 18.18
Choosing between creating a new postoffice or administering an existing workgroup postoffice.

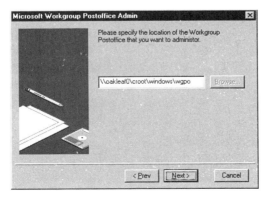

Fig. 18.19
Specifying the path to the postoffice directory in a peer-to-peer or Windows NT 3.5 Server network.

The final step in the process is to enter your mailbox name and password. If you are creating a new postoffice, the wizard adds your name to the Postoffice Address List as the administrator. To administer an existing workgroup postoffice, you must enter the mailbox ID and password of the person who originally created the postoffice. (Workgroup postoffices allow only one administrator.) When you enter the correct administrator mailbox ID and password, the current Postoffice Address List appears as shown in figure 18.20. Click the Add User button to open the Add User dialog box shown in figure 18.21. The postoffice administrator can edit user details (such as changing a forgotten password), delete a user, and inspect the status of shared folders.

Fig. 18.20
The list of existing postoffice users that appears when you enter your administrative mailbox ID and password.

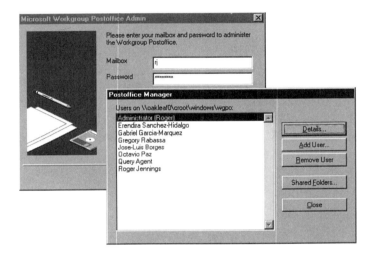

Fig. 18.21
Adding a new user to the workgroup postoffice.

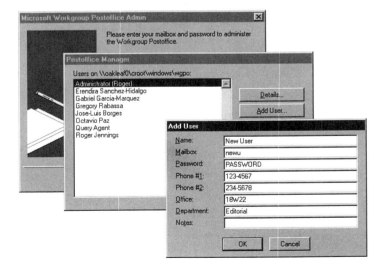

Setting Up Multiple Messaging Profiles

If you use a notebook computer at home, on the road, and in the office, the preferred messaging settings for each location will likely differ. In the office, you'll be connected directly to the network; at home, you might have an ISDN connection to the network; and on the road, you'll use a conventional or cellular telephone modem. When you're on the road, you may want to download only the message headers, not the entire set of messages, including junk e-mail, into your notebook PC's inbox. You can create as many profiles as you need, using the methods described earlier in this chapter, to suit your away-from-the-office needs. Select the profile you want to use from the When Starting Microsoft Exchange, Use This Profile, as shown in figure 18.22.

Fig. 18.22
Selecting the default messaging profile to use when starting Microsoft Exchange.

Alternatively, you can launch the Exchange client and choose Options for Microsoft Exchange from the Tools menu to display the properties sheet for Exchange. This properties sheet adds three new pages—General, Read, and Send—to Control Panel's Microsoft Exchange Profiles properties sheet. You can choose the profile to use when you open exchange from the Automatically Open Default Profile list (see fig. 18.23), or select the Choose Profile to Open option. The latter option displays a dialog box from which you choose the profile you want each time you launch the Exchange client.

Fig. 18.23
Selecting the default Exchange profile from the General page of the Exchange client's properties sheet.

The Read properties page lets you alter what happens to open items when you move or delete them and the options for replying to messages you receive. Figure 18.24 shows the default property values for reading and replying to messages. The Send properties page, shown in figure 18.25, establishes the default values for messages you compose. You can set the default message font; the priority of your messages to High, Normal, or Low; the sensitivity level of your messages; and obtain receipt messages when the message is delivered to the recipient, as well as when the recipient opens the message for reading. The values you set in the Read and Send properties pages apply to all of your Exchange messaging profiles.

Fig. 18.24
Setting the default properties for messages you receive in the Read properties page.

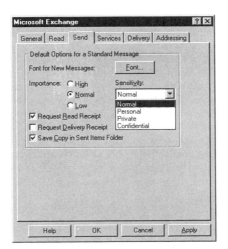

Fig. 18.25
Establishing
default properties
for the messages
you compose in
the Send proper-
ties page.

IV

Networking Windows 95

Sending and Receiving CompuServe Mail through Exchange

One of the favorite events of Microsoft's Windows 95 "road show" is demon-strating the capabilities of Exchange to use third-party on-line messaging services. At the Information Exchange Conference (formerly the Microsoft Mail User's Group meeting) in late June 1994, Bill Gates demonstrated Exchange's capability to connect to CompuServe and download waiting mes-sages. Although the content of the received message was uninspiring, to put it mildly, the demonstration proved that CompuServe's new 32-bit MAPI driver, originally developed in a 16-bit version for Windows for Workgroups 3.1+, also works with Windows 95. It's a good bet that the CompuServe driver, together with drivers for other on-line service providers, such as AT&T Mail and MCI Mail, will be included on the Windows 95 distribution floppy disks. If not, you can be certain that the major e-mail service providers will send you a copy (probably at no charge) on request. It's likely that America Online, Prodigy, and other on-line information services also will supply TAPI drivers to integrate their e-mail services into the Exchange client.

If you have a CompuServe (CIS) account and you install the CIS MAPI driver, you can integrate CIS mail into your Exchange messaging profile. The CIS MAPI driver uses the logon script and address book created by CompuServe's navigational utilities, such as DOSCIM, WINCIM, or CSNAV. Thus, you must have installed one of these applications under Windows 95 (or under Win-dows 3.1+ in a dual-boot configuration) before you can add CIS mail to your messaging profile. To add CIS mail to your profile, launch Microsoft Exchange Profiles, select the messaging profile, click the Add button and select CompuServe Mail from the Available Information Services list box of the Add Service to Profile dialog box (see fig. 18.26). When you click the Add button, the CompuServe Mail Transport Settings dialog box appears. Clicking the CompuServe Dir button opens the Select Location for CIS.INI dialog box shown in figure 18.27. To send messages to CompuServe members, you also need to add the CompuServe Address Book to your messaging profile. When you add the CompuServe Address book, you are asked to provide its location by a dialog box similar to that of figure 18.27.

Fig. 18.26
Adding the CompuServe Mail service to an existing messaging profile.

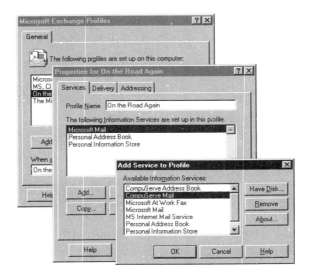

Fig. 18.27
Specifying the location of your existing CIS.INI file to provide the parameters for your CompuServe connection.

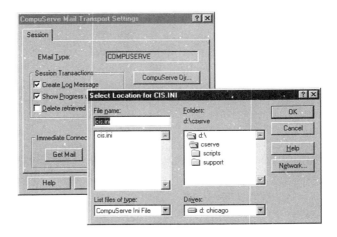

Clicking the Communications button of the Transport Settings dialog box opens the Setup Session Settings dialog box, shown in figure 18.28, that displays the connection information obtained from your CIS.INI file. You can modify the CIS.INI information if necessary; however, any modifications you make also will affect WINCIM or other CompuServe applications that rely on CIS.INI. Clicking the Connection Times button opens the Setup CompuServe Session dialog box, shown in figure 18.29. The Session dialog box lets you choose when you connect to CompuServe mail to receive and send messages.

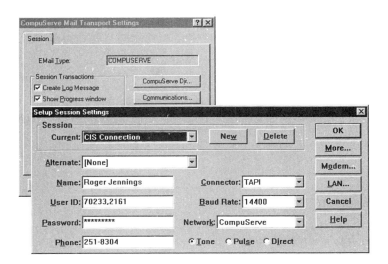

Fig. 18.28
Specifying the location of your existing CIS.INI file to provide the parameters for your CompuServe connection.

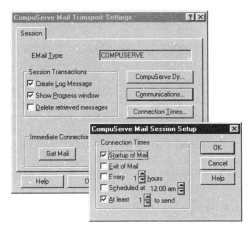

Fig. 18.29
Setting the time(s) at which you connect to CompuServe mail.

After your CIS mail session is complete, a list of the messages you received appears in Exchange's Inbox window. Double-clicking the message header displays the received message (see fig. 18.30). When you reply to a message, you can choose to include the header and text of the received message along with your reply. (This helps the recipient remember what you're replying to.) Figure 18.31 shows a reply to a message received from an Internet host via CompuServe. The person to whom you send the reply doesn't need to be listed in your CompuServe address list, but a CompuServe address list entry for the recipient is required to originate CIS mail.

Fig. 18.30
Displaying a message received from CompuServe.

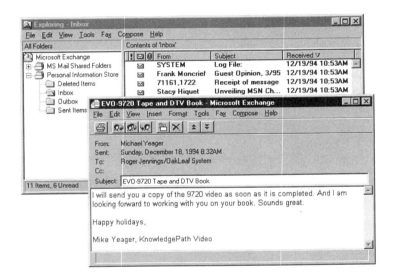

Fig. 18.31
Creating a reply to a CompuServe Mail message.

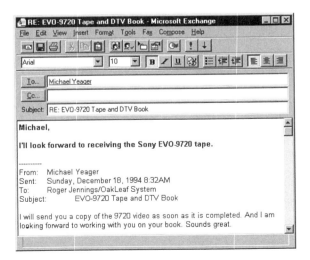

> **Note**
>
> The procedures described in this chapter for setting up and running Microsoft Mail and using the CompuServe MAPI driver were valid for the M7 beta version of Windows 95 used to write this book. Procedures and the appearance of property-setting dialog boxes will likely change in the retail version of Windows 95.

Looking Forward to Using Windows 95 with Microsoft Exchange Server

Shared-file systems, such as Microsoft Mail 3.x and Lotus cc:Mail, where postoffice files are stored on a conventional network file server, dominate today's e-mail market. Although shared-file e-mail systems have enjoyed widespread commercial success, adapting these systems to large-scale, enterprise-wide e-mail systems with thousands of users has proven to be no easy task. As Microsoft Mail and cc:Maii evolved into their current versions, Microsoft and Lotus appended a variety of new user features, administrative and maintenance applications, and gateways to their existing e-mail products. (Mail gateways provide connectivity with "foreign" mail systems.) Neither of these two popular e-mail systems has undergone a fundamental restructuring since its inception.

Microsoft hopes to make a fundamental change to enterprise messaging and workgroup computing with its new Exchange Server product now expected to appear in mid-1995, probably after the retail release of Windows 95. Exchange Server will be one of the elements of the new Microsoft BackOffice server suite that presently includes the following components:

- *Microsoft Windows NT 3.5 Server* for networking and to serve as the application server for the other BackOffice components

- *Microsoft SQL Server 4.21a*, a client-server relational database management system (RDBMS), to be upgraded to SQL 95 when it becomes available

- *Microsoft SNA Server 2.1*, which provides connectivity to IBM mainframes and AS/400 series minicomputers via IBM's System Network Architecture

- *Microsoft Systems Management Server* (SMS, formerly code-named Hermes), for distributing software and tracking client software

■ *Microsoft Mail Server 3.2*, to be upgraded to Microsoft Exchange Server when it becomes available

Exchange Server is designed to bring client-server computing to large e-mail systems. Instead of the myriad of individual files required for shared-file systems, Exchange stores messages, user directories, address books, and other mail-related information in an "intelligent database," called an Information Store, running as a process under Windows NT 3.5 Server. Taking the client-server approach to e-mail should alleviate most of the installation and administration headaches of today's e-mail systems. Exchange uses international standards, such as X.400 for messages and X.500 for directory services, which is vital to today's international messaging environment. Windows 95's Exchange is designed for compatibility with Microsoft Exchange and is very likely to become the client of choice for most Exchange users.

> **Note**
>
> Smaller organizations can use Windows 95's built-in share-file workgroup messaging system. As the number of e-mail users grows, you can quickly convert to Microsoft Exchange using migration tools to be included with Exchange Server.

One of the most important features of Exchange Server's Message Store is the capability to create Public Folders to which individual users can subscribe. Public Folders, similar to forums on CompuServe or conferences on electronic bulletin board systems, provide the collaborative (workgroup) computing capability that has made Lotus Notes a very successful product. Public folders can contain messages, files, and documents (in the form of OLE 2 objects), as well as custom-designed, fill-in-the blanks electronic forms. Enterprise-wide e-mail requires that up-to-date public folders and user directories be available on individual servers at geographically dispersed locations, a process called *replication*. (Having a local copy of the data provides far better performance than obtaining the data over a telephone line or satellite link from a central source; thus, replication also is used for periodically updating multiple client-server databases.) The advantage of the client-server approach to replication is that it's easy to duplicate only those elements of a public folder that have changed since the last replication, a process called *selective replication*.

To take advantage of all the new features of Microsoft Exchange, such as access to and creation of public folders and electronic forms, Windows 95 users likely will need to install the Microsoft Exchange Client, an extended version of the Exchange client included with Windows 95. When this book was written, Microsoft Exchange was in the beta testing stage, and Microsoft hadn't disclosed the Exchange feature set to be supported by Windows 95's Exchange client. Based on information divulged by Microsoft at the mid-1994 Exchange Conference, mentioned earlier in this chapter, Microsoft will take maximum advantage of Windows 95's unique Exchange client to demonstrate that Microsoft Exchange Server is a practical alternative to Lotus Notes for implementing workgroup computing throughout the enterprise.

Chapter 19

Synchronizing Your Notebook Computer with Briefcases

Notebook and laptop computers are a great convenience—they let you take your work with you wherever you go. Using a notebook or laptop typically involves one major inconvenience, however. Most people who use notebook and laptop computers also use a desktop computer on which they do the bulk of their work, using the notebook computer only when they are away from the office. As a result, most notebook computer users find it necessary to synchronize the documents on their desktop computer with copies of the same documents stored on their notebook computer. The same problem arises for people who work both in an office and at home.

Manually synchronizing different versions of your documents is an error-prone operation—it's easy to make a mistake that wipes out hours or days of work. Windows 95, however, solves that problem by including a special mechanism—called a *Briefcase*—to help you reliably and easily synchronize multiple copies of the same document on two or more computers. Briefcases simplify the task of making sure that each computer you use has the most up-to-date version of a particular document.

What Is a Briefcase?

Windows 95, throughout its design, tries to make your computer easier to use and understand by modeling real objects in the world around you—such as the desktop itself. A Briefcase is another of these models.

Essentially, a Windows 95 Briefcase works the same way a real briefcase does—you put documents that you want to take with you into the briefcase, and then take the briefcase with you when you go to another location. When you return, you remove the documents from your briefcase and return them to wherever they came from.

Specifically, a Windows 95 Briefcase is a system folder—similar to the Control Panel and Printers folders—in which you put documents that you want to work with on a different computer. The Briefcase folder, in addition to holding whatever documents you put into it, also contains a special database file. Windows 95 uses this database file to automatically keep track of where the documents in the Briefcase came from, and when the files were last modified.

To work with the documents on a different computer, you simply move the Briefcase folder to that computer. The Briefcase's special database lets Windows 95 automatically synchronize the documents in the Briefcase with the original documents on your computer whenever you request it.

Creating a Briefcase

Creating a Briefcase is easy—all you have to do is make sure that you've installed the optional Briefcase component for Windows 95. If you chose "Portable" as your Setup Type when you installed Windows 95, then you already have a Briefcase (named My Briefcase) on your Windows 95 desktop. If you don't already have Briefcase installed in Windows 95, you can add it by using the Add/Remove Programs applet in the Control Panel. Whenever you install Briefcase, Windows 95 automatically creates the My Briefcase icon shown in figure 19.1 on your Windows 95 desktop.

Fig. 19.1
Windows 95 lets you create a Briefcase named My Briefcase on your desktop.

My Briefcase

> **Tip**
>
> You can create additional Briefcases by choosing the New command on any desktop window's File menu, and then choosing Briefcase from the resulting submenu.

Figure 19.2 shows the informational dialog box that Windows 95 displays the very first time you open any new Briefcase (you won't see this dialog box the next time you open the Briefcase).

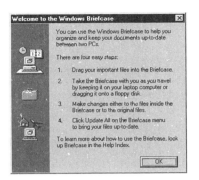

IV

Networking Windows 95

Fig. 19.2
Briefcase displays
an informational
dialog box the
first time you
open a particular
Briefcase folder.

Although it is possible to create more than one Briefcase, in general, you
should create only one Briefcase for each computer. If you create more than
one Briefcase, you're likely to end up confusing yourself as to which Briefcase
contains which files. You may even end up confusing Windows 95 if you
have more than one Briefcase that contains copies of the same document.

Using a Briefcase

A Briefcase folder, despite its special icon, behaves pretty much like any other
folder on the Windows 95 desktop. You can drag the folder to another location, open it, copy files to it, delete files from it, and so on. Figure 19.3 shows
an open Briefcase folder.

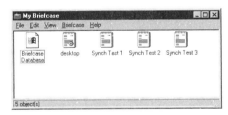

Fig. 19.3
Briefcase folders
behave—and dis-
play documents—
much the same as
any other folder,
with a few excep-
tions. Notice the
Briefcase menu
available in this
Briefcase window.

To make use of the Briefcase folder, you first have to put some documents
into it, and then "take it with you." You put documents into the Briefcase
folder simply by dragging them into the Briefcase (or onto its icon)—Windows 95 understands that it should copy files into the Briefcase, rather than
create a shortcut or move them. You can put documents into the Briefcase
individually, or you can put entire folders into it. To take your Briefcase
folder with you, move the Briefcase to one of the following:

- A notebook or laptop computer

- A floppy disk

- Another computer connected to yours on a local area network

- Another computer connected to yours with dial-up networking (also called remote access service or RAS)

▶ See Chapter 20, "Using Windows 95's Dial-Up Networking"

You then can perform any task by using the documents in the Briefcase on the other computer. (If you put the Briefcase on a floppy disk, you can take the disk to any other computer running Windows 95—or Windows 3.1+ —to work with the Briefcase documents.)

After you edit the documents and are ready to update them on your primary working computer, you don't need to copy the document files back to your computer. Instead, you update the documents from the Briefcase by using the update options on the Briefcase menu in the Briefcase's window (refer to fig. 19.3).

Editing Documents in a Briefcase

You edit documents in a Briefcase the same way you would any other document on your system. If the Briefcase is on your notebook (or another) computer's hard disk, simply edit the documents directly from the Briefcase folder. If you've put the Briefcase on a floppy disk, you can copy the documents from the Briefcase to another computer's hard disk for greater speed while editing.

Once you've completed whatever changes you want to make to the Briefcase documents, you can update the documents (as described later). If your Briefcase is on a floppy disk and you copied the documents to another computer's hard disk, you must first update the Briefcase from the computer that holds the modified document files, and then use the Briefcase to synchronize the files on the master computer.

> **Note**
>
> If you rename a document file while editing it in a Briefcase, the Briefcase won't be able to keep the file synchronized—changing the name of the document (or editing a renamed copy of the document) breaks the link between the document in the Briefcase and the original source document.

Updating Briefcase Documents

When you update the original document from a Briefcase, you don't copy the files from the Briefcase, nor do you copy the Briefcase folder itself. Instead, you leave the Briefcase folder on the notebook, floppy disk, or network computer where you put it after you first created the Briefcase.

To update the original documents from the Briefcase, you open the Briefcase folder and then use the Briefcase command on the folder's menu bar. The Briefcase menu command gives you three choices:

- *Update All.* This command causes Briefcase to synchronize all the documents in the Briefcase folder with their corresponding documents on the master computer.

- *Update Selection.* This command causes Briefcase to synchronize only the selected document(s) in the Briefcase.

- *Split.* This command breaks the connection between the selected document in the Briefcase folder and its corresponding master document.

Exactly how Briefcase updates documents depends on which version of the document has changed:

- If the document in the Briefcase folder has changed, the Briefcase update replaces the master document with the new version from the Briefcase.

- If the master version of the document has changed, Briefcase replaces the document in the Briefcase folder with another copy of the master document.

- If the master version of the document *and* the Briefcase version of the same document have changed, Briefcase displays a red-colored curved arrow. If you perform an update with the red-colored arrow, Briefcase does not actually change either document, but *does* mark both documents as updated.

Figure 19.4 shows the dialog box that Briefcase displays when you update files. The left column shows information about the document in the Briefcase folder, the right column shows information about the document outside the Briefcase, and the middle column indicates which update actions Briefcase intends to perform. A right-pointing arrow indicates that Briefcase will update the master document from the version in the Briefcase, a left-pointing arrow indicates that Briefcase will update the document in the Briefcase from the master document. A red, downward-curving arrow (as shown in the last pair of files in fig. 19.4) indicates that Briefcase will skip the update—that is, it will mark the files as updated, but not actually make any changes.

Fig. 19.4
Windows 95's Briefcase tells you which documents it will update, and asks for your confirmation.

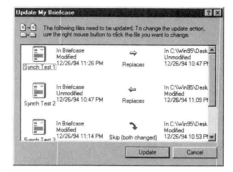

In figure 19.4, in the first pair of documents, the document inside the Briefcase was changed, and Briefcase is asking to confirm an update of the document file outside the Briefcase. In the second pair of documents, the document outside the Briefcase was changed, and Briefcase is asking to confirm an update of the document file inside the Briefcase. In the third and last pair of documents, Briefcase is indicating that both the document outside and inside the Briefcase changed, and Briefcase will skip any update.

You can manually override the way that Briefcase updates files, if you want, or you can skip the update altogether. Right-clicking the update document displays the pop-up menu shown in figure 19.5. Use this menu to choose which document should really be replaced (Briefcase updates the document that the arrow in the center column points to), or to skip updating the document at this time. The What's This? menu choice displays the properties sheet for that document.

Fig. 19.5
Choose from the pop-up menu which document should be replaced.

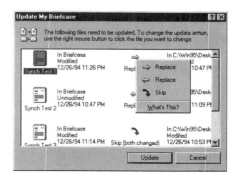

If you want, you can check the status of documents in a Briefcase without actually trying to update them. Document files in a Briefcase have an additional tab on their properties sheet: Update Status. Figure 19.6 shows the Update Status tab for a pair of documents that are up-to-date, whereas figure 19.7 shows the Update Status page for a pair of files that do need to be updated.

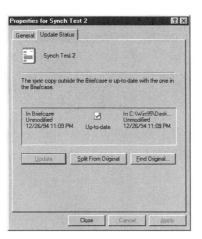

Fig. 19.6
Check the update status of your documents on the Update Status page on the properties sheet of the Briefcase copy of the document.

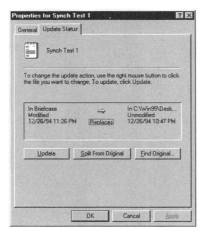

Fig. 19.7
The Update Status page also lets you update the documents as shown, split the Briefcase document from its original, or find the original document.

In rare circumstances, you may want to break the link between a document in the Briefcase and its original file—for example, you may want to move the master document to another computer, and you don't want Briefcase to continue updating the document on your computer. The Briefcase menu's Split command and the Split from Original button on the Update Status page both let you break the link between a Briefcase document and its original file.

If you do break the link between a Briefcase document and its original file, you can never again update the file via the Briefcase—unless you make another copy of the original file in your Briefcase folder. Breaking the link doesn't delete the document from the Briefcase folder, but the Update Status page in the properties sheet will indicate that the particular document in the Briefcase folder is an "orphan." Figure 19.8 shows the Update Status properties sheet page for an orphaned Briefcase document.

Fig. 19.8
You can't use the Briefcase to update orphaned documents.

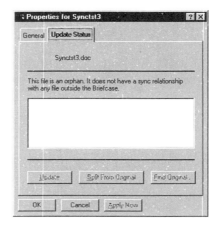

Chapter 20

Using Windows 95's Dial-Up Networking

The proliferation of laptop and notebook PCs and telecommuting workers makes remote access to PC networks and e-mail systems a necessity for corporate computing. Virtually all manufacturers and assemblers of desktop PCs now include a 14,400 bps fax modem as a standard component, and the price of PCMCIA fax modems for notebook PCs dropped dramatically in 1994. Almost all hotels and large motels have room telephones with a "data" connection, and aircraft equipped with air-to-ground telephone service usually have seat-back phones with a data port. The increasing geographic coverage and low cost of 128 Kbps ISDN lines, discussed in the earlier chapters of this book, give home telecommuters about 10 times the data rate of a standard modem. ISDN makes it practical to perform data-intensive operations, such as running remote queries against enterprise-wide databases.

Windows for Workgroups 3.11 included client-only remote access service (RAS) that let you connect to a Windows NT 3.5 Server with RAS enabled but not to NetWare or UNIX servers. To connect to a UNIX server, you had to install a TCP/IP application, such as the Shiva client, which connects to a Shiva LanRover network router. Connecting to a MS Mail postoffice required an add-on to MS Mail for PC Networks 3+, plus additional software and a license for each remote client. All told, providing dial-up networking services to Windows 3.1+ users created PC support headaches bordering on migraine.

> **Note**
>
> Commencing with the Beta 2 version (M7) used to write this book, Microsoft uses the term *dial-up networking* to describe Windows 95's remote access services (RAS). This chapter makes use of the more common *RAS* terminology used by Windows for Workgroups 3.11, Windows NT 3.5, and other third-party remote connectivity products.

Windows 95 takes the pain out of RAS. Windows 95's remote access features for mobile computing are built into the operating system, not tacked onto DOS as TSR (terminate-and-stay resident) programs loaded by entries in your AUTOEXEC.BAT file. Windows 95 uses a 32-bit, protected-mode device driver, PPPMAC.VXD, together with TAPI to provide its dial-up networking services. Windows 95 RAS includes built-in remote connectivity to Windows, NetWare, and UNIX servers that support PPP (Point-to-Point Protocol), so you won't have to deal with third-party software to connect to about 85 to 90 percent of the networks of 1995+. Also, Windows 95 includes its own RAS host (server) features; this means you can dial into your office computer from home or the field. If your office computer's on a network, you can gain access to all the network resources available at work. Thus, you don't have to wait for your network administrator to set up RAS on the network server; you can do it yourself with Windows 95.

This chapter explains the fundamentals of remote access, how to set up remote access to your network and e-mail postoffice, and how to configure your PC to deliver Windows 95's RAS host features.

Understanding How RAS Works

In principle, remote access services substitute modems for network interface cards (NICs). Once you establish a dial-up connection to the RAS host computer—traditionally a network server—the server shares are accessible to your PC, just as when you are physically connected to the network by an NIC. Figure 20.1 shows the following three most common types of remote access:

■ A home PC using an ISDN modem for telecommuting connected to one of a bank of ISDN modems at a corporate site. Typically, firms install multiple Primary Rate Interface (PRI) ISDN lines that provide twenty-three 64 Kbps (N*64) bearer (B) channels, plus one 64 Kbps signaling channel. (The 24 channels have a combined bandwidth of 1.544 Mbps, equivalent to a North American T-1 trunk.) You combine two N*64 channels to create one 128 Kbps channel; thus, it takes two PRI lines to provide twenty-three 128 Kbps incoming lines. Windows NT 3.5 Server can handle up to 256 simultaneous RAS connections. The same setup is used for NetWare servers running NetWare Connect.

■ A notebook PC connected to a networked desktop PC running Windows 95 with RAS host services enabled. Although PCMCIA modems are the most common, you also can use a battery-powered fax modem connected to the PC's serial port. Hosting RAS sessions requires that you set your office PC's modem to auto-answer mode before leaving for home or going on the road.

■ A notebook PC connected to a UNIX network by a modem-router combination. A router, such as a Shiva LanRover, is required between the modem and Unix networks. The router provides each connected RAS client with a temporary TCP/IP host address and resolves named hosts to their TCP/IP address.

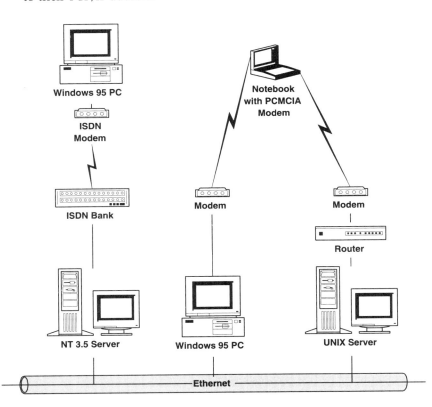

Fig. 20.1
A diagram of a multiple-server network with remote access services.

Note

If you're considering installing your first network (or are planning to upsize a Windows for Workgroups 3.1+ network) and want to provide RAS host capability, Windows NT 3.5 Server offers the best combination of price and performance of any network operating system (NOS) available when this book was written. Microsoft has priced Windows NT 3.5 Server substantially below the Novell NetWare product line, undoubtedly in an attempt to gain NOS market share. Even if you now have a NetWare 3+ network running, you may find it more economical to provide RAS via a supplemental Windows NT 3.5 Server installation. Windows NT 3.5 Server provides full compatibility with NetWare 3+ and 4+ networks.

Setting Up a Windows 95 RAS Client

If your employer now has an RAS-enabled network, it's easy to set up Windows 95 to connect to the network server(s). The simplest method is to open My Computer's window, double-click the Dial-Up Networking folder, and then double-click the New Connection button and let Windows 95 automatically install the required Microsoft Point-to-Point Protocol (PPP) driver for you. Alternatively, you can add the PPP driver from the Networks feature of Control Panel and then add your modem and dialing data. The example setup described in the following two sections uses the latter approach.

Adding the Microsoft PPP Driver as an Adapter

Windows 95 treats the PPP driver-modem combination as a network adapter card. You open the Network properties sheet, select the Configuration page, and then click the Add button to display the Select Network Component dialog (see fig. 20.2). Selecting Adapters from the list box and clicking the Add button opens the Select Network Adapters dialog; Microsoft supplies the PPP driver, so you select Microsoft from the Manufacturers list box and Microsoft Dial-Up Adapter in the Network Adapters list box, as shown in figure 20.3. When you click OK, The Microsoft Dial-Up Adapter is added to the list of installed networking components (see fig. 20.4).

IV

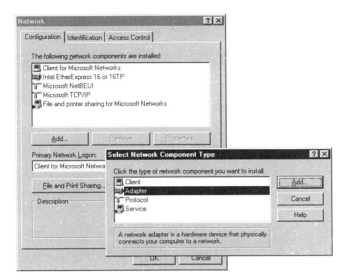

Fig. 20.2
The Network properties Config-uration page and Select Network Component type dialog for a typical Windows Network before adding the PPP driver.

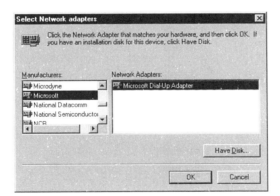

Fig. 20.3
Adding the Microsoft Dial-Up Adapter to the installed network adapters.

Note

In addition to installing the Dial-Up Adapter, the preceding process automatically installs the protocol(s) to be used by the PPP driver. Thus, it is important that you install all of the network client services you plan to use prior to setting up the PPP driver. Figure 20.4 shows two protocols, Microsoft NetBEUI (the default) and Microsoft TCP/IP, bound to the Dial-Up Adapter. If your network uses Novell's NetConnect for NetWare, you must install the Client for IPX/SPX Networks prior to configuring the PPP driver.

Fig. 20.4
The Network
properties sheet
after adding the
Dial-Up Adapter.

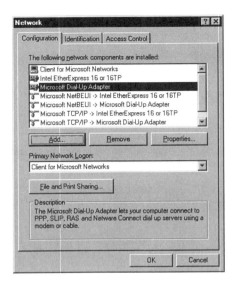

After you add the PPP driver, you can review the Properties for Microsoft Dial-Up Adapter sheet for the driver. The sheet has two pages:

■ The Driver Type page lets you select between Windows 95's built-in driver and real-mode drivers if you installed real-mode drivers in your CONFIG.SYS or AUTOEXEC.BAT file (see fig. 20.5).

■ The Bindings page lets you choose which protocols to use for remote access if you have more than one protocol installed. For communication with computers running the Microsoft Windows network, only NetBEUI is necessary. If you want to use RAS with NetWare or UNIX servers, you previously need to have installed the IPX/SPX and TCP/IP protocols, respectively. At least one check box in the Bindings page must be marked. Figure 20.6 shows the Bindings page with only the NetBEUI protocol selected.

Setting Up the RAS Connection Parameters

The final step of the RAS setup process is to enter the RAS server's telephone number and set your modem's communication parameters to correspond with those of the server's modem. The modem configuration features are provided by the Telephony API (TAPI), which is also used with the Dialer applet in Windows 95's Accessory folder. (The next section describes how to set up your modem for RAS client operations.) Windows 95 provides a mini-wizard to aid you in setting up your PPP connection. Figure 20.7 shows the first dialog of the Make New Connection "wizard" in which you enter the name of the connection, and select the modem to use. When you click the Next button, the second Make New Connection dialog appears in which you enter the telephone number of your RAS server (see fig. 20.8).

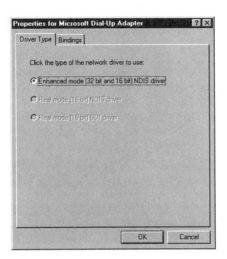

Fig. 20.5
The Driver Type page of the Properties for Microsoft Dial-Up Adapter sheet with no real-mode drivers installed.

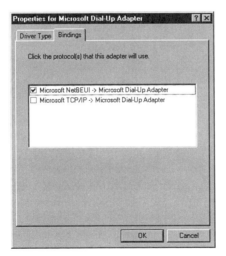

Fig. 20.6
The Bindings page of the Properties for Microsoft Dial-Up Adapter sheet with a single protocol installed.

Fig. 20.7
Entering the connection name and selecting a modem in the first dialog of the Make New Connection wizard.

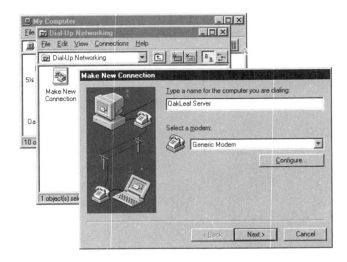

Fig. 20.8
Entering the telephone number of the RAS server in the second Make New Connection wizard.

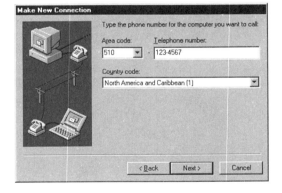

If your area code at home or on the road differs from the area code of the RAS server's modem, Windows 95 adds the 1+*AreaCode* digits to the dialing string; if you're in the same area code, the dialer doesn't send the 1+*AreaCode* digits. Clicking the Next button displays the third Make New Connection dialog that confirms you've completed the process. Clicking the Finish button adds the new connection to the Dial-Up Networking window of My Computer.

> **Note**
>
> If your firm uses an 800 number for RAS network connections, you enter 800 as the area code and then enter 1-800-PPP-NNNN as the number to call. You can add authorization codes as necessary by separating the code(s) from the phone number with commas. Each comma adds a half-second delay between strings of dialing digits.

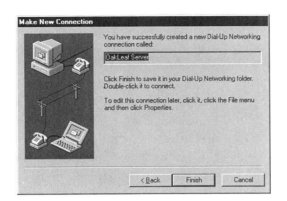

Fig. 20.9
Confirming completion of your RAS connection in the third dialog of the Make New Connection wizard.

Configuring Your Modem for RAS Dial-Out

If you haven't previously set up the modem you intend to use for dial-up networking, you should review the modem's settings. Clicking the Configure button of the first Make New Connection dialog opens the properties sheet for your modem. Figure 20.10 shows the General page of the Properties for Generic Modem sheet; this is a typical internal or external 14,400 bps Hayes-compatible faxmodem installed on COM port 2. The General page lets you set the modem's speaker volume, if the volume is adjustable, and to select the COM port to which your modem is connected. The Connection page lets you set the modem's communication parameters (see fig. 20.12). Almost all RAS connections use 8 data bits, no parity and 1 stop bit, the default values supplied by Windows 95. Clicking the Advanced button of the Connection page displays the Advanced Connection Settings dialog, shown in figure 20.12. The default properties for your modem from Windows 95's MODEM.INF file usually make the connection, but you may have to set the Flow Control method to match that used by the server's modem. Hardware flow control uses request-to-send/clear-to-send (RTS/CTS) protocol and is the most common flow control method; software flow control uses the XON/XOFF protocol. The Use Error Control options appear only for modems whose entries in MODEM.INF indicates that the modems support error correction and data compression. The Advanced Connection Settings dialog includes an Extra Settings dialog in which you can type a special setup string for your modem. In the majority of cases, additional setup commands are not necessary. (Some ISDN modems require special setup strings.)

Fig. 20.10
The General page of the modem's properties sheet.

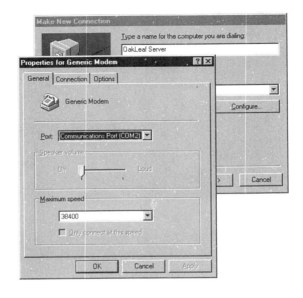

Fig. 20.11
The Connection page of the modem's properties sheet.

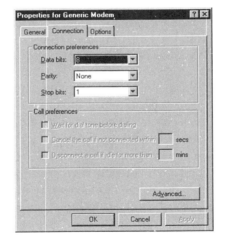

Fig. 20.12
Setting the modem's communication parameters in the Advanced Connection Settings dialog.

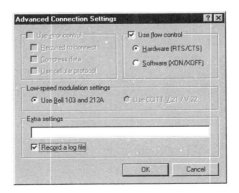

> **Note**
>
> The Advanced Connection Settings dialog includes a Record a Log File option, which you can use for troubleshooting RAS connections. Entries are made in the \WIN95\MODEMLOG.TXT file for each step in the RAS connection process. An example of entries for a connection made with Windows 95's CompuServe MAPI driver appears in Chapter 12, "Connecting to the Outside World." After you've corrected any problems with your RAS connection, make sure to turn off log file recording feature; MODEMLOG.TXT can become very large if you make extensive use of Windows 95's dial-up networking.

Connecting to and Using a RAS Network Server

Once you've established all the settings needed for your RAS connection and closed the properties sheets, the Dial-Up Networking window of My Computer displays an icon for the connection (see fig. 20.13). Double-clicking the connection's icon opens the Connect To dialog to enter your user ID and password for the server. When you click the OK button, RAS dials the server, authenticates your user ID and password, and establishes the connection, as shown in the three message boxes of figure 20.14. Once you're connected to the server, the server shares appear in your Network Neighborhood window (see fig. 20.15). You can browse the shares in the same manner as with a direct network connection; the primary difference is that browsing files with RAS at 14,400 bps is much slower than a direct network connection that operates in the 8 Mbps range.

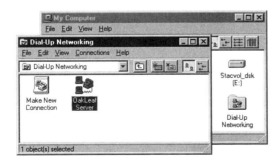

Fig. 20.13
The icon for a RAS connection in the Remote Access window of Network Neighborhood.

Fig. 20.14
The three steps
in making the
connection to a
RAS server.

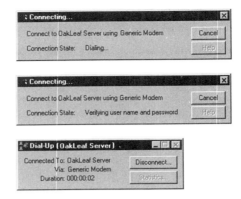

Fig. 20.15
Server shares
connected by RAS.

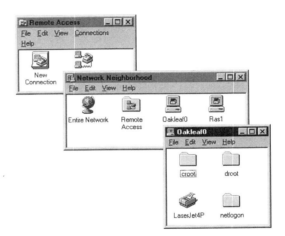

Users of notebook computers with PCMCIA NICs ordinarily map one or more
network shares to local-drive designators on startup when connected to the
office network. If you take your notebook computer home, Windows 95 notifies you that the wired network isn't available and offers the option of using a
RAS connection to attach the network share (see fig. 20.16). Clicking the Yes
button brings up a dialog that lets you select the connection for the RAS
server, as shown in figure 20.17, if you have created more than one RAS
connection.

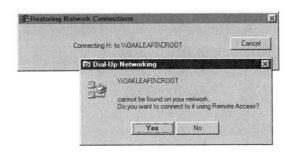

Fig. 20.16
The Dial-Up
Networking
message box
offering RAS as an
alternative to
network connec-
tion with an NIC.

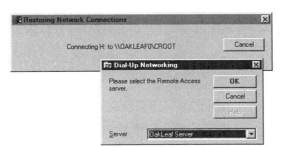

Fig. 20.17
Selecting the RAS
server connection.

Adding Windows 95 RAS Host Capability to Your PC

Making your Windows 95 PC a RAS host so that you or others can dial into your PC—and, optionally, into the server shares that your PC has access to—is a simple process. Choosing Dial-Up Server from the Connections menu of My Computer's Dial-Up Networking window (see fig. 20.18) opens the Dial-Up Server dialog. Choose the Allow Caller Access option to enable your PC as a dial-up networking host. Clicking the Change Password button opens the Dial-Up Networking dialog, shown in figure 20.19, which provides a text box to enter a common password that all dial-in users must enter to connect to your PC. If you don't enter a password, anyone who knows the telephone number of your RAS computer can gain access to your shared files, but not to files on the network (if network access is password-protected).

Clicking the Server Type button displays the Server Types dialog in which you can specify the server protocols you want to use (see fig. 20.20). The Default choice in the Type of Dial-Up Server drop-down list lets RAS clients negotiate with the server to determine automatically the appropriate proto-col. The default selections to Enable Software Compression and Require Encrypted Password are appropriate for the RAS server types supplied with Windows 95.

◀ See Chapter 17, "Creating Workgroups with Windows 95's Peer-to-Peer Networking"

Fig. 20.18
The menu choice to set up dial-in access to your PC.

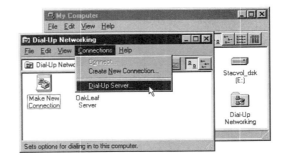

Fig. 20.19
Setting the Allow Caller Access option and setting the common dial-up password.

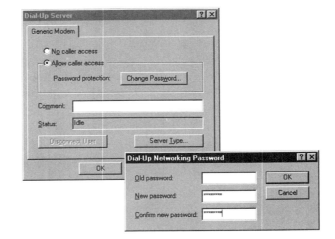

Fig. 20.20
Specifying the server types and options for your dial-up server.

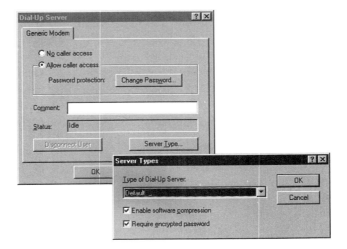

To complete the dial-up networking installation, you must take the following two steps:

1. Create local (peer-to-peer) server and printer shares for all resources you want to make available to dial-up networking users, including yourself.

2. Leave your computer turned on to make dial-up networking functional. (If you use an external modem, it too must be powered up.)

You can turn off dial-in services by selecting the No Caller Access option of the Dial-Up Server dialog, or open the System Policy Editor for your computer and click the Disable dial-in check box that appears under the Remote Access item of the Network category. If you implement systemwide policies, you can prevent all Windows 95 users from enabling their computers as RAS servers by clicking the Disable dial-in check box for the Default Computer profile (see fig. 20.21). Setting systemwide policies is the subject of the next chapter.

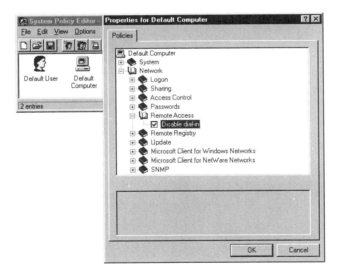

Fig. 20.21
Disabling all Windows 95 users from setting up dial-in RAS servers with the System Policy Editor's entry for Default Computer.

Chapter 21

Managing Networked PCs with Windows 95

The ability to manage Windows 95 clients over the network is a major incentive for organizations with 50 or more PCs to adopt Windows 95 as the standard operating system for their Windows users. Industry-wide studies indicate that the cost of PC network administration and support is substantially greater than the combined cost of PC hardware, software, and user training.

Much of the support cost accrues as a result of users installing non-standard software, such as games and Windows utility applications, on their workplace computers. Shareware and freeware games are the primary source of computer viruses that can infect the company's entire network. Utilities such as File Manager and Program Manager replacements sometimes wreak havoc with network client operations. Thus, management looks to centralized administration of network resources and attached client PCs (workstations) to reduce operating costs. This chapter provides an overview of the new features of Windows 95 that are intended to make network client administration more efficient and less costly.

Improving Network Manageability with Windows 95

Windows 95 includes a variety of new features that help network managers and PC support people keep trouble tickets to a minimum. Many of these features are modeled on the network management structure of Windows NT 3.5 Server. The following list describes the capabilities of Windows 95's new administrative features for networked PCs:

■ Allow users to define their own desktop configuration or impose a pre-defined configuration on all networked workstations. Although imposing a single configuration on all users (or particular groups of users) has a heavy-handed ring, a single desktop and common set of applications greatly simplifies network administration and PC support.

■ Provide all users with their own desktop configuration, stored on the server, that appears automatically when they log on to the network from any networked workstation.

■ Duplicate the operation of a Windows 95 workstation with its new Remote Administration features.

■ Remotely manage server resources with the Net Watcher applet.

■ Observe the performance of individual Windows 95 workstations with the System Monitor applet or with an SNMP (Simple Network Management Protocol) console. Windows 95 doesn't include an SNMP console application; Microsoft offers System Management Server and a variety of ISVs (independent software vendors) to provide network management software using the SNMP protocol.

■ Automatically back up fixed disks of client workstations connected to Windows NT 3.5 Server and Novell NetWare networks. (Backing up clients on NetWare networks requires third-party backup software.)

A basic description of each of the preceding administrative feature sets is included in the following sections. Most of the features are implemented by remote procedure calls (RPCs) that manipulate entries in Windows 95's new Registry database, the subject of Chapter 24, "Replacing WIN.INI, SYSTEM.INI, and REG.DAT with Registry."

Administering Workstation Policies

Workstation administration is handled by the System Policy Editor application, POLEDIT.EXE (called PolEdit in this chapter), which is *not* installed by default in the Administrative Tools folder of the Applications folder. To use PolEdit, place a shortcut to \WIN95\POLEDIT.EXE on your desktop or in the \WIN95\Start\Programs\Accessories\System Tool directory. The System Policy Editor's most important function is to establish central configuration templates for networked Windows 95 workstations and user groups. The default template, ADMINCFG.ADM, is designed for use only by network

administrators and provides the foundation for creating central policy files
(*FILENAME*.POL). As an example, a policy file for users who don't have administrative authority shouldn't allow access to the System Policy Editor or
the Registry Editor applications. The following sections describe how to set
up and enforce systemwide policies for networked Windows 95 users.

Creating a Windows 95 User Policy File

You choose the New command of the System Configuration Editor's File
menu to create a new, untitled policy file based on the administrative template. Figure 21.1 shows the Properties for Default User sheet in the process of
establishing user properties that apply to all new Windows 95 users using
network logon. You determine the wallpaper for users' desktops and whether
users can be prevented from sharing files and printers with other users in a
peer-to-peer network. Check boxes filled with a hatched pattern indicate that
no policy is set for the associated item; "no policy" is the default setting until
you establish a policy. The Properties for Default User sheet lets you set a
variety of restrictions on what individual users may access, including each of
Control Panel's functions.

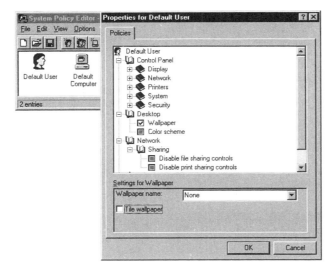

Fig. 21.1
Setting the Default
User properties for
Windows 95
network users.

> **Note**
>
> The policies you set for the Default User and Default Workstation don't apply to the administrative copy of Windows 95 you use to establish the policies. The policy file you create is applicable only to non-administrative network installations of Windows 95 you create for other users.

Figure 21.2 shows the Properties for Default Computer sheet with its hierarchical list of policies that apply to each networked PC running Windows 95, regardless of who's using the PC. You must specify the location for the Network Path for Windows Setup property from which users run the setup application to install Windows 95 on their local PCs. All users must have at least read-only access to the specified setup directory.

Fig. 21.2
Specifying the location of the network setup directory for Windows 95.

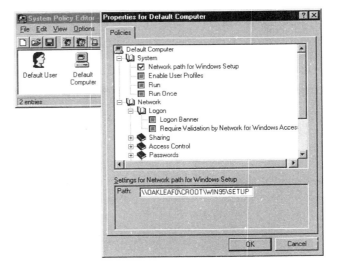

> **Note**
>
> As you can when setting up Windows 3.1+, you can choose to have users install a full copy of Windows 95 on their local fixed disk drives from the network installation copy or run Windows 95 from a network server. To enforce the policies you've established, you must select one of these two installation methods. Otherwise, you must manually set the UNC path to the location of the network policy file on each workstation as described later in this chapter.

Figure 21.3 shows setting network policies for workstations. You can specify a logon banner; the default banner is Important Notice: Do not attempt to log on unless you are an authorized user. You can change the caption and the message in the property sheet's text boxes to establish a more friendly or a more forbidding tone. The Require Validation by Network for Windows Access option (underneath the Logon Banner option) requires that the user's password be authenticated by the user/password list on a network domain controller. The rest of the policies relate to the workstation's capability to share files and printers, password security, RAS dial-in, and administrative updates to policy files. After you've specified the policies for network users, you save the policy file on the server so that it's accessible to all workstations (see fig. 21.4).

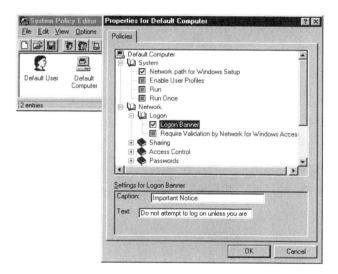

Fig. 21.3
Setting up
Windows 95
networking
policies.

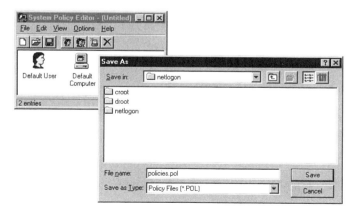

Fig. 21.4
Saving the system
policy file for new
users.

Activating Administrative Policy Updates

After you establish the policies, you use PolEdit's Update.Remote Update feature to set up administrative updating. Administrative updating lets you change policies for all user workstations as the need arises. Figure 21.5 shows the Update page of the Properties for Security sheet. If you specify Manual Update Mode, the workstation policy file is updated from the shared policy file located in the server directory you specify in the Path for Manual Update text box each time workstation network services start. A logical server share in which to place the policy file is the directory of the server that provides logon services (*SERVERNAME*\NETLOGON for Windows NT 3.5 Server networks).

Fig. 21.5
Turning on administrative updating of workstation policies.

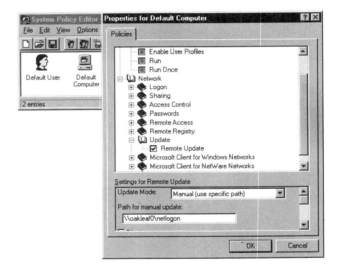

Setting Up Uniform Desktops and Remote Administration

You use the Profiles page of Control Panel's Passwords sheet to specify that all users share a common desktop folder (directory) with a predetermined set of icons (see fig. 21.6). As noted earlier in the chapter, providing all users with a standard desktop setup minimizes PC support costs.

Alternatively, you can let users design their own desktops and save the USER.DAT file on a network server; in this case, if a user logs on to another workstation, his or her custom desktop appears. When you log on from your home computer by RAS, you see the same desktop as on your workplace computer.

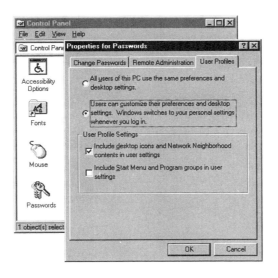

Fig. 21.6
Choosing between providing users a common desktop and providing custom desktop transportability.

IV

Networking Windows 95

Windows 95 lets you, as an administrator, operate a remote networked PC just as though you were sitting at the PC's keyboard. (You can't, however, reboot the computer remotely.) You enable remote administration by marking the check box of the Remote Administration page of the Properties for Passwords sheet (see fig. 21.7). You establish a special password for remote PC administration that applies to all the workstations on your network. You also can specify a single password to log on to Windows 95 and your network server (see fig. 21.8).

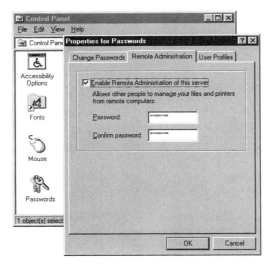

Fig. 21.7
Enabling and setting the password for remote administration of a workstation.

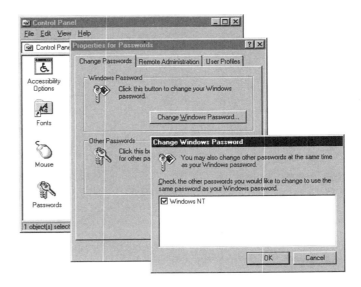

Controlling and Monitoring Remote Windows 95 Workstations

Windows 95 provides a System Administration folder that contains three primary tools for managing and monitoring PCs: the Administrative Configuration Tool, Net Watcher, and System Monitor. The Administrative Configuration Tool opens the System Policy Editor described earlier in this chapter. The following sections briefly describe the Net Watcher and System Monitor tools, plus Windows 95's SNMP agent.

Using Net Watcher to Control Local and Remote Servers

Net Watcher is an administrative tool that lets you perform the following functions:

■ Observe the status of server shares on local and remote Windows 95 workstations, including the names of computers connected to server shares

■ Create a shared resource on a local or remote Windows 95 computer

■ Stop access to a shared resource on a local or remote computer

When you open Net Watcher from the Administrative Tools submenu of the Accessories menu, Net Watcher displays the status of resources shared by your local computer. When you select a specific share, the name(s) of the computer(s) using the share appears in the list box on the right. To administer server shares on a remote Windows 95 computer, you select the folder for the computer in Network Neighborhood and right-click. If remote administration is enabled on the computer, the Admin File System menu choice appears, so you can open Net Watcher attached to the selected computer. Figure 21.9 shows Net Watcher on the OAKLEAF0 computer displaying the three shares of a remote workstation, RAS1. OAKLEAF0 is connected to the WINDOWS 95 share.

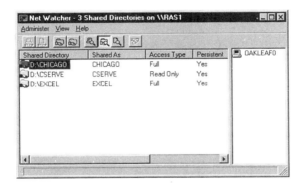

Fig. 21.9
Using Net Watcher to administer shares of a remote workstation.

Checking Windows 95's Performance with System Monitor

Windows 95's System Monitor is designed for both curious and serious computer users. You can track virtually any set of operating parameters of your local or remote PC with the System Monitor. Figure 21.10 shows the System Monitor tracking the speed of disk reads and writes in bytes per second, plus the amount of free memory available to the virtual memory manager, VMM32. Choosing Add Item from System Monitor's Edit menu displays the Add Item dialog (see fig. 21.11). Microsoft expects to expand the number of items in the Category list box in the retail version of Windows 95. System Monitor offers the time-based charts shown in figures 21.10 and 21.11, and a bar-chart display of instantaneous values.

Fig. 21.10
Displaying
performance
parameters of a
local computer on
a time base.

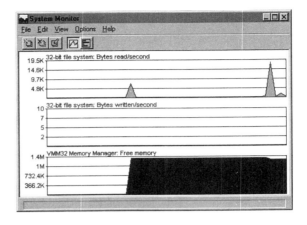

Fig. 21.11
Adding a new
chart to System
Monitor's
window.

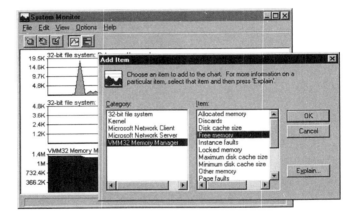

Understanding Windows 95's SNMP Agent

◄ See Chapter 16, "Using Windows 95 Clients with Existing Networks"

The Simple Network Management Protocol (SNMP) was designed by members of the Internet Engineering Task Force (IETF) in the late 1980s as an interim standard for monitoring network devices connected to the Internet while the more complex OSI (Open Systems Interconnection) network management model was being developed. By the time the ISO-standard OSI model was defined (1993), SNMP had become the *de facto* network monitoring standard for IP (Internet Protocol) networks, including those using TCP/IP.

SNMP isn't a network-management console (application); SNMP defines a set of *agents* that third-party network management applications use to obtain information on the operating status of network devices, including hubs, bridges, routers, and individual PC workstations. SNMP uses MIBs (Management Information Bases) to define individual network devices.

> **Note**
>
> Windows 95's implementation of SNMP is called version 1, because version 2 of SNMP was in the development process when this book was written. SNMP-2 adds a number of features to SNMP-1, the most important of which is improved security to prevent unauthorized persons from "snooping" on an SNMP-enabled network.

Windows 95 implements the SNMP agent as a Win32 service using the Windows Sockets (WinSock) API. To use SNMP, you need to install Windows 95's TCP/IP or IPX/SPX protocol, either of which is compatible with the WinSock API. Windows 95 implements the IETF's RFC (Request For Comments) 1156 Extension Agent, which provides for proprietary MIBs that define the capabilities of a specific, proprietary device, such as a Windows 95 workstation. After installing the TCP/IP protocol, you enable SNMP on a Windows 95 workstation by entering **snmp.exe** in the Command Line text box of the Run dialog or by moving SNMP.EXE to the Startup folder.

Microsoft's Systems Management Server (SMS), which had just been released as a component of the Microsoft BackOffice server suite when this book was written, uses SNMP but carries the network management console one step further. SMS also can inventory the adapter cards and software installed on individual PCs. SMS's SHIC (Software/Hardware Inventory Collector) runs as an agent, supplementing SNMP, on each workstation and server on the network. SHIC creates MIF (Management Information Format) files defined by the Desktop Management Task Force (DMTF) and stores the MIF data in a Microsoft SQL Server for Windows NT database.

> **Note**
>
> If you felt lost in a sea of SNMP abbreviations and acronyms in the preceding paragraphs, don't worry. After you start using TCP/IP to connect to the Internet, you'll become accustomed to the seemingly incomprehensible, cryptic code names favored by the UNIX community, such as *grep*, *gnu*, and *gopher*.

All third-party SNMP console applications will likely support Windows 95 when it's released as Windows 95 or shortly thereafter. According to an article in the Aug. 15, 1994, issue of *Information Week* titled, "NT Gains Support," SynOptics Communication, Inc. plans to port its Optivity network management software from UNIX to Windows NT and also will make Optivity available for networked Windows 95 workstations. Like other network management systems, Optivity can manage SynOptics' network hubs,

switches, and routers, as well as other manufacturers' devices that support
SNMP. All told, about 30 network management application suppliers had
committed to support Windows 95's SNMP agent when this book was
written.

Backing Up Windows 95 Clients from NetWare Servers

Windows NT 3.5 includes a built-in provision to automatically back up the
fixed disks of Windows 95 client workstations to a backup tape or magneto-
optical disk drive. Novell NetWare doesn't include this capability as a
standard feature. Two of the leading suppliers of NLMs (NetWare Loadable
Modules) for automatic client backup are Arcada Software, Inc. and Cheyenne Software, Inc. Windows 95 includes a client backup agent for Arcada
Back Exec (both Single-Server and Enterprise editions) and Cheyenne
ARCserve for NetWare.

Part V

Digging into the Windows 95 Operating System

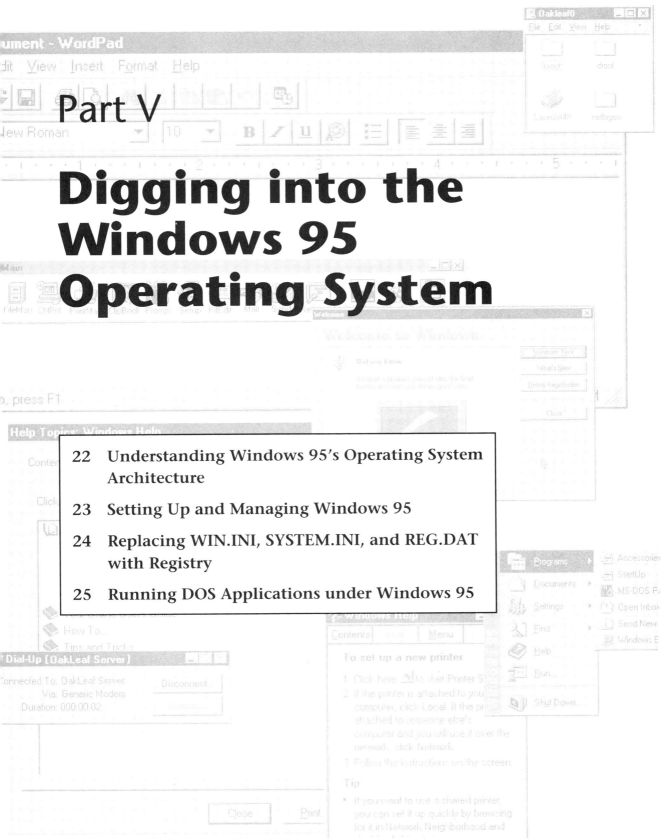

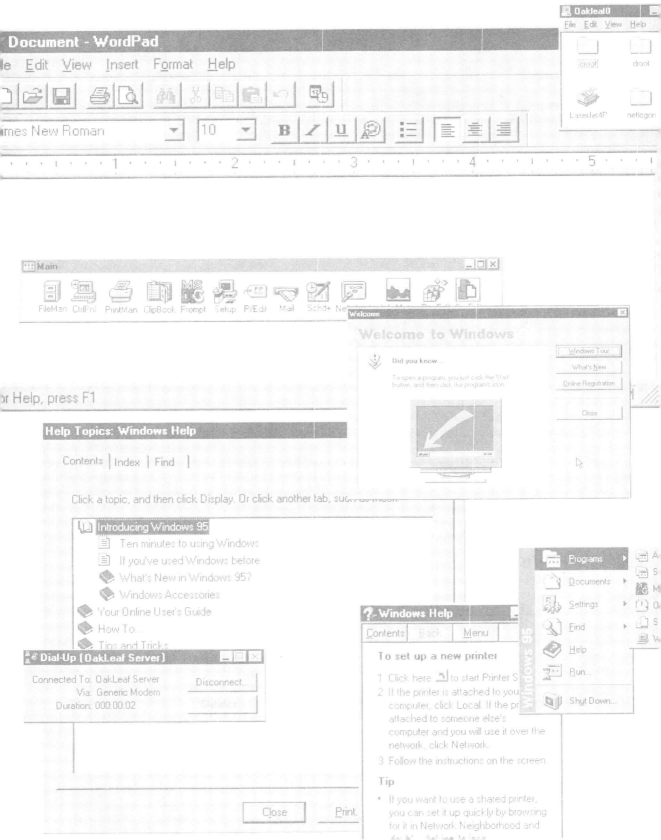

Chapter 22

Understanding Windows 95's Operating System Architecture

Microsoft is very proud of Windows 95's new 32-bit operating system architecture, much of which is derived from the effort Microsoft developers expended to make Windows NT 3.5 an outstanding, bulletproof 32-bit operating system. The reaction of most computer press columnists to early beta versions of Windows 95 has been very favorable. Some press reports, however, decry the fact that Windows 95 isn't entirely a 32-bitter; some of the code of the graphic device interface (GDI.EXE) and the library that provides basic user services (USER.EXE) retain the 16-bit code necessary to provide backward compatibility with Windows 3.1+ applications. According to Microsoft, the 16-bit code that remains in Windows 95 has been extensively optimized during the four-plus years of Windows 3+'s existence; thus, providing full 32-bitness wouldn't add a great deal to Windows 95's performance.

This chapter and the remaining chapters of this book are directed primarily to information systems managers, PC support personnel, Windows power users, and developers who want to gain a better understanding of how the Windows 95 operating system differs from its DOS predecessors. Although many of the preceding chapters have dealt with specific new operating system features as they affect the subject matter of each chapter, this chapter summarizes Windows 95's new operating system features at a greater level of technical detail.

Putting It All in One Place

Version 4 of the *Microsoft Windows 95 Reviewer's Guide*, which provided valuable assistance in the writing of this book, incorporates a list of what Microsoft considers the most important new features of the Windows 95 operating system. The list that follows is derived from the *Reviewer's Guide*, with some editorial commentary added:

■ *Integrated 32-bit protected-mode operating system,* including memory management, process scheduling, and process arbitration, which eliminates the need for a separate copy of DOS. Ultimately, users can get rid of DOS's CONFIG.SYS and AUTOEXEC.BAT files. It's likely that Windows 95 will carry a price tag less than the combination of DOS 6+ and Windows 3.1+ license fees.

■ *Preemptive multitasking and support for multithreading* (within individual 32-bit applications), which improves application responsiveness and makes background processing—especially high-speed data communication operations—less obtrusive.

■ *32-bit installable file systems,* which perform far better than their 16-bit counterparts in Windows 3.1+. Windows 95 includes the VFAT (virtual file allocation table for fixed disks), CDFS (CD-ROM file system), and network redirectors for IPX/SPX and NetBEUI protocols. If Microsoft chooses, it can add the Windows NT File System (NTFS) or OS/2's High-Performance File System (HPFS) to Windows 95, though either is unlikely to find its way into Windows 95. Third parties can create their own installable file systems, if needed. Say good-bye (and good riddance) to real-mode MSCDEX.EXE for CD-ROM drives.

■ *32-bit dynamic, protected-mode device drivers* available to all processes running on the system, which are loaded into memory when needed and are unloaded when all processes are finished with them. You no longer need entries in SYSTEM.INI to load all your device drivers on startup. Plug and Play sets up the driver for each device automatically. Even without a Plug and Play BIOS and adapter cards, Windows 95 automatically handles installation of drivers for popular cards. Most DOS applications get their full 640K of operating memory because you no longer need real-mode DOS device drivers.

- *32-bit background print spooling,* which minimizes disruption of your work while you're printing large documents. If you have a fast laser printer, you'll notice a definite speedup, especially when printing detailed graphic elements.

- *More robust operation,* such as automatically cleaning up allocated memory after a 32-bit application ends or crashes. You don't have to reboot Windows 95 to regain system resources, but you do need to close all 16-bit Windows applications to regain 16-bit resources after one Windows 3.1+ application crashes.

- *Dynamic environmental tuning,* which eliminates the need for users to set up permanent swap files and to tweak operating system parameters. You can also forget about installing EMM386 and SmartDrive, loading DOS high, and the other vagaries associated with DOS memory management and disk caching.

- *Increased system resource (heap) limits,* which makes running several simultaneous applications practical. Developers who use OLE Automation with two or more OLE 2 mega apps will especially appreciate this improvement. Note, however, that Windows 3.1+'s 64K heap limit hasn't disappeared; Windows 95 just moves as many instructions and as much data as it can outside the application's graphic (GDI) and window management (USER) heap.

- *Antialiasing of TrueType fonts,* which removes the "jaggies" associated with the display of large fonts in Windows 3.1 and improves the readability of smaller fonts, especially from those type families with serifs.

As mentioned in the introduction to this book, you can't make valid performance comparisons between an early beta of a new operating system and retail versions of updates to more mature operating systems. But the real argument for upgrading to Windows 95 is this: everything but the application software and special hardware drivers is contained within the operating system itself, not tacked onto the operating system as an afterthought. Unless there are some hidden problems with Windows 95, none of which surfaced during the course of writing of this book, Microsoft will have a unified Windows operating system which they can justifiably call "way cool." Steve Gibson said it best in his "Gibson's Guide to Windows 95" article that appeared in the June 27, 1994, issue of *InfoWorld*: "Without question, Windows 95 will prove to be the single most significant software system ever created by man."

V

Digging into the OS

Grabbing the Brass Ring

Intel microprocessors, beginning with the 80386 series, provide for protected-mode operation. Microsoft and IBM versions of OS/2 were the first operating systems to take advantage of protected-mode operation of the Intel chips. Neither of these two products was wildly successful for a variety of reasons, a discussion of which is beyond the scope of this book. With Windows 3+ running on Intel 80x86 processors under good old real-mode, 16-bit DOS took the PC market by storm. Intel maintained its 85 percent or so share of the PC processor market, and Microsoft ended up with a similar share of the operating system business, together with the graphic interface market. To most users, "Intel Inside" is synonymous with the PC.

The internal architecture, called microcode, of Intel 80x86 processors provides a series of rings in which various types of code can operate. Ring 3 (brass) provides the memory management necessary for protected-mode operation; the operating system can assign each application its own virtual machine (VM). Ring 0 (platinum, to maintain the metallurgical analogy) provides the low-level connections to the system BIOS and the required boot devices; a crash in the ring 0 code brings the entire system down. Rings 1 (gold) and 2 (silver) are involved in real-mode operations that share memory under DOS and Windows 3+. One of the original complaints about Novell's NLMs (NetWare Loadable Modules) was that the NLMs ran in ring 0; thus, a crash of an NLM brought down the entire server. The advantage of running all code in ring 0 is that ring transition operations (which require extra processor cycles) are eliminated, making NLMs run faster. Structures such as rings are what contribute to the description of Intel and similar processors: complex instruction set computing (CISC).

Figure 22.1 shows a simplified block diagram of Windows 95 simultaneously running multiple 32-bit protected-mode and 16-bit real-mode Windows applications in one VM and two DOS applications, each running in its own VM. Each DOS application gets a full 640K of memory if your computer has enough free RAM. The operating system's ring 3 code allocates each VM blocks of RAM that other VMs can't touch. (One of the most common causes of system crashes in DOS and windows is when one application accidentally steps on another application's block of RAM.) If an unruly application tries to use RAM in another application's memory space assigned by Windows 95, you receive a System Integrity Violation message, and Windows 95 immediately terminates the offending application. Windows 95 minimizes ring transitions, thereby improving performance, by running code only in ring 0 and ring 3.

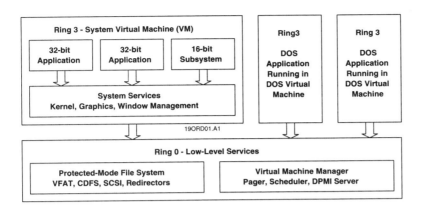

Fig. 22.1
A simplified diagram of Windows 95's method of managing virtual machines.

> **Note**
>
> One of the primary features that distinguishes Windows NT 3.5 from Windows 95 is that Windows NT has an additional layer, called the hardware abstraction layer (HAL), that operates at the bottom of ring 0. By substituting processor-specific HALs, Windows NT 3.5 can run on Intel CISC chips, as well as reduced instruction set computing processors such as the MIPS, DEC Alpha, and IBM-Apple PowerPC chips. Windows 95 doesn't have a replaceable HAL; thus, Windows 95 runs only on Intel-compatible hardware. Microsoft states that it has no intention of adding a replaceable HAL to Windows 95; if you want full cross-platform compatibility with a single operating system, you must use Windows NT 3.5 or one of the few flavors of UNIX that offers true cross-platform capabilities.

Handling 16-Bit Windows Applications in a 32-Bit System

By the time you read this book, Microsoft will have sold about 70 million copies of Windows 3+. There's some controversy regarding the number of active Windows 3+ users; estimates range between 15 million and 40 million. There are at least 50 million copies of mainstream Windows 16-bit productivity applications such as word processing and spreadsheet software in use. Thus, the primary goal of Microsoft's Windows 95 developers was to provide total compatibility with existing 16-bit Windows 3.1+ applications. There are three methods of running 16-bit Windows applications within a 32-bit operating system:

■ Run 16-bit applications in their own copy of Windows 3.1 running in a virtual machine. IBM's OS/2 Warp uses this approach, if you have enough RAM to accommodate the memory overhead of virtual machines.

■ Add a 16-bit Windows 3.1 emulator on top of a 32-bit Windows operating system. Windows NT 3.5 uses this approach with its WOW (Windows on Windows) methodology. UNIX operating systems also use Windows 3.1 emulation techniques with varying degrees of success.

■ Use a 16-bit Windows subsystem to provide 16-bit applications a unified address space within the same virtual machine that runs 32-bit applications. Windows 95 uses this method.

The first two choices of the preceding list carry a high memory overhead penalty. Although today's "standard" PC for running Windows applications has an 80486DX processor with 8M of RAM, a very substantial number of 4M 80386 computers remain in use. The only way to achieve equal or better performance of 16-bit Windows applications running in a 32-bit environment on the same hardware is to create a 16-bit subsystem. The Windows 95 16-bit Windows subsystem uses as much of the 32-bit operating system code as possible to avoid a big-time memory hit.

Chapter 5, "Running Your Current Applications under Windows 95," provides a brief explanation of how Windows 95 handles 16-bit Windows applications. The sections that follow describe in greater detail the methods Windows 95 uses to handle fundamental 16-bit Windows operations.

Queuing Windows Messages and Managing Heaps

Multitasking operating systems use messages to communicate between applications and the operating system, as well as to pass requests for services between elements of the operating system. A message identifies the originating application or operating system element and specifies the action that initiated the message. A typical Windows message, WM_MOUSEDOWN, is created when you click a mouse button. The message includes the handle (numeric identifier) of the active window, the coordinates of the mouse pointer, and a code that indicates which button you pressed. Windows puts messages in a message queue, a FIFO (first-in, first-out) stack. As you move the mouse while holding a button down, a stream of WM_MOUSEDOWN messages with different coordinates ends up in the queue. The operating system processes the message; in this case, for example, the graphic device interface, GDI.EXE, might drag a bit-mapped object from one window to another. As each message is processed, it's removed from the queue.

> **Note**
>
> Technically, Windows 3.1+ is an operating environment, not an operating system. DOS is Windows 3.1+'s operating system. Unless specifically distinguished, this chapter uses the term operating system to encompass both DOS/Windows 3.1+ and Windows 95.

To minimize memory required to run Windows 16-bit (Win16) applications, the 16-bit Windows subsystem uses a common message queue and common memory heap (also called graphic and system resources) for all open Win16 applications. Thus, Win16 applications cooperatively multitask under Windows 95 but don't gain the benefits of preemptive multitasking discussed in Chapter 6, "Upgrading to 32-Bit Productivity Applications." Out-of-memory messages can still occur when you run multiple Win16 applications, even if your computer has 16M of RAM because Win16 apps share a common memory heap. (Microsoft calls Windows 95's heap a *unified address space*.) 32-bit applications have their own protected memory area that holds each app's message queue and heap. Figure 22.2 is a diagram showing the differences between the real-mode Win16 applications running in the 16-bit subsystem and protected-mode Win32 apps running directly under Windows 95.

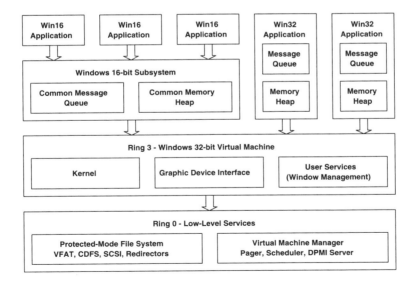

Fig. 22.2
Windows 95's message queues and memory heaps for 16-bit and 32-bit applications.

As mentioned in Chapter 5, Win16 applications must deallocate their heap memory blocks on closing. If a Win16 application crashes, it usually leaves orphaned memory blocks in the common heap. In Windows 3.1+, applications that don't properly deallocate their heap memory create memory leaks. (Beta software commonly is afflicted with memory leakage.) Ultimately, your system resources dwindle to a few percent, and Windows 3.1+ refuses to launch applications. Your only choice in this situation is to close and relaunch Windows.

One of the principal benefits of running Win16 applications under Windows 95 is that Windows 95 automatically cleans up the common heap when you close all your Win16 apps. If an errant Win16 application brings down the 16-bit Windows subsystem, currently running 32-bit applications are unaffected. In most cases, you'll be able to shut down a hung Win16 task with a three-fingered salute (Ctrl+Alt+Delete) to display the task list, then select the hung task and click the End Task button.

One of the issues raised during early computer press reports on the Windows 95 operating system was that both Win16- and Win32-based applications share the same graphic (GDI) and window-management system (USER) heaps. Thus, it's still possible to run out of GDI or system resources when running 32-bit applications. Microsoft has moved a substantial amount of objects out of the 16-bit heap and into the 32-bit heap; the 32-bit heap is never likely to run out of memory. Microsoft removed graphic region objects from the 64K 16-bit GDI heap into a 32-bit heap; this greatly helps graphic-intensive operations, such as moving a selection in Paint. Microsoft also relocated menu and window handles to the 32-bit USER heap; the 200-handle limit of Windows 3.1 is now increased to 32,767 menu handles, plus 32,767 window handles per process. Thus, you're not likely to run out of either menu or window handles under Windows 95.

Thunking Your Way between 16 and 32 Bits

One of the words you are likely to hear more often as Win32 applications become plentiful is *thunking*. 32-bit Windows applications use 32-bit (long) integers for window handles (hWnd) and most other Windows object identifiers and 32-bit memory addresses for the flat memory model of full 32-bit protected-mode operation. 16-bit applications, on the other hand, use conventional 16-bit (short) integers for handles and expect the 16-bit paged memory model used by the Intel 80x86 processors in real mode. Windows 95's 16-bit Windows subsystem provides a thunking layer that handles the conversion from 16-bit to 32-bit handles and addresses. Windows 95's thunking layer is especially important when you use a 16-bit OLE client application with a 32-bit OLE server (or vice versa).

Installing Multiple File Systems

One of the most interesting new features of Windows 95 is its Installable File System (IFS), shown in the diagram in figure 22.3. Providing an installable file system lets network operating system vendors supply their own 32-bit protected-mode redirectors for Windows 95 clients. It wouldn't be surprising if Novell were to supply their own IFS redirector to take advantages of the new features of NetWare 4.1. Another example of an IFS candidate is SunSelect's PC-NFS (Network File System) that lets you share files stored on a UNIX server. PC-NFS can be (and is likely to be) implemented as just another 32-bit IFS, replacing the present-day real-mode DOS TSR. Microsoft and third-party file systems that provide file compression can also be added to the IFS collection. Stac Electronics' Stacker 3.1, which is used on one of the drives of the computer used to write this chapter, now requires loading real-mode DOS drivers in CONFIG.SYS.

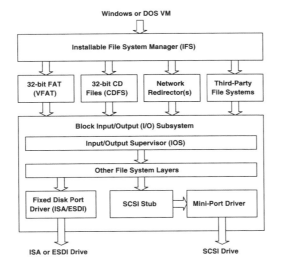

Fig. 22.3
A simplified diagram of Windows 95's Installable File System.

Windows 95's Installable File System consists of the following basic components:

- The Installable File System (IFS) Manager arbitrates access to the individual installable file system components. When your application needs access to a network file, the IFS manager chooses the appropriate redirector for the network in use.

■ The file-system drivers layer is where new drivers are installed. The file-system drivers supplied with Windows 95 include a driver for file allocation table (FAT) based disk devices, (VFAT) CD-ROM file systems (CDFS), and drivers to redirect Windows and NetWare network device support. Windows 95 supports DoubleSpace disk compression within the VFAT driver.

■ The block I/O subsystem deals with the physical disk device. This subsystem handles Plug and Play identification of ISA, EISA, and SCSI drives; substitutes 32-bit protected-mode drivers for real-mode DOS drivers (when practical); and supports mini-port drivers that are compatible with Windows NT 3.5+.

Both the 32-bit VFAT and CDFS drivers use Windows 95's new 32-bit protected-mode cache driver, VCACHE. VCACHE replaces the 16-bit real-mode Smart-Drive disk caching software Microsoft supplies with DOS and Windows 3.1. According to Microsoft, the VCACHE driver uses a more intelligent caching algorithm than SmartDrive, resulting in improved performance for reading information from and writing to the cache. VCACHE uses a dynamic memory pool, the size of which is based on the amount of available free system memory. Thus, you no longer need to set aside a permanent block of memory for use solely as a disk cache.

Printing with Windows 95

Windows 95 includes a 32-bit print subsystem that uses a multithreaded, preemptive spooler architecture that's similar to the Windows NT 3.5 print subsystem. In Windows 3.1, Print Manager handled printing; printing used code incorporated in several Windows components. Windows 95 implements the print spooler with 32-bit virtual device drivers (VxDs) that offer the following advantages over Window 3.1+'s Print Manager:

■ A new 32-bit print subsystem, modeled after that of Windows NT 3.5, makes background printing almost transparent on Windows 95 workstations.

■ Built-in support for more than 800 different printer models and all PostScript Level II printers via Windows 95's new printer mini-drivers, which also are compatible with Windows NT 3.5.

■ Spooling MS-DOS print jobs together with jobs from Windows-based applications, eliminating the conflicts that often hung Windows 3.1+ print jobs.

■ Image color matching to eliminate differences between the hue and luminance of the display and the printed version of an image.

■ Deferred printing that lets users of notebook computers spool printing jobs. When you dock the notebook, the deferred jobs print automatically.

■ Easier installation of printers with Plug and Play support.

■ Improved integration of networked printing, including support for automatic installation of printer drivers from Windows 95, Windows NT, or Novell NetWare servers.

Tests of printing graphics and text with a Hewlett-Packard LaserJet 4P with an installed PostScript Level II SIMM decreased local and network printing time under Windows 95 by about 25 to 35 percent, compared with using Windows for Workgroups 3.11's Print Manager for the same job. One of the reasons for the improvement is Windows 95's enhanced Metafile system, which creates a standard print file structure, regardless of the type of printer in use, and sends the temporary print file to the spooler. The print spooler then sends the enhanced Metafile to the print driver for translation into the language used by a specified printer. Figure 22.4 shows the differences between the structure of the Windows 3.1+ print subsystem (left) and that of Windows 95 (right). Windows 95 returns you to your application more quickly because Windows 95 bypasses the printer translation step.

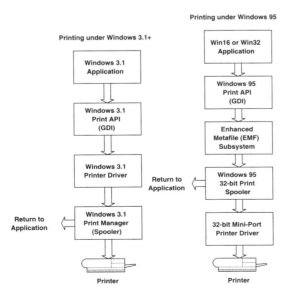

Fig. 22.4
Comparing Windows 3.1's and Windows 95's printing subsystems.

Improving TrueType Rasterizing

TrueType typefaces are created by a set of outlines, each of which is represented by a set of mathematical vectors. An operating system component, called the rasterizer, converts the vector-based images comprising a TrueType font to the bit map required to display (render) text in a window. Windows 95's rasterizer is a 32-bit component, which speeds text rendering. Microsoft claims that the rasterizer delivers better fidelity from the vector to the bit-mapped image, plus better performance for rendering TrueType fonts on your printer.

Windows 95 provides better-appearing TrueType text on your display with a technique called antialiasing. Antialiasing, also called type smoothing, makes type appear to have smoother edges by changing the intensity level of the pixels at edges and corners of characters to produce a resulting image that appears much smoother than the unsmoothed image. Windows 95's support for antialiasing TrueType fonts requires 256-color mode (or higher) to support the different intensity. Font-smoothing support in Windows 95 is independent of the TrueType type family you use, including pre-Windows 95 typefaces.

Chapter 23

Setting Up and Managing Windows 95

You'll have to make two basic choices when you install Windows 95. First and most important, you must decide whether you'll install Windows 95 as an upgrade to your current DOS/Windows 3.1+ operating system or if you'll install Windows 95 parallel to your current operating system, thus creating a dual-boot system. Second, you must choose which of three different standard installations you want, or whether you want to make a custom setup. The first two sections of this chapter explain the significance of the choices you make.

Later in this chapter, the section "Getting Ready for Windows 95 Setup" discusses issues you should consider in preparing for a safe and sane Windows 95 installation. Although Windows 95 promises a clean and automatic installation process for all software and hardware drivers, actual installation may provide a few surprises. Early upgraders to Windows 95 will install Windows 95 on computers that contain (or are entirely made up of) legacy hardware for the ISA bus and BIOS that doesn't support Plug and Play hardware detection and configuration. As a result, you can expect that installing Windows 95, while still easier than installing DOS or Windows 3.1+, won't always be a seamless "start it and forget it" operation—at least until all the hardware you'll likely encounter meets Plug and Play standards.

This chapter describes what the Windows 95 Setup program does and how the installation process alters the system files on your computer for dual-boot operation. The final section of this chapter, "Managing Windows 95's Configuration over the Long Term," describes the long-term maintenance mechanisms built into Windows 95 and its Setup program.

◀ See Chapter 2, "Making Hardware Plug and Play"

Deciding How to Install Windows 95: Upgrade or Dual-Boot System?

The foremost decision you must make—once you decide to take the plunge into the brave new world of Windows 95—is whether you want to upgrade your existing Windows 3.1+ system or install Windows 95 as a second (or third) operating system on your computer.

> **Note**
>
> Windows 95 installation requires that a DOS or DOS/Windows 3.1+ operating system already be on your computer. You can't install Windows 95 from within Windows NT or OS/2—only from the DOS command line or from within Windows 3.1+.
>
> If you use either Windows NT or OS/2, you must configure your computer to multi-boot with MS-DOS (if it doesn't already) before installing Windows 95. Also, you can't install Windows 95 into a directory with a shared Windows 3.1+ and Windows NT configuration—you'll have to use a different directory.
>
> If you start your computer from an MS-DOS floppy disk, and then install Windows 95, you won't be able to start either Windows NT or OS/2 from your hard disk. In this case, you can restore the Windows NT and OS/2 startup from your hard disk by using the Repair option on your Windows NT boot/repair disk, or by using OS/2's FDISK utility.

Installing Windows 95 as an upgrade or as a dual-boot option both have their merits and their drawbacks. The next two sections discuss the pros and cons of each approach.

Upgrading Windows 3.1+ to Windows 95: Your Best Bet for Convenience

Without doubt, installing Windows 95 as an upgrade to an existing Windows 3.1+ system provides the greatest convenience in switching to the new operating system. When installed as an upgrade, Windows 95 converts everything from your Windows 3.1+ installation.

During an upgrade installation, Windows 95's Setup program converts all your existing Program Manager program groups into a Windows 95 format. In this case, *all* really does mean every program group, including your Startup group. This conversion means that all your existing Windows 3.1+ applications (and their configurations) are available to Windows 95, without any need to reinstall or reconfigure those applications. Installing Windows 95 as an upgrade even preserves and transfers settings such as which Windows screen saver you're using and the screen saver's configuration.

If your computer is connected to a network, installing Windows 95 as an upgrade to your existing Windows 3.1+ system also converts your network configuration information (such as the computer and workgroup name)—although you may need to transfer some other information (such as user names and password lists) manually.

Freedom from any need to reinstall or reconfigure your existing software after migrating to Windows 95 is the most important argument in favor of installing Windows 95 as an upgrade. An upgrade installation of Windows 95 will likely provide an almost transparent transition, saving you the (possibly substantial) effort involved in reinstalling and reconfiguring your productivity applications. As a minor second benefit, installing Windows 95 as an upgrade uses slightly less disk space (about 10M) than a dual-boot installation.

◀ See Chapter 17, "Creating Workgroups with Windows 95's Peer-to-Peer Networking," and Chapter 21, "Managing Networked PCs with Windows 95"

The main argument *against* installing Windows 95 as an upgrade is that, after you do so, you can't easily go back to using your Windows 3.1+ system. In an upgrade installation, the Windows 95 Setup program consolidates its new software components into the same disk directory as your original Windows 3.1+ system, replacing the old components and retaining only those few items from Windows 3.1+ that make the upgrade process seamless—such as printer and certain other device drivers.

The inability to go back to Windows 3.1+ from a Windows 95 upgrade is mitigated by these factors:

- Even when you install Windows 95 as an upgrade, you can still dual-boot back to your original version of DOS by pressing the F4 key. Although booting back to your original version of DOS still won't make it possible to run Windows 3.1+, you'll be able to execute DOS programs, if any, that don't operate under Windows 95.

- Unlike some operating system upgrades, the Windows 95 upgrade doesn't make any changes in your disk partitions or their structure. If you follow maximum safety procedures, you'll make a full backup of your hard drive(s) before installing Windows 95, anyway—as you always should before any major change in your system's software or hardware. If you do upgrade to Windows 95 and then decide, for some reason, that you need to go back to Windows 3.1+, you can restore your original system and configuration from your backup without having to reformat or repartition your disk drives. By selectively restoring directories or prohibiting overwrites of existing files, you can preserve any data files that may have changed after you installed Windows 95.

■ Whether you'll ever have a need to return to Windows 3.1+ is debatable. Microsoft would obviously have problems selling an operating system that doesn't allow its buyers to use a substantial percentage of their existing investment in productivity software. As described in the preceding chapter, the Windows 95 operating system has built-in mechanisms specifically for running Windows 3.1+ applications. Given that Windows 3.1+ will cease to be available as a retail product the same day that Windows 95 is released (and the Windows 3.1+ software market will begin to dwindle correspondingly), you can expect most software publishers to rapidly climb on the Windows 95 bandwagon by providing new versions, updates, or patches for their products. In the event that you end up unable to use some Windows 3.1+ products in Windows 95, you can probably expect a fix or work-around on the near horizon.

◀ See Chapter 1, "Building the 'Information Appliance' of the 1990s"

◀ See Chapter 6, "Upgrading to 32-Bit Productivity Applications"

◀ See Chapter 22, "Understanding Windows 95's Operating System Architecture"

▶ See Chapter 25, "Running DOS Applications under Windows 95"

As you can see, upgrading to Windows 95 doesn't completely shut out the possibility of returning to Windows 3.1+. Also, the savings in time and effort obtained by not having to reinstall or reconfigure your software applications is almost certain to outweigh the fact that an upgrade doesn't allow you to immediately return to Windows 3.1+—especially because the potential need to return to a 3.1+ system may not be clearly justified.

Dual-Boot Installation: Only When Necessary

The primary purpose of a dual-boot installation is to satisfy those users who want to migrate to Windows 95 but have misgivings about making an absolute commitment to the new system all at once. When you create a dual-boot installation with Windows 95, you essentially set up Windows 95 in parallel with your existing DOS/Windows 3.1+ system. The dual-boot Setup option leaves your original Windows 3.1+ system intact and untouched. As a result, you can bypass the Windows 95 boot process and use your original DOS and Windows 3.1+ system as though Windows 95 had never been installed.

Note

This chapter uses the term *dual-boot* for consistency with Microsoft's documentation. A more accurate term might be *multi-boot* because—depending on whether you have another operating system, such as Windows NT or OS/2, on your computer—you might actually be creating a triple-boot system.

A dual-boot Windows 95 setup doesn't convert any existing Windows 3.1+ program groups, printer, or other device drivers or any other configuration information to Windows 95. If you make a Windows 95 dual-boot installation, you *must* reinstall all your Windows 3.1+ software and install new printer and device drivers for Windows 95. You must also reenter (or confirm the accuracy of) all your network configuration information.

Unless you use only one or two applications, the effort involved in reinstalling all your software will likely take hours, if not days. To further complicate the process, you must make sure that you reinstall your applications under Windows 95 into exactly the same directories/folders as they were in under Windows 3.1+—otherwise, you'll end up with duplicate copies of program components scattered throughout your system. Having duplicate program components installed not only wastes a lot of disk space, but also the duplicated program components may interfere with each other's operation, possibly making the application unusable in *both* your new Windows 95 and your old Windows 3.1+ installations.

Also, if you run programs from a network server that have local configuration files, those applications will also have to be reinstalled for your computer. Reinstalling network programs can usually be done only by a network administrator—who probably already has enough to do. These facts alone should be enough to make you think long and hard about whether you really need to create a dual-boot installation.

> **Note**
>
> The need to reinstall your software in Windows 95 when you make a dual-boot installation has one basic purpose: to allow Windows 95 to "see" the application so that it can create the appropriate entries in the Registry and in the Programs folder.

The main argument in favor of creating a dual-boot installation with Windows 95 is that many users are the type of people who prefer to test the waters gradually, rather than jump right in. These users will feel more comfortable making a dual-boot installation and working in Windows 95 intermittently until they gain experience and confidence. There's nothing wrong with choosing to move into Windows 95 this way—just be aware that you're making an essentially aesthetic decision and make sure that you're really willing (and able) to go through the extra work involved.

If you're responsible for upgrading and supporting several different computers in your company, you might upgrade a single computer as a training and

◀ See Chapter 3, "Exploring the Windows 95 Interface"

▶ See Chapter 24, "Replacing WIN.INI, SYSTEM.INI, and REG.DAT with Registry" practice station. After your users have a chance to gain some experience using Windows 95, and you have a chance to prove that all your existing programs still work—especially the in-house or custom applications that you might be worried about the most—you can go ahead and upgrade all your computers, without ever having to create a dual-boot and reinstalling everyone's existing software.

> **Note**
>
> Avoid a dual-boot installation if you use disk compression software that *doesn't* preload the compression device driver (such as versions of Stacker before 3.1) and your boot disk is compressed. Any disk compression software used with versions of DOS before Version 6 *doesn't* preload its compression device drivers—only DOS 6.0 and higher can preload compression device drivers.
>
> For Windows 95's dual-boot to work, Windows 95 must be able to rename your IO.SYS, MSDOS.SYS, CONFIG.SYS, AUTOEXEC.BAT, and COMMAND.COM files. Unless the disk compression device driver is preloaded, Windows 95 can't access these files on the compressed disk and renames only the files on the compressed disk's host drive. As a result, the disk compression software will complain that your AUTOEXEC.BAT and CONFIG.SYS files aren't synchronized; also, Windows 95 will end up loading the wrong version of COMMAND.COM, resulting in a boot failure. Refer to the section "Getting Ready for Windows 95 Setup" later in this chapter for more information about installing Windows 95 on computers using disk compression.

Deciding Whether to Use a Standard or Custom Setup

The Windows 95 Setup program provides four alternatives to setting up Windows 95: a choice of three predefined standard setups and a Custom Setup. The three standardized installation choices install a predetermined suite of DOS and Windows utility programs and applets, depending on the type of installation you choose. The DOS programs and utilities that Windows 95 Setup installs are replacements for the external DOS commands from your previous DOS version—LABEL, FORMAT, SCANDISK, CHKDSK, and so on. Windows 95 doesn't include replacements for DOS utilities such as DOSSHELL, because there's no need for them.

The predefined standard setup options are:

◀ See Chapter 4, "Using the Built-In Accessory Applets"

- *Typical.* Use this installation type for most computers. Setup will install all of the basic Windows 95 components, along with most of the accessory applets.

- *Portable.* Use this installation type for laptop, notebook, or other portable computers. Setup will install special options for portable computers, such as the Briefcase utility, support for PCMCIA cards, power-saver utilities, and so on.

- *Compact.* Use this installation option if you are low on disk space. A typical Windows 95 installation requires approximately 39M of disk space; a compact installation requires only 28M. Not all of the accessory applets are installed in a compact installation.

The Custom Setup option allows you to perform the following actions:

- Tell Windows 95 *not* to search for certain specific hardware components in your system.

- Verify or change the hardware configuration for your display (the video adapter board in your computer), monitor (the actual video picture tube), mouse, keyboard, sound board, Pen Windows extensions, network options, and so on.

- Select which optional components to install or skip—such as accessory applets, Dial-Up Networking, wallpaper files, screen savers, mail facilities, media players, and so on.

None of the choices in the Custom Setup option are particularly unusual; they're all pretty much what you'd expect of any software installation program.

V

Digging into the OS

> **Note**
>
> You can use any of the standardized Setup options (Typical, Portable, Compact) or the Custom option to create an upgrade or dual-boot Windows 95 installation.

For most situations, one of the standardized Setup options will work just fine. Use the Custom Setup installation if you want to do either of the following:

- Save disk space and disk copying time by skipping the installation of screen savers, wallpaper, or other optional components that you know you don't want or won't use.

■ Force Setup to install components that you know you'll want or need to use in the future but won't otherwise be installed. For example, the Microsoft Exchange and MAPI utilities won't be installed on your system unless you use Customize Setup and specifically tell Windows 95 you want to install them. Microsoft Exchange and MAPI are used with electronic mail and computer FAX; if you don't use them now but intend to in the near future, you might want to use the Custom option to install Microsoft Exchange and MAPI now rather than later.

If any of these situations apply to you, use the Custom Setup option.

> **Note**
>
> Custom Setup allows you to choose whether Windows 95 should use Windows 3.1+ file compatibility. If you select this option, Windows 95 doesn't allow you to use long file names. Because long file names is one of the important new features in Windows 95, you'll probably want to avoid using the Windows 3.1+ file compatibility option.

Getting Ready for Windows 95 Setup

Supposedly, installing Windows 95 is a "start it and forget it" operation, requiring little more from you than to mount a CD-ROM disk or feed floppy disks through the machine. In reality, setting up Windows 95 is somewhat more complex than that, and Setup may deliver a few surprises if you don't prepare adequately ahead of time.

The most significant source of complications in a Windows 95 installation is the involvement of legacy hardware and BIOS that doesn't fully support Plug and Play technology. As a result, you can expect that Windows 95 Setup will need your help to identify or configure some hardware devices; therefore, you need to make sure that you have information about your computer's hardware and its configuration at hand before starting Windows 95 Setup. Things you'll need to know before you start Setup are discussed later in the section "Other Things You Really Should Know Before You Start."

Because you're making a major change to your system, make sure that you take all the usual safety precautions:

■ Use the SCANDISK utility provided with Windows 95, CHKDSK, or another disk diagnostic tool to ensure that your existing disk drives and file system are in good working order. Although Windows 95 Setup checks the disk drive on which you install Windows 95 for damage, you should check all of your disk drives and partitions yourself—Setup checks only for cross-linked files on only the disk on which Windows is to be installed. Lost clusters, cross-linked files, and files unreadable due to disk surface defects are all disasters waiting to happen.

■ Make sure that you have a verified bootable DOS disk (for your current DOS version) that contains all the device drivers necessary to operate your system, along with suitable CONFIG.SYS and AUTOEXEC.BAT files—this is especially important if you use disk compression software and the hard drive you boot from is compressed.

■ Do a complete backup of your system.

Recommending these precautions does not imply a lack of faith in the Windows 95 Setup program. You should always gird yourself for the worst when making a substantial change to your system or risk losing everything. No matter how sophisticated or reliable a piece of software is, the world is still (to quote Kurt Vonnegut) "a busy place where accidents happen"—accidents such as power failures.

To speed up the installation process somewhat, you may also want to defragment your hard disk before installing Windows 95. Having all the free space on your disk in a contiguous block makes it easier for DOS to copy files (it doesn't have to spend as much time searching for free clusters) and may make it easier for Windows 95 to set up its virtual memory swap file.

Tip

During Windows 95's Setup, you'll have a chance to create an emergency boot floppy disk; you should definitely do so. Have a blank, formatted disk compatible with your drive A ready before you start Setup.

Minimum Disk Space and Other System Requirements

Although it may seem fairly obvious, don't even think of installing Windows 95 unless your computer meets or exceeds the minimum system requirements: a 25 MHz 386SX with 4M RAM and about 30M to 40M of free disk space.

V

Digging into the OS

Note

If you're going to upgrade your hardware for Windows 95 but can't afford to completely replace your system, adding more RAM may deliver the best improvements, dollar for dollar, in Windows 95's performance. Swapping virtual memory to disk takes the greatest toll on Windows 95's speed.

In addition to the disk space required for a completed Windows 95 installation, Setup needs working room on the disk. You'll need an additional 6M to 10M of free disk space on your boot drive, regardless of which drive you actually install Windows 95 on. That is, if you install Windows 95 in a directory on drive D, you'll still need 6M to 10M of space on drive C (the typical boot drive).

Note

Some of Windows 95's optional components—such as the TCP/IP software, Microsoft Exchange, and possibly others—actually require an additional 7M to 10M of free disk space (used for virtual memory swapping) to operate successfully.

If you have MS-DOS 6.x and use a preloading disk compression software (such as Stacker 3.1/4.0, Microsoft DriveSpace, or DoubleSpace), you need to make sure that at least 10M of free disk space is on the *uncompressed* host drive before you install Windows 95. If you don't have 10M of free space on the host drive, you'll have to resize your compressed drive.

Note

You may need to alter the drive letter exchanges made by your disk compression software if the drive letter for the host drive of your compressed boot disk is hidden, swapped, mapped, or overlaid by another drive letter—such as a network drive. For example, if your configuration mounts a compressed drive as drive C, creates drive D as the host drive, and then subsequently remaps drive D as a network drive (making the host drive inaccessible or reassigning it to yet another drive letter), Windows 95 Setup may not work. If this is your case, you may need to change the configuration of your disk compression software and the configuration of your network drives. A better solution might be to decompress your boot drive, if possible.

Clean Up CONFIG.SYS and AUTOEXEC.BAT before Installation

Microsoft recommends that you inspect your CONFIG.SYS and AUTOEXEC.BAT files after you install Windows 95. In many circumstances, it's probably better—or even necessary—to make changes in CONFIG.SYS and AUTOEXEC.BAT *before* you install Windows 95.

> ### Tip
>
> Always make backup copies of CONFIG.SYS and AUTOEXEC.BAT before making changes in them.

16-Bit Device Drivers Loaded in CONFIG.SYS

In general, Windows 95 *will* install its own 32-bit device drivers to replace device drivers that load from your CONFIG.SYS file—with some exceptions. Windows 95's installation documentation recommends that you remove any 16-bit real-mode device drivers from your CONFIG.SYS file before you install Windows 95. You can't, of course, remove device drivers that are essential for your computer's startup, and Microsoft recommends against removing network device drivers. You should also *avoid* removing device drivers for devices such as hand or flatbed scanners for which Windows 95 will unlikely have replacement drivers.

> ### Note
>
> If you use DoubleSpace or DriveSpace disk compression, Windows 95 will install the appropriate 32-bit protected mode device driver for your compressed disk. If you use another disk compression scheme, Windows 95 will continue to use the 16-bit real-mode device driver.
>
> To protect your compressed disk drives, Windows 95 Setup disables the old SCANDISK and DEFRAG programs in your DOS directory by renaming them, and then installs a batch file that tells you how to use the new Windows 95 equivalents.
>
> Setup also installs the Microsoft DriveSpace disk compression program, in case you want to add disk compression to your system.

◀ See Chapter 7, "Interacting with Windows 95 Multimedia"

◀ See Chapter 8, "Using CD-ROM Drives with Windows 95"

◀ See Chapter 9, "Playing and Recording Hi-Fi Sound and Music"

COMSPEC and SHELL Statements

A SHELL or COMSPEC command in CONFIG.SYS that refers to DOS's own command interpreter won't cause any problems. If you use COMSPEC to replace DOS's COMMAND.COM with another command interpreter (such as

V

Digging into the OS

Norton's NDOS), however, Windows 95's setup may not operate correctly. If you use a command interpreter other than the one supplied with DOS, you should first make sure there is a copy of the DOS COMMAND.COM file in the root directory of your boot disk, and then remove the COMSPEC command from CONFIG.SYS.

Windows 95 Setup will remove any SHELL or COMSPEC commands that it finds in CONFIG.SYS. When you install Windows 95 on your computer, it updates your DOS system files and the command interpreter (COMMAND.COM) in the root directory of your boot disk but doesn't remove your old DOS program files. As a result, any attempt to load the old command interpreter will result in an error message complaining that you're using an incorrect DOS version. Windows 95 Setup removes the COMSPEC and SHELL commands from CONFIG.SYS specifically to prevent such disturbing (but essentially harmless) error messages, and to ensure that the correct version of COMMAND.COM is always in use.

DOS 6 Multiple-Configuration Menus

If you use the DOS 6 feature that lets you create multiple configurations for your computer, be aware that Windows 95 makes extensive changes in your menu and configuration blocks. Windows 95 Setup makes every section of the multi-config into a Windows 95 section. Many of the old DOS CONFIG.SYS commands are no longer meaningful in Windows 95—they're not needed because of new file and memory management features in Windows 95. As a result, Setup may remove several commands from your CONFIG.SYS file, such as: FILES, STACKS, LASTDRIVE, SHELL, COMSPEC, and others. Don't be surprised if your CONFIG.SYS file suddenly gets somewhat smaller after installing Windows 95.

Because Windows 95 *is* the operating system, your computer will always boot directly into Windows 95. You can't use a multi-config menu to avoid starting Windows 95—you must use the F4 key (for dual-boot to your previous DOS version) or the F8 key (for conditional CONFIG and AUTOEXEC execution) to bypass loading the graphical interface portion of Windows 95.

Disk Caches

Windows 95 provides its own built-in disk caching system and doesn't use external disk caches. Remove any disk cache programs from CONFIG.SYS or AUTOEXEC.BAT. Although Microsoft recommends that you do this after installing Windows 95, you might as well do it ahead of time, while you're making other changes or checks in CONFIG.SYS and AUTOEXEC.BAT. The Setup program won't suffer from the lack of a disk cache.

Mouse Drivers

Windows 95, like Windows 3.1+ before it, uses an internal mouse driver. In Windows 3.1+, you need to load a DOS mouse driver in CONFIG.SYS or AUTOEXEC.BAT only if you want to use your mouse in a DOS program running in a Windows 3.1+ DOS window. Because DOS is now an integrated part of the Windows 95 operating system, Windows 95's mouse driver is available to all DOS programs running in a Windows 95 DOS window. Windows 95 doesn't need or use an external mouse driver for any reason—as a result, you should remove or disable any statements in your CONFIG.SYS or AUTOEXEC.BAT files that load a DOS mouse driver—Windows 95 Setup won't do it for you.

Protected-Mode Expanded Memory Managers

Protected-mode expanded memory managers include products such as QEMM, 386MAX, and Microsoft's own EMM386, among others. You should disable or remove these expanded memory managers from your CONFIG.SYS file before installing Windows 95 for a couple of reasons: to avoid any possible memory problems during Windows 95 Setup, and because Windows 95 provides its own expanded memory manager for applications that need it. (In fact, the MEM utility, when run in a Windows 95 DOS window, always shows a total amount of EMS memory equivalent to the actual amount of contiguous memory in the computer.)

▶ See Chapter 25, "Running DOS Applications under Windows 95"

> **Note**
>
> Windows 95 automatically disables all lines in CONFIG.SYS that refer to EMM386, but may not do so for other protected-mode memory manager software.

Other Things You Really Should Know Before You Start

Before you run Setup, you should gather some information about your computer's peripherals and adapter boards, because if Windows 95 Setup can't identify or fully determine the configuration of your legacy hardware, you'll need to enter the information yourself. You should prepare a list of all the ISA or other non-Plug and Play adapters and peripheral devices installed in your computer, and their respective IRQs, base I/O addresses, memory addresses, and DMA channels. (Not every device in your computer will use all these settings at once).

V

Digging into the OS

If your computer contains a network interface card (NIC), you should also make sure that you know not only the network card type but also its transceiver type. If you're making a dual-boot Windows 95 installation on a network computer, you should be prepared to reenter your computer's name and workgroup name. Whether you install Windows 95 as an upgrade or as a dual-boot installation, you'll also need to reenter all user names and password lists.

> **Tip**
>
> For network interface cards, you can get the IRQ, I/O address, DMA channel, and transceiver type information from your PROTOCOL.INI or NET.CFG file.

> **Note**
>
> Although Windows 95's Setup documentation recommends that your network software be running at the time you install Windows 95, tests indicate that the only necessity is that the network interface card be physically present in your computer during Windows 95 Setup. Windows 95 Setup will detect the network card during its hardware detection phase and install the correct device drivers or ask you which network device drivers to install.

Be aware before you start Setup that Windows 95's conflict detection for IRQs, I/O addresses, and DMA channels is excellent—so excellent that Windows 95 may detect IRQ or other conflicts that you didn't know existed and didn't affect the previous operation of your computer. If this is your case, you may need to alter your hardware configuration before using some devices in Windows 95. In one system, for example, Windows 95 correctly determined that an unused SCSI controller in the computer had an IRQ conflict with another device in the system, although this conflict caused no operating problems in the existing Windows 3.1+ installation.

> **Note**
>
> Many computers have a BIOS Setup program that allows you to specify which disk drive the computer tries to boot from first. Some of these BIOS Setup programs also allow you to specify that the computer should try to boot only from a hard disk. If your computer has this type of BIOS, you should make sure that the computer is set to look for boot files on drive A first and then drive C. In the unlikely event that something horrible should go wrong with your Windows 95 installation, you may have to start your computer from the floppy drive—something with which the BIOS boot drive settings may interfere.

The final *caveat* that you should consider before installing Windows 95 relates to various Windows 3.1+ desktop management programs. (Desktop management programs are programs that enhance or replace the Windows 3.1+ Program Manager, such as Norton Desktop or Quarterdeck's Sidebar.) If the desktop manager is started as a Windows 3.1+ application (that is, from a `load=` line in WIN.INI, from the Startup group, or by double-clicking an icon in Program Manager), it probably won't cause any problems. If the desktop manager actually replaces PROGMAN.EXE (that is, by altering the `shell=` line in SYSTEM.INI), Windows 95 Setup may not run correctly. To be safe, you should probably disable or uninstall desktop management programs before you run Setup. A Program Manager enhancement for Windows 3.1+ won't likely give you much benefit in Windows 95 anyway, since the Windows 95 user interface gives you most or all of the functionality that such desktop managers provide—program shortcuts, file viewers, and so on.

What Windows 95 Setup Does

Windows 95's Setup program performs a three-phase process, using a series of "Wizard" style dialog boxes for each step in the installation process. Each dialog box in the Setup Wizard asks you for specific information or specific choices that Setup needs you to supply in order to complete its task. Each of the dialog boxes in the Setup Wizard contains command buttons that allow you to do the following:

- Return to previous dialog boxes to correct or change the choices or information you provided.

- Continue on to the dialog box for the next step of the installation.

- Cancel the installation.

> **Tip**
>
> Up until the point at which you confirm the restarting of your computer, you can use the Back command button in the Setup Wizard dialog boxes to return to any previous step of the installation.

In the first phase, Setup gathers information about your computer by asking you questions and making its own search for installed hardware and software. Setup then copies files to your hard disk in the second phase and, in the last phase, restarts your computer, completing the installation process.

Figure 23.1 shows a flow chart depicting the course of the Windows 95 Setup program's execution.

Fig. 23.1

Windows 95 Setup first determines whether you started it from the Windows 3.1+ or from the DOS command line, and then performs a three-step installation process.

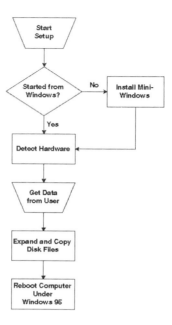

Three-Phase Setup

Typically, you start the Windows 95 Setup program the same way you start any Windows 3.1+ installation program: start Windows and use the File menu's Run command. If you want to install Windows 95 on a computer that doesn't already have Windows 3.1+ installed on it, you can also start the Windows 95 Setup program from the DOS command line. If you start Setup from the DOS command line, Setup (after obtaining confirmation) installs a special "mini" version of Windows and then continues executing Setup from within this mini-Windows program (refer to fig. 23.1).

If you're installing from floppy disks, Windows 95 Setup will need to read files from the first two installation floppy disks before it's fully loaded. After an initialization period, Windows 95 Setup displays the opening screen shown in figure 23.2. (If you have other Windows programs running, Setup displays a dialog box that asks you to shut them down before continuing.)

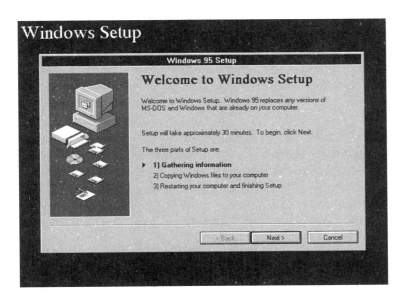

Fig. 23.2
Windows 95 Setups
opening screen.

Choosing the Setup Type and Installation Directory

The first step in the Setup Wizard, after you pass the opening screen, is to choose the type of setup you want. Figure 23.3 shows the dialog box in which you choose the Setup Type. The purpose of each setup type was discussed earlier in this chapter. You can use *any* of these setup types to create either an upgrade or dual-boot Windows 95 installation.

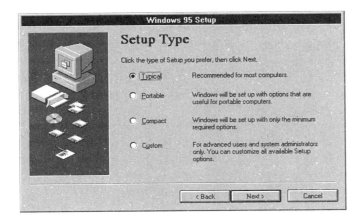

Fig. 23.3
You must choose one of the four possible setup types: Typical, Portable, Compact, or Custom.

V

Digging into the OS

After you select the type of installation you want, Setup asks you to choose whether you want to install Windows 95 in your current Windows directory, or in another directory. Choosing installation into your current Windows directory upgrades your current Windows 3.1+ software. Installing Windows 95 into another directory creates a dual-boot installation. If you choose to install Windows 95 into a directory other than your current Windows directory, Setup asks you to enter the directory name.

At this point, Setup checks the hard disk on which you're installing Windows 95 for cross-linked files. If Setup detects any problems on the disk, it will inform you and then terminate the installation. If you followed the preparation guidelines given earlier, this won't happen to you; if it does, you can use the SCANDISK utility provided with Windows 95 to correct problems on your disk drive, and then run Setup again.

After checking your hard disk, Setup prepares the directories on your hard disk, retrieves setup information, and checks for available disk space. Setup displays a progress chart for each test and procedure, so you don't have to wonder if your computer has hung. If you don't have enough available disk space, or your disk space is low, Setup displays a dialog similar to the one in figure 23.4. In most cases, you should cancel the installation, free up more disk space, and then restart Setup. Although you can go back to try installing Windows 95 in a different directory, that means you'll have to create a dual-boot installation, which may not be what you want. In some cases, Setup will allow you to continue when your disk space is low, but will *not* install accessory applets—probably not what you want, either.

Fig. 23.4
Windows 95 Setup warns you if you don't have enough disk space, or your disk space is low.

System Analysis/Hardware Detection

After making its initial tests to see whether it's possible and safe to install Windows 95, Setup asks you for your user information (your name and your company's name), and then proceeds to analyze your computer.

If you're using one of the standard setup options, Setup immediately proceeds to analyze your computer's hardware. Setup detects physical hardware and software device drivers installed in your computer system, and identifies which system resources (IRQs, I/O addresses, DMA channels, and so on) are present in your computer. Setup determines which system resources are already in use, which are available, and whether there are any conflicts between various devices. Setup also begins building the hardware-related portions of the Registry database at this time.

To detect legacy hardware devices, Windows 95 Setup uses a database of signature characteristics belonging to various hardware devices made by a wide variety of manufacturers. Windows 95 Setup also queries your system for any Plug and Play devices that may be installed.

V

Digging into the OS

> **Note**
>
> Setup's detection of legacy hardware devices is very good—so good, in fact, that you may end up surprised at what Setup tells you is installed in your computer. In many cases, Setup successfully detects the OEM (original equipment manufacturer) chipset used on an adapter board in your computer. This may be a little confusing when you review the hardware determinations that Setup makes. For example, in one installation, Setup correctly identified the video display adapter's chipset as manufactured by Cirrus Logic, although the adapter board itself was bought under a different brand name.

If you elected to make a Custom installation, Setup asks you whether to automatically check for *all* possible makes and models of hardware installed in your computer, or if you want to manually specify for which hardware Setup should search. Setup will install Windows 95's protected-mode device drivers for any hardware devices that it finds in your computer. Usually, you should let Setup perform its automatic search, and use the new device drivers. Choose the manual selection method only if, for some reason, there is some hardware device that you don't want Windows 95 to be able to use. If you choose to manually specify which hardware Setup searches for, it displays a dialog box similar to the one in figure 23.5. Clearing a check box in either list causes Setup to *skip* any tests for that device.

Fig. 23.5
You can tell Setup
to skip the search
for a particular
hardware device.

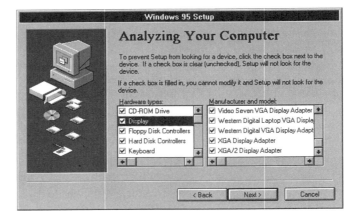

Whether you chose Typical, Portable, Compact, or Custom installation, Setup may ask you to confirm its search for certain hardware devices, anyway. Figure 23.6 shows the Analyzing Your Computer dialog for a system where Setup was unsure whether to try testing for the presence of a CD-ROM drive or a multi-media card.

Fig. 23.6
Setup may need
you to confirm its
search for some
hardware devices.

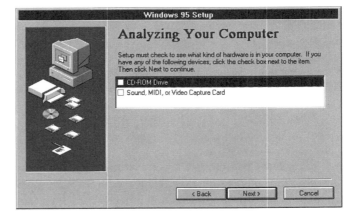

After making any choices about which hardware Setup should test for, Setup begins the actual analysis of your computer system. This part of the Windows 95 Setup can take a fairly long time. To let you know that Setup is still working, it displays a progress bar-chart while it analyzes your system. Have patience with this part of the process. If you believe that Setup has hung up while detecting hardware, check to see whether there is any disk activity, and to see whether the progress chart changes at all before rebooting your computer.

If you elected to make a Custom installation, Setup displays a couple of dialog boxes that let you review or change the software components and network options that Setup will install and to review or change the hardware and device driver settings that Setup detected in your system. Figure 23.7 shows the Select Components dialog box, which allows you to select exactly which Windows 95 accessories and options to install (applets, wallpaper, screen savers, telecommunications and network accessories, backup utilities, and so on). Figure 23.8 shows the Network Configuration dialog box, which allows you to add to, remove, or modify the settings of the network device drivers, protocols, clients, file and printer sharing, and so on that Setup will install.

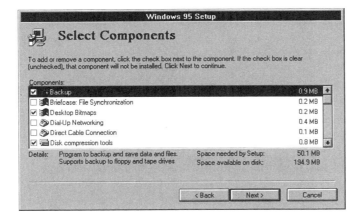

Fig. 23.7
In a Custom Setup, you can manually choose the Windows 95 components you want to install.

V

Digging into the OS

Tip

Setup asks whether you want to create an emergency boot disk for Windows 95. You definitely should do so. This emergency startup disk contains all the files needed to start your computer with Windows 95, except for Windows 95's graphical user interface.

Fig. 23.8
In a Custom installation, you can also control how your network hardware and software are set up.

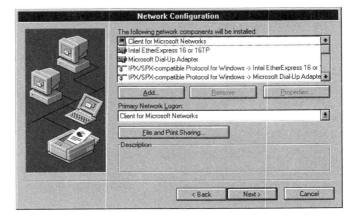

Note

If your computer is on a network, you'll need to confirm or enter the name of your computer, your workgroup, and a description of your computer—regardless of the Setup type you chose.

At this point, Setup is almost ready to begin copying files. In a Custom setup, however, two steps remain in the information gathering process. Figure 23.9 shows the Computer Settings dialog box. Use this dialog box to verify the computer hardware that Setup detected during its analysis of your computer. If necessary, you can also use this dialog box to change the types of specific devices. For example, on most systems, Setup will determine that you have an unknown monitor—which is reasonable, since there usually isn't a way to tell what brand of monitor you have plugged into your computer. You would use the Computer Settings dialog box to set a particular monitor type, so that Windows 95 can take full use of the monitor's capabilities.

The final step in a Custom setup is to select Advanced Options (see fig. 23.10). The Advanced Options dialog allows you to force Windows 95 to maintain a Windows 3.1+ compatible file mode—that is, it prohibits Windows 95 from using long file names.

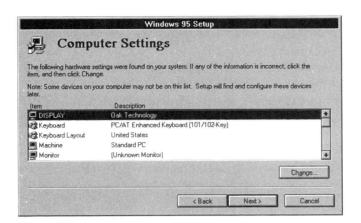

Fig. 23.9
A Custom installation lets you verify or change the specific types of hardware devices that Setup detected in your computer.

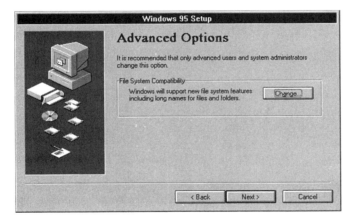

Fig. 23.10
Use the Advanced Options dialog in a Custom setup to choose which file system Windows 95 will use.

V

Digging into the OS

Note

Choosing the Windows 3.1 compatible file mode will prohibit Windows 95 from using long file names; you probably shouldn't select this option.

Windows 95 Setup may also ask you for information about any devices in your computer that Setup had trouble identifying or configuring. Windows 95 Setup displays a separate dialog asking you about each particular component.

Copying Files

When you've reached the end of the Setup Wizard's requests for information, Setup displays the dialog box shown in figure 23.11. As soon as you click the Finish command button, Setup proceeds to the file copying phase. If you're installing Windows 95 from CD-ROM, you have nothing to do but wait while Setup copies files to your hard disk; if installing from floppy disks, you merely have to feed disks to your computer in the correct order. Setup shows the percent of completion as it copies files to your hard disk. (If you elected to make a Windows 95 emergency startup disk, Setup will prompt you to insert a blank diskette into drive A, and then make the startup disk, as soon as it has copied the necessary startup files onto your hard disk.)

System Restart

When all the Windows 95 program and device driver files are copied to your hard disk, Setup restarts your computer after prompting you to remove all disks from your floppy drives. Restarting your computer at this point loads the Windows 95 operating system, basically completing your installation.

Windows 95 now updates your configuration and system files, performs a second hardware detection process (Windows 95 checks for changes in hardware every time you boot your computer), and installs and configures all the necessary device drivers. If you're making a dual-boot installation, Windows 95 will ask you to configure your printers and possibly some other devices. You'll also need to set the current time and select your time zone.

> **Note**
>
> Windows 95 occasionally detects hardware devices in the restart phase that it didn't detect during the initial system analysis phase and may ask you to reinsert one or more of your distribution disks so that it can get any additional device drivers Windows 95 may need. Although this circumstance isn't common, it isn't particularly unusual, either, and isn't a cause for alarm.

Don't be upset if this system restart phase seems to take an inordinately large amount of time. This restart isn't a typical Windows 95 boot—Windows 95 is completing its construction of the Registry database and (if you upgraded an existing Windows 3.1+ system) converting all your Windows Program Manager program groups into their Windows 95 equivalents.

Windows 95 is now installed on your computer. When Windows 95 has finished loading, it displays the Welcome to Windows 95 dialog box shown in figure 23.11 (the Online Registration command button appears only if you used Custom setup to install the Microsoft Online optional component). Windows Tour and What's New are discussed in Chapter 3, "Exploring the Windows 95 Interface."

Fig. 23.11
Windows 95 displays the Welcome dialog when its installation is complete.

> **Note**
>
> If your AUTOEXEC.BAT file contained the WIN command to start Windows 3.1+, Windows 95 Setup removes it.

What Happens if Setup Fails

During installation, Windows 95 Setup keeps a detailed log of its progress through each phase of the setup process. If you cancel Setup or Setup fails or locks up for any reason during any portion of the installation process, you can restart your computer and rerun Setup. Windows 95 Setup uses its log to determine exactly which step in the process failed and picks up at that point. When you rerun Windows 95 Setup after a setup failure, Setup displays the SmartRecovery dialog shown in figure 23.12—to recover a failed Setup, make sure that you select the Use SmartRecovery (Recommended) option button.

If you select the Use SmartRecovery (Recommended) option button, Setup skips the specific test that it failed on, and asks you to manually supply information about the device(s) it was trying to detect when it failed. If Setup failed during the disk-copying phase, it resumes copying files with the last file successfully copied, so it doesn't have to unnecessarily recopy files from the installation disks or CD-ROM.

Fig. 23.12
Windows 95
Setup's Smart-
Recovery allows
you to pick up
where a failed or
cancelled installa-
tion left off.

> **Note**
>
> When Windows 95 installation is complete, you need to reenter user names and passwords as well as reconfigure any persistent network connections, network file sharing, and network device sharing. Windows 95 Setup doesn't convert these settings, even in an upgrade installation.

Understanding Windows 95's Changes to Your System Files

When you install Windows 95, whether as an upgrade or as a dual-boot installation, Setup doesn't delete your original DOS system files, CONFIG.SYS, and AUTOEXEC.BAT. Instead, Setup renames the existing system files, giving them all a DOS file name extension before copying the Windows 95 replacement files to your hard disk. This action is the key to how Windows 95's dual-boot system works. The following table lists all the DOS system files affected by Windows 95's installation, showing the original file name and its new name.

Original DOS Name	New Windows 95 Name
IO.SYS	IO.DOS
MSDOS.SYS	MSDOS.DOS
COMMAND.COM	COMMAND.DOS
CONFIG.SYS	CONFIG.DOS
AUTOEXEC.BAT	AUTOEXEC.DOS

Whenever you boot your computer, you can skip loading Windows 95 and revert to your previous DOS version (but not necessarily your Windows 3.1+ version, unless you actually installed Windows 95 as a dual-boot system) by pressing the F4 key. When you press the F4 key, Windows 95 first renames its own system files to have the file extension W95, restores the original names to your original DOS system files, and continues the boot process, effectively restoring the previous DOS version. The following table shows the new names of the Windows 95 system files that appear in the root directory of your boot drive when you dual-boot back to your previous DOS version. (When you dual-boot back to your old DOS version, Windows 95 uses the WINBOOT.SYS file to store the startup I/O system; when you boot Windows 95, this file is named IO.SYS.)

Original Windows 95 Name	New DOS Name
IO.SYS	WINBOOT.SYS
MSDOS.SYS	MSDOS.W95
COMMAND.COM	COMMAND.W95
CONFIG.SYS	CONFIG.W95
AUTOEXEC.BAT	AUTOEXEC.W95

Note

Don't delete any files in your boot drive's root directory that end with the DOS extension while running Windows 95, or you'll make it impossible for Windows 95 to dual-boot back to your old DOS version. Similarly, you should avoid deleting any files in your boot drive's root directory that end with the W95 file extension while using your previous DOS version, or you'll make it impossible for your computer to boot into Windows 95.

V

Digging into the OS

If Windows 95 finds the system files with the W95 extension on your disk when you boot your computer, it renames them again so that the Windows 95 operating system loads into memory (unless you press the F4 key again).

You may also see some of Windows 95's special log files in your boot disk's root directory: DETCRASH.LOG, DETLOG.TXT, SETUPLOG.TXT, and BOOTLOG.TXT. Windows 95 uses these log files to determine what hardware is installed in your computer, whether installation completed successfully, and whether your computer successfully completed the boot process the last time you started it.

Managing Windows 95's Configuration over the Long Term

Windows 95 has some useful built-in long-term management features. First and foremost, Windows 95 creates a database of installed components during Setup. Whenever Windows 95 starts, it uses this database to verify the integrity of installed software components in your system. If you have problems with deleted or corrupted device drivers (or other Windows 95 software components), you just run the Windows 95 Setup program again and ask it to verify installed components. Setup uses its setup log and installed components database to run through the setup process again, only installing missing or corrupted components. Setup verifies that each Windows 95 component is present and compares it to the source files on the distribution disks or CD-ROM. If a component is missing or corrupted, Setup automatically reinstalls it. This feature can make a great difference in support in large companies—the amount of time required to identify and restore missing or damaged components is minimal.

> **Note**
>
> You can add or remove individual Windows 95 utilities and applets with the Add/Remove Programs icon in the Control Panel any time after you install Windows 95.

Also, Windows 95 examines your system each time you boot your computer to detect changes in your hardware configuration. If Windows 95 detects new or removed hardware, it will automatically try to install the additional required device drivers or disable the unused device drivers. You can also use Control Panel to add or remove device drivers at any time—Windows 95 provides the New Device Installation Wizard, Add Printer Wizard, and other features to help make installing new devices easier for both novice and experienced users.

To further simplify matters, Windows 95 remembers its installation source—whether it was installed from disk or from a network drive. If you use the maintenance mode of the Setup program or add new device drivers with Control Panel, Windows 95 tries to obtain the additional or replacement software components from the original installation source. (Windows 95's maintenance mode starts automatically whenever you run Setup on a computer that already has a working installed copy of Windows 95.) This feature may be a boon for network administrators, since you can perform system maintenance without having to insert disks, assuming that the Windows 95 program installation files still reside in the same directory on the network. This feature also makes it possible for network workstations to be at least partially maintainable by their local users, without necessarily requiring attention from the network administrator or PC support personnel.

V

Digging into the OS

Chapter 24

Replacing WIN.INI, SYSTEM.INI, and REG.DAT with Registry

Windows 3.1+ relies on a variety of initialization files to load real-mode and 32-bit virtual device drivers (VxDs) during the DOS boot and the Windows loading process. Applications often have private initialization files, usually placed in your WINDOWS directory, designed to store program-specific data. As you add or update new Windows applications under Windows 3.1+, your WIN.INI and SYSTEM.INI files grow—often to unmanageable sizes—and contain mysterious entries for applications you deleted a year or two ago. The WIN.INI file of the computer used to write this chapter, for example, is about 26K; roughly 50 percent of the content of this file is devoted to sections for applications no longer in use.

Windows NT 3.1 introduced the *Registry*, a central database that contains system and application data. Both Windows 95 and Windows NT 3.5 use the Registry to store this type of information. The Registry is intended ultimately to replace AUTOEXEC.BAT, CONFIG.SYS, WIN.INI, and SYSTEM.INI, as well as the *PRIVATE*.INI files, such as WINWORD.INI, used by individual Windows applications. Windows 95 reads WIN.INI and SYSTEM.INI during the boot process to maintain backward compatibility with Windows 3.1+ applications that expect to find application-specific information in INI files. When the 32-bit millennium arrives, a clean installation of Windows 95 and its applications won't need WIN.INI or SYSTEM.INI.

Windows 95's Registry also encompasses the functions performed by the registration database, REG.DAT, used by Windows 3.1+'s Program Manager to associate file extensions with applications and register OLE (object linking and embedding) server applications. Most Windows 3.1 users have never even looked at the entries in REG.DAT; there's little or no user documentation describing the mysterious entries in the REG.DAT file. This chapter describes Windows 95's Registry, the Registration Database Editor (RegEdit), and the remote Registry management features of Windows 95 networks.

Components of the Windows 95 Registry

Windows 3.1+'s REG.DAT file is a fragile entity that often becomes corrupted when adding or deleting OLE servers, especially servers that implement OLE 2, such as Microsoft Excel 5.0 and Project 4.0, as well as OLE 2 servers from ISVs such as Shapeware's Visio 3.0. The Windows 95 Registry—a much more robust database system than REG.DAT—is less subject to corruption. The Windows 95 Registry uses the following three files:

- SYSTEM.DAT describes an individual PC's configuration and information on applications installed on a single PC. SYSTEM.DAT stores information on Plug and Play devices, including the I/O base address, IRQ level, and DMA channel assigned to the device during Windows 95's boot process.

- USER.DAT defines user preferences—such as the configuration of the user's desktop—and application setup information specific to a user. Multiple user preferences can be stored on a single computer.

- POLICY.POL stores on a network server administrative policies set by the PC administrator. Information in POLICY.POL overrides specific user settings contained in a local or network version of USER.DAT. Chapter 20, "Managing Networked PCs with Windows 95," describes how to set policies for non-administrative users.

USER.DAT can be stored on the local PC or on a network server. POLICY.POL, which can be renamed so long as the POL extension is maintained, always is located on a network server. SYSTEM.DAT, whose entries are specific to the PC's hardware, is stored locally. To take advantage of Windows 95's capability to provide users with their custom desktop configuration, regardless of which workstation they use, you must store USER.DAT on a server. Similarly,

POLICY.POL (or whatever you name the policies file for non-administrative users) must be located on a server that's accessible to the workstations to which the policies apply. The server can be a Windows 95 workstation that shares the directory where the *.DAT and POLICY.POL files are located or a dedicated network server.

> **Note**
>
> Registry files have the read-only, hidden, and system file attributes set so that you can't delete or modify these files from the DOS command line without taking extraordinary steps. Registry data is in binary format, so the files aren't easily readable with conventional text-editing applications.

During the Windows 95 installation process, the Setup program examines the hardware installed on your computer and makes the appropriate entries in SYSTEM.DAT. If you set up Windows 95 over an existing Windows 3.1+ installation, Setup copies entries from your REG.DAT file into SYSTEM.DAT. When you open Control Panel's Properties for System sheet, the entries that appear are supplied by SYSTEM.DAT (see fig. 24.1). When you first enter your user ID and password, Setup stores this information in USER.DAT. (Passwords are encrypted for security purposes.) Even if your computer authenticates users from a domain controller, a copy of your user information is stored locally so you can log on to Windows 95 without connecting to a domain controller.

Fig. 24.1
Displaying entries from SYSTEM.DAT in Control Panel's Properties for System sheet.

> **Note**
>
> Entries are required in the SYSTEM.DAT file for most Windows productivity applications, especially those that act as OLE servers. Because of the need for Registry entries for application software, you have to reinstall most of your Windows 3.1+ applications if you set up Windows 95 in a dual-boot configuration. Applications add their entries to the Registry when the Updating system data message appears at the end of the setup process. When you use the application's uninstall feature, which is required for software that carries the "Designed for Windows 95" logo, the uninstall feature removes the Registry entries for the software.

Using the Windows 95 Registration Database Editor

Windows 95's Registry Editor (RegEdit), like Windows 3.1+'s Registration Database Editor (also named RegEdit), doesn't appear by default in any program group. This is Microsoft's way of discouraging users from casually editing or deleting entries in the Registry. To launch RegEdit, you double-click RegEdit's icon in the Windows folder (or the directory where you installed Windows 95). When the Registry Editor's window appears, it displays the seven root entries (called keys) of the Registry. If you run REGSERVE.EXE (from WINDOWS) and then choose Connect from RegEdit's File menu, you can view and edit part of SYSTEM.DAT and USER.DAT on a remote computer. Figure 24.2 shows RegEdit displaying the root keys for the local computer and a remote Windows 95 server.

Fig. 24.2
Displaying the root Registry keys for a local and a remote computer.

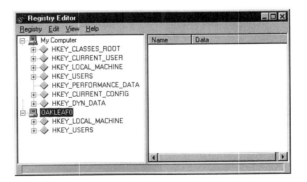

Root key names are in uppercase and each carries the HKEY_ prefix. This naming convention is based on the name of the symbolic constant assigned to each set of key values by the Registry functions of the Win32 API. Following is a list of the root keys, organized by the file where the Registry data is stored:

- HKEY_USERS maintains a list of all users and their passwords contained in the local computer's password list. Information on each user's preferences is stored under the HKEY_USERS key. HKEY_USERS is one of the two keys accessible from remote computers.

- HKEY_CURRENT_USER contains information on the user now logged on the local workstation, including the user's logon ID and cached (stored) password. (The password entry is hidden.) When a user logs on to Windows 95, the information for the user is copied to HKEY_CURRENT_USER from the corresponding entry in HKEY_USERS. HKEY_USERS and HKEY_CURRENT_USER information is stored in USERS.DAT.

- HKEY_CURRENT_CONFIG stores the data that defines the current user's desktop configuration, most recently used (MRU) documents, and other information about the current user's Windows 95 setup.

- HKEY_CLASSES specifies the name of the file type based on the file extension of each application you install that uses files. When you first install Windows 95, for example, RTF (rich text format) files are associated with WordPad. If you later install Microsoft Word, the RTF association changes to launch Word when you double-click an RTF file. HKEY_CLASSES, which is stored in SYSTEM.DAT, replaces the [Extensions] section of WIN.INI, which associates an application with the file extension. HKEY_CLASSES is especially important because it registers OLE 2 servers. (Windows 95's desktop shortcuts rely on OLE 2.) HKEY_CLASSES contains entries similar to those found in Windows 3.1+'s REG.DAT file.

- HKEY_LOCAL_MACHINE stores hardware data for the local computer. Keys under this root, which is contained in SYSTEM.DAT, are used to provide the information on the type of hardware installed on the PC, the drivers required by the hardware, and software configuration information.

- HKEY_PERFORMANCE_DATA stores the choices available to and the selections you make in the System Monitor applet.

V

Digging into the OS

■ HKEY_DYN_DATA stores in memory the data necessary to accommodate dynamic activities, such as docking or undocking a portable PC, and installing or removing a PCMCIA card in a laptop. HKEY_DYN_DATA keys are associated primarily with Plug and Play support.

The Registry Editor's Hierarchical Key Display

RegEdit displays Registry data in a hierarchical structure of keys (at the root level) and subkeys. Depending on the root key you select, you may have to open several additional subkey levels to get to the point where you find the data for the item of interest. Figure 24.3 shows some of the subkeys of the HKEY_CURRENT_USER key; the subkeys for the persistent (mapped) network connection for the local H drive appear in the right panel of RegEdit. Figure 24.4 shows a deeply nested subkey for the MCI aux(iliary) device provided by Microsoft's driver, "mssb16.drv," for the Sound Blaster 16 audio adapter card. If you spend enough time exploring the Registry with RegEdit, you ultimately can identify all the VxDs and other driver software associated with your computer's hardware.

Fig. 24.3
A subkey that defines a persistent (mapped) network connection on a local computer.

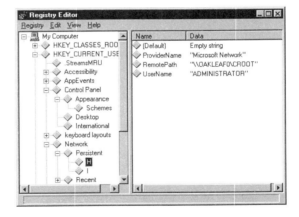

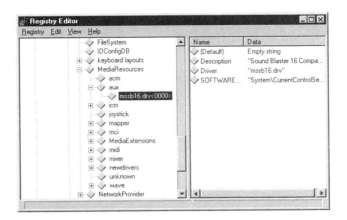

Fig. 24.4
A deeply nested
subkey that defines
the MCI aux device
and the driver
required to
implement the
device.

Editing, Adding, or Deleting Registry Subkey Values

If you experience problems with your hardware or an application, you may be asked by one of Microsoft's product support specialists or an ISV's technical support person to edit, add, or delete a Registry subkey value. Unless you are very sure of what you're doing, this is the only circumstance under which you should try to edit the Registry database with RegEdit. If you incorrectly modify an entry or add a wrong entry, Windows 95 may refuse to run and you may have to reinstall the entire operating system.

> **Tip**
>
> Windows 95 creates a backup version of your Registry files as USER.DA0 and
> SYSTEM.DA0 in your WINDOWS directory. These backup files are created when
> Windows 95 loads successfully and represent the "last known good" versions of
> USER.DAT and SYSTEM.DAT. If your Registry files become corrupted and Windows 95
> does not automatically restore USER.DAT and SYSTEM.DAT from the last known
> good version, you can copy the USER.DA0 to USER.DAT and SYSTEM.DA0 to
> SYSTEM.DAT, after executing the MS-DOS ATTRIB -r -s -h *.DA? command in
> your WINDOWS directory. Return the files to their original attribute state with an
> ATTRIB +r +s +h *.DA? command when you're done.

You add a new subkey by selecting the key or subkey and then choosing Add Key from RegEdit's Edit menu. When you add a new subkey, RegEdit assigns New Key #1 as the subkey name. You can edit the subkey immediately after you add it, or you can change the subkey name by right-clicking the new entry and choosing Rename from the shortcut menu (see fig. 24.5).

V

Digging into the OS

Fig. 24.5
Renaming a new
Registry subkey.

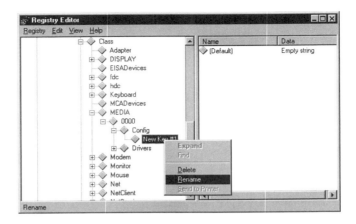

After you've created a new subkey, you need to assign the subkey a value. Figure 24.6 shows the New String Value dialog box in which you enter the value required by the subkey. You delete the new test subkey you entered or delete a subkey you're replacing with a new value by selecting the key and pressing Delete. You are warned before the deletion occurs (see fig. 24.7). To delete a subkey and all the subkeys below it, select the subkey and press Delete; again you are warned before RegEdit deletes the subkey(s), as shown in figure 24.8.

Fig. 24.6
In the New String
Value dialog, enter
the value required
by the subkey.

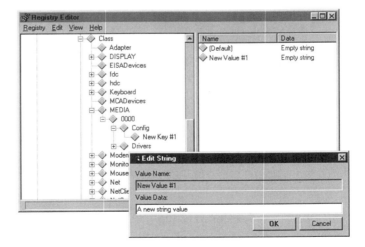

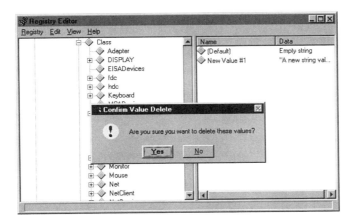

Fig. 24.7
Deleting a subkey value.

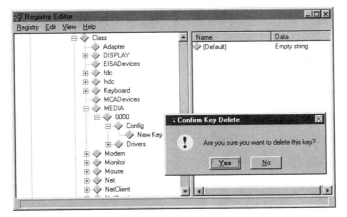

Fig. 24.8
Deleting a subkey and its member subkeys.

V

Digging into the OS

Note

Editing the Registry with Windows 95's Registry Editor is similar to the process you use to edit REG.DAT with Windows 3.1+'s Registration Info Editor. There are differences, however, in the method of entering subkey values. Windows 3.1+'s RegEdit also asks you to confirm changes when you exit, giving you the option of discarding changes; Windows 95's Registry Editor makes the changes to the DAT file(s) as you add or delete entries. The changes are stored in the file cache (RAM) until Windows 95 flushes its file buffers, at which point the changes are written to the DAT files.

Printing Registry Data

One of the most common complaints by users of Windows 3.1+'s RegEdit application is the inability to print registration database entries for review, as well as for backup purposes. Windows 95's Registry Editor includes a Print choice in its file menu, which opens the Print dialog (see fig. 24.9). You can choose to print all Registry data (have plenty of paper on hand) or just the selected branch of the Registry with all the branch's subkeys.

Fig. 24.9
The Print dialog box for printing the contents of the Registry or a branch and its subkeys.

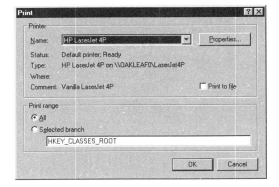

> ### Tip
>
> Before making any changes to the registry, print the branch that contains the subkey whose value you want to change. If your changes don't work, use the printed version to restore the previous values.

Chapter 25

Running DOS Applications under Windows 95

Because Windows 95 is a complete operating system, there's little need for new computer users to learn about or use MS-DOS, except to format disks or prepare an emergency startup disk. Hobbyists with many DOS-based game programs, as well as businesses with existing DOS-based applications that they want to (or must) continue using under Windows 95, will find more reasons to use the DOS command line. Many other users—particularly those with many computer hours of experience—may find that some activities are simply easier for them to perform at the DOS command line.

This chapter describes how to access DOS in Windows 95 and how Windows 95's architecture influences DOS and DOS-based applications.

Getting to DOS

There are two ways you can gain access to DOS:

- Run a DOS Virtual Machine (VM) from Windows 95. This is, by far, the most frequent technique you'll employ to use a DOS application in Windows 95. (DOS VMs are often referred to colloquially as DOS *boxes*.)

- Bypass loading Windows 95's graphical interface by either starting your computer from a floppy disk or by pressing the F8 key while Windows 95 is loading (right after the Loading Windows... message appears).

Usually, you won't use this technique unless something is wrong with Windows 95 or you have a situation such as that described in the section "Using DOS-Based Games under Windows 95" at the end of this chapter.

Starting DOS Applications with Windows 95

Windows 95 recognizes the common file extensions for executable files: EXE, COM, and BAT. (The EXE extension is used to indicate executable files for both DOS and Windows.) As a result, you can conveniently start any DOS application or DOS batch file directly from within Windows 95. Figure 25.1 shows a desktop folder window opened on a directory that contains only DOS batch files.

Fig. 25.1
You can run DOS programs and batch files by double-clicking the icon that appears in the folder window.

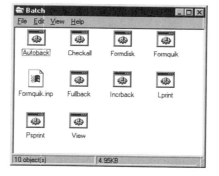

Windows 95 displays a special icon for the executable batch files and similar icons (without the gear picture at the center of the icons) for .EXE and .COM files so you can distinguish them from registered Windows programs and document files. To start any DOS batch file or DOS-based application from Windows 95, just double-click the icon. Windows 95 starts a DOS virtual machine (explained in the next section) and executes the batch file or application program. When the batch file is complete or when you exit the DOS application, Windows 95 closes the DOS virtual machine.

As explained later in this chapter, you don't really have to worry about the program information files (PIFs) that were so important in Windows 3.1+. Windows 95 automatically creates a PIF with appropriate settings for your DOS programs as you run each DOS application from Windows 95—you'll need to worry about PIF configuration only in a few unusual circumstances or if you want to customize the way a particular DOS-based application's virtual machine behaves in Windows 95.

◄ See Chapter 3,
"Exploring the
Windows 95
Interface"

Note

Unlike Windows 3.1+, Windows 95, by default, runs DOS applications in a window and enables background execution for the DOS application. These defaults are the opposite of Windows 3.1+—apparently, these two items are the first thing that most Windows 3.1+ users change for their DOS applications.

Tip

You can also execute a DOS-based program by using the Run command from the Start menu on the Task Bar, just as you can execute a DOS-based program in Windows 3.1+ by using the Run command on the Program Manager's File menu.

You can place a Shortcut for a DOS program in the Programs folder so that the DOS program appears on the Programs submenu on the Start menu of the Task Bar. Starting your DOS-based applications directly from Windows 95 is the easiest and simplest way to use DOS programs in Windows 95.

Using the DOS Command Line under Windows 95

There are a few times when you'll want to execute DOS commands and run DOS programs directly from the DOS command line. In particular, starting DOS applications directly from Windows 95 doesn't allow you to specify different command-line parameters (sometimes called switches) each time you execute the DOS-based program.

Although you can change a DOS-based program's properties to include command-line switches, the switches are the same every time you run the program. If you want to change the program's switches each time you run it, you'll need to create a different Shortcut for each different command-line switch, or execute the program directly from the DOS command line. (Be sure to read the section "Poof! No More PIF...Almost" later in this chapter for information about program properties.)

To open an MS-DOS virtual machine and display the DOS prompt, click the Start button on the Task Bar, and then choose MS-DOS Prompt from the Programs menu. Figure 25.2 shows a DOS virtual machine displaying the DOS command-line prompt. You can create a Shortcut icon to start a DOS prompt by creating a Shortcut for COMMAND.COM, the DOS command interpreter.

Fig. 25.2
Windows 95
allows you to start
a DOS prompt, as
in Windows 3.1+.

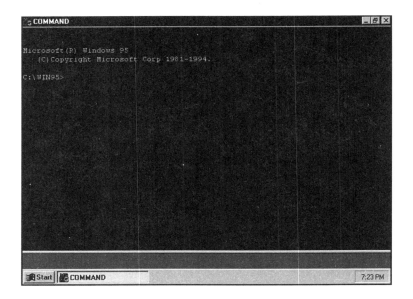

> **Note**
>
> In figure 25.2, notice that the familiar `Type EXIT and press ENTER to quit`
> this `MS-DOS prompt and return to Windows` message no longer appears in the
> Windows 95 DOS box. Now, you can just close the window that contains the DOS
> box to end the DOS session—although typing EXIT and pressing the Enter key will
> still end the DOS session.

Starting DOS without Windows 95

On very rare occasions, you may need or want to perform operations at the
DOS prompt without Windows 95's full graphical interface loaded into
memory. You might need to do this if something's wrong with Windows
95—such as a corrupted file that affects operation of the desktop. Some very
few DOS game programs simply won't run in a DOS virtual machine (so far),
and you may have to load them without loading the full Windows 95 interface and its protected-mode device drivers. (See "Using DOS-Based Games
under Windows 95" later in this chapter.)

◀ See Chapter 23,
"Setting Up
and Managing
Windows 95"

To use the DOS command line without fully loading Windows 95, you'll
need to either boot Windows 95 from a floppy disk (such as the emergency
disk you created when you installed Windows 95) or press the F8 key to

bypass loading the Windows 95 graphical interface. In either case, your computer boots up into a real-mode version of DOS.

When you skip loading the full Windows 95 interface, whether by booting your computer with a floppy disk or by using F8, DOS runs in real mode, and none of Windows 95's 32-bit protected-mode device drivers are loaded into memory. Only the real-mode device drivers loaded through CONFIG.SYS get loaded into memory. If the DOS application that you want to run requires external device drivers—such as a mouse driver or a driver for a CD-ROM drive—you'll have to make sure that your boot floppy has CONFIG.SYS and AUTOEXEC.BAT files to load the desired device drivers. Obviously, it's more convenient to run your DOS applications directly from Windows 95 or from a DOS command line running in a DOS virtual machine under Windows 95.

> **Note**
>
> As a matter of interest, whether you skip loading the full Windows 95 interface or use the DOS command line in a DOS virtual machine inside Windows 95, the VER command in DOS reports that the DOS version is Windows 95, not DOS 7. To make matters even more confusing, a DOS program that asks what version of DOS it is running under receives 7 as the answer—as a result, some of your DOS programs may report that they are running under DOS 7.

DOS Window Viewing Options

Windows 95's DOS windows provide a couple of significant conveniences over running a DOS application in Windows 3.1+. (Specific enhancements to the internal operation of Windows 95's DOS virtual machines are described separately in the later section "Windows 95's Enhancements to the DOS Virtual Machine.") The most notable new additions to the DOS virtual machine in Windows 95 are the capabilities to display a toolbar for the DOS window and scale the DOS window.

The DOS Window Toolbar

Like every other desktop window in Windows 95, you can display a windowed DOS session with a toolbar. You do so by altering the properties of the window—click the icon at the left of the window's title bar to get access to the properties sheet for the window. Figure 25.3 shows a DOS window with its toolbar displayed.

Fig. 25.3
Windows 95's
DOS windows can
display a toolbar
that provides rapid
access to various
options and
controls for the
DOS session and
its window.

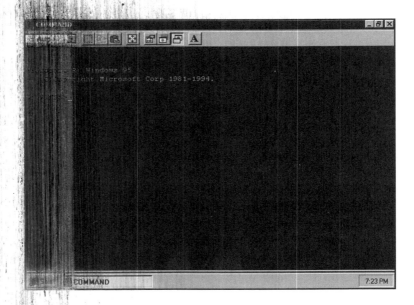

The DOS window toolbar gives the DOS window most of the same features
you find in any other desktop window, specifically:

- Quick access to the Mark, Cut, Copy, and Paste operations. Copying
  and pasting information to or from a Windows 95 DOS session is the
  same as in Windows 3.1+ —you use the Paste command to insert information from the Clipboard into the DOS window or use the Mark command to mark a region of the DOS screen and then Cut or Copy the
  information onto the Clipboard.

- The ability to easily switch from a windowed to full-screen DOS session.
  The Alt+Enter keystroke combination still toggles between both windowed and full-screen modes, as well.

- Quick access to the properties sheet for the DOS session.

- The ability to "hot-switch" the DOS session's multitasking properties,
  allowing you to dynamically change the DOS session to exclusive or
  foreground processing.

- The ability to easily change the DOS session's font options and font size
  by using the drop-down list at the left of the toolbar or the font selection button at the right of the toolbar.

While the DOS window's toolbar isn't earthshaking in its innovation, it does reduce the number of menus and mouse clicks necessary to perform common operations.

DOS Window Fonts and Scalable DOS Windows

The font options just mentioned are completely new to Windows 95's DOS session windows—there's no equivalent feature in Windows 3.1+. In Windows 3.1+, every DOS session uses the same fixed font—in full-screen mode, DOS sessions use the bit-mapped hardware font of your video display; in a windowed session, a smaller bit-mapped font is used.

Windows 95 allows you to specify—via the properties sheet for the DOS window—any bit-mapped font available for your system or any TrueType font you've installed on your computer. You can also select the font size that Windows 95 uses for the text in the DOS session. The font option settings affect the appearance of the DOS session whether the session is running full-screen or in a window. Figure 25.4 shows the properties sheet for setting the font typeface and size used in a DOS session.

The result of this feature is twofold. First, you can choose a font that you find pleasing and that produces the least amount of eyestrain for you. If you think the DOS command line looks better in Arial, for example, you can switch to that font. If you find that the sizes of the letters are too small, increase the size of the font for better readability.

Fig. 25.4
Changing the typeface and font size allows you to increase the readability of text in your DOS windows or scale the DOS window while keeping all the text visible.

V

Digging into the OS

The second—and much more significant—aspect of this feature is that it lets you scale the size of the DOS window. One of the available font size options is Auto (refer to fig. 25.4). This option allows Windows 95 to automatically choose the font size depending on the size of the DOS window. Figure 25.5 shows two different windowed DOS sessions; the smaller window has the Auto font size property set and has been reduced in size so that other windows on the desktop are visible. Notice that full 80-character width of the DOS screen is still visible in the smaller window.

Fig. 25.5
The Auto font size option makes it possible to scale your DOS session windows.

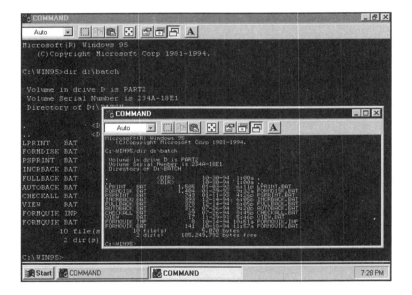

Poof! No More PIF... Almost

In Windows 3.1+, one of the most annoying aspects of using many DOS applications is the necessity to manually create and configure the DOS program's information file (PIF). If a DOS application needs special handling by Windows, the only way Windows can get that information is through a PIF. Windows 95, however, can automatically create PIFs for any applications that might need one. Windows 95 uses intelligent defaults and a database of known applications to determine the settings for the PIF.

Windows 95 gracefully removes the PIF from your attention by treating all the settings in the PIF—and the PIF file itself—as properties of the DOS program object. You set all the options for a DOS application the same way you set properties for any object on the Windows 95 desktop—by selecting the object and choosing Properties from the File menu, or by right-clicking the object to get at its properties sheet.

> **Note**
>
> Because you change a DOS application's PIF settings by altering the DOS program object's properties, Windows 95 has no need for the PIF Editor that experienced Windows 3.1+ users are used to. Don't bother looking for the Windows 95 PIF Editor—there isn't one. Just right-click on the DOS application's icon in Windows 95 to create or change its PIF.

In fact, you are altering settings in an external PIF, but Windows 95 stores all PIFs in a hidden PIF folder in the Windows 95 installed directory. (If Windows 95 is installed in the WIN95 directory, all your PIFs are in \WIN95\PIF.) The great convenience of this system is that average users, although they may need to be aware of the DOS program's properties at some time, never need to be aware of the PIF and its relationship to the DOS program—they just alter the program's properties directly from the program's icon. Windows 95 creates or changes the PIF automatically.

Windows 95's Enhancements to the DOS Virtual Machine

Running DOS applications or a DOS prompt from inside Windows 95 is essentially the same as running a DOS application or DOS prompt from inside Windows 3.1+, and uses the same basic technology. When you run a DOS application or open a DOS prompt, Windows 95 creates a virtual machine (VM), loads a copy of the DOS COMMAND.COM command interpreter, and either executes the DOS application you specified or leaves the VM running at the DOS prompt.

A virtual machine takes advantage of capabilities built into the hardware of the Intel 80386, 80486, and Pentium CPUs. Each of these processors can set aside a certain amount of protected memory and then use that memory to execute programs as though a separate 8088 CPU was inside your real CPU. The VM can run programs without affecting any other operations in the CPU. Because DOS is a 16-bit operating system, it runs just fine in the 16-bit virtual 8088 machine created for it.

In Windows 95, your DOS applications run in a DOS VM whether they are windowed or full-screen and whether you started the application by double-clicking its icon in Windows 95 or started it from the DOS prompt in a DOS window. Only if you start DOS without Windows 95 (as described earlier) does MS-DOS run in real mode—it has to because the full Windows 95 multitasking kernel hasn't been loaded.

◀ See Chapter 5, "Running Your Current Applications under Windows 95"

◀ See Chapter 22, "Understanding Windows 95's Operating System Architecture"

Windows 95, like Windows 3.1+, allows you to have several DOS applications or DOS prompts running at the same time (referred to as *multiple-concurrent DOS sessions*). All of these DOS sessions run in a VM. Windows 95's DOS virtual machines are preemptively multitasked with any other applications (whether DOS or Windows) that Windows 95 is now executing—whether your DOS application runs in a window or full screen.

Windows 95 has many improvements and enhancements to the internal operation of its DOS virtual machines. These enhancements make DOS VMs in Windows 95 easier to use and more reliable. The following list summarizes these enhancements:

- Windows 95's 32-bit protected-mode virtual device drivers (mouse, CD-ROM, SCSI drive, etc.) are shared by all DOS VMs, freeing up potentially substantial amounts of conventional memory for use by applications in the DOS VM.

- Windows 95 uses its virtual memory management capabilities to provide every DOS VM with (by default) an amount of expanded (EMS) memory and of extended (XMS) memory equivalent to the total RAM in your computer. Frequently, this is more EMS or XMS memory than your DOS application would have available in real-mode DOS, with corresponding improvements in performance. (You can change the amount of EMS and XMS available for a particular DOS application by modifying the settings on the Memory page of the properties sheet for that application.)

- Graceful forced shutdown of DOS applications. If one of your DOS applications crashes or hangs, it doesn't kill Windows 95 at the same time (crashing DOS applications frequently disable or corrupt Windows 3.1+). You can either leave the DOS VM running (and ignore it) until you shut down Windows 95, or you can force Windows 95 to shut down the DOS VM that contains the crashed DOS application. (For this last option to work, you must set the Allow Close while Active property for that particular DOS VM.)

- Global memory protection for known "buggy" DOS applications. This optional feature allows you to protect the DOS system area in a VM if an application crashes or otherwise misbehaves, further reducing the likelihood that a "bad" DOS application will also bring down Windows 95.

- The ability to individually and automatically customize the environment for each individual DOS VM.

- Windows 95 permits DOS applications that use VGA video modes to run in a window, instead of the full-screen mode mandatory in Windows 3.1+.

- Availability of a Single Application mode for DOS applications that absolutely must run in real mode. (Single Application mode is described later.)

The major result of these improvements to the internal operation of Windows 95's DOS virtual machines is that you'll rarely, if ever, need to leave Windows 95 to run a DOS application. In fact, since you can start DOS applications directly from icons on Windows 95's desktop, from folder windows, or from the Task Bar's Program menus, you'll rarely need to even explicitly start a DOS VM. In this way, Windows 95 blurs the distinction between DOS applications and Windows applications that was so important in Windows 3.1+.

Note

Experience with running various DOS applications under Windows 95 supports Microsoft's claim that DOS applications that wouldn't run in a Windows 3.1+ DOS box will run under Windows 95. One DOS application that the authors tested, for example, often crashed Windows 3.1 when exiting from the application. No such crashes have occurred under Windows 95.

In particular, Windows 95 is better able to accommodate those DOS applications that assume they're the only process running on the computer—like many DOS game programs and some other graphic—or time-critical applications such as telecommunications packages. Windows 3.1+ typically can't run such programs in a DOS VM because they usually try to take direct control of your computer's hardware devices and memory resources, interfering with Windows 3.1+ operation. For example, many programs make direct reads and writes to video memory rather than use DOS or BIOS services to put data in or get data from the video display. Other programs alter the state of your system's low-level hardware settings (such as timers, sound cards, and interrupt addresses). Windows 95 makes more of these actual hardware devices into virtual devices than does Windows 3.1+. This means that Windows 95 can keep track of most of the low-level resources that any particular DOS application might try to use and permit the DOS application to use those system resources without disrupting Windows 95's operation. Windows 95 protects its resources and just lets the DOS application think it has sole control.

Improved Memory Management

Windows 95 makes several improvements in memory management for DOS VMs, and does a better job of protecting itself and other applications from ill-behaved DOS applications that may try to overwrite another program's memory areas.

Every DOS program has a global memory protection property that you can set to make Windows 95 protect the DOS system area in a particular DOS VM. When this property is set, DOS applications can't write into the DOS system area's memory locations. This prevents a crashing DOS application from corrupting any code or data stored by DOS in that particular VM. (Setting DOS program attributes is described later in the section "Customized Environments for Individual VMs.") As part of the global memory protection property, Windows 95 also checks any disk input/output operations that a DOS application makes through DOS Int21h. (Int21h is known to DOS system-level programmers as the primary interrupt used to request various services from DOS, such as reading data from or writing data to disk files.) Presumably, this additional screening provides safeguards against a DOS application that might corrupt the DOS FAT.

Because the global memory protection and Int21h screening requires additional code and processor overhead, this feature isn't a default setting—you must explicitly turn this option on by changing the DOS program's properties, as described at the end of this chapter.

Finally, Windows 95 makes sure that all memory allocated by an application in a DOS VM is deallocated and made available for use by other applications. Windows 3.1+ has trouble deallocating DPMI (DOS Protected Mode Interface) memory in particular. Microsoft asserts that Windows 95's memory management for DOS VMs corrects this problem.

Single Application Mode

Although Windows 95 can better accommodate applications that try to directly control your computer's hardware, you may encounter a few aggressive

DOS programs that still won't run in a DOS VM because they insist on 100 percent control of your system's hardware and resources. For these applications, Windows 95 provides the Single MS-DOS application mode property.

Running a DOS application in single application mode is the same as running that application in real-mode DOS without Windows 95. In fact, when you run a DOS application in single application mode, Windows 95 shuts down all other running tasks, unloads itself from memory, and runs the DOS application in real mode, where the DOS application has full access to your system. (A stub of Windows 95 remains in memory so that Windows 95 can reload itself into memory when you exit the DOS application.)

You probably won't need this feature, but it's reassuring to know it's available, should the need arise. Using single application mode has one big disadvantage, however. When you start a DOS application in single application mode, all currently executing tasks must be shut down. (Obviously, if Windows 95 is going to change to a real-mode environment, it can't maintain operation of its protected-mode devices and applications.) Windows 95 will ask for confirmation before shutting down running applications, and you'll get an opportunity to save any documents that may be open.

When Windows 95 reloads itself at the end of a single application mode DOS session, however, it's just like booting Windows 95 from scratch—you'll have to log on again, and although Windows 95 remembers which folder windows you had open on the desktop, you'll have to restart or reopen any applications or documents you were using before starting the DOS application in single application mode.

To use the single MS-DOS application mode, you must turn on the corresponding program property in the properties sheet for the DOS application described earlier in the section "Poof! No More PIF... Almost."

Customized Environments for Individual VMs

As in Windows 3.1+, every Windows 95 DOS VM receives a copy of the DOS environment that was in effect at the time Windows 95 loaded into memory. Any terminate-and-stay-resident (TSR) programs or other memory-resident software (such as real-mode device drivers) and environment strings (created with the SET command—SET TEMP, SET PATH, and so on) that are loaded via CONFIG.SYS and AUTOEXEC.BAT are duplicated in all DOS virtual machines.

Windows 95 allows you to specify, as part of the DOS program's properties, the name of a batch file to run whenever that particular DOS program is started. Windows 95 executes the specified DOS batch file and then executes the specified DOS application. This way, you can individually customize the environment for a particular DOS VM.

Use this batch file to make any changes in the DOS environment that the particular DOS application might need—such as environment variables, a TSR program, a different PATH statement, and so on. You can even use the batch file option to execute several DOS applications or batch files with a single double-click of an icon on the Windows 95 desktop or in a folder window. Essentially, this feature provides the equivalent of individual AUTOEXEC.BAT files for each DOS VM.

> **Note**
>
> You can't use the batch file for customizing the DOS VM's environment to load additional real-mode device drivers. A real-mode device driver loaded in a DOS VM may or may not conflict with a corresponding protected-mode driver loaded by Windows 95. The real-mode device driver or Windows 95 may or may not be able to detect the conflict. So far, testing done by the authors shows that either Windows 95 or the real-mode device driver can detect a potential conflict, but you shouldn't count on it. For example, loading a real-mode mouse device driver conflicts with Windows 95's virtual mouse driver. Usually, your DOS applications will be able to use the protected-mode device drivers provided by Windows 95.

Windows 95's New and Enhanced DOS Commands

Windows 95's file system now incorporates several new features. A couple of these features—long file names and built-in network connectivity—require Windows 95 to enhance existing DOS commands so that these new features are usable at the DOS command line.

> **Note**
>
> Windows 95 creates a folder named COMMAND in its installed directory and places all the Windows 95 DOS external commands in this directory. If you installed Windows 95 in a directory named WIN95, the DOS command files are in \WIN95\COMMAND.

All DOS file commands—DIR, COPY, XCOPY, RENAME, and so on—have been extended to use long file names. You can use either the DOS name fo a file, the file's long name, or a mixture of long and DOS file names. To use a long file name, you only have to enclose the file name in double quote marks (" "):

```
COPY "new document" "another document"
```

The DIR command, in particular, has been expanded to accommodate long file names. Figure 25.6 shows a directory listing made with the DIR command. Notice that the first six columns in the directory listing show the familiar DIR information: the file's DOS name, extension, the file's size or an indicator showing that the entry is a subdirectory, and the date and time the file was last modified. A new column is added to the directory listing, however, that shows the file's long file name.

◀ See Chapter 3, "Exploring the Windows 95 Interface"

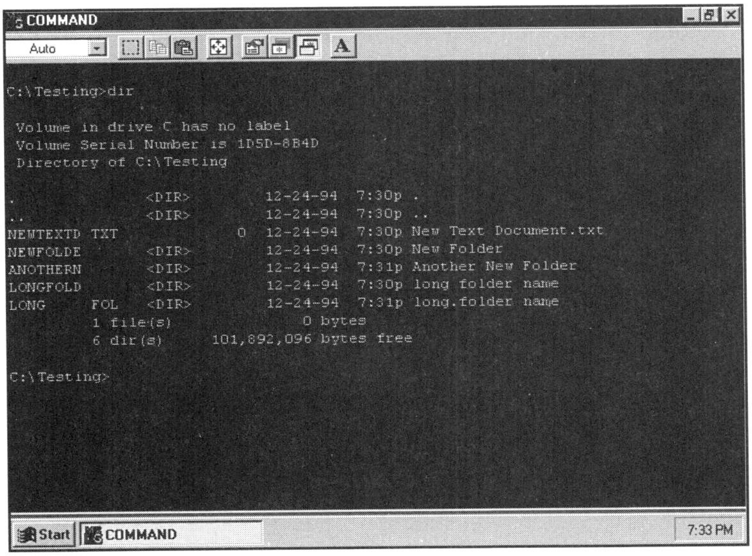

Fig. 25.6
The DOS DIR command shows a file's DOS name and its long name.

V

Digging into the OS

The DIR command also has a new command-line switch: /v. This switch produces a verbose directory listing that contains information about the file's attributes and when it was last accessed (in addition to information about when the file was last modified).

To accommodate Windows 95's built-in networking capabilities, Windows 95 also supports UNC (universal naming conventions) at the DOS command line for accessing network computers and resources. Universal naming conventions make it a bit easier to work with resources on a network because they relieve you from having to remember the specific drive letter on your computer that represents a network computer. You can use UNC with DOS commands such as DIR or COPY or to run a program stored on another computer.

◀ See Chapter 17, "Creating Workgroups with Windows 95's Peer-to-Peer Networking"

Windows 95's DOS includes a new command—START. The START command supports both Windows 95's document orientation and Windows 95's ongoing blurring of the distinction between DOS and Windows applications. The START command allows you to start a Windows- or DOS-based application from the DOS command prompt (provided the command prompt is in a DOS VM) by specifying either the name of the program you want to start or a document name:

```
START word
START "Letter to Dave.doc"
```

Each command starts the MS Word for Windows application. The first command just starts Word—MS Word loads and displays the usual empty new document. The second command starts Word and causes Word to load or create the document file name Letter to Dave—the .DOC extension in the file name tells Windows 95 that this is an MS Word document (provided, of course, that MS Word is correctly installed and registered).

As you can see, if you specify the name of a document whose file type has an association in the Windows 95 Registry, Windows 95 starts the corresponding application and loads the document—just as though you had double-clicked the document in a window on the Windows 95 desktop.

If you use the DOS START command to start a DOS application, Windows 95 creates a new DOS VM and runs the DOS application in the new VM. You can still run an application by typing its name directly at the DOS prompt. If you type the name of a Windows application by itself, Windows 95 loads and executes that application as though you had used the START command. If you type the name of another DOS application directly at the DOS command prompt, Windows 95 just runs that application in the current DOS VM.

Using DOS-Based Games under Windows 95

In general, DOS-based games—particularly, graphic-intensive games—are likely to be the most cantankerous of Windows 95's DOS citizens. Most DOS game programs require 100 percent control of your computer's hardware resources and external real-mode device drivers (such as a mouse driver).

These requirements can still pose problems for Windows 95, despite its improved handling of such demanding programs. One DOS-based game program from a prominent commercial games publisher that one of the authors tested, for example, simply refused to run in a Windows 95 DOS VM. This program, for some reason, couldn't recognize Windows 95's virtual mouse driver and refused to load because it requires a mouse. At the same time, it wasn't possible to install a real-mode mouse driver because the mouse driver refused to load in memory—it recognized Windows 95's virtual mouse driver and complained that there was already a mouse driver installed.

To complicate matters further, it isn't possible to load a real-mode device driver through CONFIG.SYS before Windows 95 loads because Windows 95 disables any real-mode device drivers that conflict with installed protected-mode drivers.

If you get stuck in this kind of circular situation, you'll probably have to make a bootable floppy disk with a CONFIG.SYS file that loads any device drivers the DOS application needs, and then use this floppy disk to start your computer so you can run that particular DOS application.

This workaround isn't as burdensome as it might seem at first—many DOS-based graphic-intensive games have such stringent memory requirements that most game players have already made a special bootable floppy disk with minimum devices to prepare their computer for game playing.

V

Digging into the OS

Index

Symbols

... (ellipsis) following commands, 51
10BASE-T cabling, 341
14, 400 modems, 16
16-bit
  applications, 421-426
    heaps, 422-424
    messages, 422-424
    multiple file systems, 425-426
    thunks, 424-425
  operating systems, 18
  subsystem
    memory, 122
    software compatibility, 121-123
32-bit applications
  APIs, 124
  CD file system, 140
  protected-mode, 18, 418
  upgrading, 125-127
    availability, 132-135
    improvements, 127-129
    multithreading, 130-132
    preemptive multi-tasking, 129-130
    requirements, 134
386MAX, 441
80x86 architecture, 33-42
  EISA bus, 35
  IDE (Integrated Drive Electronics), 40-41
  ISA bus, 35
  MCA bus, 38-39
  PCI bus, 37-38
  SCSI (Small Computer System Interface), 39-40
  system requirements, 41-42
  VLB (Vesa Local Bus), 35-36

A

Accessibility features, 93-94
Accessibility Options applet, 74
ACM (Audio Compression Manager), 178-180
Adaptec SCSI interface, 160
Add Printer Wizard, 347
Add Service to Profile dialog box, 302
Add/Remove Programs applet, 75, 102
Address Book, 105
address entries (AWFax), 307-308
address space, 130
administrative tools, 27, 319
administrative updating, 408
ADPCM CODEC, 179
ADPCM compression, 165, 169
Advanced Gravis UltraSound card, 174
Advanced Options dialog box, 450
Advanced page, 331
analog audio, 155, 167
analog video, 196, 208-211
  system requirements, 208-209
  VCR command set, 209-211
animation titles (CD-ROM), 161
antialiasing, 419
APIs
  32-bit DSP, 178
  Common Mail Calls API, 356
  MAPI, 354-358
  networking, 336
  ODBC, 229
  Print, 336
  software compatibility, 124
  TAPI, 229-231
  VIM (Vendor-Independent Messaging) API, 356
  Win32 Winnet, 336
  WinG, 142
  WinSock, 413
APM specification (Plug and Play), 44

PLUG YOURSELF INTO...

The MCP Internet Site

Free information and vast computer resources from the world's leading computer book publisher—online!

Find the books that are right for you!

A complete online catalog, plus sample chapters and tables of contents give you an in-depth look at *all* our books. The best way to shop or browse!

- ✦ **Stay informed** with the latest computer industry news through discussion groups, an online newsletter, and customized subscription news.
- ✦ **Get fast answers** to your questions about MCP books and software.
- ✦ **Visit** our online bookstore for the latest information and editions!
- ✦ **Communicate** with our expert authors through e-mail and conferences.
- ✦ **Play** in the BradyGame Room with info, demos, shareware, and more!
- ✦ **Download software** from the immense MCP library:
    - Source code and files from MCP books
    - The best shareware, freeware, and demos
- ✦ **Discover hot spots** on other parts of the Internet.
- ✦ **Win books** in ongoing contests and giveaways!

Drop by the new Internet site of Macmillan Computer Publishing!

To plug into MCP:

World Wide Web: http://www.mcp.com/
Gopher: gopher.mcp.com **FTP:** ftp.mcp.com

GOING ONLINE DECEMBER 1994!